#중학실전영문법
#내가바로문법고수

바로 문제
푸는 문법

바로 시리즈 검토에 도움을 주신 분들

홍정환 선생님(영어의 힘)
박용철 선생님(PK대치스마트에듀)
원영아 선생님(멘토영어)
원지윤 선생님(아잉카영어)
이성형 선생님(해윰학원)
김란숙 선생님(샘앤아이영어)
이차은 선생님(BOB영어)

박주경 선생님(PK대치스마트에듀)
주은숙 선생님(원클래스 학원)
김도희 선생님(원클래스 학원)
Kyle 선생님(한스터디)
윤지원 선생님(고려학원)
김현욱 선생님(동광학원)
이형언 선생님(훈성학원)

박은영 선생님(PK대치스마트에듀)
김지혜 선생님(Epic English)
박지혜 선생님(다이나믹 학원)
이민정 선생님(BMA 어학원)
채효석 선생님(빅터 아카데미)

원어민 검토

Stephanie Berry, Matthew D. Gunderman

Chunjae
Makes
Chunjae

▼

[바로 문제 푸는 문법] LEVEL 3

기획총괄	남보라
편집개발	김미혜, 신현겸, 우래희, 이지은, 이근영
디자인총괄	김희정
표지디자인	윤순미, 안채리
내지디자인	디자인뮤제오
제작	황성진, 조규영

발행일	2022년 5월 15일 2판 2025년 2월 1일 2쇄
발행인	(주)천재교육
주소	서울시 금천구 가산로9길 54
신고번호	제2001-000018호
고객센터	1577-0902
교재 내용문의	(02)3282-8834

시험이 쉬워지는 중학 실전 영문법

바로 문제 푸는 문법

LEVEL 3

이 책의 구성과 특징

01 학교 시험에 출제되는 문제
유형 파악 & 핵심 문법 확인

02 오답률별 기출 문제 풀이로
단기간에 내신 대비 마무리

STEP 1 만만한 기초
대부분의 학생들이 맞히는
아주 쉬운 문제로 구성

STEP 2 오답률 40~60% 문제
100명 중 40명~60명이 맞히는
중하 수준의 문제로 구성

STEP 3 오답률 60~80% 문제
100명 중 20명~40명이 맞히는
중상 수준의 문제로 구성

STEP 4 실력 완성 테스트
고난도 수준의 통합형 문제로 구성

STEP 2, 3에서는
선택형과 서술형을
구분하여 집중 연습

03 문장을 비교하며
핵심 문법 최종 정리

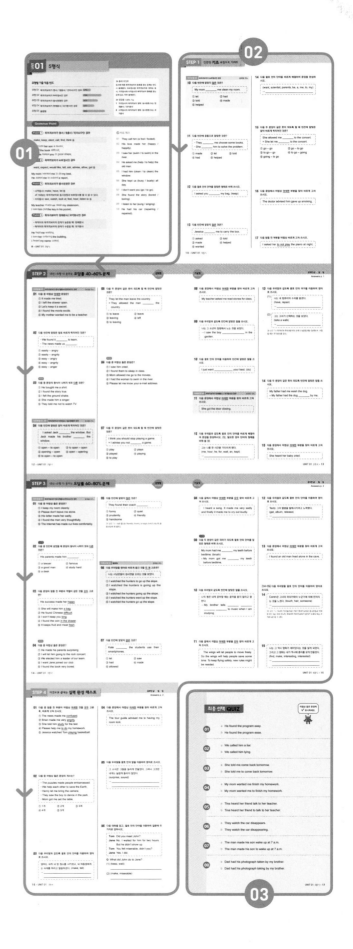

이 책의 차례

바로 쓰는 문법과
함께 공부하며
학습 효과 2배로 올리기

문법 항목별 출제 빈도

*해당 문법이 13종 교과서에서 몇 번 나오는지 확인할 수 있습니다.

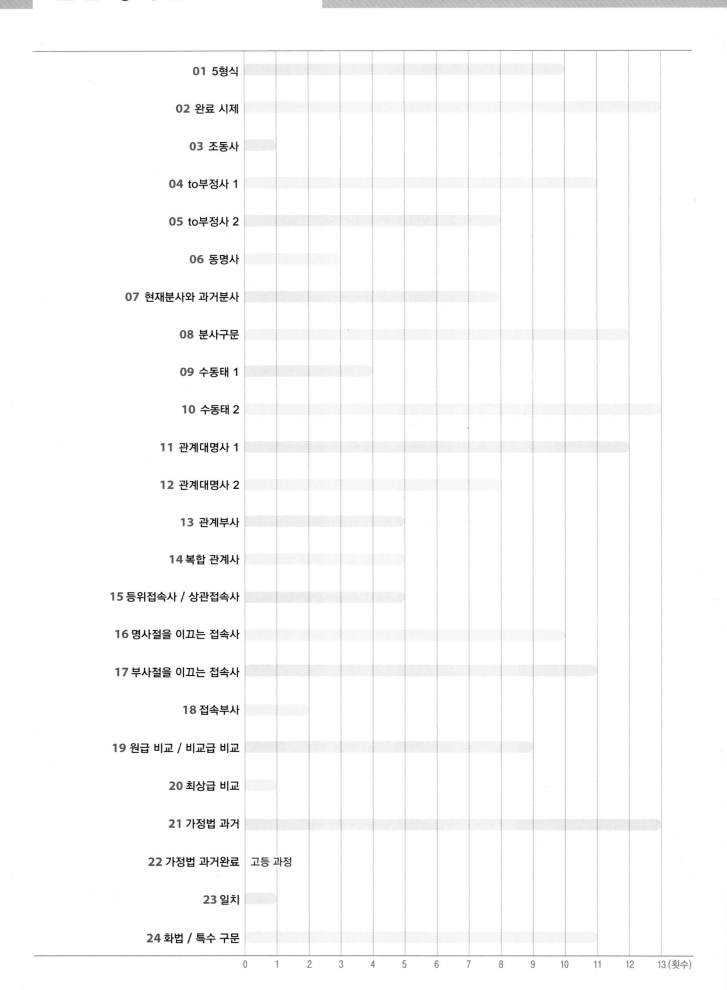

	횟수
01 5형식	10
02 완료 시제	12
03 조동사	1
04 to부정사 1	9
05 to부정사 2	8
06 동명사	
07 현재분사와 과거분사	
08 분사구문	11
09 수동태 1	4
10 수동태 2	11
11 관계대명사 1	11
12 관계대명사 2	
13 관계부사	5
14 복합 관계사	
15 등위접속사 / 상관접속사	5
16 명사절을 이끄는 접속사	9
17 부사절을 이끄는 접속사	10
18 접속부사	2
19 원급 비교 / 비교급 비교	8
20 최상급 비교	
21 가정법 과거	12
22 가정법 과거완료	고등 과정
23 일치	
24 화법 / 특수 구문	

0　1　2　3　4　5　6　7　8　9　10　11　12　13 (횟수)

바로 푸는 문법 공부 계획표

단원 목차	공부한 날 월 / 일	복습한 날 월 / 일	나의 성취도 체크 (∨) 개념이해	문제풀이	오답점검	누적복습
01 5형식						
02 완료 시제						
03 조동사						
04 to부정사 1						
05 to부정사 2						
06 동명사						
07 현재분사와 과거분사						
08 분사구문						
09 수동태 1						
10 수동태 2						
11 관계대명사 1						
12 관계대명사 2						
13 관계부사						
14 복합 관계사						
15 등위접속사 / 상관접속사						
16 명사절을 이끄는 접속사						
17 부사절을 이끄는 접속사						
18 접속부사						
19 원급 비교 / 비교급 비교						
20 최상급 비교						
21 가정법 과거						
22 가정법 과거완료						
23 일치						
24 화법 / 특수 구문						

중학교 교과서 문법 연계표 3학년

단원	천재(이재영)	천재(정사열)	동아(윤정미)	동아(이병민)	미래엔(최연희)	능률(김성곤)	비상(김진완)
1	• 관계대명사 what [11] • 5형식(지각동사+목적어+동사원형) [1]	• 간접의문문 [16] • 계속적 용법의 관계대명사 [12]	• 접속사 if, whether [16] • to부정사 형용사적 용법 [5]	• It ~ for ...+to부정사 [4] • 관계대명사 what [11]	• 관계대명사 what [11] • 접속사 although [17]	• 현재완료진행 [2] • 관계대명사 what [11]	• 관계대명사 what [11] • 관계부사 [13]
2	• 명사를 수식하는 분사 [7] • 접속사 since, though [17]	• 과거완료 [2] • 비교급 강조 [19]	• 5형식(사역동사+목적어+동사원형) [1] • so that(목적) [17]	• 부분을 나타내는 표현 • 조동사가 있는 수동태 [9]	• It ~ that 강조구문 [24] • 계속적 용법의 관계대명사 [12]	• 계속적 용법의 관계대명사 [12] • 명사를 수식하는 분사 [7]	• to부정사의 의미상 주어 [4] • 현재완료진행 [2]
3	• 현재완료진행 [2] • so ~ that [17]	• enough+to부정사 [5] • not only A but also B [15]	• 계속적 용법의 관계대명사 [12] • 가주어 It ~ that [16]	• 5형식(사역동사+목적어+동사원형) [1] • It ~ that 강조구문 [24]	• 명사를 수식하는 분사 [7] • 강조의 do [24]	• 과거완료 [2] • 부사절을 이끄는 접속사 [17]	• 접속사 if, whether [16] • 과거완료 [2]
4	• 관계부사 [13] • 접속사 if, whether [16]	• 분사구문 [8] • 관계대명사 what [11]	• 현재완료진행 [2] • 의문사+to부정사 [4]	• The+비교급, the+비교급 [19] • 접속사 since [17]	• 간접의문문 [16] • 과거완료 [2]	• 접속사 if, whether [16] • 조동사가 있는 수동태 [9]	• 명사를 수식하는 분사 [7] • 가목적어(it) ~ to부정사 [4]
5	• 과거완료 [2] • It ~ that 강조구문 [24]	• 가정법 과거 [21] • 관계대명사 whose [11]	• 명사를 수식하는 분사 [7] • 원급 비교 [19]	• 가정법 과거 [21] • 의문사+to부정사 [4]	• 분사구문 [8] • not only A but also B [15]	• to부정사의 의미상 주어 [4] • 관계부사 [13]	• 분사구문 [8] • so that(목적) [17]
6	• It ~ for ...+to부정사 [4] • 가정법 과거 [21]	• The+비교급, the+비교급 [19] • It ~ that 강조구문 [24]	• 과거완료 [2] • 관계대명사 what [11]	• so that(목적) [17] • enough+to부정사 [5]	• 관계부사 [13] • 접속부사 however, thus [18]	• The+비교급, the+비교급 [19] • 분사구문 [8]	• It ~ that 강조구문 [24] • 5형식(사역동사+목적어+과거분사) [1]
7	• 분사구문 [8] • 조동사가 있는 수동태 [9]	• 간접화법 [24] • 명사절을 이끄는 접속사 if [16]	• 분사구문 [8] • 접속사 as [17]	• 관계대명사 whose [11] • 접속사 while [17]	• 관계대명사 whose [11] • 가정법 과거 [21]	• 가정법 과거 [21] • so that(목적) [17]	• 접속사 as [17] • 부분을 나타내는 표현
8	• 조동사+have+p.p. [3] • 계속적 용법의 관계대명사 [12]	• 부정대명사 • 5형식(동사+목적어+to부정사) [1]	• It ~ for ...+to부정사 [4] • 가정법 과거 [21]	• 분사구문 [8] • 과거완료 [2]			• 가정법 과거 [21] • with+(대)명사+분사 [8]
9							

YBM(박준언)	YBM(송미정)	지학사(민찬규)	능률(양현권)	금성(최인철)	다락원(강용순)
• 강조의 do [24] • 관계대명사 what [11]	• too ~ to부정사 [5] • to부정사의 부정 [4]	• 관계대명사 what [11] • 5형식(지각동사+목적어+현재분사) [1]	• It ~ for ...+ to부정사 [4] • 계속적 용법의 관계대명사 [12]	• 5형식(사역동사+목적어+동사원형) [1] • 동명사의 관용 표현 [6]	• 최상급 [20] • 접속사 since [17] • 관계대명사 what [11]
• 현재완료진행 [2] • 명사를 수식하는 분사 [7]	• 분사구문 [8] • 접속사 if, whether [16]	• It ~ for ...+ to부정사 [4] • 명사를 수식하는 분사 [7]	• It ~ that 강조구문 [24] • 5형식(동사+목적어+목적격보어) [1]	• The+비교급, the+비교급 [19] • to부정사의 의미상 주어 [4]	• 5형식(동사+목적어+to부정사) [1] • 명사를 수식하는 분사 [7] • 관계대명사 whose [11]
• It ~ that 강조구문 [24] • 5형식(have+목적어+과거분사) [1]	• The+비교급, the+비교급 [19] • It ~ that 강조구문 [24]	• not only A but also B [15] • 관계부사 [13]	• 관계대명사 what [11] • 5형식(사역동사+목적어+동사원형) [1]	• not only A but also B [15] • I wish 가정법 과거 [21]	• 목적격 관계대명사 [11] • 조동사가 있는 수동태 [9] • 가정법 과거 [21]
• to부정사의 의미상 주어 [4] • 가정법 과거 [21]	• 접속사 although [17] • seem to [5]	• 과거완료 [2] • to부정사 부사적 용법 [5]	• 과거완료 [2] • 분사구문 [8]	• 과거완료 [2] • 원급 비교 [19]	• 현재완료 [2] • enough+to부정사 [5] • The+비교급, the+비교급 [19]
• 과거완료 [2] • so that(목적) [17]	• 관계대명사 what [11] • 현재완료진행 [2]	• 부정대명사 one • 분사구문 [8]	• 의문사+to부정사 [4] • The+비교급, the+비교급 [19]	• so ~ that [17] • 5형식(지각동사+목적어+동사원형/현재분사) [1]	• 강조 [24] • 접속사 while [17] • 과거완료 [2]
• 계속적 용법의 관계대명사 [12] • to부정사의 부사적 용법 [5]	• 원급 비교 [19] • 과거완료 [2]	• It ~ that 강조구문 [24] • 접속부사 however [18]	• 화법 전환 [24] • 5형식(지각동사+목적어+현재분사) [1]	• It ~ that 강조구문 [24] • 분사구문 [8]	• be worth -ing [6] • 접속사 whether [16] • to부정사의 명사적 용법 [4]
• 간접의문문 how [16] • The+비교급, the+비교급 [19]	• 가정법 과거 [21] • so that(목적) [17]	• 가정법 과거 [21] • 5형식(동사+목적어+형용사) [1]	• 가정법 과거 [21] • so ~ that [17]	• enough+to부정사 [5] • 도치(so+동사+주어) [24]	• 계속적 용법의 관계대명사 [12] • the+형용사 [23] • 가목적어 it ~ to부정사 [4]
• 분사구문 [8] • be worth -ing [6]	• not only A but also B [15] • 접속사 while [17]	• too ~ to부정사 [5] • 부정 구문		• 간접의문문 [16] • It is time + 가정법	• feel like -ing [6] • 도치 [24] • 부정대명사
				• It ~ that 강조구문 [24] • 5형식(have+목적어+과거분사) [1] • I wish 가정법 과거 [21]	

유형별 기출 적용 빈도

유형 01 목적격보어가 명사 / 형용사 / 전치사구인 경우 10%

유형 02 목적격보어가 to부정사인 경우 25%

유형 03 목적격보어가 동사원형인 경우 20%

유형 04 목적격보어가 현재분사 / 과거분사인 경우 15%

유형 05 통합형 30%

≫ 출제 포인트
동사에 따른 목적격보어의 종류를 묻는 문제는 반드시 출제된다. to부정사를 목적격보어로 취하는 동사, 지각동사와 사역동사의 목적격보어 형태를 묻는 문제 등도 자주 출제된다.

≫ 정답률 100% Tip
1 지각동사의 목적격보어 형태: 동사원형 또는 현재분사 / 과거분사
2 사역동사의 목적격보어 형태: 동사원형 또는 과거분사

Grammar Point

Point ① 목적격보어가 명사 / 형용사 / 전치사구인 경우

make, keep, elect, call, find, think 등

She made her son a doctor.
I found the book difficult.
Exercise keeps you in good shape.

Point ② 목적격보어가 to부정사인 경우

want, expect, would like, tell, ask, advise, allow, get 등

My mom wanted me to do my best.
He asked me to submit a report.

Point ③ 목적격보어가 동사원형인 경우

• 사역동사: make, have, let 등
  cf. help는 목적격보어로 동사원형과 to부정사를 둘 다 쓸 수 있다.
• 지각동사: see, watch, look at, feel, hear, listen to 등

My teacher made us clean my classroom.
I saw him put the key in his pocket.

Point ④ 목적격보어가 현재분사 / 과거분사인 경우

• 목적어와 목적격보어의 관계가 능동일 때: 현재분사
• 목적어와 목적격보어의 관계가 수동일 때: 과거분사

He kept me waiting.
I saw her entering the building.
Kate had her hair dyed blonde.

✔ 바로 체크

01 They call him (a fool / fooled).

02 His love made her (happy / happily).

03 I saw her (swim / to swim) in the river.

04 He asked me (help / to help) the old man.

05 I had him (clean / to clean) the window.

06 She kept us (busy / busily) all day.

07 I don't want you (go / to go).

08 She found the story (bored / boring).

09 I listen to her (sung / singing).

10 He had his car (repairing / repaired).

대표유형 01 목적격보어가 명사/형용사/전치사구인 경우 출제율 10%

01 다음 빈칸에 알맞은 것으로 바르게 짝지어진 것은?

> • I found the girl _____.
> • The song made me _____.

① happy – sad ② happily – sadly
③ happy – sadly ④ happiness – sad
⑤ happily – sadness

02 다음 빈칸에 알맞지 <u>않은</u> 것은?

> The movie made me _____.

① cry ② laugh ③ upset
④ bored ⑤ gladly

03 다음 중 어법상 <u>어색한</u> 문장은?

① We call him John.
② I found him very wise.
③ Keep your hands cleanly.
④ I made my mom depressed.
⑤ He often leaves the door open.

04 다음 우리말과 같도록 괄호 안의 단어를 알맞은 형태로 바꿔 쓰시오.

> 나는 그 주제가 대단히 흥미롭다는 것을 알았다.
> → I found the subject _____. (fascinate)

05 다음 문장의 밑줄 친 lead를 알맞은 형태로 고쳐 쓰시오.

> We elected him our new <u>lead</u>.

06 다음 중 문장의 형식이 나머지 넷과 <u>다른</u> 것은?

① He called me a baby.
② He made me a lawyer.
③ I sent him a present.
④ They elected me president.
⑤ We considered her a strong woman.

07 다음 빈칸에 알맞은 것은?

> He got me _____ big trouble.

① at ② for ③ in
④ on ⑤ with

08 다음 대화의 빈칸에 알맞은 말을 쓰시오.

> **A** How do you stay healthy?
> **B** Exercise keeps me _____ good shape.

09 다음 대화에서 어법상 <u>어색한</u> 부분을 찾아 바르게 고쳐 쓰시오.

> **A** Thank you for inviting me.
> **B** Please sit down and make yourself in home.

10 다음 빈칸에 알맞지 <u>않은</u> 것은?

> My mom _____ me clean my room.

① let   ② had
③ told   ④ made
⑤ helped

11 다음 빈칸에 공통으로 알맞은 것은?

> • They _____ me choose some books.
> • She _____ him to solve the problem.

① made   ② let   ③ told
④ had   ⑤ helped

12 다음 괄호 안의 단어를 알맞은 형태로 바꿔 쓰시오.

> I asked you _____ my bag. (keep)

13 다음 빈칸에 알맞지 <u>않은</u> 것은?

> Jessica _____ me to carry the box.

① asked   ② told
③ made   ④ helped
⑤ wanted

14 다음 괄호 안의 단어를 바르게 배열하여 문장을 완성하시오.

> (want, scientist, parents, be, a, me, to, my)
> → _____

15 다음 두 문장이 같은 뜻이 되도록 할 때 빈칸에 알맞은 말이 바르게 짝지어진 것은?

> She allowed me _____ to the concert.
> = She let me _____ to the concert.

① go – go   ② go – to go
③ to go – go   ④ to go – going
⑤ going – to go

16 다음 문장에서 어법상 <u>어색한</u> 부분을 찾아 바르게 고쳐 쓰시오.

> The doctor advised him gave up smoking.

17 다음 밑줄 친 부분을 어법상 바르게 고쳐 쓰시오.

> I asked her <u>to not play</u> the piano at night.

대표유형 03 목적격보어가 동사원형인 경우　　　　출제율 20%

18 다음 빈칸에 알맞은 것은?

> I heard her _____ a song.

① sing　　　② sang　　　③ sung
④ sings　　　⑤ to sing

19 다음 우리말과 같도록 괄호 안의 단어를 바르게 배열하여 문장을 완성하시오.

> 나는 그가 길을 건너는 것을 보았다.
> (street, him, the, cross, saw, I)
> → _____

20 다음 우리말과 같도록 할 때 빈칸에 알맞은 것은?

> 나는 그녀에게 카메라를 고치게 했다.
> → I made her _____ the camera.

① fix　　　② fixed　　　③ fixing
④ fixes　　　⑤ to fix

대표유형 04 목적격보어가 현재분사 / 과거분사인 경우　　　　출제율 15%

21 다음 우리말과 같도록 괄호 안의 단어를 알맞은 형태로 바꿔 쓰시오.

> 나는 내 노트북을 도난당했다.
> → I had my laptop _____. (steal)

22 다음 중 밑줄 친 부분의 쓰임이 어법상 어색한 것은?

① I found him wounded.
② I must get my hair cut.
③ Don't leave her waited in the rain.
④ He felt a hand touching his shoulder.
⑤ I saw a man sitting alone on the grass.

23 다음 우리말과 같도록 괄호 안의 단어를 바르게 배열하여 문장을 완성하시오.

> 그는 그의 차가 세차되도록 했다.
> (car, had, washed, his, he)
> → _____

24 다음 빈칸에 알맞은 말이 바르게 짝지어진 것은?

> • I listened to the song _____ by the band.
> • I found her _____ on a sofa.

① play – sleep　　　② play – slept
③ played – slept　　　④ played – sleeping
⑤ playing – sleeping

25 다음 괄호 안 단어의 형태로 알맞은 것은?

> I heard my name (call).

① called　　　② calling　　　③ calls
④ be called　　　⑤ to call

대표유형 01 목적격보어가 명사/형용사/전치사구인 경우   출제율 10%

01 다음 중 어법상 <u>어색한</u> 문장은?

① It made me tired.

② I left the drawer open.

③ Let's keep it a secret.

④ I found the movie excite.

⑤ My mother wanted me to be a teacher.

02 다음 빈칸에 알맞은 말로 바르게 짝지어진 것은?

> · We found it _____ to learn.
>
> · The news made us _____.

① easily – angry

② easily – angrily

③ easy – angry

④ easy – angrily

⑤ easy – anger

통합형

03 다음 중 문장의 형식이 나머지 넷과 <u>다른</u> 것은?

① He bought me a shirt.

② I found the story true.

③ I felt the ground shake.

④ She made him a singer.

⑤ They told me not to watch TV.

대표유형 02, 03 목적격보어가 to부정사 / 동사원형인 경우   출제율 25%

04 다음 빈칸에 알맞은 말이 바르게 짝지어진 것은?

> I asked Jack _____ the window. But Jack made his brother _____ the window.

① open – to open   ② to open – open

③ opening – open   ④ open – opening

⑤ to open – to open

05 다음 두 문장이 같은 뜻이 되도록 할 때 빈칸에 알맞은 것은?

> They let the man leave the country.
>
> = They allowed the man _____ the country.

① to leave   ② leave

③ leaving   ④ left

⑤ to leaving

통합형

06 다음 중 어법상 옳은 문장은?

① I saw him cried.

② I found them to sleep in class.

③ Mom allowed me go to the movies.

④ I had the woman to swim in the river.

⑤ Please let me know your e-mail address.

07 다음 두 문장이 같은 뜻이 되도록 할 때 빈칸에 알맞은 것은?

> I think you should stop playing a game.
>
> = I advise you not _____ a game.

① play   ② plays

③ played   ④ playing

⑤ to play

08 다음 문장에서 어법상 <u>어색한</u> 부분을 찾아 바르게 고쳐 쓰시오.

My teacher asked me read stories for class.

09 다음 우리말과 같도록 빈칸에 알맞은 말을 쓰시오.

나는 그 소년이 정원에서 노는 것을 보았다.
→ I saw the boy _____ in the garden.

10 다음 괄호 안의 단어를 이용하여 빈칸에 알맞은 말을 <u>3단어</u>로 쓰시오.

I just want _____ your best. (do)

대표유형 04 목적격보어가 현재분사 / 과거분사인 경우 　　출제율 15%

11 다음 문장에서 어법상 <u>어색한</u> 부분을 찾아 바르게 고쳐 쓰시오.

She got the door closing.

12 다음 우리말과 같도록 괄호 안의 단어를 바르게 배열하여 문장을 완성하시오. (단, 필요한 경우 단어의 형태를 바꿔 쓸 것)

그는 나를 한 시간을 기다리게 했다.
(me, hour, he, for, wait, an, kept)
→ _____

13 다음 우리말과 같도록 괄호 안의 어구를 이용하여 영어로 쓰시오.

(1)
나는 내 컴퓨터의 수리를 맡겼다.
(have, repair)
→ _____

(2)
그는 그녀가 산책하는 것을 보았다.
(take a walk)
→ _____

≫ 실전 Tip 목적어와 목적격보어의 관계가 능동일 때는 현재분사, 수동일 때는 과거분사를 쓴다.

14 다음 두 문장이 같은 뜻이 되도록 빈칸에 알맞은 말을 쓰시오.

My father had me wash the dog.
= My father had the dog _____ by me.

15 다음 문장에서 어법상 <u>어색한</u> 부분을 찾아 바르게 고쳐 쓰시오.

She heard her baby cried.

대표유형 01   목적격보어가 명사/형용사/전치사구인 경우   출제율 10%

01 다음 중 어법상 옳은 문장은?

① I keep my room cleanly.
② Please don't leave me alone.
③ His letter made her sadly.
④ I found the man very thoughtfully.
⑤ The Internet has made our lives comfortably.

〔신유형〕

02 다음 중 빈칸에 넣었을 때 문장의 형식이 나머지 넷과 다른 것은?

His parents made him _____.

① a lawyer   ② famous
③ a good man   ④ study hard
⑤ a desk

03 다음 문장의 밑줄 친 부분과 역할이 같은 것을 모두 고르면?

His success made her happy.

① She will make him a bag.
② He found Chinese difficult.
③ I won't keep you long.
④ I found the coin in the drawer.
⑤ It keeps fruit and meat fresh.

〔통합형〕

04 다음 중 어법상 옳은 문장은?

① He made his parents surprising.
② I will let him going to the rock concert.
③ We elected him a leader of our team.
④ I want Jane joined our club.
⑤ I found the book very bored.

05 다음 빈칸에 알맞지 않은 것은?

They found their coach _____.

① funny   ② quiet
③ prudently   ④ friendly
⑤ handsome

》 실전 Tip -ly로 끝나는 friendly, lovely, lonely는 부사가 아니라 형용사임에 유의한다.

대표유형 05   통합형   출제율 30%

06 다음 우리말을 영어로 바르게 옮긴 것을 두 개 고르면?

나는 사냥꾼들이 경사면을 오르는 것을 보았다.

① I watched the hunters to go up the slope.
② I watched the hunters is going up the slope.
③ I watched the hunters going up the slope.
④ I watched the hunters went up the slope.
⑤ I watched the hunters go up the slope.

07 다음 빈칸에 알맞지 않은 것은?

Kate _____ the students use their smartphones.

① let   ② saw
③ had   ④ made
⑤ allowed

08 다음 글에서 어법상 어색한 부분을 모두 찾아 바르게 고쳐 쓰시오.

I heard a song. It made me very sadly and finally it made me to cry out loudly.

신유형

09 다음 두 문장이 같은 의미가 되도록 괄호 안의 단어를 알맞은 형태로 바꿔 쓰시오.

My mom had me _____ my teeth before bedtime. (brush)
= My mom got me _____ my teeth before bedtime.

10 다음 우리말과 같도록 빈칸에 알맞은 말을 쓰시오.

나의 형은 내게 공부할 때는 음악을 듣지 말라고 말한다.
→ My brother tells _____ _____ _____ _____ to music when I am studying.

11 다음 글에서 어법상 어색한 부분을 모두 찾아 바르게 고쳐 쓰시오.

The wings will let people to move freely. So the wings will help people save some time. To keep flying safety, new rules might be needed.

12 다음 우리말과 같도록 괄호 안의 단어를 이용하여 영어로 쓰시오.

Ted는 그의 앨범을 발매시키려고 노력했다.
(get, album, release)

→ _____

13 다음 문장에서 어법상 어색한 부분을 찾아 바르게 고쳐 쓰시오.

I found an old man lived alone in the cave.

[14-15] 다음 우리말을 괄호 안의 단어를 이용하여 영어로 쓰시오.

14

Caren은 그녀의 머리카락이 누군가에 의해 만져지는 것을 느꼈다. (touch, hair, someone)

→ _____

≫ 실전 Tip 지각동사라고 해서 목적격보어로 동사원형과 현재분사만 쓰는 것이 아니라, 목적어와 목적격보어의 관계가 수동일 때는 과거분사도 쓸 수 있다.

15

나는 그 역사 영화가 재미있다는 것을 알게 되었다. 그리고 그 영화는 내가 역사에 흥미를 갖게 만들었다.
(find, make, interesting, interested)

→ _____

_____

01 다음 중 밑줄 친 부분이 어법상 어색한 것을 모두 고른 후, 바르게 고쳐 쓰시오.

① The news made me <u>confused</u>.
② Brian made me very <u>angrily</u>.
③ She told him <u>study</u> for the test.
④ Please help me <u>to do</u> my homework.
⑤ Jessica watched Tom <u>playing</u> basketball.

02 다음 중 어법상 옳은 문장의 개수는?

- The puzzles made people embarrassed.
- We help each other to save the Earth.
- Henry let me bring the camera.
- They saw the boy to dance in the park.
- Mom got me set the table.

① 1개   ② 2개   ③ 3개
④ 4개   ⑤ 5개

03 다음 우리말과 같도록 괄호 안의 단어를 이용하여 영어로 쓰시오.

엄마는 내게 내 방 청소를 시키셨고, 내 여동생에게 는 숙제를 하라고 말씀하셨다. (make, tell)

→ _____

_____

04 다음 문장에서 어법상 어색한 부분을 모두 찾아 바르게 고쳐 쓰시오.

The tour guide advised me to having my room lock.

05 다음 우리말을 괄호 안의 말을 이용하여 영어로 쓰시오.

그 소식은 그들을 놀라게 만들었다. 그러나 그것은 내게는 놀랍게 들리지 않았다.
(surprise, sound)

→ _____

_____

06 다음 대화를 읽고, 괄호 안의 단어를 이용하여 질문에 두 가지로 답하시오.

Tom Did you meet John?
Jane No. I waited for him for two hours. But he didn't show up.
Tom You felt miserable, didn't you?
Jane Yes, I did.

Q What did John do to Jane?
(1) (keep, wait)

_____

(2) (make, miserable)

_____

01
a He found the program easy.

b He found the program ease.

02
a We called him a liar.

b We called him lying.

03
a She told me come back tomorrow.

b She told me to come back tomorrow.

04
a My mom wanted me finish my homework.

b My mom wanted me to finish my homework.

05
a Tina heard her friend talk to her teacher.

b Tina heard her friend to talk to her teacher.

06
a They watch the car disappears.

b They watch the car disappearing.

07
a The man made his son wake up at 7 a.m.

b The man made his son to wake up at 7 a.m.

08
a Dad had his photograph taken by my brother.

b Dad had his photograph taking by my brother.

유형별 기출 적용 빈도

유형 01	현재완료	35%
유형 02	과거완료	20%
유형 03	미래완료	10%
유형 04	완료 진행	5%
유형 05	통합형	30%

》 출제 포인트

현재완료와 과거완료의 용법을 묻는 문제는 반드시 출제된다. 현재완료와 함께 쓸 수 없는 표현에 관한 문제 등도 자주 출제된다.

》 정답률 100% Tip

1 과거를 나타내는 부사(구)와 when은 현재완료 시제와 같이 쓸 수 없음
2 현재완료 have gone to는 '~에 가버렸다'는 결과를 나타내고, have been to는 '~에 가 본 적이 있다'는 경험을 나타냄

Grammar Point

Point 1 현재완료

- 형태: have[has] + 과거분사
- 용법: 경험(ever, never, before 등과 자주 쓰임), 완료(already, yet, just 등과 자주 쓰임), 계속(for, since 등과 자주 쓰임), 결과

I have been to the airport before. 〈경험〉
He has finished his homework already. 〈완료〉
She has lived here for two years. 〈계속〉
He has returned to New York. 〈결과〉

Point 2 과거완료

- 형태: had + 과거분사 / 용법: 경험, 완료, 계속, 결과

I had gone to the flower festival before. 〈경험〉
When I arrived at the theater, she had already left. 〈완료〉

Point 3 미래완료

- 형태: will have + 과거분사
- 용법: 미래의 어느 시점까지 완료되거나 영향을 미칠 동작이나 상태를 나타냄

He will have finished the project by tomorrow.

Point 4 완료 진행

시제	형태	용법
현재완료 진행	have[has] been + 현재분사	과거에 시작된 일이 현재에도 계속 진행되고 있는 상태('~하는 중이다')
과거완료 진행	had been + 현재분사	과거 기준 시점 이전에 시작된 일이 과거의 기준 시점에도 계속 진행되고 있었던 상태('~하던 중이었다')

It has been raining since last weekend.
She had been waiting for him for 30 minutes.

✅ 바로 체크

01 My friends haven't arrived (yet / just).

02 He (knew / has known) his partner since last year.

03 The new car has arrived (already / yesterday).

04 Henry (went / has gone) to London last year.

05 When I met Kate, she (talked / had talked) with him for 3 hours already.

06 When I got home, I found I (lost / had lost) my wallet.

07 They (have / had) never met the man before then.

08 We (have known / will have known) each other 3 years next year.

09 She (is working / has been working) for 2 hours.

대표유형 01 현재완료   출제율 35%

01 다음 중 어법상 어색한 문장은?

① I have lost my key.

② She has been there many times.

③ We have visited the island two years ago.

④ They have played soccer as a team.

⑤ Have you finished your homework?

02 다음 괄호 안의 단어를 알맞은 형태로 바꿔 쓰시오.

> Minsu _____ _____ here since he was little. (live)

03 다음 중 〈보기〉의 밑줄 친 부분과 쓰임이 같은 것은?

> 보기 He <u>has done</u> what has to be done.

① She <u>has</u> not <u>finished</u> her work yet.

② <u>Have</u> you <u>noticed</u> anything wrong?

③ He <u>has lost</u> the ring I gave to him.

④ They <u>have done</u> many things since then.

⑤ I <u>have seen</u> the picture before.

04 다음 대화의 밑줄 친 부분을 바르게 고쳐 쓰시오.

> **A** How have you been?
> **B** I <u>be</u> just fine. How about you?

05 다음 밑줄 친 부분 중 어색한 것은?

① He <u>has gone</u> to his friend's house many times.

② He <u>has not been</u> there.

③ She <u>has shown</u> me many good places.

④ I <u>have known</u> him for a long time.

⑤ We <u>have spent</u> quite a lot of money.

06 다음 우리말과 같도록 괄호 안의 단어를 바르게 배열하여 문장을 완성하시오.

> 당신은 전에 그 영화를 본 적이 있습니까?
> (you, watched, movie, have, ever, before, the)
> → _____

07 다음 중 밑줄 친 부분의 쓰임이 나머지 넷과 다른 것은?

① I <u>have repeated</u> the song for a week.

② I <u>have learned</u> Chinese for two years.

③ I <u>have been</u> to the airport several times.

④ I <u>have cleaned</u> my room since I was a kid.

⑤ I <u>have stayed</u> here during the whole vacation.

08 다음 두 문장이 같은 뜻이 되도록 빈칸에 알맞은 말을 쓰시오.

> James went to Spain and he is not here.
> → James _____ _____ to Spain.

09 다음 대화의 빈칸에 알맞은 것은?

> **A** Have you _____ read this book?
> **B** Yes, I have.

① now   ② ago

③ yesterday   ④ already

⑤ last month

10 다음 우리말과 같도록 빈칸에 알맞은 말을 쓰시오.

> 우리는 지금껏 최고의 축구 경기를 펼쳐왔다.
> → We _____ _____ the best soccer games so far.

대표유형 02 과거완료   출제율 20%

11 다음 중 〈보기〉의 밑줄 친 부분과 쓰임이 같은 것은?

> 보기   He <u>had learned</u> French for one year.

① I <u>had swum</u> in the pool for two hours.
② They <u>had lost</u> their friends in the accident.
③ I <u>had painted</u> the wall before he got back.
④ He lost the wallet that I <u>had bought</u> the day before.
⑤ When I arrived at the hall, she <u>had</u> already <u>left</u>.

12 다음 중 어법상 옳은 문장은?

① He has gone to Paris before I got back.
② We had built the town successfully.
③ I had found some books that he had left.
④ She had lived here for ten years until now.
⑤ They has spent much energy on this project.

13 다음 괄호 안의 단어를 알맞은 형태로 바꿔 쓰시오.

> I (lose) my watch. So I didn't have it then.

14 다음 중 어법상 <u>어색한</u> 문장은?

① Had you met him?
② We had run a coffee shop there.
③ Had he finished his homework then?
④ She has already arrived when I got there.
⑤ Had you visited his place before last Christmas?

15 다음 괄호 안의 단어를 바르게 배열하여 문장을 완성하시오.

> _____ until I bought a new one. (I, my, old, had, kept, book)

16 다음 빈칸에 공통으로 알맞은 말을 쓰시오.

> • He had _____ a great time.
> • I _____ met him before I left my hometown.

[17-18] 다음 빈칸에 알맞은 것을 고르시오.

17
> We _____ the laptop for two years before it broke down.

① have   ② had been
③ have had   ④ had had
⑤ have been had

18

When I visited my grandparents this winter, they told me that they _____ sick for days.

① were
② are
③ have been
④ could be
⑤ had been

19 다음 문장에서 어법상 어색한 부분을 찾아 바르게 고쳐 쓰시오.

I have reached the place before he got there.

대표유형 03 미래완료   출제율 10%

20 다음 대화의 빈칸에 알맞은 것은?

A How long have you been in Toronto?
B Well, I _____ in Toronto for 3 weeks by next month.

① will be
② have been
③ will have been
④ will be staying
⑤ am going to be

21 다음 우리말과 같도록 괄호 안의 단어를 알맞은 형태로 바꿔 쓰시오.

그녀는 5시까지 그녀의 숙제를 끝마칠 것이다.
→ She _____ _____ _____ her homework by five o'clock. (finish)

22 다음 문장에서 어법상 어색한 부분을 찾아 바르게 고쳐 쓰시오.

I have taken a walk by this time tomorrow.

대표유형 04 완료 진행   출제율 5%

23 다음 대화의 밑줄 친 ①~⑤ 중 어법상 어색한 것은?

A ① How long ② has Lily ③ talking with her friend on the phone?
B She has been talking ④ with him on the phone ⑤ for two hours.

24 다음 대화의 빈칸에 알맞은 것은?

A Why didn't you come to the party last night?
B My car broke down. It _____ for a long time.

① runs
② has run
③ is running
④ has been running
⑤ had been running

25 다음 대화의 밑줄 친 be를 올바른 형태로 고쳐 쓰시오.

A Have you be cooking all evening?
B Yes, I have. I'm almost finished.

대표유형 01, 02 현재완료 / 과거완료   출제율 35%

01 다음 중 어법상 옳은 문장은?
① When have you met him?
② I have joined that club long ago.
③ Kelly have known him for a long time.
④ How have you been during the vacation?
⑤ I don't have my bag because I had lost it.

02 다음 대화의 우리말을 영어로 바르게 옮긴 것은?

> **A** 넌 얼마나 오래 피아노를 쳐 왔니?
> **B** For seven years.

① How long do you play the piano?
② How long did you play the piano?
③ How long had you played the piano?
④ How long have you played the piano?
⑤ How long have you been played the piano?

03 다음 중 〈보기〉의 밑줄 친 부분과 쓰임이 같은 것은?

> 보기   They have been married for 10 years.

① He has heard this news before.
② I have just arrived at the store.
③ She has gone to Europe to travel.
④ Have you ever read the book?
⑤ I have suffered from a headache since last week.

04 다음 빈칸에 알맞은 말로 바르게 짝지어진 것은?

> Yesterday I _____ the ticket that I _____ the day before.

① lose – buy   ② lost – had bought
③ losing – bought ④ had lost – buying
⑤ have lost – had bought

05 다음 빈칸에 알맞은 것은?

> The train _____ the station when I got there.

① leaves   ② left
③ will leave   ④ has already left
⑤ had already left

[06-07] 다음 빈칸에 알맞은 말이 바르게 짝지어진 것을 고르시오.

06
> • Jason _____ a bad injury two weeks ago.
> • Julie _____ for her exam since last week.

① has – studies
② had – studied
③ had – has studied
④ had – had studied
⑤ has had – has studied

≫ 실전 Tip 과거를 나타내는 부사인 ago는 현재완료 시제와 함께 쓸 수 없고, since는 주로 현재완료 시제와 함께 쓰인다.

07
> • I found that nobody _____ a call.
> • Since I was young, I _____ to music.

① had received – had listened
② had received – have listened
③ has received – was listening
④ have received – listened
⑤ has received – listened

[08-09] 다음 우리말과 같도록 괄호 안의 말을 바르게 배열하여 문장을 완성하시오. (단, 필요한 경우 단어의 형태를 바꿔 쓸 것)

08
> 나는 이 연극을 본 적이 있다.
> (have, this, I, play, see)
> → _____

09
> Alice는 나을 때까지 오랫동안 아팠었다.
> (Alice, get better, be, sick, until, a long time, she, for, had)
> → _____

≫ 실전 Tip 과거의 두 사건 간의 전후 관계를 정확하게 파악하여 과거보다 이전에 일어난 일을 과거완료 시제로 표현한다.

10 다음 글에서 어법상 <u>어색한</u> 부분을 찾아 바르게 고쳐 쓰시오.

> I started to swim three years ago. I still swim every weekend. So I had swum for three years. I love to swim.

대표유형 03, 04 미래완료 / 완료 진행   출제율 10%

11 다음 대화의 빈칸에 괄호 안의 단어를 알맞은 형태로 바꿔 쓰시오. (단, 완료 시제와 완료 진행시제를 한 번씩 쓸 것)

> **A** I _____ in model cars for years. (interested)
> **B** Me, too. I _____ a gorgeous one for two weeks. (make)

신유형

12 다음 두 문장을 아래와 같이 바꿔 쓸 때 빈칸에 알맞은 말을 쓰시오.

> Please visit my office today. I'm going on vacation tomorrow.
> → I _____ _____ _____ on vacation by this time tomorrow.

13 다음 우리말과 같도록 빈칸에 알맞은 말을 쓰시오.

> 내가 그곳에 방문했을 때 그들은 두 시간째 춤을 추고 있었다.
> → They _____ _____ _____ for two hours when I visited there.

14 다음 두 문장을 같은 의미의 한 문장으로 바꿔 쓸 때 빈칸에 알맞은 말을 쓰시오.

> She started looking for her glasses 40 minutes ago. She is still looking for them.
> → She _____ _____ _____ _____ her glasses for 40 minutes.

15 다음 문장에서 어법상 <u>어색한</u> 부분을 찾아 바르게 고쳐 쓰시오.

> Robin will work here for nine years by the end of this year.

대표유형 05 통합형   출제율 30%

01 다음 빈칸에 알맞은 말이 바르게 짝지어진 것은?

- Call back at 2 p.m. She _____ her lunch by then.
- We _____ each other for five years.

① has finished – know
② had been finished – have known
③ had been finished – are known
④ will have finished – have known
⑤ will have finished – are known

02 다음 빈칸에 들어갈 말이 나머지 넷과 다른 것은?

① I _____ never worn a suit until I turned 20.
② We will _____ arrived at the station by 7 p.m.
③ I _____ already finished my homework when Mom arrived.
④ He _____ lived in Seoul until he moved to Ulsan.
⑤ My sisters gave me cookies that they _____ bought in Japan.

03 다음 중 어법상 옳은 문장은?

① I had forgotten what you did yesterday.
② Jack has left before we arrived in Paris.
③ I fell asleep before I finished the project.
④ He found his ring after he had bought a new one.
⑤ She didn't want to see the movie because she seen it before.

04 다음 중 어법상 어색한 문장은?

① After the guests had left, I went to bed.
② I felt a little better after I had taken the pill.
③ He has been playing a game for three hours.
④ We were late, and Mina had left by the time we got there.
⑤ You're a new student. How long had you been in this town?

[05-06] 다음 대화의 빈칸에 알맞은 것을 고르시오.

05

A Where is Rose?
B She isn't here. She _____ the museum.

① has been to   ② had been to
③ have been to   ④ has gone to
⑤ had gone to

≫ 실전 Tip have been to는 '~에 가 본 적이 있다'는 경험을 나타내고, have gone to는 '~에 가고 없다'는 결과를 나타낸다는 점에 유의한다.

06

A My brother and I are reading some books.
B Oh, how many books have you read?
A If I finish reading this book, I _____ ten books.

① have read   ② had read
③ will be read   ④ have been reading
⑤ will have read

07 다음 빈칸에 알맞은 말이 바르게 짝지어진 것은?

- When I got home, my family _____ their dinner.
- Janet _____ 17 next year. She expects a wonderful year.

① finished – has been
② have already finished – will be
③ have already finished – will have been
④ had already finished – will be
⑤ had already finished – has been

08 다음 글에서 어법상 어색한 부분을 찾아 바르게 고쳐 쓰시오.

> I have a sister. She is a good runner. She was so fast that I couldn't beat her and she still runs fast. She also paints well. She paints many pictures since she was little.

신유형

09 다음 질문에 알맞은 답을 괄호 안의 어구를 이용하여 완성하시오.

> **Q** Why did Sally call the police?
> **A** She called the police because _____ _____ _____ _____ her house last night. (a robber, break into)

10 다음 우리말과 같도록 빈칸에 알맞은 말을 쓰시오.

> 그는 다음 달이면 세 달 동안 병원에 있을 것이다.
> → He _____ _____ _____ in the hospital for three months by next month.

≫ 실전 Tip 「by+미래」, 「next+시간」, tomorrow 등은 미래완료 시제와 함께 자주 쓰이는 표현이다.

11 다음 대화의 밑줄 친 우리말을 괄호 안의 단어를 이용하여 영어로 쓰시오.

> **A** Have you thought about the problem?
> **B** Yes. 나는 그것에 대해 심각하게 생각해왔어. (seriously)

→ _____

12 다음 두 문장을 현재완료 진행시제를 사용하여 한 문장으로 바꿔 쓰시오.

> • I began to play computer games an hour ago.
> • I am still playing computer games.
> → _____ for an hour.

13 다음 두 문장을 한 문장으로 바꿔 쓸 때 빈칸에 알맞은 말을 쓰시오.

> • Dave had waited for her for two hours.
> • He was still waiting for her.
> → _____ for more than two hours.

[14-15] 다음 문장에서 어법상 어색한 부분을 찾아 바르게 고쳐 쓰시오.

14

> It has been snowing for three hours when we went out.

15

> Annie had been lying on the sofa since I came.

01 다음 우리말과 같도록 대화를 완성하시오.

> **A** _____ _____ _____ what the statement said just now? (방금 전에 발표에서 뭐라고 했는지 들었어?)
> **B** No, _____ _____. I _____ _____ _____ since two o'clock.
> (아니. 나는 2시부터 계속 TV를 보고 있었어.)

02 다음 문장 중 어법상 옳은 것끼리 묶은 것은?

> ⓐ I have been in Sydney in 2015.
> ⓑ She's been listening to music all day.
> ⓒ They have been played cards since 5 p.m.
> ⓓ He has finished painting the wall by tomorrow.
> ⓔ I had never visited an art gallery before last Sunday.

① ⓐ, ⓒ   ② ⓑ, ⓓ   ③ ⓑ, ⓔ
④ ⓐ, ⓑ, ⓔ   ⑤ ⓐ, ⓒ, ⓓ

03 다음 표를 보고, 아래의 질문에 대한 대답을 완전한 문장이 되도록 완성하시오.

Name	basketball	Chinese	piano
Minsu	1 year	3 years	×
Tim	×	×	2 years
Chris	6 years	4 months	×

> **A** How long has Minsu played basketball?
> **B** (1)_____
> **A** How long has Chris learned Chinese?
> **B** (2)_____
> **A** How long has Tim played the piano?
> **B** (3)_____

04 다음 그림을 보고, 소년이 어렸을 때 무엇을 했는지에 대해 묻고 답하는 대화를 과거완료 시제를 사용하여 완성하시오.

> **A** _____
> **B** _____

05 다음 우리말을 현재완료 진행시제를 이용하여 영어로 쓰시오.

(1)
> 그녀는 3시간 동안 케이크를 만들고 있다.

→ _____

(2)
> 그는 2시간 동안 그의 방을 청소하고 있다.

→ _____

06 다음 글의 밑줄 친 우리말을 괄호 안의 어구를 이용하여 영어로 쓰시오.

> Jessica is going to start running because she thinks she is too fat. 그녀는 이번 겨울이면 살이 빠질 것이다.

→ _____
(lose weight, by, winter)

01
- a He remained abroad since 2014.
- b He has remained abroad since 2014.

02
- a I have heard about him before.
- b I have heard about him two days ago.

03
- a She left the airport before I got there.
- b She had left the airport before I got there.

04
- a We have never seen the girl before then.
- b We had never seen the girl before then.

05
- a They will have known each other for two years next month.
- b They have known each other for two years next month.

06
- a If I go to Japan again, I will be there four times.
- b If I go to Japan again, I will have been there four times.

07
- a Mom has been baking cookies since you called her.
- b Mom had been baking cookies since you called her.

08
- a Before we got to the concert, many people have already started standing in line.
- b Before we got to the concert, many people had already started standing in line.

유형별 기출 적용 빈도

유형 O1 had better / would rather ▐ 25%
유형 O2 used to / would ▐ 25%
유형 O3 조동사 + have + p.p. ▐ 50%

》출제 포인트

조동사와 「조동사 + have + p.p.」의 종류에 따른 의미와 쓰임을 묻는 문제는 반드시 출제된다. used to와 would의 차이를 묻는 문제도 자주 출제된다.

》정답률 100% Tip

1 「be[get] used to + 동명사」는 '~에 익숙하다'의 의미를 나타냄
2 used to의 부정은 used not to / didn't use(d) to로 씀

Grammar Point

Point ① had better / would rather

You had better put on warm clothes. 〈~하는 것이 낫다〉
You had better not change your schedule. 〈~하지 않는 것이 낫다〉
I would rather drink milk than have some food. 〈would rather + 동사원형[A](+ than + 동사원형[B]): B하느니 차라리 A하겠다〉

Point ② used to / would

I used to[would] swim in this river. 〈과거의 습관〉
There used to be a tall tree around here. 〈과거의 상태〉
There would be a tall tree around here. (×) 〈would는 과거의 상태는 나타내지 못함〉

Point ③ 조동사 + have + p.p.

must have p.p.	~했음에 틀림없다
may[might] have p.p.	~했을지도 모른다
cannot have p.p.	~했을 리가 없다
should have p.p.	~했어야 한다
shouldn't have p.p.	~하지 말았어야 한다
could have p.p.	~할 수 있었을 텐데, ~했을지도 모른다

He must have seen the movie six or seven times.
She may[might] have said so.
They cannot have gone to the party.
I should have studied harder.
The police could have found it.

✅ 바로 체크

01 He had better (do / does) his homework first.

02 You (had not better / had better not) go outside.

03 We would rather sleep (or / than) read the book.

04 She (used to / is used to) go bowling every Friday.

05 There (would / used to) be a park here.

06 Eric (must / should) have forgotten his key. He can't go inside.

07 She (cannot / may) have looked cold, but she has a warm heart.

08 There were no tickets left. They (cannot / could) have gone to the concert.

09 I (should / shouldn't) have fallen asleep. I missed my favorite TV show.

대표유형 01 had better / would rather · 출제율 25%

01 다음 빈칸에 알맞은 말이 바르게 짝지어진 것은?

> · He _____ rather die than surrender.
> · You _____ better go to bed early.

① would – should
② used to – had
③ would – had
④ should – could
⑤ would – have

02 다음 대화의 밑줄 친 우리말을 영어로 바르게 옮긴 것은?

> **A** Harry, why don't we take a music class together?
> **B** I'm not interested in music. 난 음악 수업을 듣느니 차라리 역사 수업을 들을래.

① I will take a history class not a music class.
② I should take a history class than a music class.
③ I used to take a history class than a music class.
④ I would rather take a history class than a music class.
⑤ I must take a history class than a music class.

03 다음 밑줄 친 부분 중 어색한 것은?

① You'd better stop smoking.
② I'd better call her right now.
③ We had better go home now.
④ We had better make a reservation.
⑤ You had not better swim in the deep river.

04 다음 우리말을 영어로 바르게 옮긴 것은?

> 우리는 지금 당장 출발하는 것이 좋겠다.

① We had to start right now.
② We had better start right now.
③ We would start right now.
④ We used to start right now.
⑤ We had better not start right now.

05 다음 빈칸에 알맞은 말이 바르게 짝지어진 것은?

> I would rather _____ a walk in the park than _____ fishing in the river.

① take – go
② taking – go
③ to take – going
④ go for – going
⑤ going for – to go

06 다음 우리말과 같도록 괄호 안의 말을 바르게 배열하여 문장을 완성하시오.

> 길이 미끄러우니 너는 속도를 줄이는 것이 좋겠다.
> (better, slow down, the road, had, You, because, is, slippery)
> → _____

07 다음 우리말과 같도록 괄호 안의 단어를 이용하여 빈칸에 알맞은 말을 쓰시오.

> 나는 쇼핑을 가느니 차라리 집에 있겠다. (stay)
> → I _____ _____ _____ home than go shopping.

대표유형 02 used to / would · 출제율 25%

08 다음 대화의 빈칸에 알맞은 것은?

> **A** What's your favorite fruit?
> **B** I _____ like apples, but now I like grapes.

① should
② might
③ ought to
④ used to
⑤ could

09 다음 밑줄 친 부분과 바꿔 쓸 수 있는 것은?

> I used to play computer games a lot.

① could　　② might　　③ would
④ should　　⑤ had to

10 다음 〈보기〉의 밑줄 친 부분과 쓰임이 같은 것은?

> 보기　After lunch he would take a nap.

① Would you like a sandwich?
② She asked me if I would help her.
③ He would be a fool to accept it.
④ Every morning we would take a walk.
⑤ Would you mind opening the window?

11 다음 중 밑줄 친 부분의 쓰임이 나머지 넷과 다른 것은?

① I used to be a teacher.
② They used to be models.
③ She used to get up early.
④ He used to watch TV a lot.
⑤ It is used to clean the floor.

12 다음 글에서 어법상 어색한 부분을 찾아 바르게 고쳐 쓰시오.

> I am used to share a room with my brother. But now I have my own room.

13 다음 우리말과 같도록 빈칸에 알맞은 말을 쓰시오.

> 예전에 이 근처에 병원이 있었다.
> → There ＿＿＿＿＿＿＿＿＿＿＿＿
> 　around here.

14 다음 빈칸에 알맞은 말로 바르게 짝지어진 것은?

> • People used to ＿＿＿＿ that the Earth was flat.
> • I am not used to ＿＿＿＿ on the left.

① believe – drive
② believe – driving
③ believe – drove
④ believing – drive
⑤ believing – driving

15 다음 두 문장이 같은 뜻이 되도록 할 때 빈칸에 알맞은 것은?

> I'm sure that she didn't break the window.
> = She ＿＿＿＿ have broken the window.

① must　　② cannot　　③ may
④ could　　⑤ should

16 다음 중 어법상 옳은 문장은?

① Jane may have feel bad.
② He cannot have be rich.
③ They might have seen us.
④ You should have ate lunch.
⑤ She must has seen the movie.

17 다음 대화가 자연스럽도록 괄호 안의 단어를 이용하여 빈칸에 알맞은 말을 쓰시오.

> A Why was Tom absent yesterday?
> B He ＿＿＿＿ ＿＿＿＿ ＿＿＿＿ sick.
> (must)

18 다음 문장 뒤에 이어질 말로 자연스러운 것은?

> The player was given the red card and off the field.

① He must have played fair.
② He might have played fair.
③ He cannot have played fair.
④ He shouldn't have played fair.
⑤ He may have played fair.

19 다음 빈칸에 공통으로 알맞은 것은? (단, 대·소문자 무시)

> • _____ I borrow your pen?
> • She doesn't look well. She _____ have caught a cold.

① Can[can]
② May[may]
③ Will[will]
④ Should[should]
⑤ Ought to[ought to]

20 다음 빈칸에 알맞은 것은?

> I missed the train. I _____ have come earlier.

① must
② may
③ might
④ should
⑤ cannot

21 다음 두 문장이 같은 뜻이 되도록 할 때 빈칸에 알맞은 것은?

> I'm sorry that I didn't tell the truth.
> = I _____ have told the truth.

① must
② should
③ might
④ should not
⑤ cannot

22 다음 우리말을 영어로 바르게 옮긴 것은?

> 너는 나를 도와줄 수도 있었는데.

① You should have helped me.
② You may have helped me.
③ You cannot have helped me.
④ You could have help me.
⑤ You could have helped me.

23 다음 빈칸에 알맞은 것은?

> I had diarrhea all night. I _____ the food yesterday.   *diarrhea 설사

① should eat
② should be eaten
③ should have eaten
④ should not be eaten
⑤ should not have eaten

24 다음 문장에서 <u>어법상</u> 어색한 부분을 찾아 바르게 고쳐 쓰시오.

> He could have came here.

25 다음 대화의 빈칸에 괄호 안의 단어를 이용하여 알맞은 말을 쓰시오.

> **A** You know what? Jane won the contest.
> **B** I know. It's great. She _____ _____ _____ a lot. (practice)

대표유형 01, 03 had better / would rather / 조동사+have+p.p. 출제율 50%

01 다음 우리말과 같도록 괄호 안의 단어를 배열할 때 네 번째로 오는 단어로 알맞은 것은?

> 너는 너무 자주 밖에 나가지 않는 것이 좋겠다.
> (had, go, you, better, out, not, often, too)

① go ② not ③ had
④ out ⑤ better

≫ 실전 Tip had better의 부정은 had better not으로 쓴다.

02 다음 우리말을 영어로 바르게 옮긴 것은?

> 나는 춤을 추느니 차라리 노래를 부르겠다.

① I had better sing a song than dance.
② I used to sing a song than dance.
③ I would rather sing a song to dance.
④ I would rather singing a song than dancing.
⑤ I would rather sing a song than dance.

03 다음 중 어법상 옳은 문장은?
① You'd better taking a rest.
② You'd better not stay here.
③ I had better to get up early.
④ You don't had better eat snacks before dinner.
⑤ Kevin had better not plays computer games too much.

04 다음 빈칸에 알맞은 것은?

> Think of your health first. You _____ a balanced diet to stay healthy.

① had better keep ② used to keep
③ may have kept ④ would keep
⑤ shouldn't have kept

05 다음 두 문장이 같은 뜻이 되도록 할 때 빈칸에 알맞은 말은?

> I'm sure that she locked the door on purpose.
> = She _____ the door on purpose.

① might have locked
② should have locked
③ must have locked
④ cannot have locked
⑤ could have locked

대표유형 02 used to / would 출제율 25%

06 다음 빈칸에 알맞은 말로 바르게 짝지어진 것은?

> I _____ go fishing with my dad when I _____ young.

① could – am ② might – were
③ had to – been ④ would – was
⑤ used to – have been

07 다음 대화의 빈칸에 알맞은 것은?

> A Excuse me. Does Cindy live in this apartment?
> B She _____ live here, but she does not anymore.

① could ② might
③ would ④ should
⑤ used to

08 다음 문장에서 어법상 어색한 부분을 찾아 바르게 고쳐 쓰시오.

> There would be a mailbox in front of my house.

09 다음 우리말과 같도록 빈칸에 알맞은 말을 쓰시오.

> 그는 어렸을 때 몇 시간씩 축구를 하곤 했다.
> → When he was young, he _____ _____ soccer for hours.

대표유형 01, 03 | had better / would rather / 조동사+have+p.p. 출제율 50%

10 다음 두 문장이 같은 뜻이 되도록 괄호 안의 단어를 이용하여 빈칸에 알맞은 말을 쓰시오.

> I think it is impossible that he was there then.
> = He _____ _____ _____ there then. (cannot)

11 다음 밑줄 친 부분을 내용이 자연스럽도록 바르게 고쳐 쓰시오.

> I was blamed by my mom for coming home late without calling her. I <u>should call</u> my mom.

12 다음 내용이 자연스럽도록 괄호 안의 단어를 이용하여 빈칸에 알맞은 말을 쓰시오.

> The streets are all wet. It _____ _____ _____ all day long. (rain)

13 다음 우리말과 같도록 괄호 안의 단어를 이용하여 빈칸에 알맞은 말을 쓰시오.

> 그에게 무슨 일이 생겼을지도 모른다.
> → Something _____ _____ _____ to him. (happen)

14 다음 글에서 어색한 부분을 찾아 내용이 자연스럽도록 바르게 고쳐 쓰시오.

> He drove the car carelessly. His car hit the tree. He must have been more careful while driving.

통합형

15 다음 중 어법상 어색한 문장을 고른 후, 잘못된 부분을 바르게 고쳐 쓰시오.

> ⓐ Would you open the door?
> ⓑ My car wouldn't start this morning.
> ⓒ I would rather joined the reading club.
> ⓓ Would you please stay with me?
> ⓔ I would like to find a job.

_____ : _____ → _____

대표유형 01, 02 had better / would rather / used to / would   출제율 25%

01 다음 질문에 대한 응답으로 알맞은 것은?

> Can I park here although it says, "No Parking," here?

① Yes, you should.
② No, you'd rather.
③ No, you didn't use to.
④ No, you'd better not.
⑤ Yes, you have to.

02 다음 빈칸에 들어가기에 <u>어색한</u> 것은?

> As you know, overeating is bad for your health. You _____ stop overeating.

① must   ② ought to
③ had better   ④ should
⑤ are able to

03 다음 밑줄 친 ①~⑤ 중 어법상 <u>어색한</u> 것은?

> I ① used to have a good time ② with Rick. But these days, I ③ wouldn't rather talk ④ to him ⑤ in person.

04 다음 대화의 빈칸에 알맞은 것은?

> A You _____ slow down.
> B You are right. I ought to drive slowly and carefully.

① had better   ② hadn't to
③ used to   ④ had better not
⑤ would rather than

05 다음 대화의 빈칸에 알맞은 말로 바르게 짝지어진 것은?

> A How will you go there?
> B I'm not sure whether to go by plane or by train.
> A You _____ better go by plane. The plane is faster and more comfortable.
> C The plane _____ to be. But now the train takes less time and it is cheaper. I would _____ go there by train.

① have − use − rather
② have − used − rather
③ had − use − rather
④ had − used − rather
⑤ had − used − than

대표유형 02, 03 used to / would / 조동사 + have + p.p.   출제율 50%

06 다음 두 문장을 의미가 통하도록 한 문장으로 바꿔 쓸 때 빈칸에 알맞은 것을 <u>모두</u> 고르면?

> · He often visited my office before.
> · However he doesn't visit anymore.
> → He _____ my office.

① wouldn't visit   ② would visit
③ used to visit   ④ would rather visit
⑤ is used to visiting

07 다음 두 문장이 같은 뜻이 되도록 할 때 빈칸에 알맞은 것은?

> It doesn't seem that Ben studied anything about mathematics and science.
> → Ben _____ anything about mathematics and science.

① may have studied
② must have studied
③ cannot have studied
④ should not have studied
⑤ may not have studied

08 다음 글의 밑줄 친 ①~⑤ 중 어법상 어색한 것을 고른 후, 바르게 고쳐 쓰시오.

> He ① would be a family man. He ② would often wash the dishes. Also, he ③ usually ④ did the washing. So he ⑤ was used to the house chores.

09 다음 문장에서 어법상 어색한 부분을 찾아 바르게 고쳐 쓰시오.

> Roy used to not take a shower in the morning.

10 다음 글에서 어법상 어색한 부분을 모두 찾아 바르게 고쳐 쓰시오.

> There would be a church here. Every Sunday I used to coming here to pray. I also would meet my old friends and chatted with them.

11 다음 글에서 어색한 부분을 찾아 바르게 고쳐 쓰시오.

> Ted must have failed the final exam. He cannot have studied harder.

12 다음 대화의 내용이 자연스럽도록 괄호 안의 단어를 이용하여 빈칸에 알맞은 말을 쓰시오.

> **A** I saw Jack entering the store. But he wasn't there.
> **B** Wasn't he at the store? Then he _____ (go) out the back door. The store has a back door, too.

13 다음 대화에서 어색한 부분을 찾아 바르게 고쳐 쓰시오.

> **A** Why was Mike absent from school?
> **B** He may have been sick.
> **C** No way. Mike must have been sick. My mom saw him going into a PC game room. He must have played hooky.
>
> *play hooky 학교를 빼먹다

14 다음 문장을 같은 의미가 되도록 괄호 안의 어구를 이용하여 다시 쓰시오.

> I regret that I spent the money foolishly.
> → _____
> (should not)

15 다음 글의 빈칸에 알맞은 말을 쓰시오.

> Look at his car. It is very expensive. He must be rich. Was he rich in the past? I don't think so. He _____ rich. Look at his shabby clothes in the picture.
>
> *shabby 남루한

≫ 실전 Tip 과거의 일에 대한 확실한 추측은 긍정의 내용일 경우에는 must have p.p., 부정의 내용일 경우에는 cannot have p.p.를 쓴다.

01 조동사를 이용하여 다음 문장과 의미가 통하는 문장을 다시 쓰시오.

> It is certain that I put down the address wrong.
>
> → _____

02 다음 글을 읽고, 어법상 <u>어색한</u> 곳을 <u>모두</u> 찾아 바르게 고쳐 쓰시오.

> There would be a tall tree around here. I am used to climbing it up and down with my friends when I was a child. I would often reads books under it.

03 다음 글을 읽고, 마지막 질문에 알맞은 답을 괄호 안의 어구를 이용하여 완전한 문장으로 쓰시오.

> A man who has a serious problem in his lung and coughs a lot is now with a doctor. When the doctor advises him to quit smoking, what should the doctor say? (had better)
>
> → _____

04 다음 글의 빈칸 (a)~(c)에 알맞은 말로 바르게 짝지어진 것은?

> The girl ___(a)___ be fat, but she is thin now. I'm sure she ___(b)___ have exercised a lot. On the other hand, the boy was fat, and he is still fat. He ___(c)___ have exercised more.

① would – must – should
② would – must – shouldn't
③ used to – should – cannot
④ used to – must – should
⑤ used to – might – shouldn't

05 다음 밑줄 친 우리말을 조동사와 괄호 안의 어구를 이용하여 영어로 쓰시오.

> <u>그녀가 직접 그 편지를 썼을 리가 없다.</u> (by oneself)
> She must have had the letter written.
>
> → _____

06 다음 글을 읽고, 마지막 질문에 알맞은 답을 주어진 〈조건〉에 맞게 완성하시오.

> Yesterday she had an important interview. But she was late for the interview. So she lost a chance to work. She regrets that she was late for the interview. What would you say to her about yesterday's situation?

> [조건] 조동사와 not을 사용하여 과거의 일에 대한 후회를 나타낼 것

→ You _____.

01

a You had better not go to bed late.

b You had not better go to bed late.

02

a I would rather sleep than go to the movies.

b I would rather sleeping than going to the movies.

03

a He would to go hiking every Sunday.

b He would go hiking every Sunday.

04

a My sister would be very shy when she was young.

b My sister used to be very shy when she was young.

05

a He doesn't have a card. He must have lost it.

b He doesn't have a card. He cannot have lost it.

06

a The festival was a lot of fun. You might have come.

b The festival was a lot of fun. You should have come.

07

a Teddy is very honest. He could have stolen my smartphone.

b Teddy is very honest. He cannot have stolen my smartphone.

08

a There was a lot of traffic on the roads. He may have been late for work.

b There was a lot of traffic on the roads. He should have been late for work.

유형별 기출 적용 빈도

유형 01 명사적 용법   35%

유형 02 to부정사의 부정   10%

유형 03 의문사 + to부정사   20%

유형 04 가주어, 의미상 주어, 가목적어   25%

유형 05 It takes ~ to부정사   10%

>> 출제 포인트
to부정사의 용법을 구분하는 문제는 반드시 출제된다. to부정사의 의미상 주어를 나타낼 때 for와 of를 구별하는 문제와 「의문사 + to부정사」에서 어순 및 의문사의 종류를 묻는 문제는 학교 시험에서 단골로 출제된다.

>> 정답률 100% Tip
1 사람의 성격을 나타내는 형용사가 보어로 쓰였을 때 의미상 주어는 'of + 목적격'
2 가목적어의 위치 주의하기

Grammar Point

Point 1 명사적 용법

to부정사는 명사처럼 문장의 주어, 보어, 목적어 역할을 할 수 있으며 '~하는 것, ~하기'라고 해석한다. to부정사의 부정은 「not [never] + to부정사」의 형태이다.

Point 2 의문사 + to부정사

명사처럼 쓰이며 「의문사 + 주어 + should + 동사원형」으로 바꿔 쓸 수 있다.

what + to부정사	무엇을 ~할지	when + to부정사	언제 ~할지
where + to부정사	어디로 ~할지	how + to부정사	어떻게 ~할지, ~하는 방법
which + to부정사	어느 것을 ~할지	who(m) + to부정사	누가[누구를] ~할지

Point 3 가주어, 의미상 주어, 가목적어

가주어	to부정사가 주어일 때 가주어 it을 사용하여 「It ~ to부정사(구) ~」의 형태로 쓰고, 이때 it은 해석하지 않는다.
의미상 주어	to부정사가 나타내는 동작의 주체를 의미상 주어라고 한다. It ~ 일반적인 형용사 + for + 목적격 + to부정사(구) ~ It ~ 성격을 나타내는 형용사 + of + 목적격 + to부정사(구) ~ ＊성격을 나타내는 형용사: kind, wise, brave, polite, rude 등
가목적어	5형식에서 to부정사가 목적어일 때 가목적어 it을 사용하여 「주어 + 동사 + it + 목적격보어 + to부정사(구) ~」의 형태로 쓰고, 이때 it은 해석하지 않는다. • I found it difficult to pass the test.

Point 4 It takes ~ to부정사

「It takes + 목적격 + 시간 + to부정사」는 '~가 …하는 데 시간이 걸리다'라는 의미이고, 「It takes + 시간 + for + 목적격 + to부정사」로 바꿔 쓸 수 있다.

✅ 바로 체크

01 Her dream is <u>to become</u> a pilot.
　　　　(주어 / 목적어 / 보어)

02 The boy wants <u>to buy</u> the toy.
　　　　(주어 / 목적어 / 보어)

03 It is hard for (his / him) to make friends.

04 It is not easy (for / of) me to take care of my dog.

05 Try (to not stay / not to stay) up late.

06 I don't know how I should get there.
　= I don't know how _____ _____ there.

07 To live without air is impossible.
　= _____ is impossible to live without air.

08 It took me an hour to complete the puzzle.
　= It took an hour _____ _____ to complete the puzzle.

대표유형 01 명사적 용법   출제율 35%

01 다음 문장 중 어법상 <u>어색한</u> 것은?

① All I want is to be with you.
② He tried to make up with her.
③ This bench needs to be painted.
④ Relieve stress helps you sleep better.
⑤ His plan for this year is to lose 5 kilograms.

02 다음 빈칸에 들어갈 말로 알맞은 것은?

> The important thing is _____ what you have now.

① appreciates
② appreciated
③ to appreciate
④ being appreciate
⑤ to appreciating

03 다음 우리말과 같도록 괄호 안의 단어를 이용하여 문장을 완성하시오.

> 나는 과학자가 되고 싶다. (want)
> → I _____ _____ _____ a scientist.

04 다음 〈보기〉의 밑줄 친 부분과 쓰임이 같은 것은?

> 보기   My dream is <u>to be</u> a weather forecaster.

① Do you want <u>to take</u> a rest?
② His goal is <u>to have</u> a balanced diet.
③ I would like <u>to take</u> a trip to Australia.
④ <u>To be</u> or not to be, that is the question.
⑤ You promised me <u>to clean</u> your room.

05 다음 빈칸에 알맞지 <u>않은</u> 것은?

> I _____ to stay at home all day.

① planned
② hated
③ decided
④ hoped
⑤ minded

06 다음 괄호 안의 표현을 이용하여 우리말을 영작하시오.

> 그들은 영화관에 가기로 결정했다.
> (decide, go, the theater)

→ _____

07 다음 괄호 안의 표현을 바르게 배열하여 문장을 완성하시오.

> Jane really wanted _____
> (her mom, praised, be, by, to).

08 다음 〈보기〉에 주어진 단어를 이용하여 빈칸에 알맞은 말을 쓰시오.

> 보기   help   become

> Sam liked _____ sick people.
> So, he decided _____ a doctor.

대표유형 02 to부정사의 부정   출제율 10%

09 다음 우리말과 같도록 할 때 not이 들어가기에 알맞은 곳은?

> 소방관은 사람들에게 집으로 들어가지 말라고 명령했다.
> → The firefighter (①) ordered (②) people (③) to (④) enter (⑤) the house.

10 다음 우리말과 같도록 괄호 안의 단어를 이용하여 빈칸에 알맞은 말을 쓰시오.

> 우리는 그 정보를 밝히지 않는 데 동의했다.
> → We agreed _____ _____ _____ the information. (not, reveal)

11 다음 우리말과 같도록 괄호 안의 단어를 바르게 배열하여 문장을 완성하시오.

> 엄마는 내가 만화책을 너무 많이 읽지 않기를 원하셨다.
> → My mother _____ (me, to, read, wanted, not) comic books too much.

대표유형 03 의문사 + to부정사   출제율 20%

12 다음 빈칸에 공통으로 알맞은 것은? (단, 대·소문자 무시)

> • Do you know _____ to get to the post office?
> • _____ about a cup of tea?

① what [What]   ② where [Where]
③ when [When]   ④ how [How]
⑤ which [Which]

13 다음 두 문장의 의미가 같도록 빈칸에 알맞은 말을 쓰시오.

> I don't know what I should do next.
> = I don't know _____ _____ _____ next.

14 다음 〈보기〉에서 알맞은 말을 골라 대화를 완성하시오.

> 보기   where   when   watch   put

(1) **A** Please tell me _____ _____ _____ this flower pot.
     B Next to the bookshelf.

(2) **A** Did you decide to watch the movie?
     B Yeah, but we haven't decided _____ _____ _____ it.

15 다음 문장에서 어법상 어색한 부분을 찾아 바르게 고쳐 쓰시오.

> I couldn't decide to choose which between the two.

대표유형 04 가주어, 의미상 주어, 가목적어   출제율 25%

16 다음 빈칸에 알맞지 않은 것은?

> It is _____ for me to do that.

① interesting   ② hard   ③ careless
④ dangerous   ⑤ impossible

17 다음 빈칸에 들어갈 말이 순서대로 바르게 짝지어진 것은?

> _____ is natural _____ parents _____
> want to protect their children.

① It – for – to   ② It – of – to
③ It – for – that   ④ This – of – to
⑤ This – of – to

18 다음 빈칸에 알맞지 <u>않은</u> 것은?

> It was _____ of you to behave like that.

① rude   ② polite   ③ wise
④ smart   ⑤ important

19 다음 우리말과 같도록 괄호 안의 단어를 바르게 배열하시오.

> 나는 그녀를 이해하기 어렵다고 느꼈다.
> (I, to, her, hard, understand, found, it)

→ _____

20 주어진 문장과 의미가 같도록 빈칸에 알맞은 말을 쓰시오.

> To swim in the river is not safe.
> → _____ _____ _____
>   _____ _____ in the river.

21 다음 우리말을 괄호 안의 표현을 이용하여 <u>7단어</u>로 영작하시오.

> 음식물 쓰레기를 줄이는 것은 필수적이다.
> (necessary, reduce, food waste)

→ _____

22 다음 우리말을 영어로 옮긴 문장의 빈칸에 들어갈 말로 알맞은 것은?

> 기술은 전 세계의 사람들을 연결시키는 것을 더 쉽게 만들었다.
> → Technology _____ with people
>   around the world.

① made easier to connect
② made it easier to connect
③ made easier connecting it
④ made connect it easier
⑤ made to connect it easier

대표유형 05 It takes ~ to부정사   출제율 10%

23 다음 빈칸에 들어갈 말로 알맞은 것은?

> It took me only one minute _____
> the problem.

① solve   ② solving
③ to solve   ④ to be solved
⑤ having solved

24 다음 두 문장의 의미가 같도록 빈칸에 알맞은 말을 쓰시오.

> It will take him some time to make up his mind.
> = It will take some time _____ _____
>   to make up his mind.

25 다음 우리말과 같도록 괄호 안의 표현을 바르게 배열하시오

> 그녀가 이 조각품을 완성하는 데 세 달이 걸렸다.
> (three months, took, her, this sculpture, to, finish, for, it)

→ _____

대표유형 01   명사적 용법   출제율 35%

01 다음 중 빈칸에 to를 쓸 수 <u>없는</u> 것은?

① This song is easy _____ sing.

② I helped my little brother _____ do his homework.

③ My mother agreed _____ buy a digital camera.

④ Why did you decide _____ quit working?

⑤ Jason's jokes always make me _____ laugh.

02 다음 문장 중 어법상 옳은 것은?

① She refused going back together.

② He promised calling me every day.

③ They enjoyed to walk along the street.

④ She loves to hang out with her friends.

⑤ He practices to paint for amusement.

03 다음 중 밑줄 친 부분의 쓰임이 나머지 넷과 <u>다른</u> 것은?

① I want <u>to sign</u> up for a yoga class.

② <u>To learn</u> a foreign language is not easy.

③ Ellen studied hard <u>to pass</u> the exam.

④ I have decided <u>to be</u> a baseball player.

⑤ My dream is <u>to become</u> a great computer programmer.

대표유형 02   to부정사의 부정   출제율 10%

04 다음 문장 중 어법상 <u>어색한</u> 것은?

① I tried not to make any noise.

② I told him never to speak ill of others.

③ I hope to not be late for the festival.

④ Josh decided not to eat too many sweets.

⑤ You have to wash your hands not to catch a cold.

05 다음 우리말과 같도록 할 때 빈칸에 알맞은 것은?

> Mom, I'm OK. Tell Dad _____.
> (엄마, 저는 괜찮아요. 아빠에게 걱정하지 말라고 말 씀드려 주세요.)

① not worry

② not worrying

③ to not worry

④ not to worry

⑤ to worry not

대표유형 03   의문사 + to부정사   출제율 20%

06 다음 중 밑줄 친 부분의 쓰임이 어법상 <u>어색한</u> 것은?

① I can't find <u>how to get</u> to the museum.

② Can you tell me <u>when to start</u> the class?

③ He doesn't know <u>what to eat</u> for dinner.

④ I want to know <u>what to fix</u> this machine.

⑤ Does he know <u>where to experience</u> Korean culture?

07 다음 문장 중 어법상 <u>어색한</u> 것은?

① I don't know why to do it.

② Tell me which way to go.

③ I wonder when to visit his office.

④ Do you know how to set the alarm?

⑤ I don't know what to say about the topic.

대표유형 04 가주어, 의미상 주어, 가목적어   출제율 25%

08 다음 괄호 안의 표현을 바르게 배열하여 문장을 완성하시오.

> Frankly speaking, _____
> _____. (me, it is, learn, difficult, for, to, English)

09 다음 〈보기〉와 같이 두 문장을 의미가 통하는 한 문장으로 쓸 때 빈칸에 알맞은 말을 쓰시오.

> 보기   She can solve the problem. She is smart.
> → It is smart of her to solve the problem.

(1) He helped me with my homework. He was kind.
    → It was _____.

(2) I should take care of my sister. It is not easy.
    → It is _____.

10 다음 우리말을 괄호 안의 표현을 이용하여 영작하시오.

> 네가 스트레스를 관리하는 법을 배우는 것은 중요하다.
> (it, important, you, how, manage stress)

→ _____

신유형
11 다음 괄호 안의 단어를 활용하여 빈칸에 알맞은 말을 쓰시오.

> • It is not always easy _____ _____ to say "no." (I)
> • It is polite _____ _____ to give them a thank-you letter. (he)
> • I want _____ to do the dishes. (she)

대표유형 05 It takes ~ to부정사   출제율 10%

12 다음 우리말을 괄호 안의 표현을 이용하여 두 개로 영작하시오.

> 내가 아빠를 위한 선물을 찾는 데 두 시간이 걸렸다.
> (took, find a present for Dad)
> → _____
> → _____

13 다음 우리말과 같도록 빈칸에 알맞은 말을 쓰시오.

> 그녀가 어디로 가야 할지 정하는 데 시간이 걸릴 것이다. (will, take, some time, decide)
> → _____
>   where to go.

14 다음 괄호 안의 정보를 이용하여 질문에 완전한 문장으로 답하시오.

> **A** How long will it take you to get ready for the party? (30분)
> **B** _____

신유형
15 다음 빈칸에 공통으로 알맞은 말을 쓰시오.

> • It took me one hour _____ a bath.
> • He didn't allow me _____ a rest.
> • I want _____ a picture with you.

대표유형 04 가주어, 의미상 주어, 가목적어 출제율 25%

01 다음 문장 중 어법상 <u>어색한</u> 것은?

① It is stupid of you to think so.
② It is not easy for my uncle to get a job.
③ It is nice of you to send me an email.
④ It is difficult of me to make a speech.
⑤ It is very important for drivers to slow down in school zones.

02 다음 중 빈칸에 들어갈 말이 나머지 넷과 <u>다른</u> 것은?

① It was rude _____ her to yell at the waiter.
② It is natural _____ him to be kind to everyone.
③ It was careless _____ my mother not to lock the door.
④ It was brave _____ her to travel alone.
⑤ It was wise _____ you to call 119.

03 다음 우리말을 영어로 바르게 옮긴 것은?

나는 혼자서 그 상황을 감당하는 것이 불가능하다고 생각했다.

① I thought it is impossible handle the situation by myself.
② I thought handle the situation by myself is impossible.
③ I thought impossible to handle the situation by myself.
④ I thought it to handle the situation by myself impossible.
⑤ I thought it impossible to handle the situation by myself.

통합형

04 다음 중 밑줄 친 It의 쓰임이 나머지 넷과 <u>다른</u> 것은?

① It will be nice to meet you again.
② It took me so long to write the essay.
③ It is difficult but interesting to learn another language.
④ It is hard for the elderly to use smartphones.
⑤ It was useless to argue with him.

대표유형 05 It takes ~ to부정사 출제율 10%

05 다음 문장 중 어법상 <u>어색한</u> 것은?

① It takes him two hours to get to the airport.
② It will take a whole day her to clean the house.
③ It took me an hour to finish the homework.
④ It took her a month to recover from the injury.
⑤ It will take each of you a different amount of time to solve this puzzle.

06 다음 글의 밑줄 친 ① ~ ⑤ 중, 어법상 <u>어색한</u> 것은?

John lives in New York. He is ① going to Miami today. It is time ② for him ③ to leave for the airport. It will ④ take one and a half hours for him ⑤ arriving at the airport.

07 다음 우리말을 영어로 바르게 옮긴 것을 <u>모두</u> 고르면?

그가 그녀를 용서하기로 결심하는 데 오랜 시간이 걸렸다.

① He took a long time to decide to forgive her.
② It took for him a long time to decide to forgive her.
③ It took him a long time to decide to forgive her.
④ It took a long time for him decide to forgive her.
⑤ It took a long time for him to decide to forgive her.

대표유형 01 명사적 용법   출제율 35%

08 다음 표현을 바르게 배열하여 문장을 완성하시오.

> they, get, agreed, with, to, along, each other

→ _____

09 다음 대화에서 어법상 <u>어색한</u> 부분을 찾아 바르게 고쳐 쓰시오.

> **A** When are you going to leave?
> **B** We expect leaving tomorrow.

10 다음은 담임선생님이 학생들에게 남긴 쪽지이다. 〈보기〉와 같이 문장을 완성하시오.

> Do your homework. (1) Do not make any noise. (2) Turn off the lights and fans when you go out. (3) Do not make a mess.

> **보기**   The teacher told us to do our homework.

(1) The teacher asked _____ .

(2) The teacher wanted _____

_____ .

(3) The teacher ordered _____ .

대표유형 02 to부정사의 부정   출제율 10%

11 다음 대화를 한 문장으로 요약할 때 빈칸에 알맞은 말을 쓰시오.

> **Andy** Do not go out alone at night.
> **Betty** Why?
> **Andy** You know, it's not safe at night in New York.

→ Andy told Betty _____
in New York because it's not safe.

신유형

12 다음 대화의 내용과 일치하도록 대화에 있는 표현을 이용하여 빈칸에 알맞은 말을 쓰시오.

> **A** Should we buy a new house?
> **B** No, I don't think that's a good idea right now.
> **A** I think you're right.

→ They decided _____ .

대표유형 03 의문사 + to부정사   출제율 20%

13 다음 두 문장의 의미가 같도록 빈칸에 알맞은 말을 쓰시오.

> I couldn't find which way I should go.
> = I couldn't find _____ _____
> _____ _____ .

14 다음 대화의 밑줄 친 우리말을 to부정사를 이용하여 영작하시오.

> **A** <u>나는 내 컴퓨터를 고치는 방법을 모르겠어.</u>
> **B** Hmm... How about asking Steve for help? He's a computer geek.
> **A** Good idea.

→ _____

15 다음 주어진 〈조건〉에 맞게 우리말을 두 개로 영작하시오.

> 우리는 오늘밤에 어디에서 머물지 아직 결정하지 못했다.
> → _____
> → _____

> [조건] **1.** 현재완료 시제를 쓸 것
> **2.** decide, yet, stay를 활용할 것

01 다음 문장 중 어법상 <u>어색한</u> 것을 <u>모두</u> 고르면?

① I felt my knees to shake with fear.
② I didn't expect him to come to the party.
③ Her doctor ordered her to rest for a week.
④ How generous of you to say so!
⑤ It takes for the flower 10 weeks to bloom.

02 다음 중 어법상 옳은 문장의 개수는?

ⓐ He decided not to wait any longer.
ⓑ It is foolish for me to trust him.
ⓒ I wanted him to stay with me as long as possible.
ⓓ It is dangerous to play with a ball on the street.
ⓔ It is hard to concentrate for me when there is a lot of noise.
ⓕ I promised never to tell a lie again.

① 2개   ② 3개   ③ 4개
④ 5개   ⑤ 6개

03 다음 그림을 보고 괄호 안의 단어를 이용하여 대화를 알맞게 완성하시오.

(1)

A Can you show me _____ _____ _____ this copy machine? (use)
B Sure. Let me help you with it.

(2)

A Which dress are you going to wear to the party?
B Well, I can't decide _____ _____ _____ _____. (wear)

04 다음 문장 중 어법상 옳은 것끼리 짝지어진 것은?

ⓐ Does he know to how cook *pad thai*?
ⓑ She tries not to put on weight.
ⓒ I found difficult to exercise every day.
ⓓ It is convenient for me to read e-books.

① ⓐ, ⓑ   ② ⓐ, ⓒ   ③ ⓐ, ⓓ
④ ⓑ, ⓒ   ⑤ ⓑ, ⓓ

05 다음 두 문장을 한 문장으로 바꿀 때 빈칸에 알맞은 말을 쓰시오.

(1) He lost his passport. He was careless.
→ It was _____.

(2) She wants to win the audition. It is impossible.
→ It is _____.

[06-07] 다음 그림을 보고 주어진 질문에 완전한 문장으로 답하시오.

06

Q How long did it take for Jane to paint the picture?
A _____

07

Q How long did it take for Steven to wash the car?
A _____

01

a Make new kinds of food are not easy.

b To make new kinds of food is not easy.

02

a My wish is to travel around the world by bike.

b My wish is travels around the world by bike.

03

a He promised to calling me once a week.

b He promised to call me once a week.

04

a My homeroom teacher told me not to be late for school.

b My homeroom teacher told me never be late for school.

05

a The actress found it hard to memorize her lines.

b The actress found hard to memorize her lines.

06

a He knows how to play the violin.

b He knows to how play the violin.

07

a It is hard of me to sleep when the light is on.

b It is hard for me to sleep when the light is on.

08

a It took a long time for me to choose where to live.

b It took for me a long time to choose where to live.

유형별 기출 적용 빈도

유형 01 형용사적 용법   20%

유형 02 「be + to부정사」   10%

유형 03 부사적 용법   25%

유형 04 too ~ to / enough to   30%

유형 05 seem to   15%

>> 출제 포인트

to부정사의 용법을 구분하는 문제와 to부정사를 이용한 문장 전환 문제가 자주 출제된다.

>> 정답률 100% Tip

1 형용사적 용법으로 쓰인 to부정사의 어순에 주의하기
2 too ~ to와 enough to를 「so ... that ~ can [can't] + 동사원형」을 이용하여 바꿔 쓸 때 주어와 시제 일치, that절에 동사의 목적어가 필요한 경우 등에 주의하기

Grammar Point

Point ① 형용사적 용법

to부정사는 형용사처럼 명사 또는 대명사를 뒤에서 수식할 수 있고, '~할, ~하는'이라는 의미를 나타낸다.

주의 -thing, -one, -body (+ 형용사) + to부정사 / (대)명사 + to부정사 + 전치사

Point ② 「be + to부정사」

「be + to부정사」는 예정(~할 예정이다), 의무(~해야 한다), 가능(~할 수 있다), 운명(~할 운명이다), 의지(~할 작정이다) 등의 의미를 나타낸다.

Point ③ 부사적 용법

to부정사는 부사처럼 동사, 형용사, 부사를 수식할 수 있으며 목적(in order to / so as to), 감정의 원인, 판단의 근거, 결과 등을 나타낸다.

Point ④ too ~ to / enough to

too + 형용사/부사(+ for + 목적격) + to부정사 → so + 형용사/부사 + that + 주어 + can't + 동사원형	…하기에 너무 ~한/하게
형용사/부사 + enough(+ for + 목적격) + to부정사 → so + 형용사/부사 + that + 주어 + can + 동사원형	…할 만큼 충분히 ~한/하게

The movie was too boring for me to watch.
Julia was kind enough to lend me the book.

Point ⑤ seem to

• 「seem to + 동사원형」은 '~인 것 같다'라는 의미이고, 「주어 + seem(s) to + 동사원형」은 「It seems that + 주어 + 동사 ~」로 바꿔 쓸 수 있다.
• 완료부정사는 「to + have + p.p.」의 형태로 to부정사의 행위가 본동사의 시제보다 이전에 일어났을 때 사용한다.

✔ 바로 체크

01 I have many chores to do.
   ☐ 형용사적 용법   ☐ 부사적 용법

02 We were glad to win the game.
   ☐ 형용사적 용법   ☐ 부사적 용법

03 He grew up to be a nurse.
   ☐ 목적   ☐ 결과

04 If you are to be rich, you have to be diligent.   ☐ 의지   ☐ 의무

05 She is so fast that she can win the race.
   → She is fast _____ _____ win the race.

06 Jack is so young that he can't drive a car.
   → Jack is _____ young _____ drive a car.

07 It seemed that Jane told a lie.
   → Jane seemed _____ a lie.

08 It seems that Sam loved her.
   → Sam seems _____ her.

대표유형 01 형용사적 용법   출제율 20%

01 다음 우리말에 맞게 빈칸에 들어갈 말로 알맞은 것은?

> 그 신혼부부는 살 집을 찾고 있다.
> → The newly-married couple is looking for a house _____.

① living   ② to live
③ to live in   ④ living in
⑤ to living in

02 다음 우리말과 같도록 괄호 안의 어구를 바르게 배열하시오.

> 그들은 돌봐야 할 많은 아이들이 있다.
> (they, children, have, look after, to, a lot of)
> → _____

>> 실전 Tip 동사구가 to부정사와 함께 쓰여 명사를 수식하는 경우에는 전치사를 빠뜨리지 않도록 주의한다.

03 괄호 안에 주어진 단어를 바르게 배열하여 대화를 완성하시오.

> A It's really hot today.
> B Yeah, it is. Let's go and buy _____
> _____. (drink, cold, to, something)

통합형

04 다음 중 밑줄 친 부분의 쓰임이 〈보기〉와 같은 것은?

> 보기 I don't have anything to wear.

① Is there a place to park my car?
② It is hard to take care of pets.
③ To earn money, I got a part-time job.
④ She grew up to become a famous singer.
⑤ The sneakers are comfortable to wear.

05 다음 중 밑줄 친 부분의 쓰임이 나머지 넷과 다른 것은?

① I want something exciting to do.
② There is little food to eat in the fridge.
③ What is the best way to persuade someone?
④ He must be a fool to believe such a story.
⑤ Joey needs someone to take care of him.

대표유형 02 「be + to부정사」   출제율 10%

06 다음 빈칸에 들어갈 말로 알맞은 것은?

> People are _____ their helmets when they ride a bike.

① wear   ② wore
③ to wear   ④ be wearing
⑤ to wearing

07 다음 밑줄 친 부분과 바꿔 쓸 수 있는 것은?

> My cousin is to stay here for a month.

① seems to   ② is going to
③ is likely to   ④ is able to
⑤ would like to

08 다음 중 밑줄 친 부분의 쓰임이 〈보기〉와 같은 것은?

> 보기 You are to report any problem to me.

① The airplane is to take off in a minute.
② She was never to meet her child again.
③ No one was to be seen in the street.
④ If you are to win, you should practice harder.
⑤ You are to hand in the essay by Friday.

대표유형 03 부사적 용법 출제율 25%

09 다음 대화의 빈칸에 들어갈 말로 알맞은 것은?

> **A** Why did you go to Italy?
> **B** I went there _____ fashion design.

① study ② studying ③ to study
④ to studying ⑤ to be study

10 다음 중 밑줄 친 부분의 쓰임이 나머지 넷과 다른 것은?

① I went to the library to return books.
② Emma left home early to get a good seat.
③ Janet turned on the computer to write a report.
④ To achieve your goals, you have to work hard.
⑤ I was so surprised to run into an old friend of mine.

[11-12] 다음 두 문장의 의미가 같도록 빈칸에 알맞은 말을 쓰시오.

11
> I was so pleased because I received her invitation.
> = I was so pleased _____ _____
> _____ _____.

12
> Jessica stopped to watch the street performance.
> = Jessica stopped _____ _____
> _____ _____ the street performance.

≫ 실전 Tip 「stop + to부정사」: ~하기 위해 멈추다(목적을 나타내는 부사적 용법의 to부정사)

13 다음 중 밑줄 친 부분의 쓰임이 〈보기〉와 같은 것은?

> 보기 She lived to be 99 years old.

① I'm sorry to bother you.
② He awoke to find himself lying on the grass.
③ Korean is so easy for me to read.
④ She goes to Lucy's to have her hair cut.
⑤ He must be rich to pay cash for the car.

≫ 실전 Tip 결과를 의미하는 to부정사와 함께 자주 쓰이는 동사에는 live, awake, grow up 등이 있다.

14 다음 우리말과 같도록 괄호 안의 어구를 바르게 배열하시오.

> 그는 경기에서 지지 않기 위해 최선을 다했다.
> (best, lose, the game, he, his, to, did, not)
> → _____

대표유형 04 too ~ to / enough to 출제율 30%

15 다음 우리말과 같도록 빈칸에 알맞은 말을 쓰시오.

> 그는 너무 지쳐서 더 이상 걸을 수 없다.
> → He is _____ tired _____ walk any farther.

16 다음 괄호 안의 단어를 바르게 배열한 것은?

> Her son is (to, old, go, enough) to school.

① enough old to go
② to old enough go
③ to go old enough
④ to go enough old
⑤ old enough to go

[17-18] 다음 문장과 같은 뜻이 되도록 빈칸에 알맞은 말을 쓰시오.

17

The shirts are so tight that Brad can't wear them.
= The shirts are _____ _____ for Brad _____ _____.

18

It is so warm that you can relax on the beach.
= It is _____ _____ for you _____ _____ on the beach.

19 다음 문장의 밑줄 친 ① ~ ⑤ 중 어법상 어색한 것은?

Jason's grades ① aren't ② enough good ③ for him ④ to apply ⑤ to Harvard.

20 다음 문장과 의미가 가장 유사한 것은?

The water was so deep that I couldn't touch the bottom.

① The water was too deep for me to touch the bottom.
② The water was too deep of me to touch the bottom.
③ The water was deep enough for me to touch the bottom.
④ The water was not too deep to touch the bottom.
⑤ The water was enough deep for me not to touch the bottom.

21 다음 문장에서 enough가 들어가기에 알맞은 곳은?

My grandma thinks (①) that (②) she is (③) still (④) healthy (⑤) to go on a trip.

대표유형 05 seem to   출제율 15%

22 다음 우리말과 같은 뜻이 되도록 빈칸에 들어갈 말로 알맞은 것은?

Laura는 여전히 내게 화난 것처럼 보인다.
→ Laura still seems _____ mad at me.

① be   ② to be
③ being   ④ to being
⑤ to have been

23 다음 두 문장이 같은 뜻이 되도록 빈칸에 들어갈 말로 알맞은 것은?

It seems that Robin did something wrong.
= Robin _____ something wrong.

① seems to do   ② seems to doing
③ seemed to do   ④ seems to have done
⑤ seemed to have done

24 다음 두 문장의 뜻이 같도록 빈칸에 알맞은 말을 쓰시오.
(1) No one seems to care about the problem.
   = _____ _____ that no one _____ about the problem.
(2) David seemed to have lost the car keys.
   = _____ _____ that David _____ _____ the car keys.

25 다음 문장과 같은 뜻이 되도록 괄호 안의 지시대로 바꿔 쓰시오.

It seemed that you were surprised.
= _____ (you를 주어로)

대표유형 01, 03 형용사적 용법/부사적 용법　출제율 25%

01 다음 중 밑줄 친 부분의 쓰임이 나머지 넷과 다른 것은?

① Everyone has a right to speak freely.
② Alex was happy to return to his country.
③ I went to the bank to open a bank account.
④ He must be rude to ignore the elderly man.
⑤ Danny's handwriting is impossible to read.

02 다음 중 빈칸에 들어갈 말이 바르게 짝지어진 것은?

· They bought their baby a toy _____.
· I rested at home _____ from the flight.

① to play – to recover
② to play – recovering
③ to play in – recovered
④ to play at – to recover
⑤ to play with – to recover

통합형

03 다음 중 빈칸에 to가 들어갈 수 없는 것을 모두 고르면?

① Everyone needs someone _____ love.
② Dad made me _____ walk the dog.
③ I nodded my head in order _____ show that I understood.
④ Dorothy awoke _____ see her baby smiling at her.
⑤ This oil soap can be used _____ washing.

04 다음 중 〈보기〉의 밑줄 친 부분과 쓰임이 같은 것은?

보기　I was pleased to meet my old friend.

① Our school has many rules to follow.
② The password is not easy to remember.
③ I visited Egypt to see the pyramids.
④ We were upset to miss out on the World Cup.
⑤ Deborah grew up to be a professional golfer.

05 다음 중 어법상 옳은 문장끼리 묶은 것은?

ⓐ We have no time to lose.
ⓑ Can you lend me a pen to write?
ⓒ Jessy was excited to get a new job.
ⓓ I have important something to tell you.
ⓔ We should reduce food waste to protect the Earth.

① ⓐ, ⓑ, ⓓ
② ⓐ, ⓒ, ⓔ
③ ⓑ, ⓒ, ⓓ
④ ⓑ, ⓓ, ⓔ
⑤ ⓒ, ⓓ, ⓔ

대표유형 02 「be+to부정사」　출제율 10%

06 다음 중 짝지어진 두 문장의 의미가 서로 다른 것은?

① Not a single word was to be heard.
= Not a single word could be heard.
② You are not to feed the animals in the zoo.
= You don't have to feed the animals in the zoo.
③ Michael is to appear in court tomorrow.
= Michael is going to appear in court tomorrow.
④ They were not to see each other again.
= They were destined not to see each other again.
⑤ If you are to win others' trust, you should be honest.
= If you intend to win others' trust, you should be honest.

07 다음 중 밑줄 친 부분의 쓰임이 나머지 넷과 다른 것은?

① This train is to leave in a minute.
② Bella and I are to meet at the library.
③ David is to join our club next week.
④ The conference is to be held next month.
⑤ If you are to be a baseball player, you should practice a lot.

대표유형 01   형용사적 용법   출제율 20%

08 다음 우리말에 맞게 괄호 안의 단어를 바르게 배열하시오. (단, 한 개의 단어를 추가할 것)

> 나는 달콤한 먹을 것이 필요하다.
> (eat, sweet, need, I, something)
> → _____

신유형

09 다음 그림을 보고, 괄호 안의 단어를 이용하여 〈보기〉와 같이 각 인물에게 필요한 것을 나타내는 문장을 쓰시오. (단, to부정사의 형용사적 용법을 이용할 것)

> 보기   (book, read)
> → I need a book to read.

(1)

(chair, sit)

→ _____

(2)

(fork, eat)

→ _____

대표유형 03   부사적 용법   출제율 25%

10 〈조건〉에 맞게 다음 문장을 바꿔 쓰시오.

> [조건] **1.** to부정사를 이용할 것
>   **2.** 주어진 말로 시작하되, 8단어를 추가하여 문장을 완성할 것

> Abbie wanted to improve her writing skills, so she kept a diary.
> → Abbie _____
> _____.

11 다음 우리말을 괄호 안의 단어를 이용하여 8단어로 영작하시오.

> 그 소년들은 바다를 보고 신이 났다.
> (excited, see, the ocean)
> → _____

대표유형 04   too ~ to / enough to   출제율 30%

12 다음 두 문장의 뜻이 같도록 빈칸에 알맞은 말을 쓰시오.

> We arrived so late that we couldn't see the film.
> = We arrived _____ _____ _____
>   _____ the film.

13 다음 두 문장을 괄호 안의 표현을 이용하여 한 문장으로 바꿔 쓰시오.

> My brother is very strong. He can move that heavy table.
> → _____
> _____ (enough to)

대표유형 05   seem to   출제율 15%

14 다음 두 문장의 뜻이 같도록 빈칸에 알맞은 말을 쓰시오.

> It seems that Alice was sick.
> = Alice seems _____ _____ _____
>   sick.

15 다음 문장과 같은 의미의 문장을 주어진 단어로 시작하여 쓰시오.

> The kids seemed to be satisfied.
> → It _____.

대표유형 01, 03 형용사적 용법 / 부사적 용법 　출제율 25%

01 다음 문장 중 어법상 <u>어색한</u> 것을 <u>모두</u> 고르면?

① I would like something spicy to eat.

② I've been looking for a roommate to live.

③ The chameleon is famous for its ability to change color.

④ We went to the hospital to do some volunteer work.

⑤ I chose my words carefully to not make any mistake.

02 다음 중 밑줄 친 부분을 in order to와 바꿔 쓸 수 있는 것끼리 묶은 것은?

ⓐ We sang a carol to please our mom.

ⓑ They were relieved to know the truth.

ⓒ They called 911 to ask for an ambulance.

ⓓ Be careful. These dogs are hard to control.

ⓔ She returned with the police, only to find him gone.

① ⓐ, ⓒ 　　② ⓑ, ⓓ 　　③ ⓒ, ⓔ

④ ⓑ, ⓒ, ⓓ 　　⑤ ⓐ, ⓒ, ⓔ

대표유형 04 too ~ to / enough to 　출제율 30%

03 다음 짝지어진 대화 중 <u>어색한</u> 것은?

① **A** How was the weather in Hong Kong?

　B Well, it was so hot that I couldn't breathe.

② **A** Olivia is too smart to take part in the quiz show.

　B Yeah, I think she'll be able to win.

③ **A** These gloves aren't big enough for me to put on.

　B I'll get you bigger ones.

④ **A** The river is too polluted for people to swim in.

　B Oh, I'm sorry to hear that.

⑤ **A** Can you teach me how to make a cake?

　B Sure. The recipe is simple enough for you to follow.

04 다음 문장의 밑줄 친 ① ~ ⑤ 중 어법상 <u>어색한</u> 것은?

She heard an elderly man ① yelling ② loudly enough ③ of her ④ to hear ⑤ through her headphones.

05 다음 중 나머지 넷과 의미가 <u>다른</u> 것은?

① I was too busy to attend the meeting.

② I was so busy that I couldn't attend the meeting.

③ I managed to attend the meeting though I was busy.

④ I was very busy, so I failed to attend the meeting.

⑤ I wasn't able to attend the meeting because I was too busy.

대표유형 05 seem to 　출제율 15%

06 다음 중 짝지어진 두 문장의 의미가 서로 같은 것은?

① James seems to be honest.

　= It seems that James was honest.

② Scott seemed to be sick then.

　= It seemed that Scott had been sick then.

③ Nick seems to have met her.

　= Nick seems that he will meet her.

④ Jenny seemed to be enjoying her job.

　= It seemed that Jenny was enjoying her job.

⑤ Sujin seemed to have been a teacher.

　= It seemed that Sujin was a teacher.

07 다음 우리말에 맞게 빈칸에 들어갈 말로 알맞은 것은?

그녀는 젊었을 때 유명했던 것 같다.

→ She _____ when she was young.

① seems to be famous

② seemed to be famous

③ seems to has been famous

④ seems to have been famous

⑤ seemed to have been famous

대표유형 01, 02 형용사적 용법 / 「be + to부정사」 출제율 20%

08 다음 괄호 안의 단어를 바르게 배열하여 대답을 완성하시오. (단, 두 개의 단어를 추가할 것)

> **A** Have you decided on a topic for your essay?
>
> **B** Not yet. I can't come up with _____ _____. (interesting, write, anything)

09 다음 두 문장의 의미가 같도록 빈칸에 알맞은 말을 쓰시오.

> (1) The president is going to visit Vietnam next month.
>
> = The   president _____ _____ _____ Vietnam next month.
>
> (2) You must not touch anything in this house.
>
> = You _____ _____ _____ _____ anything in this house.

대표유형 03 부사적 용법 출제율 25%

10 다음 문장과 의미가 통하도록 'in order to'를 이용하여 문장을 다시 쓰시오.

> I turned down the volume because I didn't want to wake the baby.
>
> → I _____
>
> _____.

11 다음 두 문장을 to부정사를 이용하여 한 문장으로 바꿔 쓰시오.

> Glen failed the audition. That's why he was disappointed.
>
> → Glen _____.

12 다음 문장과 같은 의미가 되도록 to부정사를 이용하여 문장을 다시 쓰시오.

> Kevin wrote everything down so that he could memorize it fast.
>
> = _____
>
> _____

대표유형 04 too ~ to / enough to 출제율 30%

13 다음 대화의 내용에 맞게 문장을 완성하시오. (단, 괄호 안의 단어를 이용할 것)

> **A** How was Mr. Wilson's lecture, Cathy?
>
> **B** It was very confusing, so I couldn't understand it.
>
> → Mr. Wilson's lecture was _____
>
> _____. (too, to)
>
> → Mr. Wilson's lecture was _____
>
> _____. (so, that, can)

14 다음 우리말에 맞게 괄호 안의 어구를 이용하여 문장을 완성하시오. (단, 8단어로 완성할 것)

> 그녀는 사고를 피할 만큼 충분히 운이 좋았다.
> (the crash, lucky, avoid)
>
> → _____

15 다음 우리말을 괄호 안의 단어를 이용하여 두 개의 문장으로 영작하시오.

> 그 수프는 내가 먹기에 너무 짜다. (salty)
>
> → _____
>
> → _____

01 다음 밑줄 친 부분 중 '목적'의 의미를 나타내는 것끼리 묶은 것은?

> ⓐ Families and friends gather <u>to celebrate</u> Christmas.
> ⓑ You shouldn't be afraid of making mistakes <u>to learn</u> something new.
> ⓒ Judy missed a chance <u>to meet</u> her favorite actor.
> ⓓ The article gives you some tips <u>to overcome</u> stress.
> ⓔ She was upset <u>to read</u> the negative reviews about her film.

① ⓐ, ⓑ   ② ⓐ, ⓒ   ③ ⓑ, ⓓ
④ ⓐ, ⓑ, ⓔ   ⑤ ⓒ, ⓓ, ⓔ

02 다음 중 어법상 옳은 문장의 개수는?

> ⓐ I need a pen to write.
> ⓑ Will you get me hot something to drink?
> ⓒ The suitcase is too heavy for me to carry.
> ⓓ I took a taxi in order not to be late for the meeting.
> ⓔ I am happy to having a friend like you.

① 1개   ② 2개   ③ 3개   ④ 4개   ⑤ 5개

03 다음 중 짝지어진 두 문장의 의미가 서로 <u>다른</u> 것은?

① I was too scared to say anything.
   = I was so scared that I couldn't say anything.
② They seemed to have been rich.
   = It seemed that they had been rich.
③ He seems to be hiding something.
   = It seems that he was hiding something.
④ He put on the brakes so that he would not hit the tree.
   = He put on the brakes in order not to hit the tree.
⑤ The ice was thick enough to bear the weight of a child.
   = The ice was so thick that it could bear the weight of a child.

04 다음 두 문장을 to부정사를 이용하여 한 문장으로 바꿔 쓰시오.

(1) I want some friends. I want to play soccer with them.

→ _____

(2) I was shocked. Because I found the room empty.

→ _____

05 to부정사를 이용하여 그림의 상황을 나타내는 문장을 다시 쓰시오.

(1) 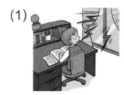 The noise is so loud that the boy can't concentrate on studying.

→ _____
_____

(2) The sofa is so comfortable that the girl can sleep on it.

→ _____
_____

신유형

06 다음 그림을 보고, 괄호 안의 표현을 이용하여 우리말을 두 개의 문장으로 영작하시오.

> 어젯밤에 비가 왔던 것 같다.
> → _____
>   (seem, that)
> → _____
>   (seem to)

01
a She has no friend to talk.

b She has no friend to talk to.

02
a Is there anything to watch fun?

b Is there anything fun to watch?

03
a You are not to bring food or drinks into the library.

b You are to not bring food or drinks into the library.

04
a I filled out the form in order to sign up for the event.

b I filled out the form in order that sign up for the event.

05
a They were disappointed to find that the shop was closed.

b They were disappointed finding that the shop was closed.

06
a The bus was so crowded for us to sit together.

b The bus was too crowded for us to sit together.

07
a This watch is cheap enough for me to buy.

b This watch is enough cheap for me to buy.

08
a My brother seems to cry last night. His eyes are red.

b My brother seems to have cried last night. His eyes are red.

유형별 기출 적용 빈도

유형 01 동명사의 쓰임	35%
유형 02 동명사와 현재분사의 구별	10%
유형 03 동명사의 의미상 주어와 시제	5%
유형 04 동명사 / to부정사를 목적어로 쓰는 동사	35%
유형 05 동명사의 관용적 표현	15%

》출제 포인트

동사의 목적어로 동명사와 to부정사 둘 중 하나를 선택하는 문제는 반드시 출제된다. 동명사와 현재분사를 구별하는 문제, 관용적으로 쓰이는 동명사 표현 등도 자주 출제된다.

》정답률 100% Tip

1 동명사(구) 주어는 단수로 취급함
2 전치사 다음에는 동명사를 씀
3 동명사와 to부정사를 목적어로 쓸 때 의미가 달라지는 동사에 주의하기

Grammar Point

Point 1 동명사

1. 동명사의 쓰임: 「동사원형＋-ing」의 형태로 명사 역할(주어, 보어, 목적어)을 하며, '~하는 것, ~하기'라고 해석한다. 부정은 「not[never]＋동명사」이다.
2. 동명사의 의미상 주어와 시제: 동명사의 행위를 하는 주체가 문장의 주어와 다를 때 「소유격[목적격]＋동명사」로 의미상 주어를 나타내고, 동명사가 문장의 시제보다 앞서 일어난 일을 나타낼 때는 「having＋p.p.」로 쓴다.
3. 동명사 vs. 현재분사: 동명사는 명사 역할을 하고, 현재분사는 진행의 의미로 쓰여 진행형을 만들거나 명사를 수식한다.

Point 2 동명사 / to부정사를 목적어로 쓰는 동사

동명사를 목적어로 쓰는 동사	enjoy, finish, keep, stop, mind, avoid, admit, deny, recommend, consider, give up, put off 등
	주의 stop＋to부정사: ~하기 위해 멈추다
to부정사를 목적어로 쓰는 동사	want, hope, expect, plan, need, decide, agree, promise, manage, pretend 등
둘 다 목적어로 쓸 수 있는 동사	의미 차이 없는 것	start, begin, like, love, hate, prefer, continue 등
	의미 차이 있는 것	forget, remember, regret, try 등

Point 3 동명사의 관용적 표현

- be busy -ing: ~하느라 바쁘다
- on[upon] -ing: ~하자마자
- be worth -ing: ~할 만한 가치가 있다
- feel like -ing: ~하고 싶다
- spend＋시간/돈＋-ing: ~하느라 시간/돈을 쓰다
- cannot help -ing: ~하지 않을 수 없다

- be used to -ing: ~하는 데 익숙하다
- look forward to -ing: ~하기를 고대하다
- make a point of -ing: ~하는 것을 규칙으로 하다
- It is no use -ing: ~해도 소용없다
- keep[prevent] ... from -ing: …가 ~하지 못하게 막다
- have trouble[difficulty] (in) -ing: ~하는 데 어려움이 있다

✓ 바로 체크

01 (Be / Being) kind to others is important.

02 Stop (to write / writing) and put your pen down.

03 I'm sorry for (not keeping / keeping not) my word.

04 I'm sure of (she / her) passing the audition.

05 I want to apologize for (not having answered / having not answered) your calls.

06 Do you mind my _____ the window? (open)

07 Don't forget _____ me when you get there. (call)

08 I'm looking forward to _____ my favorite singer. (see)

대표유형 01 동명사의 쓰임 　　　　　　　　출제율 35%

01 다음 빈칸에 들어갈 말로 알맞은 것은?

> My dream is _____ a medicine that can cure all diseases.

① invents 　　② invented 　　③ invention

④ inventing 　　⑤ to inventing

02 다음 빈칸에 들어갈 수 있는 것을 <u>모두</u> 고르면?

> Do you enjoy _____?

① go hiking

② eats spicy food

③ to listen to classical music

④ visiting new places

⑤ reading mystery novels

03 괄호 안의 단어를 알맞은 형태로 고쳐 <u>한 단어</u>로 쓰시오.

> _____ on the phone while driving is very dangerous. (talk)

04 다음 중 밑줄 친 부분의 쓰임이 〈보기〉와 같은 것은?

> 보기　My hobby is <u>taking</u> pictures of nature.

① I don't like <u>eating</u> fast food.

② Many people avoid <u>going</u> to the dentist.

③ <u>Keeping</u> a pet takes a lot of responsibility.

④ We can protect the environment by <u>reducing</u> plastic waste.

⑤ The best part of Christmas is <u>sharing</u> love and friendship.

05 다음 문장에서 어법상 어색한 부분을 찾아 바르게 고쳐 쓰시오.

> The singer is afraid of lose his popularity.

_____ → _____

06 다음 우리말에 맞게 not이 들어가기에 알맞은 곳은?

> 수업에 참석하지 못해서 죄송합니다.
> → I am (①) sorry (②) for (③) attending (④) the class (⑤).

07 다음 문장 중 어법상 <u>어색한</u> 것은?

① Meet new people is exciting.

② The man kept on talking for hours.

③ Her sister is interested in acting.

④ I hate being late for an appointment.

⑤ His plan is designing his own house.

대표유형 02 동명사와 현재분사의 구별 　　　　　출제율 10%

08 다음 중 밑줄 친 부분의 쓰임이 〈보기〉와 같은 것은?

> 보기　<u>Cooking</u> is one of my favorite hobbies.

① Whom are you <u>waiting</u> for?

② I liked <u>playing</u> soccer when I was young.

③ I saw a cat <u>following</u> a mouse silently.

④ Do you know the boy <u>talking</u> with Eva?

⑤ The children were <u>planting</u> some trees in the yard.

09 다음 중 밑줄 친 부분의 쓰임이 나머지 넷과 <u>다른</u> 것은?

① Look at the little girl <u>singing</u> on the stage.

② He was trying to calm down the <u>crying</u> baby.

③ Dad and I were <u>walking</u> the dog in the park.

④ The girl <u>waving</u> at Kate is her best friend.

⑤ Jerome was good at <u>handling</u> customer complaints.

10 다음 중 밑줄 친 부분의 쓰임이 〈보기〉와 **다른** 것은?

> 보기 They were playing basketball in the gym.

① What are you thinking about so hard?
② I saw a woman standing near the dog.
③ Her strong arms were holding her child.
④ We heard people screaming and woke up.
⑤ What I want to do now is getting some rest.

11 다음 우리말과 같도록 빈칸에 알맞은 단어를 쓰시오.

(1) 나는 수학 문제를 푸는 것을 마쳤다.
  → I finished _____ the math problem.

(2) 나는 지금 수학 문제를 푸는 중이다.
  → I'm _____ the math problem now.

대표유형 03 동명사의 의미상 주어와 시제 출제율 5%

12 다음 빈칸에 들어갈 수 **없는** 것은?

> Do you mind _____ coming in?

① my   ② me   ③ she
④ her   ⑤ their

13 다음 두 문장의 의미가 같도록 할 때 빈칸에 들어갈 말로 알맞은 것은?

> Jane had spilled coffee on my shirt, but she didn't apologize for it.
> = Jane didn't apologize for _____ coffee on my shirt.

① being spilled   ② having spilled
③ to have spilled   ④ to have spilling
⑤ having been spilled

14 다음 우리말과 같도록 괄호 안의 어구를 바르게 배열하시오.

> 나는 내 남동생이 내 물건을 사용하는 것을 싫어한다.
> (my stuff, I, using, my little brother's, hate)
> → _____

대표유형 04 동명사 / to부정사를 목적어로 쓰는 동사 출제율 35%

15 다음 빈칸에 들어갈 말로 알맞은 것은?

> My uncle _____ spending time with his family.

① hopes   ② planned   ③ enjoys
④ decided   ⑤ expects

16 다음 빈칸에 들어갈 말이 순서대로 바르게 짝지어진 것은?

> • Would you mind _____ the channel?
> • David agreed _____ me some money.
> • I have just finished _____ for the trip.

① changing – to lend – packing
② changing – to lend – to pack
③ changing – lending – packing
④ to change – lending – to pack
⑤ to change – lending – packing

17 다음 빈칸에 공통으로 들어갈 수 **없는** 것은?

> • Alice _____ to walk in the rain.
> • My son _____ studying German.

① likes   ② kept   ③ started
④ hates   ⑤ continued

18 다음 두 문장을 한 문장으로 나타낼 때 빈칸에 들어갈 말로 알맞은 것은?

> Ryan won the championship in 2015. He will always remember it.
> → Ryan will always remember _____ the championship in 2015.

① win　　　② winning　　　③ to win
④ to winning　　⑤ to having won

≫ 실전 Tip 「remember+동명사」는 '(과거에) ~한 것을 기억하다'라는 의미이고, 「remember+to부정사」는 '(앞으로) ~할 것을 기억하다'라는 의미이다.

19 다음 중 밑줄 친 부분의 쓰임이 어법상 어색한 것은?

① I didn't expect <u>to score</u> so many goals.
② Our family gave up <u>moving</u> to a big city.
③ The man managed <u>escaping</u> the fire.
④ Alicia pretends <u>to be</u> happy even though she's not.
⑤ I'm considering <u>joining</u> the photography club.

20 다음 우리말과 같도록 괄호 (1), (2)에서 알맞은 것을 각각 고르시오.

> 그는 항상 너무 많이 먹는 것을 피하려고 노력한다.
> → He always tries (1) (avoiding / to avoid)
> (2) (eating / to eat) too much.

21 다음 짝지어진 두 문장의 의미가 서로 같은 것은?

① I remembered buying the tickets.
　 I remembered to buy the tickets.
② Dad tried moving the sofa.
　 Dad tried to move the sofa.
③ He stopped talking to me.
　 He stopped to talk to me.
④ It continued to rain for 3 days.
　 It continued raining for 3 days.
⑤ I regret telling you that she won't come.
　 I regret to tell you that she won't come.

22 다음 두 문장의 의미가 통하도록 빈칸에 알맞은 말을 쓰시오.

> I needed to bring my swimsuit, but I forgot.
> → I forgot _____ my swimsuit.

대표유형 05　동명사의 관용적 표현　　　출제율 15%

23 다음 우리말을 영어로 바르게 옮긴 것은?

① 나는 산책을 가고 싶다.
　 → I feel like to go for a walk.
② Tim은 한국말을 하는 데 익숙하지 않다.
　 → Tim is not used to speaking in Korean.
③ 나는 그를 방문하기를 고대하고 있다.
　 → I'm looking forward to visit him.
④ 그들은 온종일 집을 청소하며 시간을 보냈다.
　 → They spent all day to clean the house.
⑤ 그는 그 질문을 다시 하지 않을 수 없었다.
　 → He couldn't help ask the question again.

24 다음 우리말에 맞게 괄호 안의 표현을 배열할 때, 네 번째로 오는 것은?

> 그를 탓해봤자 소용없다.
> (him, it, blaming, no use, is)

① him　　　　② it　　　　③ blaming
④ no use　　　⑤ is

25 다음 우리말을 영어로 옮긴 문장에서 어법상 어색한 부분을 찾아 바르게 고쳐 쓰시오.

> 나는 대중 앞에서 연설하는 데 어려움을 겪는다.
> → I have difficulty in to make a speech in public.

_____ → _____

대표유형 01, 02 동명사의 쓰임 / 동명사와 현재분사의 구별 출제율 35%

01 다음 빈칸에 들어갈 말로 알맞은 것은?

> Esther is interested in _____ action figures.

① collect ② collects
③ collected ④ collecting
⑤ to collect

02 다음 문장에서 어법상 어색한 부분을 찾아 바르게 고친 것은?

> Learning about other cultures make us understand each other better.

① Learning → Learn ② other → another
③ make → makes ④ us → our
⑤ understand → to understand

03 다음 중 밑줄 친 부분의 쓰임이 나머지 넷과 다른 것은?

① I love dancing to music.
② He is preparing dinner for his children.
③ She enjoys running a marathon.
④ Watching horror movies is my hobby.
⑤ What about going to the movies tonight?

04 다음 문장 중 어법상 어색한 것은?

① He was getting tired of shop online.
② Earning fame is important to him.
③ The baby kept on crying loudly.
④ Not having breakfast is bad for you.
⑤ My plan is helping the poor and the sick.

대표유형 03 동명사의 의미상 주어와 시제 출제율 5%

05 다음 빈칸에 들어갈 말로 알맞은 것은?

> Do you mind _____ your phone?

① my using ② my to use ③ me for using
④ me to use ⑤ my to using

06 다음 두 문장의 의미가 서로 다른 것은?

① I am sure that he will win the race.
  = I am sure of his winning the race.
② She is proud that her father is a firefighter.
  = She is proud of her father's being a firefighter.
③ I don't like that she calls me late at night.
  = I don't like her calling me late at night.
④ I was angry that they didn't pick me up.
  = I was angry about their not picking me up.
⑤ The player is ashamed that he made a mistake.
  = The player is ashamed of making a mistake.

대표유형 04 동명사 / to부정사를 목적어로 쓰는 동사 출제율 35%

07 다음 문장 중 어법상 옳은 것은?

① This bicycle needs to fix.
② I'm considering to take her advice.
③ We have put off to travel for so long.
④ You should avoid touching your eyes with dirty hands.
⑤ Ms. Thompson was planning attending the wedding.

08 다음 중 밑줄 친 부분의 쓰임이 옳은 것을 모두 고르면?

① I will stop being lazy this year.
② He forgot locking the door and someone broke in.
③ The lifeguard tried to save the drowning boy.
④ I forgot your name but remember to meet you last year.
⑤ I regret to fight with Jim, and I'll apologize to him.

09 다음 두 문장을 한 문장으로 나타낼 때 빈칸에 알맞은 말을 쓰시오.

> Amy always listens to pop music. She really enjoys it.

→ Amy enjoys _____ _____ _____

_____ .

10 다음 대화의 빈칸에 괄호 안의 표현을 알맞은 형태로 쓰시오.

> **A** Ted, don't forget _____ the TV before you leave the house. (turn off)
> **B** Okay, Mom. Don't worry.

11 다음 문장에서 어법상 어색한 부분을 찾아 바르게 고쳐 쓰시오.

> You need to stop to buy unnecessary things to save money.

_____ → _____

12 다음 문장 중 어법상 어색한 것을 두 개 골라 기호를 쓰고 바르게 고쳐 문장을 다시 쓰시오.

> ⓐ Chris gave up to play the guitar.
> ⓑ I expect being back in an hour.
> ⓒ The boy pretended to be sick and went to bed.
> ⓓ They practice throwing and catching the ball every day.

(1) _____ → _____

(2) _____ → _____

대표유형 05 동명사의 관용적 표현   출제율 15%

13 〈보기〉에서 알맞은 말을 골라 대화를 완성하시오.
(단, 필요 시 형태를 바꿔 쓸 것)

> 보기   get up   ride   join

> **A** I make a point of _____ a bike every morning. How about _____ me?
> **B** I'd love to, but I have difficulty _____ early.

14 괄호 안의 표현을 이용하여 우리말을 영어로 옮기시오.

> 그녀는 혼자서 여행하는 것에 익숙하다.
> (be used to, travel alone)
>
> → _____

>> 실전 Tip '~하는 데 이용되다'라는 의미의 「be used to + 동사원형」과 혼동하지 않도록 주의한다.

신유형

15 다음 대화의 내용과 일치하도록 괄호 안의 단어를 이용하여 문장을 완성하시오.

> **A** Anne, we're going to see a movie after school. Do you want to join?
> **B** Sounds good. Which movie are you going to see?
> **A** We all want to see the new *Spiderman*. You haven't seen it, have you?
> **B** Actually, I have, but it's really exciting. I'll gladly see it again.

→ Anne thinks that the movie *Spiderman*

_____ .

(worth, watch, twice)

대표유형 04 | 동명사 / to부정사를 목적어로 쓰는 동사   출제율 35%

01 다음 우리말을 영어로 바르게 옮긴 것은?

① 나는 그녀에게 답장하는 것을 잊었다.
  → I forgot writing back to her.

② 너는 우비를 챙기는 것을 기억했니?
  → Did you remember to pack your raincoat?

③ 그는 실종된 강아지를 찾기 위해 애썼다.
  → He tried finding the missing dog.

④ 그들은 그들의 차를 팔았던 것을 후회한다.
  → They regret to sell their car.

⑤ 그 전화는 계속 울렸다.
  → The phone didn't stop to ring.

02 다음 대화의 밑줄 친 ①~⑤ 중 어법상 어색한 것은?

A Do you mind ① my ② smoking?

B I do. Can't you see the "No Smoking" sign over there?

A I didn't see it. I will try ③ to stop ④ to smoke this year, anyway.

B I doubt it. You decided ⑤ to quit last year, didn't you?

03 다음 대화의 내용에 맞게 빈칸에 들어갈 말로 알맞은 것은?

A Did you see the accident, Tim?
B No, I didn't.
→ Tim _____ the accident.

① denied to see   ② denied seeing
③ admitted to see   ④ admitted seeing
⑤ pretended to see

04 다음 중 어법상 옳은 문장의 개수는?

ⓐ My sister quit to drink coffee.
ⓑ Ms. Bennet refused to accept the offer.
ⓒ Jake has decided taking part in the contest.
ⓓ I promise turning in my essay on time.

① 1개   ② 2개   ③ 3개   ④ 4개   ⑤ 없음

대표유형 05 | 동명사의 관용적 표현   출제율 15%

05 다음 빈칸에 들어갈 수 <u>없는</u> 것은?

My mom is really looking forward _____.

① to go to the concert
② to talking with you
③ to the family trip
④ to her wedding anniversary
⑤ to opening a restaurant

≫ 실전 Tip look forward to의 to는 전치사이다.

06 다음 문장 중 어법상 <u>어색한</u> 것은?

① The palace is worth visiting at least once.
② I spend two hours studying Chinese every day.
③ He looked really funny, so I couldn't help laugh.
④ I am busy preparing for an important exam.
⑤ The noise from next door kept me from sleeping.

07 다음 두 문장의 의미가 서로 <u>다른</u> 것은?

① As soon as he saw the police, he slowed down the car.
  = On seeing the police, he slowed down the car.

② I have difficulty in making new friends.
  = It is difficult for me to make new friends.

③ I feel like drinking a cup of hot cocoa.
  = I would like to drink a cup of hot cocoa.

④ David used to eat spicy food.
  = David is used to eating spicy food.

⑤ He couldn't exercise because of his back pain.
  = His back pain prevented him from exercising.

대표유형 04 동명사 / to부정사를 목적어로 쓰는 동사   출제율 35%

08 다음 문장에서 어법상 어색한 부분을 찾아 바르게 고쳐 쓰시오.

> Our family has been considering donate money to a charity.

09 〈보기〉의 단어를 이용하여 문장을 알맞게 완성하시오.

> 보기   pay   spend   inform

(1) They forgot _____ the electricity bill, so the power went off.

(2) Nick remembered _____ Christmas once at Mr. Sanders' farm.

(3) I regret _____ you that you have failed the test.

대표유형 01 동명사의 쓰임   출제율 35%

10 다음 두 문장을 동명사를 이용하여 한 문장으로 바꿔 쓰시오. (단, 의미상 주어는 생략할 것)

> • People use plastic bags.
> • It is harmful to the environment.

→ _____ to the environment.

11 다음 표의 내용과 일치하도록 〈보기〉와 같이 동명사를 이용하여 Mike를 묘사하는 문장을 두 개 쓰시오.

Name	Dream	Plan for This Year
Ella	soccer player	jog every morning
Mike	famous writer	write a fantasy novel

> 보기 • Ella's dream is becoming a soccer player.
> • Her plan for this year is jogging every morning.

(1) _____

(2) _____

12 다음 우리말에 맞게 괄호 안의 어구를 이용하여 문장을 완성하시오.

> 대부분의 사람은 직업을 갖지 못하는 것을 두려워한다.
> (afraid of, a job, get)
>
> → _____

대표유형 03 동명사의 의미상 주어와 시제   출제율 5%

13 〈보기〉와 같이 동명사를 이용하여 다음 문장을 바꿔 쓰시오.

> 보기 I can understand that she is upset.
> → I can understand her being upset.

She hates that someone talks behind her back.

→ _____

14 다음 두 문장이 같은 의미가 되도록 빈칸에 알맞은 말을 쓰시오.

(1)
> She is telling a lie. I feel angry about it.
> = I feel angry about _____
> _____ _____.

(2)
> I'm sure that he will be successful.
> = I'm sure of _____ _____.

15 〈조건〉에 맞게 우리말을 영작하시오.

> [조건] **1.** regret, study, hard를 이용할 것
> **2.** 7단어의 완전한 문장으로 쓸 것

> 그 소년은 더 열심히 공부하지 않았던 것을 후회한다.
> → _____

≫ 실전 Tip 동명사가 문장의 시제보다 앞선 일을 나타낼 때의 형태에 유의한다.

01 다음 중 동명사가 포함된 문장의 개수로 알맞은 것은?

ⓐ Will you stop treating me like a child?
ⓑ He spent a lot of money buying the car.
ⓒ The fans are shaking their heads.
ⓓ The man sitting on the bench is my dad.
ⓔ Guiding foreigners is his job.
ⓕ My grandmother is learning how to use her smartphone.

① 2개   ② 3개   ③ 4개   ④ 5개   ⑤ 6개

02 다음 문장 중 어법상 옳은 것을 <u>모두</u> 고르면?

① I think his new book is worth read.
② They felt like to eat something sweet.
③ I spend too much time checking social media.
④ Some people have difficulty to control their anger.
⑤ On arriving home, my brother took a shower.

03 동명사를 이용하여 전환한 문장 중 <u>잘못된</u> 것끼리 묶은 것은?

ⓐ I'm sure that they will not attend the party.
   → I'm sure of their not having attended the party.
ⓑ The woman admitted that she had stolen the car.
   → The woman admitted being stolen the car.
ⓒ His roommate complained that he snored.
   → His roommate complained of his snoring.
ⓓ Mr. Dean always dreamed that his daughter would be a star.
   → Mr. Dean always dreamed of his daughter's being a star.

① ⓐ, ⓑ   ② ⓐ, ⓒ   ③ ⓑ, ⓒ
④ ⓑ, ⓓ   ⑤ ⓒ, ⓓ

04 〈조건〉에 맞게 다음 문장과 같은 의미의 문장을 쓰시오.

[조건] **1.** keep, from을 이용할 것
       2. 9단어의 완전한 문장으로 쓸 것

He couldn't become a pilot because of his poor eyesight.
→ _____

05 다음은 감기에 걸린 Mike에게 의사가 하는 조언을 그림으로 나타낸 것이다. 그림에 맞게 괄호 안의 단어를 이용하여 조언을 완성하시오.

(1) You'd better _____.
    (avoid, eat)
(2) _____ hot tea.
    (recommend, drink)
(3) Don't _____.
    (forget, take, medicine)

06 〈보기〉의 단어를 각각 두 개씩 이용하여 다음 대화의 내용과 일치하도록 문장을 완성하시오.

보기   share   stop   mind   listen

(1) **Mary** The radio is too loud. I can't study at all.
    Ben Sorry. I will turn off the radio.
    → Ben will _____

(2) **Mom** Can you share your room with Tom?
    Steve No. I want to use my room alone.
    → Steve _____.

최종 선택 QUIZ

어법상 옳은 문장에
✔ 표시하세요.

01
a   Learn a new language is exciting.

b   Learning a new language is exciting.

02
a   I enjoy hanging out with my friends.

b   I enjoy to hang out with my friends.

03
a   Her dream is making the world a better place.

b   Her dream is makes the world a better place.

04
a   I blamed myself for trying not hard enough.

b   I blamed myself for not trying hard enough.

05
a   Would you mind my staying here for a while?

b   Would you mind I staying here for a while?

06
a   Will you forgive me for worn your clothes without permission?

b   Will you forgive me for having worn your clothes without permission?

07
a   She has to remember to post the letter by tomorrow.

b   She has to remember posting the letter by tomorrow.

08
a   I am looking forward to go camping with my family.

b   I am looking forward to going camping with my family.

유형별 기출 적용 빈도

유형 01 현재분사와 과거분사 `55%`

유형 02 현재분사와 동명사 `20%`

유형 03 감정을 나타내는 분사 `25%`

>> 출제 포인트
수식·서술하는 대상과 분사가 능동의 관계인지 수동의 관계인지 구별하여 현재분사 또는 과거분사를 선택하는 문제가 많이 출제된다.

>> 정답률 100% Tip
1 수식받는 명사와 분사가 능동 관계이면 현재분사, 수동 관계이면 과거분사를 쓰는 것에 주의하기
2 현재분사는 형용사 역할, 동명사는 명사 역할

Grammar Point

Point ① 현재분사와 과거분사

분사는 동사의 형태를 바꿔 형용사처럼 쓰는 것으로, 명사를 수식하거나 보어 역할을 한다. 현재분사는 진행형에, 과거분사는 완료형과 수동태에 사용된다.

	현재분사	과거분사
형태	동사원형＋-ing	동사원형＋-ed /불규칙 과거분사형
의미	• 능동(~하는) • 진행(~하고 있는)	• 수동(~되어진) • 완료(~된)

분사의 쓰임		
한정적 용법	명사 수식	Do you know the boy wearing a red cap?
서술적 용법	보어 역할	The dog sat barking up the tree. (주격보어) He had his bike fixed. (목적격보어)

주의 분사가 단독으로 명사를 수식할 때는 명사 앞에 분사를 쓰고, 다른 수식어구와 함께 쓰일 때는 명사 뒤에 쓴다.

Point ② 현재분사와 동명사

현재분사와 동명사의 형태는 「동사원형＋-ing」로 같지만 현재분사는 형용사 역할을, 동명사는 명사 역할을 한다. 명사 앞에 사용되는 경우에 현재분사는 명사의 동작이나 상태를, 동명사는 명사의 용도나 목적을 나타낸다.
Look at the sleeping child. (현재분사: The child is sleeping.)
The patient needs a sleeping pill. (동명사: a pill for sleeping)

Point ③ 감정을 나타내는 분사

주어가 감정을 유발하는 원인일 때는 현재분사를, 주어가 감정을 느끼게 되는 주체일 때는 과거분사를 쓴다.
It was an embarrassing moment.
I was embarrassed by my friend's snoring on the bus.

✔ 바로 체크

01 The (crying / cried) boy is my brother.

02 He is repairing the (breaking / broken) elevator.

03 I saw a girl (dancing / danced) in the rain.

04 She heard her name (calling / called).

05 Brian lives in a house (building / built) 20 years ago.

06 David sat (read / reading) a novel.

07 The games are very (exciting / excited).

08 I am (interesting / interested) in watching horror movies.

09 Her dream is helping the poor. (현재분사 / 동명사)

10 My sister is helping the poor. (현재분사 / 동명사)

대표유형 01 현재분사와 과거분사   출제율 55%

01 다음 빈칸에 들어갈 말을 순서대로 바르게 짝지은 것은?

> · I walked on the floor _____ with a red carpet.
> · Listen carefully to the birds _____ in the trees.

① covering – sung   ② covering – singing
③ covered – sung   ④ covered – sang
⑤ covered – singing

[02-03] 다음 밑줄 친 동사의 형태로 알맞은 것을 고르시오.

02

> The book write in French is too difficult for me.

① writes   ② wrote   ③ written
④ writing   ⑤ is written

03

> Brian usually keeps all the windows of his room lock all day.

① locked   ② locking   ③ are locked
④ to lock   ⑤ has locked

04 다음 밑줄 친 단어를 각각 알맞은 형태로 고쳐 쓰시오.

> Have you ever thought that a bee buzz around is make music?

05 다음 빈칸에 paint의 알맞은 형태를 각각 쓰시오.

> · I had the front door _____ white.
> · I had him _____ the front door white.

[06-07] 다음 밑줄 친 부분 중 어법상 어색한 것을 고르시오.

06 ① I'd like to have a baked potato.
② Don't wake up the sleeping cat.
③ Who are those people waiting outside?
④ Who is the woman catching by the police?
⑤ She bought a new dress made in Italy.

07 ① Everyone felt the ground shaken.
② There was no seat left in the theater.
③ We were looking at the shining stars.
④ I had my hair cut last weekend.
⑤ My mom sat on the sofa knitting a sweater.

08 다음 중 밑줄 친 부분의 쓰임이 나머지 넷과 다른 것은?
① My son got his finger stuck in a door.
② We saw the parade passing by.
③ My brother decided to buy a used car.
④ She heard someone whistling outside.
⑤ The roof was damaged because of the storm.

09 다음 우리말을 영어로 옮긴 문장에서 어법상 어색한 부분을 찾아 바르게 고쳐 쓰시오.

> 그녀는 버스에서 지갑을 도난당했다.
> → She had her purse steal on the bus.

_____ → _____

10 다음 우리말에 맞게 괄호 안의 표현을 바르게 배열하시오.

> 차 옆에 서 있는 남자는 나의 삼촌이다.
> (standing, by the car, the man)

→ _____ is my uncle.

11 다음 밑줄 친 단어를 알맞은 형태로 고쳐 쓰시오.

The ideas present in that magazine are reasonable.

12 다음 대화의 빈칸에 들어갈 말이 순서대로 바르게 연결된 것은?

A Has your luggage _____, Laura?
B No. I can't find my luggage. What should I do?
A I think you should go to the luggage counter and report the _____ luggage.

① arrived – lost
② arrived – losing
③ arrived – lose
④ arriving – losing
⑤ arriving – lost

13 다음 우리말에 맞게 밑줄 친 단어를 알맞은 형태로 고쳐 쓰시오.

끓는 물에 다진 감자를 넣어라.
→ Drop the (1) chop potatoes into (2) boil water.

(1) _____   (2) _____

신유형
14 〈보기〉와 같이 주어진 두 문장을 한 문장으로 바꿔 쓰시오.

보기   · I saw the girl.
      · She was flying a drone.
        → I saw the girl flying a drone.

· I heard the song.
· It was sung by a famous rock band.
  → _____

15 다음 우리말과 같도록 빈칸에 알맞은 말끼리 짝지어진 것은?

그녀는 런던에서 찍은 사진들을 응시하며 서 있었다.
→ She stood _____ at the pictures _____ in London.

① staring – taking
② staring – taken
③ stare – taken
④ stared – taking
⑤ stared – taken

16 다음 문장에서 어법상 어색한 부분을 찾아 바르게 고쳐 쓰시오.

The man had a breaking heart because his best friend lied to him.

대표유형 02   현재분사와 동명사   출제율 20%
17 다음 중 〈보기〉의 밑줄 친 부분과 쓰임이 다른 것은?

보기   Look at the dancing boys.

① Barking dogs seldom bite.
② The girl wearing sunglasses is Rachel.
③ I saw the monkey climbing up the tree.
④ They put my name on the waiting list.
⑤ The police were looking for the missing child.

18 다음 빈칸에 공통으로 들어갈 말을 run을 이용하여 쓰시오.

· She gave me a pair of _____ shoes.
· I saw a _____ man with a baseball cap in the park.

19 다음 빈칸에 들어갈 말이 순서대로 바르게 짝지어진 것은?

> • We enjoy _____ to English songs.
> • There are many sports fans _____ excitedly.

① listened – cheered
② listened – cheering
③ listening – cheer
④ listening – cheering
⑤ listening – cheered

20 다음 중 밑줄 친 부분의 쓰임이 나머지 넷과 다른 것은?

① My cousin has a talking parrot.
② We need to buy a new washing machine.
③ There are many ways to calm a crying baby.
④ You can hardly see the twinkling stars in a big city.
⑤ I was listening to the sound of the falling rain.

≫ 실전 Tip 명사 앞에 쓰인 동명사는 명사의 목적이나 용도를 나타낸다.

대표유형 03 감정을 나타내는 분사　　출제율 25%

21 다음 빈칸에 들어갈 말이 바르게 짝지어진 것은?

> Leo's explanation confused me.
> → Leo's explanation was _____ to me.
> → I was _____ by Leo's explanation.

① confused – confused
② confused – confusing
③ confusing – confuse
④ confusing – confused
⑤ confusing – confusing

[22-23] 괄호 안의 단어를 알맞은 형태로 바꿔 각 빈칸에 쓰시오.

22
> The seafood of the restaurant was _____. However, I was not _____ with the service. (satisfy)

23
> The children went to a robot show. For them, the show was _____. The _____ children jumped up and down. (excite)

24 다음 밑줄 친 부분 중 어법상 어색한 것은?

① The speech was encouraging.
② He put me in an embarrassing situation.
③ My family was disappointed at the result.
④ The hot weather makes me annoyed.
⑤ Teaching kids is a challenged job.

25 다음 밑줄 친 ①~⑤ 중 어법상 어색한 것은?

> The news ① that your team won first prize is not ② surprised to me at all. I was sure of ③ your winning ④ because I knew ⑤ how hard you had practiced. Congratulations!

대표유형 01 현재분사와 과거분사   출제율 55%

01 다음 밑줄 친 부분 중 어법상 어색한 것을 두 개 고르면?

① The rising sun was beautiful.

② I like to eat boiling eggs for breakfast.

③ The language spoken in Vienna is German.

④ There are a lot of people waiting for the taxis.

⑤ The man driven the sports car is my older brother.

[02-03] 다음 빈칸에 들어갈 말이 순서대로 바르게 짝지어진 것을 고르시오.

02
> • Most people _____ in a big city seem to be stressed.
> • I tried to recall if I'd ever met anyone _____ Bentley.

① live – called   ② lived – calling

③ living – called   ④ living – calling

⑤ lived – was called

03
> • I found my car _____ in front of the garage.
> • Does anybody know the man _____ on the sofa?

① parked – lied   ② parked – lying

③ parked – lie   ④ parking – lied

⑤ parking – lying

04 다음 괄호 안의 말이 들어갈 위치로 가장 알맞은 곳은?

> (known as *the Venus de Milo*)
> The ancient (①) statue (②) was (③) discovered in 1820 on the island of Melos, and it is (④) believed to (⑤) represent Aphrodite.

05 다음 우리말을 영어로 바르게 나타낸 것은?

> 그 방은 타버린 토스트의 냄새로 가득했다.

① The room filled with the smell of burnt toast.

② The room filling with the smell of burning toast.

③ The room was filled with the smell of burnt toast.

④ The room was filled with the smell of burning toast.

⑤ The room was filling with the smell of burnt toast.

대표유형 02 현재분사와 동명사   출제율 20%

06 다음 〈보기〉의 밑줄 친 부분과 쓰임이 다른 것은?

> 보기   Do you know that girl smiling at me?

① I saw a balloon floating high up in the sky.

② A lifeguard pulled the drowning boy out of the water.

③ The firefighter rushed to the burning house.

④ There is no smoking room in this building.

⑤ The boys dancing in the street are my friends.

07 다음 중 밑줄 친 부분의 쓰임이 나머지 넷과 다른 것은?

① My dog is running after the cat.

② Look at the girl brushing back her hair.

③ The problem is carrying water for cooking.

④ Daniel kept me waiting for so long.

⑤ Some children stood crying in the classroom.

08 다음 괄호 안의 표현을 이용하여 대화를 완성하시오.

> **A** What are you looking for?
> **B** I'm _____ .
>   (look for, sleep, bag)

09 다음 문장 중 어법상 어색한 것을 찾아 기호를 쓰고, 바르게 고쳐 쓰시오.

> ⓐ There are many dancing shoes in this shop.
> ⓑ The bridge connected the two islands has been closed.

> _____ : _____ → _____

대표유형 01 현재분사와 과거분사　　　　출제율 55%

10 다음 두 문장을 한 문장으로 바꿔 쓰시오. (단, 분사를 포함한 7단어로 완성할 것)

> We saw a castle. It was made of ice.
> → _____

11 〈보기〉에서 알맞은 말을 골라 빈칸에 쓰시오. (단, 필요 시 형태를 바꿀 것)

> 보기　　invite　　leave　　damage

> (1) They got on the plane _____ for New Zealand.
> (2) Most people _____ to the party were his old friends.
> (3) We will give you a full refund for the _____ goods.

12 다음 문장에서 어법상 어색한 부분을 두 군데 찾아 바르게 고쳐 쓰시오.

> The girl wear a blue dress is played Mozart.

> (1) _____ → _____
> (2) _____ → _____

대표유형 03 감정을 나타내는 분사　　　　출제율 25%

13 다음 밑줄 친 단어를 각각 알맞은 형태로 고쳐 쓰시오.

> The whole audience was (1) impress by the (2) amaze performance.

> (1) _____　　　　(2) _____

14 다음 빈칸에 bore의 알맞은 형태를 쓰시오.

> Rex is a _____ person. He always says something _____ .

>> 실전 Tip 주어가 사람이라고 해서 항상 과거분사를 쓰지 않도록 유의한다.

15 다음 우리말에 맞게 빈칸에 들어갈 단어를 〈보기〉에서 골라 알맞은 형태로 쓰시오.

> 보기　　depress　　annoy　　amuse

> (1) 나는 오늘 몹시 우울한 하루를 보냈다.
>   → I had a very _____ day today.
> (2) 학생들은 선생님의 이야기에 즐거워했다.
>   → The students were _____ at the teacher's story.

대표유형 01, 03　현재분사와 과거분사 / 감정을 나타내는 분사　출제율 55%

01 다음 밑줄 친 단어의 형태로 알맞은 것끼리 짝지어진 것은?

> Everyone was <u>shock</u> when several items <u>belong</u> to Mr. Green were <u>find</u> in the closet.

① shocked – belonging – found
② shocked – belonged – found
③ shocked – belonging – finding
④ shocking – belonged – found
⑤ shocking – belonged – finding

02 다음 글의 밑줄 친 ①~⑤ 중 어법상 어색한 것을 모두 고르면?

> Have you ① <u>seen</u> this movie? I saw it with my friends. The beginning was a little bit ② <u>boring</u>. As the story went on, it became so ③ <u>interested</u>, and the last scene was really ④ <u>touching</u>. All of us were deeply ⑤ <u>moving</u>.

03 다음 밑줄 친 부분 중 어법상 어색한 것을 모두 고르면?

① The cat sat <u>scratched</u> itself.
② The mystery remained <u>unsolved</u>.
③ Look at the fire <u>coming</u> out of the house.
④ My family booked a room <u>facing</u> the sea.
⑤ There is a crowd of boys <u>thrown</u> snowballs at each other.

04 다음 문장 중 어법상 옳은 것은?

① We saw him slept on the bench.
② My grandma has just had her eyes tested.
③ Their recent failure was really frustrated.
④ Anyone interesting in baseball can join us.
⑤ The truck driver hit the woman crossed the street.

05 다음 짝지어진 대화 중 자연스럽지 <u>않은</u> 것은?

① **A** What has happened to your finger?
　B I cut it on a broken glass.
② **A** Who is the girl holding a dog in her arms?
　B She is my classmate Olivia.
③ **A** I really love Adele's songs.
　B Me, too. I think her voice is amazed.
④ **A** You hate Ted, don't you?
　B Yeah, he's the most annoying person I've ever met.
⑤ **A** What was Eddie doing this morning?
　B He was sweeping the fallen leaves in the yard.

대표유형 02　현재분사와 동명사　출제율 20%

06 다음 중 밑줄 친 부분의 쓰임이 나머지 넷과 <u>다른</u> 것은?

① Sandra likes the boy <u>shooting</u> a basketball.
② Where is the <u>ringing</u> sound coming from?
③ Helen is used to <u>writing</u> with her left hand.
④ A group of sea lions is <u>lying</u> on the rocks.
⑤ Drivers <u>speeding</u> in a school zone have to pay a fine.

07 다음 〈보기〉의 밑줄 친 부분과 쓰임이 같은 것을 모두 고르면?

> 보기　Do you know the man <u>talking</u> with Alice?

① We're <u>preparing</u> a surprise party for Max.
② They wanted to buy a <u>cleaning</u> robot.
③ I heard a clock <u>ticking</u> somewhere in the room.
④ His plan for this year is <u>reading</u> 100 books.
⑤ I'm looking forward to <u>spending</u> time with you.

대표유형 01 현재분사와 과거분사   출제율 55%

08 괄호 안에 주어진 표현을 이용하여 문장을 다시 쓰시오. (단, 분사를 이용할 것)

> In 1969, scientists made a new discovery. (study bacteria)

→ In 1969, scientists _____
_____.

09 다음 문장에서 어법상 어색한 부분을 두 군데 찾아 바르게 고쳐 쓰시오.

> I had my wisdom tooth pull out last week, and since then, I haven't eat sweets.

(1) _____ → _____
(2) _____ → _____

10 다음 우리말을 주어진 〈조건〉에 맞게 영어로 옮기시오.

> 그녀는 비틀즈가 작곡한 노래들을 좋아한다.
> → _____

> [조건] **1.** 분사를 이용할 것
>   **2.** compose, by the Beatles를 이용할 것
>   **3.** 8단어로 완성할 것

11 다음 우리말에 맞게 괄호 안의 표현을 바르게 배열하시오. (단, 주어진 표현 중 하나의 형태를 알맞게 고칠 것)

> 바람에 쓰러진 나무들이 도로를 막았다.
> (blow down, the wind, by, the road, blocked, trees)

→ _____

대표유형 03 감정을 나타내는 분사   출제율 25%

12 다음 세 문장이 같은 뜻이 되도록 문장을 완성하시오.

> The result disappointed my family.
> = The result _____ _____ to my family.
> = My family _____ _____ at the result.

13 괄호 안의 단어를 이용하여 빈칸에 알맞은 말을 쓰시오.

> **A** How was your trip to Korea?
> **B** It was great. I think Korea is a _____ (fascinate) city with a lot of _____ (interest) activities to enjoy.

14 빈칸에 들어갈 단어를 〈보기〉에서 골라 알맞은 형태로 쓰시오. (단, 한 번씩만 사용할 것)

> 보기   frighten   satisfy   exhaust   embarrass

(1) I had to drive for two hours without a break, and it was _____.
(2) The boy felt _____ when everyone laughed at him.
(3) Most children are _____ of the dark.

15 다음 중 어법상 어색한 문장을 두 개 골라 기호를 쓰고, 바르게 고쳐 쓰시오.

> ⓐ A long flight is always tired.
> ⓑ The child got boring and turned on the TV.
> ⓒ The neighbors were shocked at the accident.

(1) _____ : _____ → _____
(2) _____ : _____ → _____

01 다음 밑줄 친 부분의 쓰임에 해당하는 것에 기호를 쓰시오.

ⓐ I really like her smiling face.
ⓑ Julia hates talking to complete strangers.
ⓒ I saw a goat jumping over the fence.
ⓓ The swimming pool was full of dirt.
ⓔ The ship sailing to Tallinn is leaving tonight.
ⓕ The best part of the day was riding a roller coaster.

(1) 현재분사: _____   (2) 동명사: _____

02 다음 밑줄 친 문장 중 어법상 어색한 것을 모두 고르면?

① It was a frozen cold day in February.
② Our family visited an old hot spring built in the 19th century. ③ There were many people soaking in the hot spring. ④ The hot spring water was relaxed and perfect.
⑤ We all thought the place was worth visiting.

03 다음 중 어법상 옳은 문장의 개수는?

ⓐ He saw me dancing to the music.
ⓑ I found my answer sheet tear into pieces.
ⓒ Sylvia had her computer repaired.
ⓓ I was frustrating when I failed the test.
ⓔ The picture drawn by Jim was shocked.

① 1개   ② 2개   ③ 3개   ④ 4개   ⑤ 5개

04 다음 우리말에 맞게 주어진 표현을 바르게 배열하시오.

트럭에 치인 강아지는 동물 병원으로 옮겨졌다.
(was, run over, by, to the animal hospital, taken, a puppy, a truck)

→ _____

_____

05 다음 글에서 어법상 어색한 부분을 모두 찾아 바르게 고쳐 쓰시오.

Yesterday was my sixteenth birthday. My parents made a chocolate cake for me. The cake was amazed. My sister gave me a present wrapped with a red ribbon. It was a pretty hairpin. I was pleasing with her present. We had such an excited time.

_____

_____

06 다음 그림 속 인물을 묘사하는 문장을 주어진 〈조건〉에 맞게 완성하시오.

[조건] 1. (A)와 (B)에서 각각 하나씩 골라 쓸 것
     2. (A)를 분사로 만들고 시제는 현재진행형으로 쓸 것
     3. 「관계대명사 + be동사」는 생략할 것

(A) • sit on the bench
    • wear an orange sweater
    • surround by children

(B) • make a balloon teddy bear
    • talk on the phone
    • walk his dog

(1) The boy _____
(2) The girl _____ .
(3) The woman _____ .

최종 선택 QUIZ

어법상 옳은 문장에 ✔ 표시하세요.

01
a I found fallen leaves on the ground.

b I found falling leaves on the ground.

02
a The noise is really annoying.

b The noise is really annoyed.

03
a Let me see the pictures taken on your journey.

b Let me see the pictures taking on your journey.

04
a They heard someone screaming for help.

b They heard someone screamed for help.

05
a A man is training the puppy barked at people.

b A man is training the puppy barking at people.

06
a My family booked a room facing the sea with an amazed view.

b My family booked a room facing the sea with an amazing view.

07
a Lucy is going to have her teeth examined tomorrow.

b Lucy is going to have her teeth examining tomorrow.

08
a My head is filled with depressed thoughts.

b My head is filled with depressing thoughts.

유형별 기출 적용 빈도

유형 01   분사구문의 형태와 의미   45%

유형 02   분사구문의 시제와 태   20%

유형 03   비인칭 독립분사구문   15%

유형 04   with + 명사(구) + 분사   20%

Grammar Point

Point 1 분사구문의 형태와 의미

분사구문은 부사절을 현재분사로 시작하는 부사구로 줄여 쓴 것으로 시간, 이유, 조건, 동시동작 등의 의미를 나타낸다. 부정은 「not[never] + 분사」의 형태이다.

분사구문 만드는 법	As she waved at the crowds, she came into the stadium.
① 접속사 생략	→ As she waved at the crowds, ~
② 부사절의 주어 생략 (주절의 주어와 같을 때)	→ she waved at the crowds, ~
③ 동사를 현재분사로 바꾸기	→ Waving at the crowds, ~

• 독립분사구문은 부사절과 주절의 주어가 다를 때, 부사절의 주어를 생략하지 않고 분사 앞에 남겨두는 분사구문을 말한다.
It being a holiday today, the bank is closed.

Point 2 분사구문의 시제와 태

• 완료 분사구문은 「having + 과거분사」의 형태로 부사절의 시제가 주절의 시제보다 앞설 때 사용한다. 부정은 「not[never] + having + 과거분사」이다.
• 수동태의 분사구문은 「being + 과거분사」 또는 「having been + 과거분사」로 쓴다. 이때, being과 having been은 생략할 수 있다.

Point 3 비인칭 독립분사구문

비인칭 독립분사구문은 부사절의 주어가 you, people처럼 일반인을 나타낼 때 주절의 주어와 다르더라도 주어를 생략하고 관용 표현처럼 쓰는 것이다.
e.g. frankly[strictly/roughly/generally] speaking 솔직히[엄밀히/대강/일반적으로] 말하면, speaking of ~ 이야기가 나와서 말인데, judging from ~로 판단하건대

Point 4 with + 명사(구) + 분사

「with + 명사(구) + 분사」는 '~한 채로, ~하면서'라는 의미로 명사(구)와 분사의 관계가 능동이면 현재분사를, 수동이면 과거분사를 쓴다.

✔ 바로 체크

01   (Seen / Seeing) him, the baby began to cry.

02   (Left / Leaving) in the car, the dog started barking.

03   (Eaten / Having eaten) dinner, they went out.

04   He stood in the rain with his body (shaking / shaken).

05   The bird flew away with its leg (breaking / broken).

06   As I was excited, I screamed.
→ _____ excited, I screamed.

07   When it is fine, we'll go on a picnic.
→ _____ _____ fine, we'll go on a picnic.

08   As she wasn't well, she went to the hospital.
→ _____ _____ well, she went to the hospital.

대표유형 01 분사구문의 형태와 의미   출제율 45%

01 다음 두 문장의 의미가 같도록 빈칸에 들어갈 말로 알맞은 것은?

> As I was walking along the stream, I met a group of hikers.
> = _____ along the stream, I met a group of hikers.

① Walk   ② Walked   ③ Walking
④ To walk   ⑤ Being walked

02 다음 빈칸에 들어갈 말로 알맞은 것을 <u>모두</u> 고르면?

> _____, I went to bed early.

① Tiring   ② Being tired
③ As I was tired   ④ I tired
⑤ Having tired

03 다음 우리말에 맞게 빈칸에 알맞은 말을 쓰시오.(단, 분사구문으로 쓸 것)

> White 씨는 보통 음악을 들으면서 집을 청소한다.
> → Mr. White usually cleans his house, _____ to music.

[04-06] 다음 밑줄 친 부분을 분사구문으로 바꿀 때 빈칸에 알맞은 말을 쓰시오.

04

> <u>Though I live near the beach</u>, I still can't swim well.
> → _____ near the beach, I still can't swim well.

05

> <u>As I felt frightened</u>, I hid under the desk.
> → _____, I hid under the desk.

06

> <u>Because he didn't have enough money</u>, he couldn't pay the fine.
> → _____ _____ enough money, he couldn't pay the fine.

07 다음 밑줄 친 부분 중 어법상 <u>어색한</u> 것은?

① <u>Eating chocolate</u>, Emily did her homework.
② <u>Turning to the left</u>, you will find the bank.
③ <u>Hearing his voice</u>, I realized there was something wrong.
④ <u>Being a vegetarian</u>, he doesn't eat meat.
⑤ <u>Knowing not what to say</u>, I remained silent.

08 다음 문장을 부사절을 이용하여 바꿔 쓸 때 각 빈칸에 들어갈 접속사가 바르게 짝지어진 것은?

> • Visiting our website, you can get more information.
> → _____ you visit our website, you can get more information.
> • Staying in Korea, we experienced the mud festival.
> → _____ we were staying in Korea, we experienced the mud festival.

① If – While   ② When – If
③ Before – As   ④ Because – Though
⑤ Though – As

09 다음 중 밑줄 친 부분의 쓰임이 나머지 넷과 <u>다른</u> 것은?

① <u>Opening the envelope</u>, you'll find a concert ticket.
② <u>Being very busy</u>, Sophie had to skip lunch.
③ <u>Having no keys</u>, I couldn't enter the room.
④ <u>Getting poor grades</u>, Brad was really disappointed.
⑤ <u>Thinking he was asleep</u>, I turned down the music.

10 다음 우리말에 맞게 괄호 안의 단어를 이용하여 알맞은 분사구문을 쓰시오.

> 가난했기 때문에 그들은 옷에 많은 돈을 쓰지 않았다.
> → _____ _____, they didn't spend much money on clothes. (poor)

11 〈보기〉에서 알맞은 접속사를 골라 밑줄 친 분사구문을 부사절로 바꿔 쓰시오.

> 보기   as   if   though

(1) Going upstairs, you will meet the manager.
    → _____

(2) Not feeling hungry, he skipped dinner.
    → _____

12 〈보기〉와 같이 분사구문을 이용하여 두 문장을 한 문장으로 바꿔 쓰시오.

> 보기 She was talking on the phone. At the same time, she was putting on makeup.
> → She was talking on the phone, putting on makeup.

Andy was taking a shower. At the same time, he was whistling to himself.
→ _____

13 다음 문장을 분사구문으로 바꾼 문장에서 어법상 어색한 부분을 찾아 바르게 고쳐 쓰시오.

> As there was nothing more to do, we went back home.
> → Being nothing more to do, we went back home.

_____ → _____

14 다음 두 문장의 의미가 같도록 빈칸에 알맞은 분사구문을 쓰시오. (단, 시제의 차이가 드러나도록 쓸 것)

> After I had locked the door, I went to sleep.
> = _____ _____ the door, I went to sleep.

15 다음 빈칸에 들어갈 말이 순서대로 바르게 짝지어진 것은?

> • _____ her speech, Ms. Swift headed towards the exit.
> • _____ from space, the Earth looks like a beautiful green and blue jewel.

① Finished – Seeing
② Having finished – Seen
③ Being finished – Having been seen
④ Finished – Having seen
⑤ Having been finished – Seeing

16 다음 밑줄 친 부분을 분사구문으로 바꿔 쓰시오.

> As the book was written in old English, it was not easy to understand.
> → _____, the book was not easy to understand.

17 다음 밑줄 친 부분 중 어법상 어색한 것은?

① Having read the book, I returned it to my friend.
② Being exhausted by the work, he fell asleep.
③ Destroyed by fire, the building was rebuilt.
④ Having left the party too early, we couldn't see the fireworks.
⑤ Studied Korean history in university, she knows a lot about the subject.

18 다음 밑줄 친 부분과 바꿔 쓸 수 있는 것은?

> <u>Honestly</u>, I think it is a waste of time and money.

① Compared with　② Strictly speaking
③ Considering that　④ Frankly speaking
⑤ Roughly speaking

19 다음 우리말과 같도록 빈칸에 들어갈 말로 알맞은 것은?

> 일반적으로 말해서, 부모들은 자녀들에게 좋은 것은 무엇이든지 하려는 경향이 있다.
> → _____, parents are likely to do whatever is good for their children.

① Granting　② Considering that
③ Seeing that　④ Provided that
⑤ Generally speaking

20 다음 빈칸에 공통으로 들어갈 말로 알맞은 것은?

> • Strictly _____, he doesn't deserve this prize.
> • _____ of soccer, which team do you think will win the game?

① seeing[Seeing]　② talking[Talking]
③ being[Being]　④ listening[Listening]
⑤ speaking[Speaking]

21 다음 밑줄 친 우리말을 괄호 안의 표현을 이용하여 알맞은 분사구문으로 쓰시오.

> <u>나의 경험으로 판단하건대</u>, 선의의 거짓말을 하는 것이 항상 나쁜 것은 아니다.
> → _____,
> telling a white lie is not always bad.
> (judge from, my experience)

22 다음 빈칸에 들어갈 말로 알맞은 것은?

> She danced alone _____.

① with her eyes closed
② with her eyes closing
③ with close her eyes
④ closing with her eyes
⑤ closed with her eyes

>> 실전 Tip 「with + 명사(구)+분사」 구문에서 명사(구)와 분사의 관계가 능동이면 현재분사를, 수동이면 과거분사를 쓴다.

23 다음 우리말과 같도록 괄호 안의 표현을 이용하여 문장을 완성하시오.

> 주전자가 끓고 있는 채로 우리는 아무 말 없이 서 있었다. (with, the kettle, boil)

→ We stood in silence _____.

24 다음 밑줄 친 부분 중 어법상 옳은 것은?

① I fell asleep <u>with the TV turning on.</u>
② He was lying on the beach <u>with his body covering in sand.</u>
③ The dog ran up to us <u>with its tail wagged.</u>
④ I was sitting <u>with tears running down my cheeks.</u>
⑤ She drove her car <u>with her long hair blown in the wind.</u>

25 다음 문장 중 어법상 어색한 것을 모두 고르면?

① I can't sleep with the bedroom door closing.
② With April approaching, the temperature rose.
③ She came to school with her hair dyed yellow.
④ He entered the room with everyone staring at him.
⑤ I read a book with my cat slept by my side.

대표유형 01, 02 분사구문의 형태와 의미, 시제와 태   출제율 45%

01 다음 빈칸에 들어갈 말이 순서대로 바르게 짝지어진 것은?

> • _____ for his missing dog, he called its name out loud.
> • _____ by the lightning and thunder, we screamed.

① Looking – Surprised
② Looking – Surprising
③ Looked – Being surprised
④ Looked – Having surprised
⑤ Having looked – Being surprised

02 다음 밑줄 친 부분을 알맞은 형태로 고친 것은?

> A group of young girls dashed into the sea, <u>shout</u> with excitement.

① shouts   ② shouted
③ shouting   ④ having shouted
⑤ being shouted

[03-04] 다음 두 문장의 의미가 같도록 빈칸에 알맞은 것을 고르시오.

03

> Accepting what you say, I still don't believe it.
> → _____ I accept what you say, I still don't believe it.

① If   ② When   ③ Since
④ Because   ⑤ Although

04

> As he hadn't received a reply, he decided to write her again.
> → _____ a reply, he decided to write her again.

① Not received
② Being not received
③ Having not received
④ Not having received
⑤ Having been not received

05 다음 우리말을 영어로 바르게 나타낸 것은?

> 날씨가 추워서, 우리는 수영을 갈 수 없었다.

① Being cold, we couldn't go swimming.
② It being cold, we couldn't go swimming.
③ Been cold, we couldn't go swimming.
④ It having cold, we couldn't go swimming.
⑤ Having been cold, we couldn't go swimming.

06 다음 밑줄 친 부분 중 어법상 옳은 것을 <u>두 개</u> 고르면?

① <u>Written a letter to Julia</u>, I started to doze off.
② <u>Having not a ticket</u>, I couldn't go to the concert.
③ <u>Her eyes shining with joy</u>, Grace laughed loudly.
④ <u>Chosen as the class president</u>, she was proud of herself.
⑤ <u>Having born and raised in France</u>, Leo is fluent in French.

07 다음 밑줄 친 부사절을 분사구문으로 나타낸 것 중 어법상 어색한 것은?

① <u>While I traveled in Spain</u>, I bumped into Kate.
   → Traveling in Spain
② <u>After I walked my dog</u>, I watched a movie.
   → Having walked my dog
③ <u>Since she had worked hard all day</u>, she was exhausted.
   → Having worked hard all day
④ <u>As he was trained for 3 years</u>, he is now ready to play for the team.
   → Trained for 3 years
⑤ <u>Because she wasn't invited to the party</u>, she didn't come.
   → Not having invited to the party

[08-09] 다음 밑줄 친 부분을 분사구문으로 바꿔 쓰시오.

08

> <u>While I was waiting for the bus</u>, I texted my mom.
> → _____ _____ _____, I texted my mom.

09

> <u>Because she hadn't eaten for two days</u>, she couldn't get up.
> → _____ _____ _____ _____ _____, she couldn't get up.

10 다음 문장에서 어법상 <u>어색한</u> 부분을 찾아 바르게 고쳐 쓰시오.

> Seriously injuring in the car accident, the man was taken to the hospital.

_____ → _____

대표유형 03 비인칭 독립분사구문   출제율 15%

11 빈칸에 알맞은 말을 〈보기〉에서 골라 문장을 완성하시오. (단, 한 번씩만 쓸 것)

> 보기   speaking of   judging from
> frankly speaking

(1) _____, I don't like your jokes.
(2) _____ Mr. Jones, he got fired last week.
(3) _____ her expression, she must have enjoyed her meal.

12 다음 우리말과 같도록 괄호 안의 단어를 이용하여 알맞은 분사구문을 쓰시오.

> 그의 나이를 고려하면 그는 꽤 건강한 상태이다.
> → _____, he is in pretty good health. (consider, age)

대표유형 04 with + 명사(구) + 분사   출제율 20%

13 다음 문장에서 어법상 <u>어색한</u> 부분을 찾아 바르게 고쳐 쓰시오.

> Diana walked along the beach with her dog followed her.

_____ → _____

14 다음 두 문장의 의미가 같도록 빈칸에 알맞은 말을 쓰시오. (단, with를 포함할 것)

> Cathy was listening to music, and she was crossing her legs.
> = Cathy was listening to music _____ _____ _____ _____.

15 괄호 안의 단어를 이용하여 그림 속 남자를 묘사하는 문장을 완성하시오.

> The man is leaning against the wall _____ _____ _____. (arms, fold)

대표유형 01, 02 　분사구문의 형태와 의미, 시제와 태　출제율 45%

01 다음 밑줄 친 부사절을 분사구문으로 바르게 바꾼 것을 **두 개** 고르면?

① As it snowed heavily, the hikers gave up hiking.
　→ It snowing heavily

② When I spilled coffee on the carpet, I got embarrassed.
　→ Spilled coffee on the carpet

③ As he was lost in thought, he almost ran into the bike.
　→ Losing in thought

④ Because I didn't understand his question, I couldn't answer.
　→ Not understanding his question

⑤ As I had seen the movie before, I didn't go to the theater.
　→ Having been seen the movie before

02 다음 밑줄 친 부분을 알맞은 형태로 고친 것은?

Know mainly as a poet, he has now written a successful novel.

① Knew　　　　② Knowing
③ Known　　　④ Having known
⑤ Been known

03 다음 밑줄 친 부분을 생략할 수 **없는** 것끼리 묶은 것은?

ⓐ If you are poor at math, I will help you.
ⓑ Having written his report, he took a nap.
ⓒ Though he was tired, he went on working.
ⓓ Being satisfied with the result, I nodded.
ⓔ If they are grown in the right conditions, they will bloom in early May.
ⓕ Having been scolded by his mom, he is now depressed.

① ⓐ, ⓑ　　　② ⓓ, ⓔ　　　③ ⓐ, ⓒ, ⓓ
④ ⓑ, ⓒ, ⓕ　　⑤ ⓓ, ⓔ, ⓕ

04 다음 밑줄 친 분사구문을 부사절로 바꾼 것 중 어색한 것은?

① I was reading a book, drinking a cup of coffee.
　→ while I was drinking a cup of coffee

② Using this tool, you'll be able to open the door.
　→ If you use this tool

③ Not having a car, she had to walk there.
　→ Because she didn't have a car

④ Having been warned before, he is still late for class.
　→ Though he warned before

⑤ Dressed in all black, the child was almost invisible at night.
　→ As the child was dressed in all black

대표유형 01, 03 　분사구문의 형태와 의미, with + 명사(구) + 분사　출제율 45%

05 다음 글의 빈칸에 들어갈 말이 순서대로 바르게 짝지어진 것은?

It was a gloomy day with the rain _____ down. _____ alone in the house, Josh was lying on the floor with the curtains _____.

① poured – Been left – drawing
② poured – Leaving – drawing
③ pouring – Left – drawn
④ poured – Having left – drawn
⑤ pouring – Leaving – having drawn

06 다음 중 어법상 옳은 문장의 개수는?

ⓐ Being no seat left on the bus, I had to stand the whole way.
ⓑ Not feeling too well, he left work early.
ⓒ Arriving at the party, we saw Lucy sitting alone.
ⓓ He came to school with one eye bandaged.
ⓔ The woman was sleeping with her head resting her arms.

① 1개　　② 2개　　③ 3개　　④ 4개　　⑤ 5개

대표유형 01, 02 분사구문의 형태와 의미, 시제와 태   출제율 45%

07 다음 우리말에 맞게 빈칸에 알맞은 말을 쓰시오.

> 나는 어젯밤에 한숨도 못 자서 지금 너무 피곤하다.
> → _____ _____ _____ a wink last night, I'm very tired now.

[08-10] 다음 밑줄 친 부분을 분사구문으로 바꿔 쓰시오.

08
> <u>After he had been arrested and sent to jail</u>, he wrote a letter to the judge.
> → _____,
>   he wrote a letter to the judge.

09
> <u>As the score was equal</u>, the players had to go into overtime.
> → _____,
>   the players had to go into overtime.

10
> <u>Because she realized her mistake</u>, she apologized to them.
> → _____,
>   she apologized to them.

11 다음 문장에서 어법상 <u>어색한</u> 부분을 찾아 바르게 고쳐 쓰시오.

(1) Lost his wallet yesterday, he's going to buy a new one today.
    _____ → _____

(2) Annoy at his rudeness, she didn't want to meet him.
    _____ → _____

[12-13] 주어진 〈조건〉에 맞게 우리말을 영작하시오.

12
> 나는 내 차를 세차한 후에, 쇼핑을 갔다.
> → _____

> [조건] 1. 분사구문을 포함할 것
>   2. 두 행동 사이에 시제의 차이가 드러나도록 할 것
>   3. 7단어로 완성할 것

13
> 나는 버스를 놓치고 싶지 않아서, 버스 정류장까지 뛰었다.
> (부사절로) → _____
> _____
> (분사구문으로) → _____
> _____

> [조건] 1. want, miss the bus, run을 이용할 것
>   2. 각각 부사절과 분사구문을 이용하여 쓸 것

대표유형 04 with + 명사(구) + 분사   출제율 20%

14 다음 두 문장이 같은 의미가 되도록 빈칸에 알맞은 말을 쓰시오.

(1) Freddie watched TV and his sister knitted beside him.
    → Freddie watched TV with _____
    _____.

(2) Sophia accepted my offer and her eyes were filled with tears of joy.
    → Sophia accepted my offer with _____
    _____.

15 다음 우리말과 같도록 괄호 안의 표현을 이용하여 문장을 완성하시오.

> 문이 열릴 때까지 안전벨트를 맨 채 좌석에 앉아 계십시오. (safety belt, fasten)
> → Please stay in your seat _____
> _____ until the door is opened.

01 다음 빈칸에 들어갈 말이 나머지 넷과 <u>다른</u> 것은?

① His mom _____ ill, he had to look after her.

② Not _____ confident, I remained silent.

③ _____ badly injured, she couldn't walk anymore.

④ Having _____ hit by the storm, the town was a mess.

⑤ There _____ no evidence, the man was finally released.

02 다음 문장 중 어법상 옳은 것끼리 묶은 것은?

ⓐ Ben washed the dishes, humming gently.

ⓑ Spent my childhood in China, I can speak Chinese.

ⓒ Considered the price, the hotel is really satisfying.

ⓓ Having not done my homework, I can't go camping.

ⓔ Completely confused, I had to ask her a question.

① ⓐ, ⓒ   ② ⓐ, ⓔ   ③ ⓑ, ⓓ

④ ⓐ, ⓑ, ⓔ   ⑤ ⓒ, ⓓ, ⓔ

03 다음 밑줄 친 부분을 분사구문으로 바꾼 것 중 <u>어색한</u> 것을 <u>모두</u> 고르면?

① <u>If it is sunny</u>, we will have lunch in the garden.

→ Being sunny

② <u>While she was playing tennis</u>, she sprained her wrist.

→ Playing tennis

③ <u>Though he was asked some unexpected questions</u>, he kept calm.

→ Asking some unexpected questions

④ <u>As it was written quickly</u>, it had some mistakes.

→ Written quickly

⑤ <u>After she had graduated from college</u>, she became a lawyer.

→ Having graduated from college

04 〈보기〉에서 알맞은 단어를 골라 그림 속 인물을 묘사하는 두 문장을 완성하시오. (단, 현재진행형을 쓸 것)

보기	watch with
	run eyes fix

(1) The girl _____ on the treadmill, _____ TV.

(2) The girl _____ on the treadmill _____ on the TV screen.

05 〈보기〉와 같이 의미가 통하도록 문장을 완성하시오. (단, (A)는 분사구문으로 바꾸어 문장의 앞에 쓸 것)

(A) • smile brightly	(B) • she hugged me
(1) water regularly	tightly
(2) slip on the ice	• he hurt his leg
(3) have nothing left to do	• I took a nap for a while
	• the plant will last long

보기	Smiling brightly, she hugged me tightly.

(1) _____

(2) _____

(3) _____

06 다음 우리말에 맞게 괄호 안의 단어를 바르게 배열하시오. (단, 각각 한 단어의 형태를 알맞게 고칠 것)

(1) 전에 한 번도 해외에 가 본 적이 없어서, 그는 이번 여행에 대해 매우 신이 나 있다.

→ _____,

he is so excited about this trip. (never, be, abroad, before, having)

(2) 그 도둑은 등 뒤에 손이 묶인 채로 끌려왔다.

→ The thief was brought in, _____

_____.

(with, tie, behind, his hands, his back)

최종 선택 QUIZ

어법상 옳은 문장에
✔ 표시하세요.

01
- a   Felt cold, the girl put on the coat.
- b   Feeling cold, the girl put on the coat.

02
- a   Raining hard, they canceled the game.
- b   It raining hard, they canceled the game.

03
- a   Being not tired, he continued to work.
- b   Not being tired, he continued to work.

04
- a   Raised by his grandparents, he called them Mom and Dad.
- b   Raising by his grandparents, he called them Mom and Dad.

05
- a   Finished his homework, he went out for a walk.
- b   Having finished his homework, he went out for a walk.

06
- a   Not having seen her for ages, I couldn't recognize her.
- b   Having not seen her for ages, I couldn't recognize her.

07
- a   He left home with the door unlocked.
- b   He left home with the door unlocking.

08
- a   She greeted me with her hand waved.
- b   She greeted me with her hand waving.

유형별 기출 적용 빈도

유형 01 능동태와 수동태	45%	
유형 02 수동태의 여러 가지 형태	45%	
유형 03 수동태로 쓰지 않는 동사	10%	

Grammar Point

Point 1 능동태와 수동태

능동태	동사의 동작을 하는 행위자를 주어로 함
수동태	동사의 행위를 당하는 대상을 주어로 함
	형태: 「be동사 + 과거분사(+ by + 행위자)」

A tiger attacked the traveler. 〈능동태: 호랑이가 공격했다는 것에 초점〉
→ The traveler was attacked by a tiger. 〈수동태: 여행자가 공격당했다는 것에 초점〉
행위자가 일반인이거나 분명하지 않은 경우, 또는 언급하지 않아도 알 수 있는 경우에는 「by + 행위자」를 생략할 수 있다.
English is spoken in Canada (by people).

Point 2 수동태의 여러 가지 형태

미래 시제	will be + 과거분사 / be동사 + going to be + 과거분사
진행 시제	be동사 + being + 과거분사
완료 시제	have[has / had / will have] + been + 과거분사
조동사가 있을 때	조동사 + be + 과거분사

Her book will be published in May.
His name is being called by the interviewer.
Many movies have been made by Steven Spielberg.
The bike can be repaired within a few days.

Point 3 수동태로 쓰지 않는 동사

목적어가 없는 자동사	happen, appear, disappear, occur, remain 등
상태·소유를 나타내는 타동사	have, resemble, meet, become, fit 등

Jessica resembles her mother a lot. 〈← is resembled (×)〉

✅ 바로 체크

01 The kid (broke / was broken) the window.

02 The poem (wrote / was written) by Jenny.

03 The smartphone was found by (he / him).

04 The walls (painted / were painted) green by volunteers.

05 The fence (is being fixed / is been fixed) by Kevin.

06 The dog (has been feed / has been fed) by my sister.

07 The cello (will is played / will be played) by Ann.

08 The box (should not be opened/ should be not opened) by Sam.

09 The land (will disappear / will be disappeared) within 10 years.

10 Cathy (has / is had) two daughters and a son.

대표유형 01 능동태와 수동태　　　　　출제율 45%

01 다음 두 문장의 의미가 같도록 할 때 빈칸에 알맞은 것은?

> Many people loved the actor.
> = The actor _____ many people.

① was loving
② is loved by
③ was loved by
④ was loving by
⑤ were loved by

02 다음 밑줄 친 write의 형태로 알맞은 것은?

> The letter write by Ms. Jones last night.

① wrote
② was written
③ has written
④ were written
⑤ had written

03 다음 빈칸에 알맞은 말로 바르게 짝지어진 것은?

> The museum _____ by a famous architect last year, and many tourists _____ it.

① designed – are visited
② designed – will be visited
③ was designed – visit
④ has designed – are visited
⑤ will be designed – visit

04 다음 밑줄 친 부분 중 어법상 어색한 것은?

① The zookeeper fed the elephants.
② Cacao beans are grown in West Africa.
③ The awards ceremony is seen by millions of people.
④ Walt Disney created a character named Mickey Mouse.
⑤ The speech gave by the new principal yesterday.

05 다음 능동태 문장을 수동태로 바꾼 것 중 잘못된 것은?

① Many teens read comic books.
　→ Comic books are read by many teens.
② Sophia took this picture.
　→ This picture was taken by Sophia.
③ My brother made this apple pie.
　→ This apple pie was made by my brother.
④ I drew the paintings.
　→ The paintings was drawn by me.
⑤ The Beatles sang the song.
　→ The song was sung by the Beatles.

≫ 실전 Tip 능동태를 수동태로 바꿀 때는 행위의 대상이 되는 주어(능동태 문장의 목적어)가 단수인지 복수인지, 동사의 시제가 현재인지 과거인지 반드시 확인해야 한다.

06 다음 우리말과 같도록 괄호 안의 단어를 이용하여 빈칸에 알맞은 말을 쓰시오.

> 그 집은 나의 부모님이 지으셨다. (build, by)
> → The house _____.

[07-09] 다음 능동태를 수동태로 바꾼 문장을 완성하시오.

07
> Many students wear jeans.
> → Jeans _____.

08
> The police arrested the drunk driver.
> → The drunk driver _____.

09
> She didn't break my glasses.
> → My glasses _____.

10 다음 대화의 밑줄 친 우리말과 같도록 괄호 안의 어구를 이용하여 영어로 쓰시오.

> **A** 그 꽃들은 그에 의해 구입된 거니?
> (the flowers, buy)
> **B** Yes, they were. He bought them in a shop.

→ _____

>> 실전 Tip 수동태 의문문의 형태는 「Be동사＋주어＋과거분사 ~?」이다.

11 다음 〈보기〉와 같이 괄호 안의 어구와 수동태를 이용하여 질문에 완전한 문장으로 답하시오.

> 보기 **A** Where was the mummy found?
> **B** It was found in the pyramid. (in the pyramid)

A Who invented Hangeul?
B _____ (King Sejong)

12 다음 그림과 〈보기〉를 참고하여, 빈칸에 알맞은 말을 쓰시오. (단, 괄호 안의 단어를 이용하여 현재 시제로 쓸 것)

> 보기 The steak is cooked by Mom. (cook)

(1) Mom _____ by Dad. (help)
(2) The cookies _____ by Tom. (bake)
(3) The dishes _____ by Sally. (wash)

대표유형 02 　수동태의 여러 가지 형태　　　　　출제율 45%

13 다음 빈칸에 알맞은 것은?

> The letter will _____ by my sister.

① send　　② is sent　　③ be sent
④ been sent　　⑤ has sent

14 다음 빈칸에 공통으로 알맞은 것은?

> • Was the dog _____ trained?
> • Their car is _____ fixed by the mechanic.

① has　　　② be　　　③ been
④ being　　⑤ to be

15 다음 우리말과 같도록 괄호 안의 단어를 이용하여 빈칸에 알맞은 말을 쓰시오.

> 레오나르도 다빈치의 〈모나리자〉는 파리의 루브르 박물관에서 볼 수 있다.
> → Leonardo da Vinci's *Mona Lisa* _____ _____ _____ at the Louvre Museum in Paris. (see)

16 다음 능동태를 수동태로 바꾼 문장을 완성하시오.

> They will invite Mike to the party.
> → Mike _____.

17 다음 밑줄 친 부분 중 어법상 어색한 것을 모두 고르면?

① Plastic bottles can be recycled.
② A tree is being cut down by the man.
③ Should animals kept in zoos?
④ The music will be performed by the school band.
⑤ Garlic has used as medicine for thousands of years.

18 다음 두 문장의 의미가 같도록 할 때 빈칸에 알맞은 것은?

> The staff was decorating the hall.
> = The hall _____ by the staff.

① is decorated
② was decorated
③ being decorated
④ is been decorated
⑤ was being decorated

19 다음 우리말과 같도록 괄호 안의 어구를 이용하여 영어로 쓰시오.

> 2022년 FIFA 월드컵은 카타르에서 개최될 것이다.
> (the 2022 FIFA World Cup, hold, Qatar)
>
> → _____

20 다음 두 문장의 의미가 같도록 주어진 말로 시작하여 문장을 완성하시오.

> The students have written the report.
> → The report _____.

≫ 실전 Tip 완료형 수동태의 형태는 「have[has/had/will have]+been+과거분사」이다. 이때 have 동사는 주어의 수와 인칭에 일치시킨다.

21 다음 중 어법상 옳은 문장은?

① The work should been done today.
② The house will is painted by them next week.
③ Her speech could be understand by the audience.
④ The stolen car is be chased by the police now.
⑤ Coffee has been loved for thousands of years.

[22-23] 다음 능동태를 수동태로 바꾼 문장에서 어법상 <u>어색</u>한 부분을 찾아 바르게 고쳐 쓰시오.

22

> Ms. Jones must pay the bill.
> → The bill must paid by Ms. Jones.

23

> A stranger has hurt the elderly man.
> → The elderly man has be hurted by a stranger.

대표유형 03 수동태로 쓰지 않는 동사 　　　　출제율 10%

24 다음 중 어법상 <u>어색한</u> 문장을 <u>모두</u> 고르면?

① The project will be completed by them.
② The accident was happened a week ago.
③ The suggestions are being considered now.
④ A cure was discovered by scientists.
⑤ My grandfather is had a lot of gold medals.

25 다음 빈칸에 was를 쓸 수 있는 것은?

① The lady _____ remained healthy.
② The baby _____ weighed 10kg.
③ That camera _____ belonged to him.
④ One of the tourists _____ arrived late.
⑤ Ann _____ invited to the award ceremony.

대표유형 01 능동태와 수동태   출제율 45%

01 다음 대화의 빈칸에 알맞은 말로 바르게 짝지어진 것은?

> **A** Steven Spielberg _____ *Star Wars*, didn't he?
> **B** No. It _____ by George Lucas.

① directed – was directed
② directed – been directed
③ has directed – was directed
④ was directed – directed
⑤ was directed – was directed

02 다음 빈칸에 들어갈 수 <u>없는</u> 것은?

> The dog _____ by its owner.

① was helping   ② is loved
③ was fed   ④ will be washed
⑤ was raised

03 다음 중 밑줄 친 부분을 <u>잘못</u> 고친 것은?

> ⓐ America <u>discovered</u> in 1492.
> ⓑ *The Kiss* was painted <u>with</u> Gustav Klimt.
> ⓒ Many mice <u>caught</u> by the cat.
> ⓓ The travelers <u>didn't</u> invited by the host.
> ⓔ Baobab trees <u>find</u> in the desert.

① ⓐ → was discovered   ② ⓑ → by
③ ⓒ → were caught   ④ ⓓ → weren't
⑤ ⓔ → are founded

04 다음 중 어법상 <u>어색한</u> 문장은?

① The ball was kicked by Kelly.
② My sister and I were scolded by Dad.
③ A young man was composed this song.
④ Both French and English are spoken in Canada.
⑤ The surprise party was thrown by her.

대표유형 02 수동태의 여러 가지 형태   출제율 45%

05 다음 능동태 문장을 수동태로 바르게 바꾼 것은?

> Mr. Kyle will teach German.

① German will teach by Mr. Kyle.
② German will taught by Mr. Kyle.
③ German will be taught by Mr. Kyle.
④ German will been taught by Mr. Kyle.
⑤ German will be teaching by Mr. Kyle.

06 다음 밑줄 친 부분 중 어법상 옳은 것은?

① The problem <u>might be solved</u> by her.
② I think history <u>must be not forget</u>.
③ The fire alarm system <u>is being test</u>.
④ The boy <u>has raised</u> by his grandparents.
⑤ The first performance <u>will shown</u> this Sunday.

≫ 실전 Tip 조동사가 있는 수동태의 부정은 「조동사+not+be+과거분사」로 쓴다.

07 다음 능동태 문장을 수동태로 바꾼 것 중 <u>잘못된</u> 것은?

① The teacher will praise her.
   → She will be praised by the teacher.
② The hurricane has destroyed the forest.
   → The forest has been destroyed by the hurricane.
③ The company is going to hire new workers.
   → New workers are going to be hired by the company.
④ Did the lifeguard rescue the boy?
   → Was the boy rescued by the lifeguard?
⑤ His classmates are spreading the rumor.
   → The rumor is being spreading by his classmates.

대표유형 01, 02 능동태와 수동태 / 수동태의 여러 가지 형태 출제율 45%

08 다음 두 문장이 같은 의미가 되도록 빈칸에 알맞은 말을 쓰시오.

> The fallen trees blocked the road.

→ The road _____.

09 다음 문장의 밑줄 친 부분을 수동태로 바꿔 쓰시오.

> Some people think that <u>robots will make food</u> in the future.

→ Some people think that _____
_____ in the future.

10 다음 문장을 수동태로 바꿔 쓰시오.

> The clerk is wrapping their presents.

→ _____

11 다음 문장을 주어진 〈조건〉에 맞게 바꿔 쓰시오.

> Many children celebrate Halloween.

> [조건] **1.** 수동태를 이용할 것
> **2.** 현재완료 시제를 이용할 것

→ _____

12 다음 괄호 안의 단어를 이용하여 문장을 완성하시오.

> The jewelry _____.
> (have, steal, a thief)

신유형

13 다음 글을 읽고, 문맥에 맞게 밑줄 친 동사를 알맞은 형태로 고쳐 쓰시오.

> President Lincoln was (1) <u>shoot</u> while he was (2) <u>watch</u> a play at the theater. He (3) <u>carried</u> to a house across the street, but he died the following day. The killer ran from the theater and (4) <u>catch</u> by soldiers later.

(1) _____ (2) _____
(3) _____ (4) _____

대표유형 03 수동태로 쓰지 않는 동사 출제율 10%

14 다음 문장에서 수동태의 쓰임이 어색한 부분을 찾아 각각 바르게 고쳐 쓰시오.

> (1) No one can expect what will be happened tomorrow.
> (2) A magician was suddenly appeared from behind the curtain.

15 다음 중 수동태 문장으로 바꿀 수 있는 문장과 바꿀 수 <u>없는</u> 문장을 구분하여 쓰시오.

(1) It fits you perfectly, doesn't it?
(2) Van Gogh painted *Starry Night*.
(3) His sister resembles his mother.
(4) The accident occurred in the night.
(5) Did the hacker change your password?

• 바꿀 수 있는 문장: _____
• 바꿀 수 <u>없는</u> 문장: _____

대표유형 01, 02 능동태와 수동태 / 수동태의 여러 가지 형태 　　출제율 45%

01 다음 중 어법상 옳은 문장은?

① Tickets can bought online.
② The firefighters were put out the fire.
③ The fish was being eaten by the cat.
④ The dog has adopted by Mary.
⑤ Dinner will be preparing by the host.

02 다음 빈칸에 들어갈 make의 형태가 나머지 넷과 <u>다른</u> 것은?

① A decision should be _____ right away.
② A birthday cake was being _____ by John.
③ The goods were not _____ in France.
④ The car has been _____ a strange sound.
⑤ His book will be _____ into a movie.

03 다음 빈칸에 알맞은 것은?

Keep the windows shut after dark, or you _____ by mosquitoes.

① will be bit　　② will be bitten
③ were bitten　　④ have been bit
⑤ will being bitten

04 다음 밑줄 친 ① ~ ⑤ 중 어법상 <u>어색한</u> 것은?

① Until the 18th century, eyeglasses ② had no arms, and people ③ held the frame of the eyeglasses ④ with one hand. But later, arms ⑤ added to them.

05 다음 대화의 빈칸에 알맞은 말로 바르게 짝지어진 것은?

A I heard Jim _____ by a car on his way to school. Is he okay?
B Yeah, luckily, he _____ seriously. He is now _____ in hospital.

① hit – was injured – treated
② was hit – was injured – been treated
③ was hit – wasn't injured – being treated
④ has hit – wasn't injured – be treated
⑤ was hit – didn't be injured – be treated

06 다음 중 어법상 <u>어색한</u> 문장은?

① His image was reflected in the mirror.
② Their request wasn't accepted.
③ The money will spent on the homeless.
④ The soup is being heated on the stove.
⑤ Mother Teresa was respected by many people.

07 다음 능동태 문장을 수동태로 바꾼 것 중 <u>잘못된</u> 것을 <u>모두</u> 고르면?

① Will they display her new paintings?
　→ Will her new paintings are displayed by them?
② The man didn't forgive Anna.
　→ Anna wasn't forgiven by the man.
③ Air pollution can cause health problems.
　→ Health problems can be caused by air pollution.
④ The reporter is interviewing the singer.
　→ The singer is being interviewed by the reporter.
⑤ The gardener hasn't mowed the lawn.
　→ The lawn hasn't be mowed by the gardener.

08 다음 문장을 수동태로 바꿔 쓰시오.

> We should protect wild animals.

→ _____

09 다음 두 문장의 의미가 같도록 빈칸에 알맞은 말을 쓰시오.

> The housekeeper will have mopped the floor.
> = The floor _____
>   by the housekeeper.

10 다음 문장을 수동태로 바꿔 쓰시오.

> Is the ambulance taking the victims to hospital?

→ _____

_____

_____

11 다음 빈칸에 알맞은 말을 각각 쓰시오.

> • Traffic laws must _____ obeyed.
> • Has David _____ helped by the counselor?
> • This proposal is _____ examined by the council.

12 다음 우리말과 같도록 괄호 안의 단어를 이용하여 문장을 완성하시오.

> 경기장에 도착했을 때, 우리는 경기가 취소되었다는 것을 알았다.
> → When we got to the stadium, we found that the game _____ _____
>   _____. (cancel)

13 다음 표의 (A) ~ (C)에서 알맞은 말을 골라 〈보기〉와 같이 수동태 문장을 쓰시오. (단, 한 번씩만 사용하고, will을 이용할 것)

(A)	(B)	(C)
~~the concert~~	hit	the show host
the city	~~enjoy~~	a huge earthquake
the winner's name	announce	~~all music lovers~~

> 보기 The concert will be enjoyed by all music lovers.

(1) _____

(2) _____

신유형

14 다음 그림을 보고, 괄호 안의 단어와 현재진행형을 이용하여 문장을 완성하시오.

(1) The flowers _____ by Dave. (water)

(2) The guitar _____ by Tiffany. (play)

대표유형 03 수동태로 쓰지 않는 동사   출제율 10%

15 다음 문장에서 어법상 어색한 부분을 찾아 바르게 고쳐 쓰시오.

> She will be missed by many people, and her spirit will be remained with them forever.

≫ 실전 Tip 목적어가 없는 자동사와 상태·소유를 나타내는 타동사는 수동태로 쓰지 않는다.

01 다음 중 어법상 옳은 문장의 개수로 알맞은 것은?

> ⓐ The sun was hiding by the clouds.
> ⓑ The present will deliver tomorrow.
> ⓒ Can the stars seen from the moon?
> ⓓ I found out that my idea had copied by someone.
> ⓔ Coffee introduced into Europe in the 17th century.

① 없음 ② 1개 ③ 2개 ④ 3개 ⑤ 4개

02 다음 중 어법상 옳은 것끼리 묶은 것은?

> ⓐ A new bridge is being built.
> ⓑ Something must be done to stop global warming.
> ⓒ Was the house been designed by Colin?
> ⓓ The steam engine has invented by James Watt.
> ⓔ She is resembled by her sister.

① ⓐ, ⓑ   ② ⓐ, ⓒ   ③ ⓑ, ⓔ
④ ⓐ, ⓑ, ⓓ   ⑤ ⓒ, ⓓ, ⓔ

03 다음 능동태 문장을 수동태로 바꾼 것 중 <u>잘못된</u> 것을 <u>모두</u> 고르면?

① The judge blew the whistle.
  → The whistle was blown by the judge.
② Dad is making an egg sandwich.
  → An egg sandwich is been made by Dad.
③ Ms. White will translate the book.
  → The book will be translated by Ms. White.
④ Can you deliver this package this afternoon?
  → Can this package delivered this afternoon by you?
⑤ The recent heavy storms have damaged crops.
  → Crops have been damaged by the recent heavy storms.

04 다음 안내판을 보고, 주어진 〈조건〉에 맞게 문장을 완성하시오.

[조건] should, touch를 이용할 것

→ The pictures ＿＿＿＿＿＿＿＿＿＿ in the museum.

05 다음 문장에서 어법상 어색한 부분을 <u>모두</u> 찾아 바르게 고쳐 쓰시오. (단, 과거 시제를 쓸 것)

> The little girl was seemed nervous when she left alone in the car.

06 다음은 Andy와 Jean이 현재 하고 있는 일과 앞으로 할 일을 나타낸 표이다. 표의 내용과 일치하도록 문장을 완성하시오.

Name	하고 있는 일	할 일
Andy	clean the pool	feed the dog
Jean	move the furniture	return the books

(1) The pool ＿＿＿＿＿＿＿＿＿＿
＿＿＿＿＿＿＿＿＿＿＿＿.

(2) The dog ＿＿＿＿＿＿＿＿＿＿
＿＿＿＿＿＿＿＿＿＿＿＿.

(3) The furniture ＿＿＿＿＿＿＿＿＿＿

(4) The books ＿＿＿＿＿＿＿＿＿＿

최종 선택 QUIZ

01

a　Horror movies are loved by teenagers.

b　Horror movies are loving by teenagers.

02

a　The most popular actress will be chosen by audiences.

b　The most popular actress will being chosen by audiences.

03

a　A birthday cake is been made by Mom.

b　A birthday cake is being made by Mom.

04

a　The orphans have helped been by volunteers.

b　The orphans have been helped by volunteers.

05

a　The trees were not cut down by people.

b　The trees were cut down not by people.

06

a　Your happiness can't be measured by how much money you have.

b　Your happiness can be not measured by how much money you have.

07

a　I learned what to do when an earthquake is occurred at school.

b　I learned what to do when an earthquake occurs at school.

08

a　I think plastic bags will disappear completely.

b　I think plastic bags will be disappeared completely.

유형별 기출 적용 빈도

- **유형 01** 4형식 문장의 수동태 — 30%
- **유형 02** 5형식 문장의 수동태 — 20%
- **유형 03** 주의해야 할 수동태 — 20%
- **유형 04** 통합형 — 30%

>> 출제 포인트
4형식 문장의 수동태에서 전치사의 종류, 5형식 수동태에서는 사역동사와 지각동사의 목적격보어 형태 등에 관한 문제가 자주 출제된다.

>> 정답률 100% Tip
1 5형식 문장의 수동태에서 목적격보어는 수동태의 주어가 될 수 없음
2 사역동사 중에는 make만 수동태로 씀

Grammar Point

Point 1 4형식 문장의 수동태

간접목적어와 직접목적어를 주어로 하여 두 종류의 수동태를 만들 수 있다. 직접목적어가 주어일 때는 간접목적어 앞에 전치사 to, for, of를 쓴다.

They gave the actor an award.
→ The actor was given an award by them. 〈간접목적어가 주어일 때〉
→ An award was given to the actor by them. 〈직접목적어가 주어일 때〉

• 직접목적어만 주어로 쓰는 동사: buy, make, cook, sell, read, write, choose 등

Point 2 5형식 문장의 수동태

목적어를 주어로 쓰고, 동사를 「be동사+과거분사」로 바꾼다. 목적격보어(명사, 형용사, to부정사, 분사)는 동사 뒤에 그대로 쓴다.

I named my dog Max. → My dog was named Max by me.
사역동사와 지각동사가 쓰일 때는 목적격보어인 동사원형을 to부정사로 바꾼다.
We heard her laugh. → She was heard to laugh by us.
cf. 지각동사의 목적격보어가 현재분사일 때는 그대로 동사 뒤에 쓴다.

Point 3 주의해야 할 수동태

1. 동사구의 수동태: 「동사+전치사/부사」의 동사구는 수동태로 바꿀 때 한 덩어리로 취급하여 「be동사+과거분사+전치사/부사」의 형태로 쓴다.
2. by 이외의 전치사를 쓰는 수동태

be surprised at	~에 놀라다	be covered with	~로 덮여 있다
be interested in	~에 관심이 있다	be pleased with	~에 기뻐하다
be tired of	~에 싫증나다	be accustomed to	~에 익숙하다

3. that절을 목적어로 하는 문장의 수동태
(1) 「It(가주어)+be동사+과거분사+that절」로 쓴다.
(2) that절의 주어를 문장의 주어로 쓰고, that절의 동사는 to부정사로 바꾼다.

✅ 바로 체크

01 A boy handed me letters.
→ I _____ letters by a boy.
→ Letters _____ me by a boy.

02 Dad made us spaghetti.
→ Spaghetti was made (to / for / of) us by Dad.

03 He saw her drive away.
→ She was seen _____ by him.

04 She heard the birds singing.
→ The birds _____ heard _____ by her.

05 He turned on the light.
→ The light _____ by him.

06 I'm interested _____ acting.

07 People say that he is a liar.
→ _____ is said that he is a liar.
→ _____ is said _____ a liar.

대표유형 01 4형식 문장의 수동태   출제율 30%

01 다음 문장을 수동태로 바꿀 때 빈칸에 알맞은 말을 쓰시오.

> We gave the winners flowers.

→ The winners _____ _____ _____ by us.

→ Flowers _____ _____ _____ the winners by us.

02 다음 문장을 수동태로 바르게 바꾼 것을 <u>모두</u> 고르면?

> My father taught me baseball.

① I was taught baseball by my father.
② Baseball was taught for me by my father.
③ Baseball was taught my father by me.
④ I was taught to baseball by my father.
⑤ Baseball was taught to me by my father.

[03-04] 다음 문장을 수동태로 바꿀 때 빈칸에 알맞은 것을 고르시오.

03

> The old woman asked the boy a favor.
> → A favor was asked _____ the boy by the old woman.

① to   ② of   ③ by
④ for   ⑤ with

04

> Sharon will not send Alex the files.
> → The files won't _____ Alex by Sharon.

① send to   ② send for   ③ be sent to
④ be sent for   ⑤ be sent of

05 다음 밑줄 친 부분 중 어법상 어색한 것은?

① The house <u>was sold for</u> Mr. Brown.
② Some photos <u>were shown to</u> them.
③ A doll <u>was made for</u> the baby by Jack.
④ A new sweater <u>was bought for</u> my sister.
⑤ The truth <u>was told to</u> everyone by Angelina.

06 다음 빈칸에 알맞은 것을 <u>모두</u> 고르면?

> A birthday cake was _____ for me by my friends.

① sold   ② sent   ③ baked
④ given   ⑤ bought

07 다음 문장을 주어진 말로 시작하는 문장으로 바꿔 쓰시오.

> My mother made me some cookies.
> → Some cookies _____.

08 다음 문장을 올바른 수동태 문장으로 고쳐 쓰시오.

> I was bought an interesting book by Mom.

→ _____

≫ 실전 Tip 4형식 문장에서 직접목적어만 수동태 문장의 주어로 쓰는 동사는 buy, make, cook, sell, read, write, choose 등이다.

09 다음 문장을 주어진 말로 시작하는 <u>두 개의</u> 수동태 문장으로 바꿀 때 빈칸에 알맞은 말을 쓰시오.

> Ms. Green didn't teach us English.

→ We _____ by Ms. Green.

→ English _____ _____ _____ by Ms. Green.

대표유형 02 5형식 문장의 수동태 · · · · · · 출제율 20%

10 다음 능동태 문장을 수동태로 바꾼 것 중 <u>잘못된</u> 것을 <u>모두</u> 고르면?

① They call him a champion.
   → He is called a champion by them.
② Everyone considered her a genius.
   → A genius was considered her by everyone.
③ Judy saw him stealing the car.
   → He was seen stealing the car by Judy.
④ We can hear her sing this evening.
   → She can be heard sing this evening by us.
⑤ My dad made me do my homework.
   → I was made to do my homework by my dad.

11 다음 밑줄 speak를 알맞은 형태로 바꿔 쓰시오.

> The students were made <u>speak</u> only in English by the English teacher.

12 다음 밑줄 친 enter의 형태로 알맞은 것을 <u>모두</u> 고르면?

> The famous actor was seen <u>enter</u> the building yesterday.

① enter   ② entered   ③ entering
④ to enter   ⑤ to be entered

13 다음 우리말과 같도록 괄호 안의 어구를 바르게 배열하여 문장을 완성하시오.

> 한 남자가 벽을 뛰어넘고 있는 것이 한 경찰관에 의해 목격되었다.
> (a wall, was, a man, seen, jumping, a police officer, over, by)

→ _____

[14-15] 다음 문장을 수동태로 바꿀 때 빈칸에 알맞은 말을 쓰시오.

14
> They painted the wall green.
> → The wall _____ _____ _____ by them.

15
> The teacher made the children stand in line.
> → The children _____ _____ _____ _____ in line by the teacher.

16 다음 중 어법상 <u>어색한</u> 문장을 <u>모두</u> 고르면?

① The cat was named to Kitty by its owner.
② The dancers were seen to perform on the street.
③ The meeting room was found empty by the team member.
④ The bellboy was let to carry his luggage by the guest.
⑤ They were made to leave the house because they didn't pay the rent.

대표유형 03 주의해야 할 수동태 · · · · · · 출제율 20%

17 다음 빈칸에 알맞은 것은?

> The child must _____ by you.

① take care of   ② taken care of
③ be taken care   ④ is taken care of
⑤ be taken care of

>> 실전 Tip 「동사+전치사/부사」의 동사구가 있는 문장은 동사구를 하나의 단어처럼 취급하여 수동태로 만든다.

18 다음 중 어법상 <u>어색한</u> 문장은?

① He was made fun by his classmates.

② The girl was run over by the truck.

③ The cat will be looked after by me.

④ The meeting was called off by Mr. Dean.

⑤ Your request will be turned down by them.

19 다음 문장을 수동태로 바꿔 쓰시오.

> Two men broke into his house.

→ _____

20 다음 문장의 빈칸에 알맞은 전치사를 〈보기〉에서 골라 쓰시오.

> 보기   in   of   on   for   from   with

(1) I'm interested _____ science.

(2) These boxes are made _____ wood.

(3) The city is known _____ its hot spring.

(4) His room was filled _____ many books.

21 다음 빈칸에 들어갈 말이 나머지 넷과 <u>다른</u> 것은?

① The window was opened _____ Kevin.

② The telephone was invented _____ Bell.

③ *Hamlet* was written _____ Shakespeare.

④ The mountain was covered _____ snow.

⑤ The picture was painted _____ my father.

22 다음 밑줄 친 부분 중 옳은 것을 <u>모두</u> 고르면?

① Emma seems to be tired <u>of</u> waiting.

② The bag is made <u>from</u> tough leather.

③ The customers were satisfied <u>with</u> the service.

④ Matt was surprised <u>for</u> her getting married.

⑤ Nuts are commonly known <u>by</u> healthy food.

23 다음 문장을 수동태로 바꿔 쓸 때, 빈칸에 알맞은 말로 바르게 짝지어진 것은?

> People believe that the man is innocent.
> → _____ believed that the man is innocent.
> → The man is believed _____ innocent.

① It is – to be

② It is – to have been

③ It was – to have been

④ That is – to be

⑤ That is – to have been

24 다음 빈칸에 들어갈 수 <u>없는</u> 것은?

> It is _____ that Venice is one of the most beautiful cities.

① said   ② knew   ③ believed

④ thought   ⑤ considered

25 다음 문장을 수동태로 바꿀 때, 주어진 단어로 시작하여 문장을 완성하시오.

> They say that he is a millionaire.

→ He _____ _____ _____ _____ a millionaire by them.

대표유형 01   4형식 문장의 수동태   출제율 30%

01 다음 문장을 수동태로 바르게 바꾼 것을 <u>모두</u> 고르면?

> The waiter brought him a cup of coffee.

① He was brought a cup of coffee by the waiter.
② He was brought for a cup of coffee by the waiter.
③ He was brought to a cup of coffee by the waiter.
④ A cup of coffee was brought of him by the waiter.
⑤ A cup of coffee was brought to him by the waiter.

02 다음 중 의미가 나머지 넷과 <u>다른</u> 것은?

① Katie gave Ann the pink dress.
② Katie was given the pink dress by Ann.
③ Katie gave the pink dress to Ann.
④ Ann was given the pink dress by Katie.
⑤ The pink dress was given to Ann by Katie.

[03-04] 다음 빈칸에 알맞은 말로 바르게 짝지어진 것을 고르시오.

03

> • The antique was sold _____ a millionaire by Mr. Stevens.
> • Dinner is being cooked _____ us by the host.

① to – by   ② to – for   ③ for – to
④ of – by   ⑤ of – for

04

> • A new pair of shoes was bought _____ Julia by her parents.
> • Some questions were asked _____ me by the interviewer.

① to – to   ② to – of   ③ of – for
④ for – of   ⑤ for – for

대표유형 02   5형식 문장의 수동태   출제율 20%

05 다음 문장을 수동태로 바르게 바꾼 것은?

> Mom made me take piano lessons.

① I was made take piano lessons by Mom.
② I was made taking piano lessons by Mom.
③ I was made to take piano lessons by Mom.
④ Piano lessons were made me to take by Mom.
⑤ Piano lessons were made to take me by Mom.

≫ 실전 Tip '목적어가 ~하도록 시키다'라는 뜻을 가진 동사(make, have, let 등)를 사역동사라고 하는데, 이 중 make만 수동태 문장으로 쓸 수 있다.

06 다음 능동태 문장을 수동태로 바꾼 것 중 <u>잘못된</u> 것은?

① They saw the man get on the train.
   → The man was seen get on the train by them.
② She made me carry the luggage.
   → I was made to carry the luggage by her.
③ We heard the dog barking all night.
   → The dog was heard barking all night by us.
④ The fireplace kept them warm.
   → They were kept warm by the fireplace.
⑤ The doctor advised me to give up sweets.
   → I was advised to give up sweets by the doctor.

07 다음 문장을 수동태로 바꿔 쓸 때, not이 들어갈 위치로 알맞은 곳은?

> Mr. Choi told me not to waste my life.
> → I (①) was (②) told (③) to (④) waste (⑤) my life by Mr. Choi.

대표유형 01, 02 4형식·5형식 문장의 수동태 출제율 30%

08 다음 능동태 문장을 각각 간접목적어와 직접목적어를 주어로 하여 수동태로 바꿔 쓰시오.

> Chris has offered them the job.

→ _____

(간접목적어를 주어로 한 문장)

→ _____

(직접목적어를 주어로 한 문장)

신유형

[09-10] 다음 수동태로 바꿔 쓴 문장에서 어법상 어색한 부분을 바르게 고쳐 문장을 다시 쓰시오.

09
> We considered him a hero.
> → A hero was considered him by us.

→ _____

10
> The teacher made us do extra homework.
> → We were made done extra homework by the teacher.

→ _____

[11-12] 다음 문장을 수동태로 바꿔 쓰시오.

11
> A famous chef will make you both brunch and dinner.

→ _____

12
> The man asked me to donate money.

→ _____

대표유형 03 주의해야 할 수동태 출제율 20%

13 다음 문장의 빈칸에 공통으로 알맞은 말을 쓰시오.

> • The hill was covered _____ fallen leaves.
> • The coach wasn't satisfied _____ our team's performance.

14 다음 우리말과 같도록 괄호 안의 단어를 바르게 배열하여 문장을 완성하시오. (단, 한 개의 단어를 추가하고 필요한 경우 형태를 바꿔 쓸 것)

> 그의 공연은 대부분의 팬들에 의해 비웃음을 당했다.
> (laugh, by, his, most, performance, was, fans)

→ _____

15 다음 문장을 주어진 말을 주어로 하는 <u>두 개</u>의 수동태 문장으로 바꿔 쓰시오. (단, 「by+행위자」는 생략할 것)

> People believed that the Earth was flat.

→ It _____.

→ The Earth _____.

대표유형 01, 02 | 4형식·5형식 문장의 수동태 | 출제율 30%

01 다음 빈칸에 알맞은 것은?

A love letter _____ him by someone.

① has written for
② will be wrote to
③ was written for
④ has been written to
⑤ was been written to

02 다음 빈칸에 들어갈 말이 나머지 넷과 <u>다른</u> 것은?

① Aesop's Fables were told _____ the children.
② Math will be taught _____ us by Ms. Jones.
③ Some chances will be given _____ the challengers.
④ A special discount was offered _____ me by the manager.
⑤ The earrings were bought _____ her as a birthday present.

03 다음 문장을 수동태로 바르게 바꾼 것은?

I saw him go out for a walk.

① He was seen go out for a walk by me.
② He was seen to go out for a walk by me.
③ Going out was seen him for a walk by me.
④ Going out was seen to him for a walk by me.
⑤ Going out for a walk was seen to him by me.

04 다음 문장 중 어법상 <u>어색한</u> 것을 <u>모두</u> 고르면?

① They were told sit down and wait.
② He is expected to win the game by us.
③ The building was seen burning down.
④ She was made to a doctor by her parents.
⑤ The child has been found safe by the police.

대표유형 04 | 통합형 | 출제율 30%

05 다음 능동태 문장을 수동태로 바꾼 것 중 옳은 것은?

① I can buy Bob a meal.
→ A meal can be bought of Bob by me.
② We chose him chairman.
→ He was chosen to chairman by us.
③ Thomas sent me a game CD.
→ A game CD was sent to me by Thomas.
④ My brother made me a kite.
→ I was made a kite by my brother.
⑤ They expected the meeting would attract many people.
→ The meeting was expected attract many people.

06 다음 문장 중 어법상 옳은 것끼리 묶은 것은?

ⓐ The highway was crowded with cars.
ⓑ Eva was heard crying out for help.
ⓒ Potatoes were brought to Europe by Spanish explorers.
ⓓ The lamb must be taken care by the shepherd.
ⓔ Volunteers are made participating in the learning process.

① ⓐ, ⓑ, ⓒ
② ⓐ, ⓑ, ⓓ
③ ⓐ, ⓒ, ⓔ
④ ⓑ, ⓒ, ⓓ
⑤ ⓒ, ⓓ, ⓔ

≫ 실전 Tip 지각동사의 목적격보어가 현재분사일 때는 수동태 문장에서 그대로 동사 뒤에 쓴다.

07 다음 문장을 수동태로 바르게 바꾼 것을 <u>모두</u> 고르면?

People think that foxes are clever.

① Foxes are thought to clever.
② Foxes are thought to be clever.
③ It is thought for foxes to be clever.
④ It is thought to be foxes are clever.
⑤ It is thought that foxes are clever.

신유형

08 다음 우리말과 같도록 괄호 안의 어구를 이용하여 능동태 문장으로 만든 후, 이를 다시 수동태 문장으로 바꿔 쓰시오.

> 그의 부모님은 그가 혼자 여행하는 것을 허락하셨다.
> (allow, travel alone)

→ _____ (능동태)

→ _____ (수동태)

[09-10] 다음 문장을 수동태로 바꿔 쓰시오.

09
> She encourages James to pass the test.

→ _____

10
> The flood swept away houses and cars.

→ _____

11 다음 빈칸에 알맞은 말을 괄호 안의 단어를 이용하여 각각 쓰시오.

(1) Cheese is _____ milk. (make)

(2) Are you _____ classical music? (interest)

(3) Her secret will be _____ everybody. (know)

(4) The pianist was _____ his performance. (satisfy)

12 다음 빈칸에 알맞은 말을 각각 쓰시오. (단, know를 이용할 것)

> • Jiyeon is also _____ an actress.
> • The island has _____ its beautiful beaches.

13 다음 문장을 두 개의 수동태 문장으로 바꿔 쓰시오. (단, 「by+행위자」는 생략할 것)

> They report that the sailors are missing.

→ _____

→ _____

14 다음 문장에서 어법상 어색한 부분을 바르게 고쳐 문장을 다시 쓰시오.

> The man made stop the car by the police.

→ _____

15 다음 문장을 두 가지 형태의 수동태로 바꿔 쓸 때, 빈칸에 알맞은 말을 쓰시오.

> People say that air pollution is caused by cars.

→ _____ by cars.

→ Air pollution _____.

01 다음 중 의미가 나머지 넷과 <u>다른</u> 것은?

① He will tell the police the truth.
② The police will tell him the truth.
③ The police will tell the truth to him.
④ He will be told the truth by the police.
⑤ The truth will be told to him by the police.

02 다음 문장 중 어법상 <u>어색한</u> 것끼리 묶은 것은?

ⓐ Chris was seen driving away.
ⓑ The class president was elected him by us.
ⓒ David was written a letter by Jane.
ⓓ He was bought a blue jacket by his mother.
ⓔ He will be made wash the car by his father.

① ⓐ   ② ⓐ, ⓒ   ③ ⓑ, ⓒ, ⓓ
④ ⓑ, ⓓ, ⓔ   ⑤ ⓑ, ⓒ, ⓓ, ⓔ

03 다음 빈칸에 알맞은 말이 바르게 짝지어진 것은?

• This coat was made _____ wool.
• The field trip was put _____ because of heavy rain.
• The novel was said _____ interesting to read by teenagers.

① of – on – be
② of – off – to be
③ from – on – be
④ from – off – be
⑤ from – off – to be

04 다음 문장을 주어진 〈조건〉을 참고하여 바꿔 쓰시오.

The man gives the woman the book.

[조건] 두 가지 형태의 수동태로 쓸 것

→ _____
_____

→ _____
_____

05 다음 괄호 안의 단어를 이용하여 빈칸에 알맞은 말을 각각 쓰시오. (단, 과거 시제를 이용할 것)

• Many photos _____ me by Tom. (send)
• The paper plane _____ me by her. (make)
• This question _____ all respondents. (ask)

06 다음 우리말과 같도록 괄호 안의 어구를 이용하여 능동태 문장으로 만든 후, 이를 다시 수동태 문장으로 바꿔 쓰시오.

그는 웨이터에게 물 한 잔을 가져오게 했다.
(make, the waiter, a cup of)

→ _____
_____ (능동태)

→ _____
_____ (수동태)

최종 선택 QUIZ

01
a The invitation was written to Jake by her.

b The invitation was written of Jake by her.

02
a Some clothes were bought to the orphans by the charity.

b Some clothes were bought for the orphans by the charity.

03
a The nest was kept warm by the hen.

b The nest was kept to warm by the hen.

04
a The monkey was seen climbing over the fence.

b The monkey was seen climb over the fence.

05
a He was made to stop smoking by the doctor.

b He was made stopping smoking by the doctor.

06
a She can't stand being laughed by anyone.

b She can't stand being laughed at by anyone.

07
a The old box was filled of precious treasures.

b The old box was filled with precious treasures.

08
a Vitamins are believed that good for your health.

b Vitamins are believed to be good for your health.

유형별 기출 적용 빈도

유형 O1 주격, 소유격, 목적격 관계대명사   **45%**

유형 O2 관계대명사의 생략   **20%**

유형 O3 관계대명사 what   **35%**

>> 출제 포인트

알맞은 관계대명사를 선택하는 문제, 관계대명사를 사용하여 두 문장을 연결하는 문제가 많이 출제된다. 심화 문제로 관계대명사 what의 쓰임을 묻는 문제도 출제된다.

>> 정답률 100% Tip

1 관계대명사 that은 주격과 목적격으로만 쓰임
2 전치사가 목적격 관계대명사 앞에 위치할 때는 목적격 관계대명사를 생략할 수 없음

Grammar Point

Point ① 주격, 소유격, 목적격 관계대명사

선행사	주격	소유격	목적격
사람	who	whose	who(m)
사물, 동물	which	whose, of which	which
사람, 사물, 동물	that	–	that

선행사가 「사람＋사물」 또는 「사람＋동물」인 경우, 최상급, 서수, some, any, the only, the same, all, -thing, -body, -one 등이 선행사에 포함된 경우에는 일반적으로 관계대명사 that을 쓴다.

Jack bought a shirt which was made in China. 〈주격〉
Sally is a girl whose mother is a writer. 〈소유격〉
The girl who(m) I met at the store was my classmate. 〈목적격〉
This is all the money that I have.

Point ② 관계대명사의 생략

목적격 관계대명사는 생략할 수 있고, 「주격 관계대명사＋be동사＋분사(형용사)」 구문에서 「주격 관계대명사＋be동사」는 생략할 수 있다.

The bottle (which) my mother is holding is very heavy.
Look at the people (who are) singing merrily.

Point ③ 관계대명사 what

'~하는 것'이라는 의미로 선행사를 포함하며 문장에서 주어, 목적어, 보어로 쓰이고 the thing(s) which[that]와 바꿔 쓸 수 있다.

What she made was amazing. 〈주어〉
I can't believe what he said. 〈목적어〉
This is just what I have to do now. 〈보어〉

✅ 바로 체크

01 The reporter interviewed the man (who / which) won the gold medal.

02 I have a book (which / whose) was written in French.

03 This is the house (which / whose) roof is blue.

04 The movie (whose / which) we saw yesterday was interesting.

05 He is a man (whom / whose) everybody respects very much.

06 Is there anything (what / that) I should buy?

07 Look at the girl and her dog (that / what) are swimming.

08 (That / What) he said was true.

09 He bought (what / that) his wife wanted.

대표유형 01 주격, 소유격, 목적격 관계대명사   출제율 45%

01 다음 빈칸에 알맞은 것은?

> Do you know the woman _____ is talking to Tom?

① who   ② which   ③ whose
④ whom   ⑤ what

02 다음 괄호 안에서 알맞은 것을 고르시오.

> Mother Teresa was the nun (who / which / whose) received the Nobel Peace Prize.

03 다음 빈칸에 알맞은 말을 쓰시오.

> You can make decisions _____ are right for you.

04 다음 빈칸에 알맞은 말끼리 바르게 짝지어진 것은?

> • What's the name of the film _____ you are going to see?
> • An orphan is a child _____ parents are dead.

① who – who   ② which – whose
③ which – whom   ④ whose – who
⑤ what – whose

05 다음 우리말과 같도록 빈칸에 알맞은 말을 한 단어로 쓰시오.

> 표지가 빨간 그 책은 나의 것이다.
> → The book _____ cover is red is mine.

06 다음 빈칸에 알맞은 말끼리 바르게 짝지어진 것은?

> • The volunteers can feel the pride _____ comes from helping other people.
> • He is the only man _____ I love.

① who -- who   ② which – whose
③ which – what   ④ that – which
⑤ that – that

07 다음 문장에서 어법상 어색한 부분을 찾아 바르게 고쳐 쓰시오.

> We also have our own feelings whose his music calls up in us.

08 다음 빈칸에 알맞은 것은?

> I have a monkey _____ tail is four inches long.

① who   ② which   ③ whose
④ whom   ⑤ that

09 다음 두 문장을 한 문장으로 연결할 때 빈칸에 알맞은 말을 쓰시오.

> The man is a famous singer. I met him yesterday.
> → The man _____ I met yesterday is a famous singer.

10 다음 빈칸에 알맞은 것은?

> This is my umbrella _____ the colors are pink and yellow.

① who ② which ③ what
④ whom ⑤ of which

11 다음 우리말을 영어로 바르게 옮긴 것을 <u>두 개</u> 고르면?

> 그 가게는 내가 원하는 배낭을 가지고 있지 않다.

① The store doesn't have the backpack who I want.
② The store doesn't have the backpack that I want.
③ The store doesn't have the backpack whom I want.
④ The store doesn't have the backpack which I want.
⑤ The store doesn't have the backpack whose I want.

12 다음 대화의 빈칸에 알맞은 것은?

> **A** Is there anything _____ I can do for you?
> **B** Can you help me do my homework?

① what ② that ③ who
④ whom ⑤ of which

대표유형 02 관계대명사의 생략   출제율 20%

13 다음 문장의 빈칸에 생략된 것으로 알맞은 것은?

> I met my elder sister _____ sitting in the park.

① who is ② which is ③ who was
④ who were ⑤ which was

[14-15] 다음 밑줄 친 부분 중 생략할 수 <u>없는</u> 것을 고르시오.

14 ① The picture <u>which</u> you're looking at is my favorite.
② The woman to <u>whom</u> Nick is talking is Ms. Wilson.
③ This is the cartoon <u>which</u> kids are crazy about.
④ He is my neighbor <u>whom</u> I talked about.
⑤ It is the bag <u>which</u> I lost yesterday.

15 ① I know the girl <u>that</u> likes you.
② I know the man <u>that</u> you love.
③ I read all the books <u>that</u> I wanted to read.
④ This is the bicycle <u>that</u> I bought yesterday.
⑤ This is the very book <u>that</u> I wanted to have.

16 다음 문장의 빈칸에 생략된 것으로 알맞은 것은?

> The ideas _____ presented in the book are very unique.

① who is ② who are ③ which is
④ which are ⑤ that is

17 다음 문장에서 관계대명사 that이 생략된 곳으로 알맞은 것은?

> Beethoven and other composers (①) did not (②) just (③) imitate (④) the sounds (⑤) they heard.

18 다음 중 밑줄 친 부분의 쓰임이 어법상 어색한 것은?

① I know the boy called the "Bookworm."
② The house has a window painting blue.
③ There lived a rich merchant named Mr. Lee.
④ I ran to my elder sister jogging in the park.
⑤ I like the song "Yesterday" composed by the Beatles.

대표유형 03 관계대명사 what　　　출제율 35%

19 다음 두 문장이 같은 의미일 때 빈칸에 알맞은 것은?

> This is not the thing that I wanted to have.
> = This is not _____ I wanted to have.

① that
② what
③ who
④ which
⑤ of which

20 다음 중 밑줄 친 부분의 쓰임이 나머지 넷과 다른 것은?

① What I want is to go home.
② What he asked for was this book.
③ He wants to know what your name is.
④ What she wants to be is a designer.
⑤ You can buy what you want.

21 다음 빈칸에 알맞은 것은?

> The boy did _____ he was told.

① who
② what
③ which
④ that
⑤ whose

22 다음 괄호 안의 단어를 바르게 배열하여 대화를 완성하시오.

> **A** What movie do you want to see?
> **B** This movie is _____.
>   (see, I, what, to, want)

23 다음 밑줄 친 부분을 한 단어로 바꿔 쓰시오.

> This shows the things that many people already know.

24 다음 빈칸에 공통으로 알맞은 것은? (단, 대·소문자 무시)

> • Computer games are _____ I like most.
> • _____ makes me happy is a baby's smile.
> • Please show me _____ you have in your pocket.

① that [That]
② who [Who]
③ whom [Whom]
④ which [Which]
⑤ what [What]

25 다음 중 〈보기〉의 밑줄 친 부분과 쓰임이 같은 것은?

> 보기　You must do what I told you to do.

① What did you do yesterday?
② I know what your address is.
③ What is the population of this city?
④ This is what my daughter wrote.
⑤ What shoes are you going to wear?

대표유형 01 주격, 소유격, 목적격 관계대명사 출제율 45%

01 다음 빈칸에 들어갈 말이 나머지 넷과 <u>다른</u> 것은? (단, that은 제외할 것)

① Do you know the boy _____ is crying in the street?
② He was the teacher _____ taught us math last year.
③ The room _____ was cleaned by Mike was very large.
④ Bob _____ was angry at me is okay now.
⑤ We like Kevin _____ helped us with the project.

02 다음 우리말을 영어로 바르게 옮긴 것은?

> 눈이 갈색인 그 남자는 Julie의 삼촌이다.

① The man who eyes are brown is Julie's uncle.
② The man which eyes are brown is Julie's uncle.
③ The man that eyes are brown is Julie's uncle.
④ The man whose eyes are brown is Julie's uncle.
⑤ The man of which eyes are brown is Julie's uncle.

≫ 실전 Tip of which는 선행사가 사물, 동물인 경우에 쓸 수 있는 소유격 관계대명사이다.

[03-04] 다음 빈칸에 알맞은 것을 <u>모두</u> 고르시오.

03
> Is this the dog _____ has three puppies?

① who   ② that   ③ which
④ whose   ⑤ whom

04
> The person _____ you should interview is Evan.

① who   ② that   ③ whose
④ which   ⑤ whom

05 다음 빈칸에 공통으로 알맞은 것은?

> • My father bought me a smartphone _____ is very expensive.
> • She has the box _____ I gave to her.

① who   ② whose   ③ which
④ what   ⑤ of which

대표유형 02 관계대명사의 생략 출제율 20%

06 다음 문장의 빈칸에 생략된 말로 알맞은 것은?

> This is the picture _____ painted by my mother.

① who is   ② what is   ③ which was
④ that are   ⑤ who was

07 다음 문장에서 관계대명사가 생략된 곳으로 알맞은 것은?

> A lot of books (①) I read (②) in the classroom (③) for two hours (④) provide (⑤) some information about AI.

08 다음 문장에서 생략할 수 있는 부분을 찾아 쓰시오.

> I know the girl who is playing the piano on the stage.

신유형

[09-10] 다음 문장에서 생략된 말을 〈보기〉에서 골라 알맞은 위치에 넣어 문장을 다시 쓰시오.

보기   which   which was

09 The hat my father wears is very old.

→ _____

10 My school built 30 years ago is still good.

→ _____

대표유형 03 관계대명사 what   출제율 35%

11 다음 두 문장의 의미가 같도록 관계대명사를 이용하여 빈칸에 알맞은 말을 쓰시오.

> These are the things that we need now.
> = These are _____.

12 다음 우리말과 같도록 빈칸에 알맞은 말을 쓰시오.

> 내가 원하는 것은 시험에 합격하는 것이다.
> → _____ is to pass the exam.

13 다음 문장에서 어법상 어색한 부분을 찾아 바르게 고쳐 쓰시오.

> I don't like that my brother bought at the store.

14 다음 우리말과 같도록 괄호 안의 단어를 바르게 배열하여 문장을 완성하시오. (단, 관계대명사를 추가할 것)

> 상황은 우리가 예상했던 것과 다르다.
> (expected, different, the situation, we, from, is)
> → _____

15 다음 우리말과 같도록 괄호 안의 단어를 이용하여 문장을 완성하시오.

> 아무도 내가 만들고 있는 것을 알지 못한다.
> → Nobody knows _____.
>   (make)

대표유형 01, 03 관계대명사 – 주격, 소유격, 목적격, what   출제율 45%

01 다음 빈칸에 공통으로 알맞은 것을 <u>모두</u> 고르면?

> • The song "Vincent" _____ was composed by Don McLean came from a famous painting.
> • Look at the bus _____ is covered with dust.

① who   ② whose   ③ which
④ that   ⑤ of which

02 다음 중 〈보기〉의 밑줄 친 부분과 쓰임이 같은 것은?

> 보기   <u>What</u> he needs is a piece of advice.

① Do you know <u>what</u> it is?
② I know <u>what</u> her phone number is.
③ That's not <u>what</u> I meant to say.
④ <u>What</u> is the capital of Canada?
⑤ <u>What</u> kind of music do you like?

03 다음 두 문장을 관계대명사를 이용하여 한 문장으로 바꾼 것 중 알맞은 것을 <u>모두</u> 고르면?

> Let's buy a small plant. + We can put it on the table.

① Let's buy a small plant which we can put on the table.
② Let's buy a small plant that we can put it on the table.
③ Let's buy a small plant of which we can put on the table.
④ Let's buy a small plant what we can put on the table.
⑤ Let's buy a small plant that we can put on the table.

04 다음 밑줄 친 ⓐ, ⓑ의 알맞은 형태로 바르게 짝지어진 것은?

> • My father bought a new program which ⓐ <u>work</u> on his computer.
> • She was the daughter of Italian-American parents who ⓑ <u>are</u> very poor.

① work – were   ② worked – were
③ worked – was   ④ worked – are
⑤ was worked – were

05 다음 우리말과 같도록 할 때 빈칸에 알맞은 것을 <u>모두</u> 고르면?

> 나는 비행기에서 내 옆에 앉아 있던 남자에게 이야기를 많이 하지 않았다.
> → I didn't talk much to the man _____ next to me on the plane.

① sitting   ② who was sitting
③ who is sitting   ④ that was sitting
⑤ that were sitting

06 다음 밑줄 친 ①~⑤ 중 어법상 어색한 것은?

> I want ① <u>to buy</u> ② <u>that coat</u> ③ <u>which</u> ④ <u>the price</u> ⑤ <u>is over</u> 500 dollars.

07 다음 문장을 두 문장으로 바르게 바꿔 쓴 것은?

> I saw a house whose windows were all broken.

① I saw a house. It was all broken.
② I saw a house's windows. They were all broken.
③ I saw a house. Its windows were all broken.
④ I saw a house. My windows were all broken.
⑤ I saw a house. Its was all broken.

08 다음 문장에서 어법상 어색한 부분을 찾아 바르게 고쳐 쓰시오.

> He is my neighbor whose work for a computer company.

09 다음 빈칸에 공통으로 알맞은 말을 쓰시오. (단, 대·소문자 무시)

> • _____ followed was shocking.
> • I can't believe _____ I heard yesterday.
> • This cake is _____ Mom wanted.

10 다음 두 문장을 관계대명사를 이용하여 한 문장으로 연결하시오.

> • She had left her bag behind on a bus.
> • She remembered the bag.
>
> → _____
> _____

대표유형 02 관계대명사의 생략   출제율 20%

11 다음 〈보기〉와 같이 생략 가능한 부분을 생략하여 문장을 다시 쓰시오.

> 보기   The team which was called "White Horse" won the gold medal.
> → The team called "White Horse" won the gold medal.
>
> I saw an old man who was lying on the bench.
> → _____

[12-13] 다음 문장에서 생략된 말을 알맞은 위치에 넣어 문장을 다시 쓰시오.

12

> The boy you praised last night was my little brother.
>
> → _____
> _____

13

> This is the house he was born in.
>
> → _____
> _____

>> 실전 Tip 전치사가 목적격 관계대명사 앞에 올 때는 목적격 관계대명사를 생략할 수 없다.

신유형

14 다음 두 문장을 한 문장으로 연결할 때 가능한 답을 세 개 쓰시오.

> Look at the boys. They are fighting in the street.
>
> → _____
> → _____
> → _____

15 다음 문장에서 어법상 어색한 부분을 찾아 바르게 고쳐 관계대명사를 이용한 문장으로 다시 쓰시오.

> My sister is reading a novel writing by Hemingway.
>
> → _____
> _____

01 다음 그림을 보고, 괄호 안의 말과 관계대명사를 이용하여 대화를 완성하시오.

A What is this?
B It is an opener. An opener _____
_____. (a tool, a bottle)

02 다음 그림을 보고, 괄호 안의 어구와 관계대명사(that은 제외할 것)를 이용하여 대화의 빈칸을 각각 완성하시오.

(1)

(play basketball)

(2)

(win the gold medal)

A Can you see the boys out there?
B You mean the boys (1) _____
_____?
A Yes! They are very famous.
B What's so special about them?
A They are players on the basketball team
(2) _____ in the middle school tournament last year.
B Wow! That's amazing!

03 다음 빈칸에 들어갈 말이 나머지 넷과 다른 것은? (단, 대·소문자 무시)

① _____ you need is a good job.
② I will do _____ I can for you.
③ Make sure that you understand _____ you have read.
④ This is _____ I want to say.
⑤ It is true _____ he ran away from home.

04 다음 단어와 관계되는 설명을 연결하고, 〈보기〉에서 알맞은 말을 골라 문장을 완성하시오. (단, 한 번씩만 사용하고 필요한 경우 관계대명사를 추가할 것)

(A) friend · · (a) you know well and like
(B) Internet · · (b) you give to someone on a special day
(C) gift · · (c) connect one computer to another

보기   what   a person   something

(1) A friend is _____
_____.

(2) The Internet is _____
_____.

(3) A gift is _____
_____.

05 다음 우리말과 같도록 관계대명사와 괄호 안의 어구를 이용하여 문장을 완성하시오.

너는 Sera에게 문자 메시지를 보낸 학생을 아니?
(a text message, to)

→ _____
_____

최종 선택 QUIZ

어법상 옳은 문장에 ✔ 표시하세요.

01
a I have a friend who loves to go fishing.

b I have a friend which loves to go fishing.

02
a She invented a pen who can glow in the dark.

b She invented a pen which can glow in the dark.

03
a I know a boy whom brother is a famous actor.

b I know a boy whose brother is a famous actor.

04
a He ate a cookie which his mom made.

b He ate a cookie of which his mom made.

05
a Terry is the only man that I envy.

b Terry is the only man which I envy.

06
a Amy was the person whom I could depend on.

b Amy was the person whose I could depend on.

07
a The girl who is run on the grass is my sister.

b The girl who is running on the grass is my sister.

08
a I can't remember what he promised.

b I can't remember that he promised.

유형별 기출 적용 빈도

유형 01 전치사 + 관계대명사   30%

유형 02 관계대명사의 계속적 용법   35%

유형 03 소유격 관계대명사   20%

유형 04 통합형   15%

>> 출제 포인트

전치사의 목적어로 쓰인 관계대명사에서 전치사의 위치나 쓰임을 묻는 문제, 계속적 용법으로 쓰인 관계대명사의 의미나 활용을 묻는 문제가 많이 출제된다.

>> 정답률 100% Tip

1 「접속사 + 대명사」는 계속적 용법의 관계대명사로 바꿔 쓸 수 있음

2 관계대명사 that과 what은 계속적 용법으로 쓸 수 없음

Grammar Point

Point 1   전치사 + 관계대명사

관계대명사가 전치사의 목적어로 쓰인 경우에 전치사가 관계대명사의 앞 또는 관계사절의 끝에 올 수 있다. 단, 「전치사 + that」으로는 쓰지 않는다. 또한, 전치사 뒤에는 목적격 관계대명사 whom 대신 who를 쓸 수 없다.

Terry is a true friend. I can rely on him.

→ Terry is a true friend on whom I can rely.

→ Terry is a true friend whom[that] I can rely on.

→ Terry is a true friend on that I can rely. (×)

Point 2   관계대명사의 계속적 용법

	제한적 용법	계속적 용법
형태	선행사 + 관계대명사	선행사 + 콤마(,) 관계대명사
역할	선행사를 수식	선행사에 대한 보충 설명을 함
해석	관계대명사절부터 해석함	관계대명사절 앞에서부터 해석함

My cousin recommended this novel, which(= and it) was very interesting.

I called Peter, who(= but he) didn't answer me quickly.

Point 3   소유격 관계대명사

소유격 관계대명사 whose는 선행사가 사람이나 사물, 동물일 때 모두 쓸 수 있고, of which는 선행사가 사물이나 동물일 때 사용한다.

Pick up the umbrella whose color is green.

= Pick up the umbrella the color of which is green.

= Pick up the umbrella of which the color is green.

바로 체크

01   This is a house (in which / in that) my friend lives.

02   I hate some people whom I worked (on / with).

03   That is the town (at which / in which) I was born.

04   He has three sons, (who / that) are doctors.

05   I have two bags, (that / which) are red and black.

06   There are few places to park in downtown, (which / what) is a problem.

07   I'm looking for friends (with who / with whom) I can talk.

08   She is the woman (whose / of which) husband is a lawyer.

09   We have a cat (for which / of which) the name is Lucky.

대표유형 01 전치사 + 관계대명사   출제율 30%

01 다음 빈칸에 알맞은 것은?

> This is the reason _____ we have to build up our strength.

① which   ② what   ③ that
④ for which   ⑤ for that

02 다음 우리말과 같도록 할 때 빈칸에 알맞은 것은?

> 우리가 목표를 이룰 수 있는 여러 가지 방법이 있다.
> → There are many ways _____ we can achieve our goals.

① which   ② who   ③ in which
④ what   ⑤ in that

03 다음 우리말과 같도록 괄호 안의 어구를 순서대로 배열하여 문장을 완성하시오.

> 이것은 그 남자가 장난감 뼈를 던져주었던 개이다.
> (the man, a toy bone, to which, the dog, threw)
> → This is _____
> _____.

04 다음 두 문장을 의미 변화 없이 한 문장으로 연결할 때 빈칸에 알맞은 것은?

> • The farmer carried a lot of money.
> • He wanted to buy a cow with the money.
> → The farmer carried a lot of money _____ he wanted to buy a cow.

① which   ② what   ③ with that
④ for which   ⑤ with which

05 다음 빈칸에 공통으로 알맞은 것은?

> • I am the planet Earth _____ you live.
> • I am the wet sand at the beach _____ you walk.
> • I am the grass _____ you lie down.

① which   ② on which   ③ on that
④ for which   ⑤ with which

06 다음 두 문장을 한 문장으로 연결할 때 빈칸에 알맞은 말을 쓰시오.

> • She often wears the blue blouse.
> • She looks very attractive in the blue blouse.
> → She often wears the blue blouse _____ _____ she looks very attractive.

07 다음 중 밑줄 친 부분의 쓰임이 어법상 어색한 것은?

① This is the city which I grew up in.
② This is the house in which he was born.
③ This is the bus stop at which I met her first.
④ Do you know the residence at which he is staying?
⑤ The museum at which we visited in Italy was beautiful.

08 다음 밑줄 친 부분을 바르게 고쳐 쓰시오.

> She went to the store of which she lost her bag.

대표유형 02 관계대명사의 계속적 용법   출제율 35%

09 다음 빈칸에 알맞은 것은?

> I seldom see the woman, _____ lives next door.

① who   ② what   ③ that
④ where   ⑤ which

10 다음 빈칸에 알맞은 말을 쓰시오.

> Jenny wrote an answer to my letter right away, _____ I appreciated.

11 다음 문장에서 밑줄 친 who의 의미를 바르게 나타낸 것은?

> She met the man, who told her the truth.

① and he   ② but he   ③ if he
④ though he   ⑤ unless he

통합형
12 다음 빈칸에 공통으로 알맞은 말을 쓰시오.

> • You are able to watch the TV programs, _____ will help you learn more about other countries.
> • I don't know _____ foreign language I should choose.

13 다음 두 문장이 같은 의미가 되도록 할 때 빈칸에 알맞은 말끼리 바르게 짝지어진 것은?

> • He lent me a comic book, which interested me very much.
> = He lent me a comic book, _____ it interested me very much.
> • He lent me a comic book, which I haven't read yet.
> = He lent me a comic book, _____ I haven't read it yet.

① but – and   ② and – but
③ but – but   ④ though – but
⑤ though – and

14 다음 문장을 관계대명사를 이용한 문장으로 다시 쓰시오.

> Last year, she bought a skirt, but it doesn't fit any more.
> → Last year, she bought a skirt, _____
> _____ .

15 다음 빈칸에 알맞은 말을 쓰시오.

> Minho is my best friend, _____ helps me with math.

16 다음 두 문장이 같은 뜻이 되도록 할 때 빈칸에 알맞은 것은?

> I have two close friends, and they are very different.
> = I have two close friends, _____ are very different.

① who   ② what   ③ which
④ that   ⑤ whose

17 다음 문장의 밑줄 친 부분을 알맞은 관계대명사로 바꿔 쓰시오.

My family is planning to go to China, because it is famous for the Great Wall.
→ My family is planning to go to China, _____ is famous for the Great Wall.

대표유형 03 소유격 관계대명사 　　　　　　출제율 20%

18 다음 대화의 빈칸에 알맞은 것은?

A Did you see the fashion show on TV last night?
B Yes, it was awesome. I especially liked the model _____ hair was red.

① who　　② that　　③ whose
④ which　　⑤ what

19 다음 괄호 안의 단어를 순서대로 배열하여 문장을 완성하시오.

This is the house (walls, broken, were, whose).

→ This is the house _____.

20 다음 빈칸에 알맞은 것은?

I know the boy _____ father is a popular artist.

① that　　② which　　③ who
④ whose　　⑤ whom

21 다음 문장에서 어법상 어색한 부분을 찾아 바르게 고쳐 쓰시오.

We have to find a person who language is Portuguese.

22 다음 빈칸에 들어갈 수 없는 것은?

This is a university whose _____.

① history is very long
② there are many beautiful trees
③ students are very good at science
④ cafeteria is well-known
⑤ dormitory is very nice

23 다음 두 문장의 의미가 같도록 빈칸에 알맞은 말을 쓰시오.

This is the classical music piece whose composer tried to describe nature musically.
= This is the classical music piece _____ the composer tried to describe nature musically.

24 다음 빈칸에 알맞은 말끼리 바르게 짝지어진 것은?

I have a shirt _____ buttons are red.
= I have a shirt _____ the buttons are red.

① that – whose　　② which – of which
③ what – of which　　④ whose – of which
⑤ whose – of whose

25 다음 빈칸에 공통으로 알맞은 말을 쓰시오.

• I want to meet someone _____ hobby is interesting.
• He lives in the house _____ windows are very big.

대표유형 01 전치사 + 관계대명사 출제율 30%

01 다음 빈칸에 알맞은 것은?

> This is the opportunity _____ the man has desperately searched.

① which ② in which ③ on which
④ for which ⑤ for that

02 다음 빈칸에 공통으로 알맞은 것은?

> • The 15th of May is the day _____ we will have a party.
> • The door _____ Sena is leaning is made of wood.

① which ② in which ③ on which
④ for which ⑤ on that

03 다음 대화의 빈칸에 알맞은 것은?

> **A** Where did you go last weekend?
> **B** We went to the palace _____ the kings had lived during the Joseon Dynasty.

① which ② in which ③ on which
④ for which ⑤ with which

04 다음 우리말을 영어로 바르게 옮긴 것을 두 개 고르면?

> 이것은 우리가 아이들의 나무 블록을 보관하는 상자이다.

① This is the box which we keep children's wood blocks in.
② This is the box which we keep children's wood blocks with.
③ This is the box on which we keep children's wood blocks.
④ This is the box in that we keep children's wood blocks.
⑤ This is the box in which we keep children's wood blocks.

》 실전 Tip 관계대명사가 전치사의 목적어로 쓰인 경우에 전치사는 관계대명사절의 맨 끝에 올 수도 있다.

05 다음 우리말과 같도록 할 때 빈칸에 알맞은 것을 모두 고르면?

> 저것이 그 배우가 묵고 있는 호텔이야.
> → That is the hotel _____.

① which the actor is staying at
② which the actor is staying
③ at which the actor is staying
④ that the actor is staying at
⑤ at that the actor is staying

대표유형 02 관계대명사의 계속적 용법 출제율 35%

06 다음 두 문장을 한 문장으로 만들 때 빈칸에 알맞은 것은?

> Taegwondo is one of the most exciting martial arts. It started in Korea.
> → Taegwondo, _____, started in Korea.

① who is one of the most exciting martial arts
② that is one of the most exciting martial arts
③ what is one of the most exciting martial arts
④ which is one of the most exciting martial arts
⑤ of which is one of the most exciting martial arts

07 다음 문장에서 어법상 어색한 부분을 찾아 바르게 고쳐 쓰시오.

> Sam lost his trunk, that ruined his trip.

08 다음 우리말과 같도록 빈칸에 알맞은 말을 쓰시오.

> 그녀는 Peter로부터 편지를 받았는데, 그것이 그녀를 매우 기쁘게 했다.
> → She got a letter from Peter, _____ _____ very happy.

[09-10] 다음 두 문장의 의미가 같도록 빈칸에 알맞은 말을 쓰시오.

09
> I went to see James, who wasn't at home.
> = I went to see James, _____ wasn't at home.

10
> I studied with Helen, who can speak three languages.
> = I studied with Helen, _____ can speak three languages.

대표유형 03 소유격 관계대명사 　　　　출제율 20%

11 다음 우리말과 같도록 빈칸에 알맞은 말을 쓰시오.

> 그것은 문이 하얀색 페인트로 칠해진 건물이다.
> → It's the building _____ is painted white.

12 다음 문장에서 어법상 어색한 부분을 찾아 바르게 고쳐 쓰시오.

> Kate helped her friend of which arm was broken.

13 다음 우리말과 같도록 괄호 안의 단어를 이용하여 빈칸에 알맞은 말을 쓰시오.

> 이름이 Bella인 한 공주가 살았다. (name)
> → There lived a princess _____ _____.

14 다음 두 문장을 관계대명사 whose를 이용하여 한 문장으로 바꿔 쓰시오.

> Susan is my neighbor. Her son wants to be a designer.
> → Susan is _____ _____.

15 다음 괄호 안의 어구와 관계대명사 whose를 이용하여 대화를 완성하시오.

> **A** Who is Daejin?
> **B** Daejin is a boy _____.
> (sister, love her pet cats)

대표유형 01 전치사 + 관계대명사　　　　출제율 30%

01 다음 빈칸에 알맞은 것은?

> He is the type of person _____ I want to get along.

① whom　　② with who　　③ in that
④ with whom　　⑤ for whom

02 다음 우리말과 같도록 할 때 빈칸에 알맞은 것은?

> 나는 사진을 찍을 수 있는 카메라가 필요하다.
> → I need a camera _____ I can take pictures.

① which　　② with that　　③ in which
④ for which　　⑤ with which

03 다음 우리말을 영어로 바르게 옮긴 것을 모두 고르면?

> 내가 같이 일하는 그 남자는 Kane이다.

① The man with that I'm working is Kane.
② The man with who I'm working is Kane.
③ The man with whom I'm working is Kane.
④ The man whom I'm working in is Kane.
⑤ The man whom I'm working with is Kane.

04 다음 두 문장을 한 문장으로 바꿔 쓸 때, 빈칸에 알맞은 것을 모두 고르면?

> The song was good. We listened to it yesterday.
> = The song _____ we listened to yesterday was good.

① that　　② what　　③ which
④ whom　　⑤ whose

대표유형 02, 03 관계대명사의 계속적 용법 / 소유격 관계대명사　　출제율 35%

05 다음 중 밑줄 친 부분의 쓰임이 어법상 어색한 것은?

① He fixed my suitcase whose zipper was broken.
② I have a cousin whose goes to a university.
③ Let's go to the restaurant whose menu has a lot of choices.
④ There is a boy whose mother works for a bank.
⑤ Don't sit on the chair whose legs are very weak.

[06-07] 다음 빈칸에 들어갈 말이 나머지 넷과 다른 것을 고르시오.

06 ① People watch the movie, _____ is funny.
② I'll go on a picnic, _____ will be exciting.
③ Move this sofa _____ cushion is uncomfortable.
④ Tell the truth, _____ will surprise everyone.
⑤ Invite the team _____ won the first prize.

07 ① I read the novel _____ story is about world history.
② Would you show me a shirt _____ sleeves are short?
③ Tell me a story _____ ending is a happy one.
④ They went to a town _____ bus system was very comfortable.
⑤ This is my student _____ practices for the piano contest.

대표유형 04 통합형 　　　　　　　　　출제율 15%

08 다음 빈칸에 알맞은 말을 각각 쓰시오.

> - I went to Ulsan last week, _____ is far from Seoul.
> - I read a book _____ the writer is famous.
> - The party _____ I was invited was held outside.

09 다음 문장을 관계대명사를 이용하여 연결하여 쓰시오.

(1)
> Last night, Eddie watched a movie, and it was very scary.
> → Last night, Eddie watched a movie, _____ .

(2)
> - Evelyn bought a stool.
> - She could sit on it.
> → Evelyn bought _____ she could sit.

10 다음 문장을 관계대명사 whose를 이용하여 바꿔 쓰시오.

> She was holding a cat, and the eyes of the cat were green.
> → She _____
> _____ .

11 다음 글에서 어법상 어색한 부분을 <u>모두</u> 찾아 바르게 고쳐 쓰시오.

> One of my hobbies are reading books. I read a lot of books every day, what are very good.

신유형

12 다음 그림의 내용에 맞도록 대화의 빈칸에 알맞은 말을 <u>두 단어</u>로 쓰시오.

> **A** What is the man doing?
> **B** He is checking his car _____ is flat.

[13-14] 다음 〈보기〉에서 알맞은 말을 골라 관계대명사를 이용하여 문장을 완성하시오. (단, 필요한 경우 형태를 바꿔 쓸 것)

> 보기　invent the light bulb
> 　　　is made in Vietnam

13 I admire Thomas Edison, _____
_____ .

14 She bought a new TV, _____
_____ .

15 다음 우리말과 같도록 문장을 완성하시오.

> 나는 어머니가 선생님인 두 명의 친구가 있다.
> → I have _____ .

01 다음 두 문장을 비교하는 설명으로 옳은 것은?

> (A) Harry has two uncles, who are writers.
> (B) Harry has two uncles who are writers.

① The meanings of (A) and (B) are exactly the same.
② In (B), Harry has only two uncles.
③ In (A), Harry has more than two uncles.
④ In (B), we cannot know how many uncles Harry has.
⑤ In both (A) and (B), we can know that Harry's job is a writer.

02 다음 대화를 읽고, 관계대명사를 이용하여 내용을 요약하는 문장을 완성하시오. (단, 계속적 용법으로 쓸 것)

> **A** Mr. Parker's two daughters were on TV.
> **B** Wow! What are they?
> **A** They're famous reporters.
> **B** That's great! Mr. Parker must be proud of his two daughters.

→ Mr. Parker has _____

_____.

03 다음 메모를 보고, 관계대명사를 이용하여 (1) ~ (3)의 문장을 각각 완성하시오.

> My girlfriend....
> (1) Name: Martha
> (2) I meet her after school every day.
> (3) good at telling funny stories

(1) I have a girlfriend _____.

(2) I have a girlfriend _____

_____.

(3) I have a girlfriend, _____

_____.

04 다음 대화에서 관계대명사와 주어진 어구를 이용하여 (1) ~ (3)의 빈칸을 각각 완성하시오.

> (1) talk to a foreigner now
> (2) good at jumping high
> (3) work at a flower shop

> **A** Who is Jinsu?
> **B** (1) He is my classmate, _____
>
> _____.
>
> **A** Is there anything special about him?
> **B** (2) He has a dog, _____
>
> _____.
>
> **A** Does he live with his parents?
> **B** No. (3) He lives with his grandparents,
>
> _____.

05 다음 두 문장을 관계대명사를 이용하여 한 문장으로 연결하시오.

(1) The woman is my neighbor. Her face is pale.

→ _____

_____

(2) Did you clean the room? Jackson stayed in the room for a long time.

→ Did you clean the room _____

_____

_____?

(3) The park was very quiet. We drew pictures at the park.

→ The park _____

_____.

01
a This is the village on which my grandparents grew up.

b This is the village in which my grandparents grew up.

02
a I know the boy whose Leo is talking with.

b I know the boy that Leo is talking with.

03
a Hana has a cat, which can run very well.

b Hana has a cat, that can run very well.

04
a I have two sisters, who are very different from each other.

b I have two sisters, which are very different from each other.

05
a This novel was written by Virginia Woolf, who lived a lonely life.

b This novel was written by Virginia Woolf, that lived a lonely life.

06
a The man whom wallet was stolen called the police.

b The man whose wallet was stolen called the police.

07
a I like a jacket that pocket is blue.

b I like a jacket whose pocket is blue.

08
a Buy the oven of that the price is cheap.

b Buy the oven of which the price is cheap.

UNIT 13 관계부사

유형별 기출 적용 빈도

유형 01	관계부사 when, where	35%
유형 02	관계부사 why, how	25%
유형 03	관계부사와 선행사의 생략	15%
유형 04	통합형	25%

>> 출제 포인트
문맥에 맞는 관계부사 고르기, 「전치사＋관계대명사」로의 전환 문제가 많이 출제되고, 선행사와 함께 쓰이지 않는 관계부사에 관한 문제도 자주 출제된다.

>> 정답률 100% Tip
1 관계부사는 「전치사＋관계대명사」로 바꿔 쓸 수 있음
2 관계부사 how와 선행사 the way는 함께 쓰일 수 없음

Grammar Point

관계부사는 시간, 장소, 이유, 방법을 나타내는 선행사를 수식하는 절을 이끌며 접속사와 부사의 역할을 한다. 관계부사는 「전치사＋관계대명사」와 바꿔 쓸 수 있다.

	선행사	관계부사	전치사＋관계대명사
시간	the day, the time, the week 등	when	in / at / on＋which
장소	the place, the town, the city 등	where	in / at / on＋which
이유	the reason	why	for which
방법	(the way)	how	in which

Point 1 관계부사 when, where

I can't remember the date when we took a trip to Italy.
Let's go to the stadium where a baseball game will be held this afternoon.

Point 2 관계부사 why, how

I have no idea about the reason why you left me.
Tell me how[the way] he won an award.
주의 관계부사 how와 선행사 the way는 함께 쓸 수 없다.

Point 3 관계부사와 선행사의 생략

관계부사의 선행사가 the day, the place, the reason 등과 같이 일반적일 때 관계부사와 선행사 중 하나를 생략할 수 있다.
Today is (the day) when we will start a new semester.
= Today is the day (when) we will start a new semester.
Tell me (the reason) why you didn't do your homework.
= Tell me the reason (why) you didn't do your homework.

바로 체크

01 December 5th is the day (when / where) my mom was born.

02 This is the hotel (which / where) my favorite actor stayed.

03 She went to a special school (when / where) pets get trained.

04 That's the reason (why / how) I love him.

05 This is (the way / the way how) he invented the machine.

06 Do you know (where / why) she hasn't come yet?

07 Friday is the day (on which / in which) he is free.

08 This is the place (when / where) we first met.

대표유형 01 관계부사 when, where   출제율 35%

01 다음 빈칸에 들어갈 말로 알맞은 것은?

> We know that spring is the time _____
> everything gets started.

① where   ② when   ③ which
④ how   ⑤ why

02 다음 빈칸에 알맞은 말끼리 바르게 짝지어진 것은?

> • Harvard University is near Boston _____
>   my uncle lives.
> • I still remember the day _____ I met
>   her.

① which – that   ② that – which
③ which – when   ④ when – where
⑤ where – when

03 다음 괄호 안의 단어를 알맞은 위치에 넣어 문장을 다시 쓰시오.

> This is the restaurant I had dinner
> yesterday. (where)
> → _____

04 다음 괄호 안의 어구들을 바르게 배열하여 문장을 완성하시오.

> March _____.
> (the month, my school, is, starts, when).

05 다음 대화의 빈칸에 공통으로 들어갈 알맞은 말을 한 단어로 쓰시오.

> **A** Dad, let's find a place _____ we can
>   stop and rest.
> **B** Sounds good. How about the café
>   _____ we went last Sunday?

06 다음 대화의 빈칸에 들어갈 말로 알맞은 것은?

> **A** What was your favorite holiday?
> **B** It was last Christmas _____.

① how people loved the holiday
② where I got a lot of presents
③ why my mom made a delicious cake
④ which is the biggest holiday
⑤ when I first went to a ski resort

07 다음 두 문장을 한 문장으로 연결할 때 빈칸에 알맞은 말을 쓰시오.

> • Mozart was born in the house.
> • The house is now one of the most popular
>   museums in the world.
> → The house _____ Mozart was born is
>   now one of the most popular museums
>   in the world.
> → The house _____ _____ Mozart
>   was born is now one of the most popular
>   museums in the world.

08 다음 문장에서 어법상 어색한 부분을 찾아 바르게 고치시오.

> 1948 was the year which Korea first
> participated in the Olympic Games.

_____ → _____

09 다음 빈칸에 공통으로 알맞은 것은?

> • _____ would be the best day for the event?
> • Please tell the hotel guest the exact time _____ the room will be ready.

① When [when]　　　② Where [where]
③ Which [which]　　④ How [how]
⑤ Why [why]

10 다음 빈칸에 들어갈 말이 나머지 넷과 <u>다른</u> 것은?

① The month _____ she feels most relaxed is January.
② Are there any cities _____ there are no traffic lights?
③ I can't find the box _____ I stored my savings.
④ The court _____ we usually play tennis is not available right now.
⑤ The man chose to sit in a place _____ he could easily see the speaker.

11 다음 문장의 ①~⑤ 중 관계부사 where가 들어가기에 알맞은 것은?

> Mr. Dean (①) visited (②) the high school (③) he had (④) worked (⑤) for more than 20 years.

12 다음 빈칸에 들어갈 말로 알맞은 것은?

> Do you know the reason _____ he decided to resign?

① when　　　② where　　　③ which
④ how　　　⑤ why

13 다음 빈칸에 공통으로 들어갈 알맞은 말을 쓰시오.

> • Can you tell me _____ to get to City Hall?
> • The teacher needs to tell the students _____ they should behave in the classroom.

14 다음 두 문장의 의미가 같도록 할 때 빈칸에 알맞은 것은?

> Everybody wants to know the reason why the famous actress got married to him.
> = Everybody wants to know the reason _____ the famous actress got married to him.

① which　　② on which　　③ in which
④ for which　　⑤ for why

15 다음 우리말과 같도록 빈칸에 알맞은 말을 세 단어로 쓰시오.

> 그가 항상 피곤한 이유는 수면 부족 때문이다.
> → _____ he is always tired is lack of sleep.

16 다음 밑줄 친 부분과 바꿔 쓸 수 있는 것을 <u>모두</u> 고르면?

> Social media has changed <u>how</u> people communicate with each other.

① the way　　　② the way which
③ the way in which　　④ the way of which
⑤ the way for which

[17-18] 다음 두 문장을 알맞은 관계부사를 이용하여 한 문장으로 쓰시오.

17
- I don't know the reason.
- He refused to follow the directions for that reason.
- → I don't know the reason _____

  _____.

18
- The man told us the way.
- He survived the car crash in the way.
- → The man told us _____

  _____.

대표유형 03 관계부사와 선행사의 생략   출제율 15%

19 다음 우리말을 영어로 옮긴 문장에서 생략된 말을 넣어 문장을 다시 쓰시오.

> 그녀의 아버지는 그녀에게 거짓말을 한 이유를 물었다.
> → Her father asked why she had lied to him.

→ _____

20 다음 괄호 안의 생략된 말이 알맞은 것은?

① Can you tell me (the time) why you didn't call me?
② Do you remember (the way) when we played soccer in the rain?
③ There were times (where) people didn't have cell phones.
④ This is (the place) where we used to play hide and seek.
⑤ I don't understand (the reason) how they finished the project before anyone else.

21 다음 빈칸에 들어갈 수 없는 것은?

> Can you tell me _____ you went there?

① the way   ② where   ③ how
④ why   ⑤ when

22 다음 문장의 밑줄 친 부분 중 어법상 어색한 것은?

① David is greedy. That's <u>how</u> I hate him.
② This is <u>where</u> my parents live.
③ Tell me <u>why</u> you were absent from school.
④ Do you know <u>when</u> he is going to start?
⑤ Let's go to a place <u>where</u> we can sit and talk.

23 다음 괄호 안의 단어들을 바르게 배열하여 문장을 완성하시오.

> Nobody knows _____.
> (come, he, when, will)

24 다음 빈칸에 생략된 말로 알맞은 것은?

> This is _____ where Abraham Lincoln was born.

① the day   ② the time   ③ the way
④ the place   ⑤ the reason

25 다음 문장 중 어법상 어색한 것은?

① Nobody knows why Mr. Johnson left the town.
② She told me the way how she escaped from the burning house.
③ This is the park where we're going on a picnic.
④ Tell me when we will have a meeting.
⑤ We took a trip to an island where there are more cats than people.

대표유형 01 관계부사 when, where 출제율 35%

01 다음 빈칸에 알맞은 말끼리 바르게 짝지어진 것은?

> • The owner was extra busy on days _____ his employees called out sick.
> • She missed her hometown _____ she spent her childhood.

① which – that
② why – how
③ how – why
④ when – where
⑤ where – when

02 다음 빈칸에 들어갈 말로 알맞은 것은?

> Students like _____ cheap and delicious food.

① where this cafeteria they can enjoy
② this cafeteria where they can enjoy at
③ this cafeteria where they can enjoy
④ where they can enjoy this cafeteria
⑤ this cafeteria which they can enjoy

03 다음 빈칸에 들어갈 말이 나머지 넷과 <u>다른</u> 것은?

① Let's mark the day _____ we will travel.
② Do you remember the day _____ we met first?
③ Think about a time _____ you kept trying and didn't give up.
④ That was the moment _____ changed my life completely.
⑤ July is the month _____ the summer vacation starts.

04 다음 문장의 ①~⑤ 중 관계부사 where가 들어가기에 알맞은 것은?

> When it's time (①) to lay eggs, some salmon* (②) swim (③) thousands of miles (④) to get back to the stream (⑤) they hatched.　　　　*salmon: 연어

05 다음 두 문장의 의미가 같도록 할 때 빈칸에 알맞은 것은?

> We went to the mall where we had met our friends.
> = We went to the mall _____ we had met our friends.

① of which
② at which
③ for which
④ in that
⑤ on that

대표유형 04 통합형 출제율 25%

06 다음 빈칸에 들어갈 말이 순서대로 바르게 짝지어진 것은?

> • She wants to know _____ she can please her parents.
> • The apartment _____ the couple lives in is old but neat.
> • The manager provided the customer with a list of reasons _____ the product could not be returned.

① when – how – why
② where – which – how
③ how – which – why
④ how – where – which
⑤ which – that – which

07 다음 밑줄 친 부분을 괄호 안의 말과 바꿔 쓸 수 <u>없는</u> 것은?

① Christmas is the day <u>when</u> we exchange gifts. (on which)
② The town <u>where</u> I grew up has gotten much bigger. (in which)
③ Summer is the season <u>when</u> we can enjoy many water activities. (in which)
④ Tell us right now <u>how</u> the robbers stole the money from the bank. (at which)
⑤ The scientists explained several reasons <u>why</u> the experiment had failed. (for which)

대표유형 01   관계부사 when, where   출제율 35%

08 다음 두 문장을 관계부사를 이용하여 한 문장으로 바꿔 쓰시오.

> • I will never forget the morning.
> • We climbed up the old Mayan pyramid in the morning.
>
> → _____
> _____

09 다음 우리말을 괄호 안의 표현과 관계부사를 이용하여 바르게 영작하시오.

> 네가 꽃들의 사진을 찍을 수 있는 멋진 정원으로 데려 갈게. (wonderful, take photographs)

I'll take you to _____
_____ .

대표유형 02, 03   관계부사 why, how / 관계부사와 선행사의 생략 출제율 25%

10 다음 문장에서 어법상 어색한 부분을 찾아 바르게 고쳐 쓰시오.

> Roy asked the teacher the way which he could get a good grade.

11 주어진 문장과 같은 의미가 되도록 관계대명사를 이용하여 바꿔 쓰시오.

> A severe storm was the reason why most of the houses were damaged.
> = A severe storm was the reason _____
> _____ .

12 다음 빈칸에 공통으로 알맞은 말을 쓰시오.

> • They finally found out _____ to solve the quiz.
> • That's _____ people get the tickets.

13 다음 그림을 보고, 대화의 빈칸에 공통으로 알맞은 말을 세 단어로 쓰시오.

> **A** Wow! Who sent this to you?
> **B** Bill did. But I don't know the reason _____ this to me.
> **A** Why don't you call him and ask _____ _____ it to you?

대표유형 04   통합형   출제율 25%

14 괄호 안에 주어진 표현을 바르게 배열하시오. (단, 각각 알맞은 관계부사를 추가할 것)

> **A** Bobby, you look tired. Did you have trouble sleeping last night?
> **B** Yes, I did. Actually, my roommate's loud snoring is (1) _____ .
> (couldn't, I, sleep, the reason)
> **A** Oh, no! I think you should tell him (2) _____
> _____ . (for his snoring, get, he, to visit, some treatment, can, a clinic)

15 다음 중 어법상 어색한 문장을 두 개 골라 바르게 고쳐 쓰시오.

> ⓐ My aunt runs a shop where sells traditional wooden toys.
> ⓑ Everyone wants to know the way he became successful at a young age.
> ⓒ Too much TV and not enough exercise are the reasons of which he gained weight.

(1) _____ : _____ → _____
(2) _____ : _____ → _____

대표유형 01 관계부사 when, where 출제율 35%

01 다음 빈칸에 들어갈 말이 나머지 넷과 <u>다른</u> 것은?

① The phone was still on the seat _____ I left it.
② This is the park _____ I used to play badminton with Dad.
③ She visited the town _____ she was born.
④ Venice is the city _____ I want to visit most.
⑤ She works in a small company _____ all the workers are women.

02 다음 우리말에 맞게 괄호 안의 단어를 배열할 때 <u>네 번째</u>로 오는 것은?

대통령이 머물렀던 호텔은 공항 근처에 위치해 있다.
(stayed, where, is, the president, located, near the airport, the hotel)

① stayed   ② where   ③ is
④ located   ⑤ the president

03 다음 중 어법상 옳은 것을 <u>모두</u> 고르면?

① This is the place where I play computer games.
② This is the place where I play computer games in.
③ This is the place for which I play computer games.
④ This is where I play computer games.
⑤ This is the place in where I play computer games.

04 다음 대화의 밑줄 친 ① ~ ⑤ 중 어법상 <u>어색한</u> 것은?

A Do you know your ① parents' wedding anniversary?
B Well, I ② don't know the day ③ how my parents ④ got married. How about you?
A I don't know, ⑤ either.

대표유형 04 통합형 출제율 25%

05 다음 문장 중 어법상 옳은 것을 <u>모두</u> 고른 것은?

ⓐ This is the shop in which I bought my backpack.
ⓑ Halloween is a special day when people dress up as ghosts.
ⓒ The girl always has bad dreams at night, and nobody knows why.
ⓓ She wrote an article about the way she overcame difficulties in her life.
ⓔ I'm looking for some spots how I can observe the stars.

① ⓐ, ⓑ, ⓓ   ② ⓒ, ⓓ, ⓔ   ③ ⓐ, ⓑ, ⓒ, ⓓ
④ ⓐ, ⓓ, ⓔ   ⑤ ⓑ, ⓒ, ⓓ, ⓔ

06 다음 문장 중 어법상 <u>어색한</u> 것은?

① That is the gym where we often exercise.
② That's why the man was surprised.
③ The boys want to know the time when the game starts.
④ My family didn't know how they handled the problem.
⑤ We visited Suwon where is famous for its old fortress.

신유형
07 다음 밑줄 친 부분을 어법상 알맞게 고친 것을 <u>모두</u> 고르면?

① The street <u>when</u> the accident occurred was closed for a few hours. (→ which)
② I was really impressed by <u>the way how</u> she organized everything. (→ the way in which)
③ The man unlocked the drawer <u>how</u> he kept his documents in. (→ where)
④ Last Wednesday was the day <u>at which</u> I graduated from middle school. (→ of which)
⑤ I think there are several reasons <u>of which</u> opposites attract. (→ for which)

대표유형 01 관계부사 when, where　　출제율 35%

08 다음 두 문장을 괄호 안의 지시에 따라 각각 한 문장으로 바꿔 쓰시오.

My best friend moved to another school on the day. The day was the saddest of my life.

→ _____

_____ (관계대명사 이용)

→ _____

_____ (관계부사 이용)

09 다음 세 문장의 의미가 같도록 괄호 안의 지시대로 빈칸에 알맞은 말을 쓰시오.

My school is in the village. My uncle was born there.

= _____

_____ (관계대명사 이용)

= _____

_____ (관계부사 이용)

대표유형 02, 03 관계부사 why, how / 관계부사와 선행사의 생략　출제율 25%

10 다음 두 문장을 한 문장으로 쓰시오.

• Can you tell me the way?
• You studied Chinese in that way.

→ _____

[11-12] 다음 우리말을 영작하시오.

11 그것이 내가 고양이를 키우는 이유이다.

→ _____

12 나는 그가 여기에 도착했던 방법을 알기 원한다.

→ _____

신유형

13 다음 두 문장의 의미가 같도록 관계부사를 이용하여 빈칸에 알맞은 말을 쓰시오.

I didn't visit you because I didn't know your address.

= The reason _____

is that _____.

대표유형 04 통합형　　출제율 25%

14 다음 문장 중 어법상 어색한 것을 두 개 골라 바르게 고쳐 쓰시오.

ⓐ Justin drove back to the parking lot which the accident happened.
ⓑ Sunday is the only day how Ms. Dean can spend time with her family.
ⓒ I want to find out the way in which the actress got ready for the role.
ⓓ The teacher explained why birds migrate at a particular time.

(1) _____ : _____ → _____
(2) _____ : _____ → _____

15 다음 대화에서 어법상 어색한 부분을 모두 찾아 바르게 고쳐 쓰시오.

A Hi, Julie. What is the day which we have to hand in our math homework?
B It's next Tuesday. But I'm having a hard time understanding the assignment.
A If you meet me at the library after school, I can show you the way how I completed it quickly and easily.
B That would be great. See you then.

_____

_____

01 다음 밑줄 친 문장 중 어법상 어색한 것의 개수는?

> Peter has a problem. ⓐHe wants to go on a date with Jenny, but he doesn't know how he can ask her. ⓑHe is also unaware of the day when she has free time. ⓒHe needs to find out about Jenny's schedule. ⓓHowever, he doesn't want anyone to know the reason why he wants to know her schedule.

① 1개   ② 2개   ③ 3개   ④ 4개   ⑤ 없음

02 다음 괄호 안의 문장과 관계부사를 이용하여 대화의 빈칸에 알맞은 말을 쓰시오.

(1) **A** We can see a lot of animals at the zoo.
   B That is the reason _____.
   (We go to the zoo.)

(2) **A** I could think about life and death after watching the movie.
   B That's _____.
   (We watched the movie.)

03 다음 〈보기〉와 같이 관계부사를 이용하여 자신의 경우에 맞게 질문에 답하시오.

> 보기 **A** What month were you born in?
> **B** November is the month when I was born.

(1) **A** What city were you born in?
   B _____

(2) **A** Where do you usually study?
   B _____

04 다음 대화의 밑줄 친 우리말과 같도록 관계부사를 이용하여 문장을 쓰시오.

> **A** I don't understand why he is mad at me!
> **B** (1) 네 기분이 어떨지 알아.
> **A** He was so rude when he talked to me.
> **B** Just forget it. (2) 그게 그가 사람들에게 말하는 방식이야.

(1) _____
(2) _____

05 다음은 Tom에 관한 사실들이다. 각 문장을 〈보기〉와 같이 관계부사를 이용하여 바꿔 쓰시오.

> 보기 Tom was born in 1990.
> → 1990 was the year when Tom was born.

(1) He grew up in New York.
   → New York was the place _____
   _____.

(2) He moved to Dallas in 1995.
   → 1995 was the year _____
   _____.

(3) He won first prize in the art festival in 2018.
   → The art festival was the event _____
   _____.

06 다음 문장에서 생략된 관계부사를 넣어 문장을 다시 쓰시오.

(1) She forgot the day she had to submit her report.
   → _____
   _____

(2) I don't know the reason he didn't show up.
   → _____

최종 선택 QUIZ

어법상 옳은 문장에 ✔ 표시하세요.

01
  a   Today is the day where we will start a new semester.

  b   Today is the day when we will start a new semester.

02
  a   The girl went back to the store where she had bought her pants.

  b   The girl went back to the store which she had bought her pants.

03
  a   I don't know the reason why he is angry at me.

  b   I don't know the reason how he is angry at me.

04
  a   Tell me the reason in which you canceled the appointment.

  b   Tell me the reason for which you canceled the appointment.

05
  a   That is how he overcame the crisis.

  b   That is the way how he overcame the crisis.

06
  a   This is the way I won the competition.

  b   This is the way which I won the competition.

07
  a   I don't know the place she came back home.

  b   I don't know the time she came back home.

08
  a   This is the room on which we get some rest.

  b   This is the room in which we get some rest.

유형별 기출 적용 빈도

유형 01 복합 관계대명사 `45%`

유형 02 복합 관계부사 `55%`

≫ **출제 포인트**
문맥에 알맞은 복합 관계사를 묻는 문제가 많이 출제되고, 대체 표현을 묻는 문제도 자주 출제된다.

≫ **정답률 100% Tip**
1 복합 관계대명사 주어는 단수 취급
2 「however + 형용사 / 부사 + 주어 + 동사」의 어순에 주의

Grammar Point

Point 1 복합 관계대명사

복합 관계대명사는 「관계대명사 + -ever」의 형태로 자체에 선행사를 포함한다.

복합 관계대명사	명사절	양보의 부사절
whoever	anyone who ~하는 누구든지	no matter who 누가 ~할지라도
whomever	anyone whom ~하는 누구든지	no matter whom 누구를 ~할지라도
whichever	anything which ~하는 어느 것이든지	no matter which 어느 것이[을] ~할지라도
whatever	anything that ~하는 무엇이든지	no matter what 무엇이[을] ~할지라도

You can wear whatever(= anything that) you want. 〈명사절〉
Whatever(= No matter what) he says to you, you don't have to care about it. 〈양보의 부사절〉

Point 2 복합 관계부사

복합 관계부사는 「관계부사 + -ever」의 형태로 자체에 선행사를 포함한다.

복합 관계부사	시간, 장소의 부사절	양보의 부사절
whenever	at any time when ~할 때마다	no matter when 언제 ~할지라도
wherever	at any place where ~한 곳 어디에나	no matter where 어디에서 ~할지라도
however	–	no matter how 아무리 ~할지라도

Sit wherever(= at any place where) you like. 〈장소의 부사절〉
I will follow you wherever(= no matter where) you go. 〈양보의 부사절〉
However(= No matter how) hard I tried, I couldn't achieve the goal. 〈양보의 부사절〉

주의 「복합 관계부사 however + 형용사 / 부사 + 주어 + 동사」의 어순이다.

✓ 바로 체크

01 (Who / Whoever) passes the exam, I will be happy.

02 We'll do (whatever / however) you tell us to do.

03 There are two pens. Take (which / whichever) you like better.

04 (Anything that / No matter what) you said, I didn't care.

05 I cry (whenever / however) I watch a drama.

06 (Where / Wherever) you go, I will be with you.

07 (No matter how / No matter where) tired you may be, you must submit it.

08 I can go (wherever / however) I want.

09 (However hot it is / However it is hot), I want to go hiking.

대표유형 01 복합 관계대명사   출제율 45%

01 다음 빈칸에 들어갈 말로 알맞은 것은?

> _____ calls me today, say that I'm not available.

① Who ② Whoever ③ Which
④ Whichever ⑤ What person

02 다음 괄호 안의 어구들을 바르게 배열하여 대화를 완성하시오.

> **A** Do you have any idea about how to spend this summer vacation?
> **B** No, I don't. _____ (suggest, no, what, you, matter), I'll agree to it.

03 다음 밑줄 친 부분 중 어법상 어색한 것은?

① Whoever comes, I won't open the door.
② They will buy you whatever you need.
③ She can date whomever she likes.
④ Whoever he does, his father will never be happy.
⑤ You can use this room or that one, whichever you want.

04 다음 대화의 밑줄 친 문장과 같은 의미가 되도록 빈칸에 알맞은 말을 쓰시오.

> **A** Are you going to join us?
> **B** Of course. Whatever may happen, I'm sure to come.

→ _____ _____ _____ may happen, I'm sure to come.

05 다음 우리말과 같도록 할 때 빈칸에 알맞은 것은?

> 네가 원하는 것은 무엇이든 포틀럭 파티에 가져올 수 있다.
> → You can bring _____ you want to the potluck party.

① what ② whatever ③ which
④ where ⑤ whomever

[06-07] 다음 대화가 자연스럽도록 빈칸에 알맞은 복합 관계대명사를 쓰시오.

06
> **A** What class do I have to take?
> **B** Well, _____ you choose, I don't mind at all.

07
> **A** Who do you think will score a goal?
> **B** Well, I'm not sure, but _____ scores a goal will be a hero.

08 다음 대화의 빈칸에 들어갈 말로 알맞은 것은?

> **A** Who would you like to invite to the party?
> **B** I'd like to invite _____ is funny and cheerful.

① who ② whatever ③ whoever
④ whichever ⑤ whomever

09 다음 두 문장의 의미가 같도록 빈칸에 알맞은 말을 쓰시오.

> No matter what you do today, please don't play computer games.
> = _____ you do today, please don't play computer games.

10 다음 우리말과 같도록 할 때 괄호 안의 단어들을 바르게 배열한 것을 <u>두 개</u> 고르면?

> 네가 누구라고 해도, 나는 너를 사랑한다.
> (love, I, whoever, you, you, are)

① You are whoever I love you.
② I love you you are whoever.
③ Whoever you are, I love you.
④ Whoever I love you, you are.
⑤ I love you whoever you are.

11 다음 빈칸에 들어갈 말로 알맞은 것은?

> _____ she meets, she always finds their good points.

① Who   ② Whatever   ③ Whichever
④ Whoever   ⑤ Whomever

12 다음 밑줄 친 부분을 바르게 고쳐 <u>한 단어</u>로 쓰시오.

> <u>Who</u> says so, nobody thinks it's true.

→ _____

대표유형 02 복합 관계부사   출제율 55%

13 다음 빈칸에 알맞은 말끼리 바르게 짝지어진 것은?

> • _____ late you may be, be sure to call me.
> • Please be seated _____ you feel comfortable.

① However – wherever
② Whenever – wherever
③ Whenever – whoever
④ However – whoever
⑤ Whatever – wherever

14 다음 우리말과 같도록 빈칸에 알맞은 말을 쓰시오.

> 그가 아무리 영리할지라도, 그는 이 문제를 풀 수 없다.
> → _____ _____ _____ smart he is, he cannot solve this problem.

15 다음 빈칸에 공통으로 알맞은 것은?

> • _____ I try to study, my little brother bothers me.
> • _____ Grace calls me, she makes me angry.

① Whomever   ② Whatever   ③ However
④ Whenever   ⑤ Wherever

16 다음 우리말과 같도록 괄호 안의 어구들을 바르게 배열하여 문장을 완성하시오.

> 그 문제가 아무리 어려울지라도, 나는 그것을 풀 것이다. (hard, the problem, however, be, may)
> → _____,
> I will solve it.

17 다음 우리말과 같도록 할 때 빈칸에 알맞은 것은?

> 그는 여유 시간이 있을 때마다 조부모님을 방문한다.
> → He visits his grandparents _____ he has some extra time.

① whoever ② whatever ③ however
④ whenever ⑤ wherever

18 다음 두 문장의 의미가 같도록 빈칸에 알맞은 말을 쓰시오.

> However high he jumped, he couldn't reach the branch of the tree.
> = _____ _____ _____ _____
> he jumped, he couldn't reach the branch of the tree.

19 다음 우리말과 같도록 빈칸에 알맞은 말을 쓰시오.

> 네가 그러고 싶을 때는 언제든지 넌 TV를 볼 수 있다.
> → You can watch TV _____ you want to.

20 다음 문장의 밑줄 친 ① ~ ⑤ 중 어법상 어색한 것은?

> My brother ① always ② makes friends ③ quickly, ④ where he ⑤ goes.

21 다음 괄호 안의 어구들을 바르게 배열하여 문장을 다시 쓰시오.

> Whenever (it, his, my father, car, washes, rains).
> → _____

22 다음 두 문장의 의미가 같도록 할 때 빈칸에 알맞은 것은?

> You can leave whenever you want.
> = You can leave _____ you want.

① no matter how
② no matter where
③ at any time when
④ no matter when
⑤ at any place where

23 다음 빈칸에 들어갈 말로 알맞은 것은?

> _____ hard he tries, he will never change the situation.

① Whichever ② Whatever ③ However
④ Whenever ⑤ Wherever

24 다음 우리말과 같도록 괄호 안의 어구들을 바르게 배열하여 문장을 완성하시오. (단, 부사절을 앞에 쓸 것)

> 그녀가 어디를 가더라도, 많은 사람들이 그녀를 보기 위해 기다리고 있다.
> (many people, she, to see, wherever, goes, her, are waiting)
> → _____

25 다음 빈칸에 들어갈 말로 알맞은 것은?

> Do you fasten your seat belt _____ you ride in a taxi?

① whoever ② whenever ③ however
④ whatever ⑤ wherever

대표유형 01 복합 관계대명사   출제율 45%

01 다음 빈칸에 알맞은 말끼리 바르게 짝지어진 것은?

> • I'll help _____ needs my help.
> • We have milk and orange juice in the refrigerator. Pour a glass of _____ one you would like.

① whoever – whichever
② however – whoever
③ whenever – whatever
④ whatever – whenever
⑤ whichever – however

>> 실전 Tip whichever / whatever는 명사 앞에서 명사를 꾸밀 수 있다.

02 다음 두 문장의 의미가 같도록 할 때 빈칸에 알맞은 것은?

> His mother trusts him, whatever he does.
> = His mother trusts him _____ he does.

① no matter who
② no matter what
③ no matter which
④ no matter whom
⑤ anything that

03 다음 빈칸에 공통으로 알맞은 것은?

> • _____ wishes to get an A must try hard.
> • _____ comes to my house will be welcome.

① Whomever ② Whatever ③ However
④ Whoever ⑤ Whichever

04 다음 두 문장의 의미가 같도록 할 때 빈칸에 알맞은 것은?

> The gifts will go to anyone who passes the finish line.
> = The gifts will go to _____ passes the finish line.

① whoever ② whomever ③ however
④ whatever ⑤ whichever

대표유형 02 복합 관계부사   출제율 55%

05 다음 문장의 밑줄 친 ① ~ ⑤ 중 어법상 어색한 것은?

> ① Whatever ② carefully I ③ explained the rules, he still didn't understand and kept ④ asking me ⑤ to explain them again.

06 다음 빈칸에 들어갈 말로 알맞은 것은?

> _____ she is sad, she thinks of her children and gets new strength.

① Wherever ② Whenever ③ Whatever
④ However ⑤ Whichever

07 다음 우리말과 같도록 할 때 빈칸에 알맞은 것은?

> 내가 어디를 가든지 너에게 매일 전화할게.
> → I'll call you every day, _____ I go.

① whoever ② whenever ③ wherever
④ whatever ⑤ however

복합 관계대명사   출제율 45%

08 다음 문장과 같은 의미가 되도록 복합 관계대명사를 이용하여 문장을 다시 쓰시오.

> I won't believe anything that you say.

→ _____

09 다음 대화의 빈칸에 알맞은 말을 세 단어로 쓰시오.

> A You look so tired. What happened?
> B I couldn't sleep at all last night. I had to finish the art homework.
> A Oh, no! _____ you do, you have to have a good night's rest.

10 다음 우리말을 복합 관계대명사와 괄호 안의 어구들을 이용하여 영작하시오. (단, 명사절을 앞에 쓸 것)

> 시험에서 부정행위를 하는 사람은 누구든지 벌을 받을 것이다.
> (cheat on the test, will, punish)

→ _____

≫ 실전 Tip 복합 관계대명사가 주어일 때는 단수 동사를 쓴다.

복합 관계부사   출제율 55%

11 다음 우리말과 같도록 괄호 안의 어구들을 바르게 배열하여 문장을 완성하시오. (단, 부사절을 앞에 쓸 것)

> 네가 아무리 늦게 일어나더라도, 아침 식사는 반드시 하도록 해라. (make sure, get up, late, to have, however, breakfast, you)
> → _____
> _____

12 다음 대화의 밑줄 친 부분과 바꿔 쓸 수 있는 말을 한 단어로 쓰시오.

> A What is Jessica doing now?
> B She's playing online games. Every time I see her, she's always playing online games.

→ _____

13 〈조건〉에 맞게 대화의 밑줄 친 우리말을 영작하시오.

> [조건] 1. 부사절을 앞에 쓸 것
>   2. see, smile을 활용하여 6단어로 쓸 것

> A It's certain that Sumi likes me.
> B What makes you think so?
> A 그녀는 나를 볼 때마다 웃어.

→ _____

[14-15] 다음 두 문장의 의미가 같도록 빈칸에 알맞은 말을 쓰시오.

14
> My cat follows me to any place where I go.
> = My cat follows me _____ I go.

15
> However soft the bed was, the princess could never get a good night's sleep.
> = _____ _____ _____ soft the bed was, the princess could never get a good night's sleep.

≫ 실전 Tip 복합 관계부사 however는 양보의 부사절만 이끈다.

대표유형 01 복합 관계대명사   출제율 45%

01 다음 문장 중 어법상 옳은 것끼리 묶은 것은?

ⓐ She will hire whomever she considers the most intelligent.

ⓑ It will not be easy to finish the project, whichever method you choose.

ⓒ You can bring anything whatever you want.

ⓓ Whomever volunteers to work at the festival will be accepted.

① ⓐ, ⓑ
② ⓐ, ⓒ
③ ⓑ, ⓓ
④ ⓐ, ⓒ, ⓓ
⑤ ⓑ, ⓒ, ⓓ

02 다음 우리말을 영어로 바르게 옮긴 것을 <u>모두</u> 고르면?

Evelyn이 누구와 사랑에 빠졌든지 나는 신경 쓰지 않는다.

① Whoever Evelyn fell in love with, I don't care.

② Whomever Evelyn fell in love with, I don't care.

③ No matter who Evelyn fell in love with, I don't care.

④ Anyone whom Evelyn fell in love with, I don't care.

⑤ No matter whom Evelyn fell in love with, I don't care.

[03-04] 다음 빈칸에 들어갈 말로 알맞은 것을 <u>모두</u> 고르시오.

03

_____ comes to the party will get a gift card.

① Whomever
② Whoever
③ Anyone whom
④ Anyone who
⑤ No matter who

04

_____ smartphone you choose, I will buy it for your birthday.

① Whichever
② Which
③ No matter which
④ Anything which
⑤ Anything that

대표유형 02 복합 관계부사   출제율 55%

05 다음 글의 빈칸에 들어갈 말로 알맞은 것은?

The best restaurant in the city is opening soon! _____ you visit our restaurant, you will enjoy the best dishes and the best service.

① Whenever
② Wherever
③ However
④ Whoever
⑤ Whatever

06 다음 문장의 밑줄 친 ① ~ ⑤ 중 어법상 <u>어색한</u> 것은?

① No matter what ② nicely we dress, we ③ can't be truly wonderful people ④ without good ⑤ manners.

07 다음 빈칸에 알맞은 것을 <u>모두</u> 고르면?

_____ busy you are, you have to eat regularly.

① Whatever
② Whenever
③ However
④ No matter how
⑤ No matter what

대표유형 01 복합 관계대명사 출제율 45%

08 다음 문장에서 어법상 어색한 부분을 찾아 바르게 고쳐 쓰시오.

> The shirt comes in three colors. Choose which you prefer.

09 다음 우리말에 맞게 괄호 안의 어구들을 바르게 배열하시오. (단, 알맞은 한 단어를 추가할 것)

> 일을 가장 열심히 하는 사람은 누구든지 다음 달에 승진할 것이다.
> (hardest, be, works, next month, will, promoted)

→ _____

10 〈조건〉에 맞게 대화의 밑줄 친 우리말을 영작하시오.

> [조건] **1.** 부사절을 앞에 쓸 것
>   **2.** wear, always, look, cool을 이용하여 7단어로 완성할 것

> A Kelly, do I look all right?
> B 네가 뭘 입더라도, 너는 항상 멋있어 보여.
> A It's sweet of you to say so.

→ _____

대표유형 02 복합 관계부사 출제율 55%

11 다음 우리말과 같도록 빈칸에 알맞은 말을 <u>5단어</u>로 쓰시오.

> 네가 어디를 가더라도, 너는 푸른 장미를 찾을 수 없다.
> → _____,
>   you can't find the blue roses.

〔신유형〕

12 다음 중 어법상 <u>어색한</u> 문장을 골라 바르게 고쳐 쓰시오.

① Whenever we call her, she never answers the phone.
② Wherever she travels in the world, she learns some phrases in the local language.
③ No matter where you've been, I'll forgive you.
④ No matter what small the cake is, you can't eat it all.
⑤ However much Rachel drank, she still felt thirsty.

_____ → _____

13 다음 우리말을 괄호 안의 어구들을 이용하여 영작하시오. (단, <u>11단어</u>로 완성할 것)

> 그 산이 아무리 높아도, 그는 정상에 오를 수 있다.
> (high, climb, to the top)
> → _____
> _____

≫ 실전 Tip 양보의 부사절을 이끄는 however가 쓰일 때 어순은 「however + 형용사/부사 + 주어 + 동사」로 쓴다.

[14-15] 다음 우리말과 같도록 복합 관계부사와 괄호 안의 어구들을 이용하여 문장을 쓰시오. (단, 부사절을 앞에 쓸 것)

14
> 그녀는 피곤할 때마다 커피를 한 잔 마신다.
> (tired, a cup of)
> → _____
> _____

15
> 그들은 아무리 부유해도 항상 더욱 더 많이 원한다.
> (rich, always, more and more)
> → _____
> _____

01 다음 문장 중 어법상 옳은 것의 개수는?

> ⓐ Miranda packs instant noodles in her luggage whenever she travels abroad.
> ⓑ Wherever I work, I try to do my best and help my colleagues.
> ⓒ He can eat whatever he wants, but he always stays slim.
> ⓓ However way you go, you won't arrive at the theater in time.

① 1개   ② 2개   ③ 3개   ④ 4개   ⑤ 없음

02 다음 〈보기〉와 같이 그림의 내용에 맞게 괄호 안의 어구들을 바르게 배열하시오.

> 보기
>
> (the singer, to him, his fans, goes, rush)
> → Wherever <u>the singer goes, his fans rush to him</u>.

(1)

(it, have, take, you, you, can)
→ Whatever _____.

(2)

(he, he, goes, sleepy, to school, is, on time)
→ No matter how _____
_____.

[03-04] 다음 우리말과 같도록 괄호 안의 어구들을 바르게 배열하시오. (단, 부사절을 앞에 쓸 것)

03
> 아무리 바람이 불더라도, 나는 수영하러 갈 것이다.
> (it, windy, go, is, swimming, however, I, will)
>
> → _____

04
> 나와 통화하고 싶을 때는 언제든지 내게 전화해.
> (talk, with me, a call, want, give, whenever, to, you, me)
>
> → _____

05 다음 대화의 우리말을 복합 관계사와 괄호 안의 어구들을 이용하여 영작하시오.

(1)
> A Who do you want to choose?
> B 열정이 있고 열심히 연습하는 사람은 누구든지 뽑고 싶어요. (passionate, practice hard)
>
> → _____
> _____

(2)
> A How are you going to help us?
> B 우리는 당신을 돕기 위해 필요한 일이라면 무엇이든 할 것입니다. (necessary, to help)
>
> → _____
> _____

(3)
> A When do you usually meet your girlfriend?
> B 나는 그녀가 나를 만나고 싶어 할 때는 언제든지 그녀를 만납니다. (her, want to meet)
>
> → _____
> _____

01
  a Whoever is interested in drawing can join us.

  b Whomever is interested in drawing can join us.

02
  a There are two hats. Take which you like better.

  b There are two hats. Take whichever you like better.

03
  a What you say, I don't want to work with them.

  b Whatever you say, I don't want to work with them.

04
  a Kate won't meet anyone whom she doesn't like.

  b Kate won't meet no matter whom she doesn't like.

05
  a Thomas is busy wherever I visit him.

  b Thomas is busy whenever I visit him.

06
  a No matter where she is, she thinks of her parents.

  b No matter how she is, she thinks of her parents.

07
  a You can come to my house at any time when you want.

  b You can come to my house no matter when you want.

08
  a However you run fast, you won't be able to catch up with him.

  b However fast you run, you won't be able to catch up with him.

UNIT 15 등위접속사 / 상관접속사

유형별 기출 적용 빈도

유형 01 등위접속사	15%	
유형 02 「명령문, and/or ~」	35%	
유형 03 상관접속사	50%	

>> 출제 포인트
등위접속사와 상관접속사가 쓰인 문장의 병렬구조,
수의 일치 그리고 문장 전환 문제가 자주 출제된다.

>> 정답률 100% Tip
1 「명령문, and/or ~」→ If/Unless ~
2 상관접속사를 쓸 때는 수의 일치에 주의하기

Grammar Point

Point 1 등위접속사

등위접속사는 문법적으로 대등한 역할을 하는 단어, 구, 절 등을 연결하여 병렬
구조를 이룬다.

and	but	or	so	for
~와, 그리고	그러나, 하지만	또는, 아니면	그래서	왜냐하면

She was very tired, but she finished writing the report.
I had a headache, so I couldn't sleep. 〈원인, so + 결과〉
cf. Because I had a headache, I couldn't sleep. 〈because + 원인, 결과〉

Point 2 「명령문, and/or ~」

「명령문, and ~」 (…해라, 그러면 ~할 것이다)	Take the bus, and you'll save money. → If you take the bus, you'll save money.
「명령문, or ~」 (…해라, 그렇지 않으면 ~할 것이다)	Leave now, or you'll be late. → If you don't leave now, you'll be late. → Unless you leave now, you'll be late.

Point 3 상관접속사

상관접속사는 두 개 이상의 단어가 짝을 이루는 접속사로, 상관접속사가 연결하
는 말이 주어로 쓰일 때 동사의 수는 B에 일치시킨다. 단, both A and B는 복수
취급한다.

both A and B	A 와 B 둘 다	B as well as A	A뿐만 아니라 B도
not A but B	A가 아니라 B	either A or B	A 또는 B 둘 중 하나
not only A but (also) B	A뿐만 아니라 B도	neither A nor B	A도 B도 아닌

Both Hojin and I were late for school.
Rex speaks not only Korean but also Japanese.
(= Rex speaks Japanese as well as Korean.)
Emma is either at home or at the sports center.
Neither my brother nor I like fast food.

✅ 바로 체크

01 Do you go to school by bus (and/ or) by subway?

02 It was raining heavily, (or / but) many people came to the event.

03 I caught a bad cold, (but / so) I was absent from school.

04 Go straight, (and / or) you'll find the park.

05 Never waste your time, (and / or) you'll regret it.

06 Yoga is good for both body (and/ or) mind.

07 Not only Leo but also Tim (have / has) no money left.

08 The man neither ate (or / nor) drank for days.

09 All of her friends as well as Ann (is / are) kind.

10 The powder can be taken with either water (and / or) milk.

대표유형 01 등위접속사   출제율 15%

01 다음 빈칸에 들어갈 말이 순서대로 바르게 짝지어진 것은?

> • Emily is a bright _____ hardworking student.
> • Would you prefer working alone _____ with others?
> • The boy fell off his bike _____ didn't hurt himself.

① and – or – but   ② but – or – and
③ or – so – and   ④ so – and – but
⑤ for – but – or

02 다음 빈칸에 들어갈 말로 알맞은 것은?

> Everybody likes Henry, _____ he is kind and good-looking.

① for   ② or   ③ but
④ so   ⑤ if

03 다음 밑줄 친 부분 중 의미상 어색한 것은?

① Dad cooked some food <u>and</u> served it to his guests.
② She tried to persuade Jack, <u>but</u> he wouldn't listen to her.
③ Using social media is useful, <u>so</u> it also causes some problems.
④ Information can be given over the phone, by email, <u>or</u> in person.
⑤ I didn't arrive on time, <u>for</u> the traffic was heavy.

04 다음 문장의 밑줄 친 부분을 어법상 알맞은 형태로 고치시오.

> They approached the car slowly and <u>silence</u>.

05 다음 밑줄 친 부분 중 어법상 옳은 것은?

① My grandfather is very old but still <u>health</u>.
② All the people in the stadium are waving and <u>shout</u>.
③ I returned from a long but <u>satisfying</u> day's work.
④ Christmas is all about celebrating love, joy, and <u>happy</u>.
⑤ Do you want to play board games or <u>reading</u> comic books?

대표유형 02 「명령문, and/or ~」   출제율 35%

06 다음 빈칸에 공통으로 들어갈 말로 알맞은 것은?

> • Ask Judy for help, _____ she will help you.
> • Be a good boy, _____ you'll be rewarded.

① or   ② and   ③ but
④ so   ⑤ that

07 다음 빈칸에 들어갈 말이 순서대로 바르게 짝지어진 것은?

> • Take this medicine after lunch, _____ your headache will get better.
> • Be quiet, _____ the baby will wake up.

① and – but   ② or – but
③ but – so   ④ and – or
⑤ or – and

08 다음 두 문장이 같은 의미가 되도록 빈칸에 알맞은 말을 쓰시오.

> Join us, and we will win this game.
> = _____ _____ _____ _____,
> we will win this game.

09 다음 문장과 의미가 가장 유사한 것은?

> Use this tool, and you'll be able to take the bolt apart.

① Unless you use this tool, you'll be able to take the bolt apart.

② If you use this tool, you won't be able to take the bolt apart.

③ When you don't use this tool, you'll be able to take the bolt apart.

④ If you don't use this tool, you'll be able to take the bolt apart.

⑤ If you use this tool, you'll be able to take the bolt apart.

10 다음 두 문장이 같은 의미가 되도록 빈칸에 알맞은 말을 쓰시오.

> Listen carefully, or you won't find the correct answer.
>
> = _____ _____ _____ _____ carefully, you won't find the correct answer.

11 다음 문장을 긍정 명령문으로 시작하여 바꿔 쓰시오.

> Unless you wear a swimming cap, you can't get into the pool.
>
> → _____
>
> _____

12 다음 우리말과 같도록 괄호 안의 말을 이용하여 빈칸에 알맞은 말을 쓰시오.

> 늦지 마, 그렇지 않으면 행사에 참석할 수 없을 거야.
> → _____
>   be able to attend the event. (don't, late)

13 다음 빈칸에 들어갈 말이 나머지 넷과 <u>다른</u> 것은?

① Get some fresh air, _____ you'll feel better.

② Return your book on time, _____ you'll have to pay a fine.

③ Respect others, _____ you will be respected.

④ Practice harder, _____ you'll become a great pianist.

⑤ Apologize to Kate first, _____ she'll forgive you.

대표유형 03 상관접속사   출제율 50%

14 다음 두 문장이 같은 의미가 되도록 빈칸에 알맞은 말을 쓰시오.

> Sleeping well is important not only for children but also for adults.
> = Sleeping well is important for adults _____ _____ _____ for children.

15 다음 빈칸에 들어갈 말로 알맞은 것은?

> Fortunately, _____ Ms. Robinson and her baby were safe.

① both   ② nor   ③ either

④ neither   ⑤ not only

16 다음 두 문장을 한 문장으로 바르게 나타낸 것은?

> • You can stay with me.
> • Or you can stay with Lily.

① You can stay both me and Lily.

② You can stay either with me or with Lily.

③ You can stay neither with me nor with Lily.

④ You can stay not with me but with Lily.

⑤ You can stay with me as well as Lily.

17 다음 빈칸에 공통으로 들어갈 말로 알맞은 것은?

- I like not only writing stories _____ drawing cartoons.
- Jason lied to me not just once _____ several times.

① but   ② and
③ or   ④ nor
⑤ for

[18-19] 다음 빈칸에 들어갈 말이 순서대로 바르게 짝지어진 것을 고르시오.

18

Alice felt both _____ and _____ at the same time.

① angry – sadly   ② happily – sadly
③ nervous – excited ④ joyful – angrily
⑤ relaxed – joy

19

A Which subject is your favorite, science or history?
B _____ science _____ history is my favorite subject. I like math best.

① Both – and   ② Either – or
③ Neither – nor   ④ Not – but
⑤ Not – only

20 다음 빈칸에 들어갈 말로 알맞은 것은?

Either you or she _____ care of the dog.

① take   ② are taking
③ have to take   ④ has to take
⑤ don't take

21 다음 우리말을 영어로 옮긴 문장을 바르게 완성하시오.

우리는 해외에서 공부하는 것의 이점과 단점 둘 다에 관해 토론할 것입니다.
→ We will discuss _____ the advantages _____ disadvantages of studying abroad.

22 다음 대화의 빈칸에 알맞은 말을 쓰시오.

A Do you know where Eva is from?
B I think she's _____ French or Italian.

23 다음 우리말과 같도록 괄호 안의 어구를 바르게 배열하시오.

이 노트북은 가격이 쌀 뿐만 아니라 매우 유용하다.
(very useful, but also, cheap, not only, is)
→ This laptop _____.

24 다음 문장을 as well as를 이용하여 바꿔 쓰시오.

Not only Wendy but also I have to do the work.
→ _____

25 다음 문장 중 어법상 어색한 것은?

① Brenda as well as I is from Busan, Korea.
② Either you or she has to pay for lunch.
③ She's not the principal but a math teacher.
④ Neither I nor he are going to dive first.
⑤ Both Yuna and Jessica are popular among boys.

대표유형 01, 03 | 등위접속사 / 상관접속사 | 출제율 50%

01 다음 문장 중 어법상 <u>어색한</u> 것은?

① It's an old car, but it's very fast.

② Both swimming and skiing is my favorite sports.

③ Which do you like better, beef or chicken?

④ She is rich, but she is not always happy.

⑤ Neither Jason nor I like doing outdoor activities.

02 다음 빈칸에 들어갈 말이 순서대로 바르게 짝지어진 것은?

> • Rachel waved at me, _____ I pretended not to notice her.
> • Leo forgot the password, _____ he couldn't log in.

① or – but   ② and – but

③ but – for   ④ but – so

⑤ so – or

03 다음 문장의 밑줄 친 ① ~ ⑤ 중 어법상 <u>어색한</u> 것은?

> ① <u>According to</u> color experts, colors not only ② <u>reflect</u> our character ③ <u>and</u> also ④ <u>have</u> a great effect ⑤ <u>on</u> us.

04 다음 우리말을 영어로 옮길 때 빈칸에 알맞은 것은?

> 우리에게 필요한 것은 용기가 아니라 신뢰이다.
> → What we need is _____.

① not courage but faith

② both courage and faith

③ courage as well as faith

④ either courage or faith

⑤ not only faith but also courage

대표유형 02, 03 | 「명령문, and/or ~」 / 상관접속사 | 출제율 50%

05 다음 빈칸에 들어갈 말이 나머지 넷과 <u>다른</u> 것은?

① Slow down, _____ you might crash.

② Hurry up, _____ you'll be late for the meeting.

③ Dry your wet hair, _____ you'll catch a cold.

④ You can either accept _____ refuse the invitation.

⑤ The 2002 World Cup was held not only in Korea _____ also in Japan.

06 다음 빈칸에 들어갈 말이 순서대로 바르게 짝지어진 것은?

> • Their new album will be released either late this year _____ early next year.
> • My left arm hurts for some reason, _____ I can't carry my bag.
> • I watched the movie twice, _____ I hardly remember anything about it.

① or – so – but   ② but – and – for

③ for – or – and   ④ nor – and – or

⑤ but – nor – so

07 다음 문장 중 어법상 <u>어색한</u> 것은?

① Mix white with red, and you'll get pink.

② Ian enjoys cycling as well as jogging.

③ I'm neither for or against your opinion.

④ Unless you do your homework, you'll be punished.

⑤ Either I or my brother has to visit our grandparents.

대표유형 02 「명령문, and/or ~」 출제율 35%

08 〈조건〉에 맞게 괄호 안의 어구를 이용하여 다음 우리말을 영어로 옮기시오.

> [조건] 1. 긍정 명령문으로 시작할 것
>   2. 10단어의 완전한 문장으로 쓸 것

> 지금 일어나라, 그렇지 않으면 학교버스를 놓칠 것이다. (wake up, miss)
> → _____

09 다음 문장을 같은 의미로 바꾼 문장에서 어법상 <u>어색한</u> 부분을 찾아 바르게 고쳐 쓰시오.

> Stop eating so much fast food, or you're going to be fat.

> → Unless you don't stop eating so much fast food, you're going to be fat.

대표유형 03 상관접속사 출제율 50%

10 다음 문장의 빈칸에 알맞은 말을 쓰시오.

> Susan couldn't go on holiday last year because she had _____ time nor money for the trip.

11 다음 우리말을 영어로 옮긴 문장에서 어법상 <u>어색한</u> 부분을 <u>두 개</u> 찾아 바르게 고쳐 쓰시오.

> Janet과 그녀의 여동생 둘 다 과학 캠프에 참가할 계획이다.
> → Both Janet or her sister is planning to participate in a science camp.

(1) _____ → _____
(2) _____ → _____

[12-13] 〈보기〉와 같이 두 문장을 상관접속사를 사용하여 한 문장으로 바꿔 쓰시오.

> 보기 I play the piano. I also play the violin.
>   → I play both the piano and the violin.

12
> We can eat out. Or we can order some food online.
> → We can _____ _____
> _____ _____ _____
> _____ online.

13
> Kate seems to be satisfied with the result. Tim seems to be satisfied with the result, too.
> → _____ _____ _____
> _____ _____ to be satisfied
> with the result.

14 다음 두 문장을 as well as를 사용하여 한 문장으로 바꿔 쓰시오.

> • I like watching cartoon movies.
> • Sam also likes watching cartoon movies.
> → _____
> _____

15 〈조건〉에 맞게 다음 우리말을 영어로 옮기시오.

> [조건] 1. Neither로 시작할 것
>   2. 과거 시제 수동태를 사용할 것
>   3. 10단어의 완전한 문장으로 쓸 것

> Andy도 나도 그녀의 생일 파티에 초대받지 않았다.
> → _____
> _____

>> 실전 Tip neither A nor B는 그 자체로 부정의 의미를 포함하고 있으므로 부정어를 반복하여 쓰지 않도록 유의한다.

대표유형 01, 03 등위접속사 / 상관접속사 출제율 50%

01 다음 문장 중 어법상 옳은 것은?

① I will buy not a book and a notebook.

② I'm really hungry, or I haven't eaten all day.

③ Who runs faster, Jake and his brother?

④ She felt cold, so she pulled the blanket over her.

⑤ Jennifer is good at not only singing but also to dance.

02 다음 대화의 내용을 나타내는 문장으로 가장 알맞은 것은?

> **Jean** Have you ever been to Australia?
> **Alex** No. How about you?
> **Jean** I haven't, either.

① Both Jean and Alex have been to Australia.

② Either Jean or Alex has been to Australia.

③ Jean as well as Alex has been to Australia.

④ Not Jean but Alex has been to Australia.

⑤ Neither Jean nor Alex has been to Australia.

03 다음 중 우리말을 영어로 바르게 나타낸 것끼리 묶은 것은?

> ⓐ 너는 계단을 오르거나 엘리베이터를 타서 꼭대기에 갈 수 있다.
>   → You can reach the top either by climbing the stairs or taking an elevator.
> ⓑ 엄마와 아빠 두 분 다 나의 선물에 기뻐하셨다.
>   → Both Mom and Dad were pleased with my present.
> ⓒ 그녀는 고기도 생선도 먹지 않는다.
>   → She doesn't eat neither meat nor fish.
> ⓓ 나는 살을 빼기 위해서가 아니라 건강해지기 위해서 운동한다.
>   → I exercise not to lose weight so to be healthy.

① ⓐ, ⓑ   ② ⓑ, ⓒ   ③ ⓑ, ⓓ

④ ⓐ, ⓓ   ⑤ ⓒ, ⓓ

04 다음 중 빈칸에 but이 들어갈 수 없는 것은?

① It is not you _____ me who is to blame.

② I neither said _____ did anything in reply.

③ Ted is not only smart _____ also funny.

④ We eat out on Sunday, _____ not often.

⑤ My sister hated the movie, _____ I thought it was great.

05 다음 문장 중 어법상 어색한 것은?

① Either you or Ben has been hiding the truth.

② Mike as well as my nieces are really good at chess.

③ Both her dog and my dog are females.

④ Not only Lydia but also I was not allowed to enter the room.

⑤ Neither the driver nor the passengers were injured.

대표유형 02 「명령문, and/or ~」 출제율 35%

06 다음 중 나머지 넷과 의미가 <u>다른</u> 것은?

① Drive not too fast, and you won't miss the details.

② Don't drive too fast, or you'll miss the details.

③ If you drive too fast, you'll miss the details.

④ Unless you drive too fast, you'll miss the details.

⑤ If you don't drive too fast, you won't miss the details.

07 다음 중 빈칸에 들어갈 말이 나머지 넷과 <u>다른</u> 것은?

① Try to keep your word, _____ everyone will trust you.

② Use less plastic, _____ it'll help save the planet.

③ Put on sunscreen, _____ you'll get a sunburn.

④ Wear your helmet, _____ you can protect yourself when you fall over.

⑤ Burn more calories than you consume, _____ you'll lose weight.

08 다음 문장을 의미가 통하도록 주어진 단어로 시작하여 다시 쓰시오.

> Make a reservation in advance, or you'll have to wait one hour or more.
> → Unless _____
>
> _____.

09 다음 세 문장이 같은 의미가 되도록 빈칸에 알맞은 말을 쓰시오. (단, 접속사를 이용할 것)

> Be honest with him, or he won't forgive you.
> = _____,
> he won't forgive you.
> = _____,
> he won't forgive you.

10 다음 우리말과 같도록 빈칸에 알맞은 말을 쓰시오.

> 동남아시아의 날씨는 더울 뿐만 아니라 습하다.
> → The weather in Southeast Asia is _____
> _____ hot _____ _____ humid.
> → The weather in Southeast Asia is humid
> _____ _____ _____ hot.

11 다음 문장에서 어법상 어색한 부분을 찾아 바르게 고쳐 쓰시오.

> You can learn lots of things by reading a book, searching the Internet, or visit a school library.

12 〈조건〉에 맞게 다음 우리말을 영어로 옮기시오.

> [조건] 1. as well as 구문으로 쓸 것
> 2. enjoy, horror movies, scare를 이용할 것

> 나뿐만 아니라 Chris도 공포영화를 보는 것과 사람들을 놀라게 하는 것을 즐긴다.
> → _____
>
> _____

[13-15] 〈보기〉와 같이 괄호 안의 표현을 사용하여 두 문장을 한 문장으로 바꿔 쓰시오.

> 보기 It is freezing. It is terribly windy, too.
> → It is both freezing and terribly windy. (both)

13

> The actress is popular in Korea. She is also popular in many other countries.
>
> → _____
>
> _____ (not only)

14

> Henry has spread the rumor. Or his brother has spread the rumor.
>
> → _____
>
> _____ (either)

15

> Emilia was not shocked by the news. She was not disappointed by the news, either.
>
> → _____
>
> _____ (neither)

신유형

01 다음 중 빈칸에 한 번도 들어가지 <u>않는</u> 것은?

ⓐ Avoid buying unnecessary things, _____ you may end up wasting a lot of money.

ⓑ The woman has gained both fame _____ money.

ⓒ She will neither call Jack _____ send him a text message anymore.

ⓓ Italy is known not only for its historical importance _____ also for its natural beauty.

① and ② or ③ but ④ nor ⑤ so

02 다음 문장 중 어법상 옳은 것끼리 묶은 것은?

ⓐ Either you or she is lying.

ⓑ Neither Mr. Patterson nor his children speaks Korean.

ⓒ You as well as Matt are responsible for the accident.

ⓓ Both Jeff and I am going to decorate the Christmas tree.

ⓔ We wear gloves not only for warmth but also protect.

① ⓐ, ⓒ   ② ⓑ, ⓓ   ③ ⓐ, ⓑ, ⓒ
④ ⓑ, ⓒ, ⓔ   ⑤ ⓒ, ⓓ, ⓔ

03 〈조건〉에 맞게 다음 문장과 같은 의미의 문장을 <u>두 개</u> 쓰시오.

If you don't arrive on time, you may not be allowed to take the test.

[조건] 1. 첫 번째 문장은 긍정 명령문으로 시작할 것
2. 두 번째 문장은 부사절을 앞에 쓸 것

→ _____
_____
→ _____
_____

04 다음 짝지어진 대화 중 <u>어색한</u> 것을 <u>모두</u> 고르면?

① A Why didn't you submit your homework?
 B Sorry, sir. I finished my homework, but I left it at home.

② A Did you enjoy the show?
 B No, it was neither funny and interesting.

③ A What are you going to do this Sunday?
 B I will either go shopping or go to the movies.

④ A Jerry made a big mess in the kitchen, didn't he?
 B It was not him and his sister who made a mess.

⑤ A I have difficulty falling asleep these days.
 B Take a warm bath before bed, and it will help you fall asleep.

05 다음 두 문장을 알맞은 상관접속사를 사용하여 한 문장으로 바꿔 쓰시오.

• I didn't go to the fast food restaurant.
• I didn't have a hamburger, either.

→ _____
_____

06 다음 표의 내용과 일치하도록 빈칸에 알맞은 말을 쓰시오.

이름	출신지	사용하는 언어
Sophia	Canada	English, French
Danny	Canada	English
Robert	Britain	English, Spanish

(1) _____ Sophia _____ Danny _____ Canadians.

(2) Sophia can speak _____ _____ English _____ _____ French.

(3) Not Danny _____ _____ can speak Spanish.

(4) _____ Danny _____ Robert can speak French.

01
a She was rich, so she could afford to buy the car.

b She was rich, but she could afford to buy the car.

02
a Avoid eating at night, and you will lose weight.

b Avoid eating at night, or you will lose weight.

03
a Don't miss the first train, and you won't be able to attend the meeting.

b Don't miss the first train, or you won't be able to attend the meeting.

04
a If you want to fail again, you'd better follow my advice.

b Unless you want to fail again, you'd better follow my advice.

05
a Both vegetables and fruit have a lot of vitamin C.

b Both vegetables and fruit has a lot of vitamin C.

06
a Either Mom and Dad are going to pick me up.

b Either Mom or Dad is going to pick me up.

07
a Calcium helps to make not only strong bones and also strong teeth.

b Calcium helps to make not only strong bones but also strong teeth.

08
a I could understand neither what she asked and what she answered.

b I could understand neither what she asked nor what she answered.

UNIT 16 명사절을 이끄는 접속사

유형별 기출 적용 빈도

유형 01	접속사 that	35%
유형 02	접속사 if / whether	20%
유형 03	간접의문문	25%
유형 04	통합형	20%

>> 출제 포인트
that의 다양한 용법 구별과 if절의 명사절/부사절 구분, 직접의문문을 간접의문문으로 바꿔 쓰는 문제 등이 자주 출제된다.

>> 정답률 100% Tip
1 명사절은 주어, 보어, 목적어 역할을 함
2 간접의문문의 어순에 주의하기

Grammar Point

Point 1 접속사 that

'~라는 것'의 의미로 명사절을 이끌며 문장에서 주어, 보어, 목적어 역할을 한다.

주어	That he lied is true.
	→ It is true that he lied. 〈It(가주어) ~ that절(진주어)〉
보어	My point is that we have no time to wait.
목적어	I think (that) she will move to another city. 〈생략 가능〉

cf. No one can deny the fact that he is guilty. 〈동격절을 이끄는 that〉

Point 2 접속사 if / whether

'~인지 아닌지'의 의미로 명사절을 이끌며 문장에서 주어, 보어, 목적어 역할을 한다. whether는 주어, 보어, 목적어로 쓰이는 절을 모두 이끌 수 있지만, if는 주어, 보어로 쓰이는 절을 이끌 수 없다.

주어	Whether she likes him (or not) is not clear.
보어	The question is whether she will say yes or no.
목적어	I don't know if [whether] she will come (or not).
	= I don't know whether or not she will come. ← if or not(×)

Point 3 간접의문문

의문문이 다른 문장의 일부(주어, 보어, 목적어)가 되는 것을 말한다.

| 의문사가 있는 경우 | 의문사 + 주어 + 동사 |
| 의문사가 없는 경우 | if[whether] + 주어 + 동사 |

I don't know. + Where is she? → I don't know where she is.

Do you know? + Does he like me?

→ Do you know if[whether] he likes me?

cf. 주절의 동사가 think, believe, guess, suppose, imagine 등일 때는 의문사를 문장 맨 앞에 둔다.

Do you think? Where was he born?

→ Where do you think he was born?

✓ 바로 체크

01 _____ the soldier is alive is certain.

02 I'm sure _____ Julia will be a great singer.

03 He hid the fact _____ he was bankrupt.

04 _____ is surprising that Max failed the test.

05 She asked me _____ I like horror movies or not.

06 Do you remember (who he is / who is he)?

07 The good news is (what / that) the child was completely cured.

08 (If / Whether) Sally will come tomorrow is doubtful.

09 I don't know (if / whether) or not Mr. Smith is married.

10 When do you (know / think) the surgery will be over?

대표유형 01   접속사 that   출제율 35%

01 다음 빈칸에 공통으로 들어갈 말로 알맞은 것은?

> • I think _____ we should help the poor.
> • It's fortunate _____ you weren't badly hurt in the accident.

① when   ② that   ③ whether
④ what   ⑤ which

02 다음 두 문장을 한 문장으로 연결할 때 빈칸에 알맞은 말이 바르게 짝지어진 것은?

> I haven't heard of you. It is strange.
> → _____ is strange _____ I haven't heard of you.

① That – it   ② It – what
③ That – if   ④ It – that
⑤ It – whether

03 다음 중 밑줄 친 that의 쓰임이 나머지 넷과 다른 것은?

① My wish is that my mother gets well.
② It is interesting that he mentioned it.
③ I know that Ms. Sandler is a math teacher.
④ He is the only man that can speak Chinese.
⑤ We believe that most people have kind hearts.

》 실전 Tip 접속사 that 다음에는 완전한 문장이 오고, 관계대명사 that 다음에는 불완전한 문장이 온다.

04 다음 중 빈칸에 접속사 that을 쓸 수 <u>없는</u> 것은?

① I want to know _____ made you sad.
② I hope _____ my missing dog will come home.
③ Megan finally admitted _____ she had lied.
④ The fact _____ he missed the class annoyed his parents.
⑤ It is quite clear _____ there is a difference between the two.

05 다음 두 문장의 빈칸에 공통으로 알맞은 말을 쓰시오.

> • Is it true _____ you've seen a UFO before?
> • The survey shows _____ global warming is getting worse and worse.

06 다음 우리말과 같도록 괄호 안의 어구를 바르게 배열하시오.

> 문제는 그가 그 영화에 관심이 없다는 것이다.
> (isn't, in, the movie, that, he, interested)
> → The problem is _____
> _____.

07 다음 〈보기〉의 밑줄 친 that과 쓰임이 같은 것은?

> 보기   The important thing is that I believe in myself.

① That's exactly what I want to hear.
② Becky is the best person that I've ever met.
③ Can't you remember that nice guy who came to dinner?
④ Everyone wants a puppy that is friendly and healthy.
⑤ His mistake was that he refused to follow her advice.

08 다음 문장에서 어법상 <u>어색한</u> 부분을 찾아 바르게 고쳐 쓰시오.

> It is not true what I said bad things about you.

대표유형 02 접속사 if / whether　　　　　출제율 20%

09 다음 빈칸에 들어갈 말이 순서대로 바르게 짝지어진 것은?

> The test will help you find out _____ you're a positive thinker _____.

① if – or so
② that – or not
③ how – or so
④ whether – or not
⑤ which – or not

10 다음 빈칸에 공통으로 들어갈 말로 알맞은 것은?

> • Is it OK _____ I use your phone?
> • I asked myself _____ I really wanted this job.

① but
② if
③ as
④ that
⑤ whether

11 다음 중 밑줄 친 if의 쓰임이 나머지 넷과 다른 것은?

① I doubt if I can write a poem.
② He doesn't know if she will join us.
③ They were not sure if the thief was a man.
④ Please tell him to call me if you see him.
⑤ She wondered if something was wrong with her.

≫ 실전 Tip if는 명사절을 이끌 때 '~인지 아닌지'라는 의미이고, 조건의 부사절을 이끌 때 '만일 ~라면'이라는 의미이다.

12 다음 우리말과 같도록 괄호 안의 어구를 바르게 배열하시오.

> 나는 Lucy가 파티에 올지 궁금하다.
> (come, the party, if, will, to, Lucy)
> → I wonder _____.

13 다음 우리말과 같도록 빈칸에 알맞은 말을 쓰시오.

> 그가 성공할지 아닐지는 알기 어렵다.
> → _____ he'll succeed or not is hard to tell.

14 다음 중 빈칸에 if가 들어갈 수 없는 것은?

① I don't know _____ Christine is honest.
② We wonder _____ we can finish the work on time.
③ He doubted _____ the bike was his sister's.
④ She asked _____ I could help her with her homework.
⑤ I'm sure _____ you can do much better next time.

15 다음 문장에서 어법상 어색한 부분을 찾아 바르게 고쳐 쓰시오.

> If or not he comes to the meeting is not important.

16 다음 우리말과 같도록 괄호 안의 어구와 현재진행형을 이용하여 문장을 완성하시오.

> 나는 그가 거짓말을 하고 있는지 아닌지 잘 모르겠다. (tell a lie)
> → I don't know _____ or not.

대표유형 03 간접의문문　　　　　　　출제율 25%

17 다음 밑줄 친 부분 중 어법상 어색한 것은?

① Nobody knows <u>what he wants</u>.

② I don't remember <u>when his birthday is</u>.

③ She asked <u>who the winner was</u>.

④ Do you have any idea <u>how much it will cost</u>?

⑤ I didn't know <u>why was my sister so angry</u>.

18 다음 빈칸에 들어갈 말로 알맞은 것은?

> I wonder _____ at the art museum.

① if stops the bus

② if the bus stops

③ whether stops the bus

④ if does the bus stop

⑤ whether does the bus stop

19 다음 밑줄 친 우리말을 영어로 바르게 옮긴 것은?

> You may have different ideas about <u>무엇이 영웅을 만드는지</u>.

① what are heros　　② a hero makes what

③ what make a hero　④ what makes a hero

⑤ what a hero makes

[20-21] 다음 두 문장을 한 문장으로 바꿔 쓸 때 빈칸에 알맞은 말을 쓰시오.

20
> • He wants to know.
>
> • When did she leave home?
>
> → He wants to know _____ _____ _____ home.

21
> • Tell me.
>
> • Will he come in time?
>
> → Tell me _____ _____ _____ in time.

22 다음 문장에서 어법상 어색한 부분을 찾아 바르게 고쳐 쓰시오.

> Tell me who the flowers sent to you.

23 다음 두 문장을 한 문장으로 만들 때 어법상 어색한 것은?

① I don't know. + Where do you live?

　→ I don't know where you live.

② Do you know? + When did she buy it?

　→ Do you know when she buy it?

③ Please tell me. + Why is the baby crying?

　→ Please tell me why the baby is crying.

④ Can you tell me? + What can I do for you?

　→ Can you tell me what I can do for you?

⑤ Would you say? + How did you make this cake?

　→ Would you say how you made this cake?

24 다음 대화의 빈칸에 들어갈 말로 알맞은 것은?

> **A** _____
>
> **B** I think it's because she is funny and friendly.

① Why do you think everyone loves her?

② Why do you think does everyone love her?

③ Why everyone loves her do you think?

④ Do you think why everyone loves her?

⑤ Do you think why does everyone love her?

25 다음 문장 중 어법상 어색한 것은?

① He asked me what I meant.

② I wonder if she has a driver's license.

③ Do you think how old the dog is?

④ Can you tell me where the police station is?

⑤ How do you suppose he solved the problem?

대표유형 01 접속사 that 출제율 35%

01 다음 빈칸에 들어갈 말이 순서대로 바르게 짝지어진 것은?

> • It is possible _____ she has forgotten the appointment.
> • Leonardo da Vinci discovered _____ sound travels in waves.

① if – if
② if – that
③ that – if
④ whether – that
⑤ that – that

02 다음 중 밑줄 친 that의 쓰임이 나머지 넷과 다른 것은?

① Everyone believes that Sarah is innocent.
② The truth is that we are short of money.
③ Isn't it amazing that he got a new job?
④ He doesn't know the fact that I'm a teacher.
⑤ Do you remember the story that I told you about?

03 다음 두 문장의 빈칸에 공통으로 알맞은 것은?

> • The news _____ the war had started shocked everyone.
> • The customer complained _____ the soup was too salty.

① if
② whether
③ that
④ what
⑤ which

대표유형 02, 03 접속사 if/whether / 간접의문문 출제율 25%

04 다음 밑줄 친 부분 중 어법상 어색한 것은?

① Ask them whether she will get well.
② I don't know when the accident happened.
③ Whether you like it or not doesn't matter.
④ I can tell how many types of sharks there are.
⑤ It is certain whether they will need supplies.

05 다음 중 밑줄 친 if의 의미가 나머지 넷과 다른 것은?

① I wonder if there's life on Mars.
② I doubt if anyone will recognize me.
③ I won't go out if it rains tomorrow.
④ I'm not sure if he really cheated on the test or not.
⑤ I don't know if they will be able to win the championship.

06 다음 두 문장을 한 문장으로 바르게 나타낸 것을 모두 고르면?

> • Do you remember?
> • Did you lock the door?

① Do you remember if you locked the door?
② Do you remember that you did lock the door?
③ Do you remember whether did you lock the door?
④ Do you remember whether you locked the door?
⑤ Do you remember if or not you did lock the door?

07 다음 문장 중 어법상 옳은 것은?

① How often she goes jogging?
② Where he was born is not known.
③ No one knows if or not her story is true.
④ I want to know what is your name.
⑤ If the writer is alive or not is still a mystery.

≫ 실전 Tip whether or not은 쓸 수 있지만 if 바로 뒤에는 or not을 쓰지 않는다.

대표유형 01, 02 접속사 that / if / whether 출제율 35%

08 다음 문장의 빈칸에 공통으로 알맞은 접속사를 쓰시오.

- We believe _____ the animals will be saved.
- All I know is _____ Robert was not American.

09 다음 우리말을 영어로 옮긴 문장에서 어법상 어색한 부분을 찾아 바르게 고쳐 쓰시오.

너는 그가 틀렸다고 확신하니?
→ Are you sure if he is wrong?

10 〈보기〉와 같이 다음 두 문장을 접속사 that을 사용하여 한 문장으로 연결하시오.

보기 The news is surprising. The movie star will visit my school.
→ The news that the movie star will visit my school is surprising.

The fact is important. All people are equal before the law.

→ _____

_____

11 다음 중 어법상 어색한 문장의 기호를 쓴 후, 잘못된 부분을 바르게 고치시오.

ⓐ If we win or lose makes no difference.
ⓑ I heard that Victoria had a car accident last week.
ⓒ We discussed whether we should move to another city.

_____ : _____ → _____

대표유형 03 간접의문문 출제율 25%

12 다음 우리말과 같도록 괄호 안의 단어를 바르게 배열하시오.

나는 그녀가 내 제안을 받아들일지 아닐지 알고 싶다.
(not, she, accept, my, will, proposal, or, if)
→ I want to know _____

_____.

[13-14] 다음 두 문장을 간접의문문을 이용하여 한 문장으로 바꿔 쓰시오.

13
Can you tell me? + How long has she been living here?

→ _____

14
I wonder. + Does John speak French?

→ _____

신유형

15 다음 대화를 읽고, 〈조건〉에 맞게 밑줄 친 우리말을 영어로 옮기시오.

[조건] 1. do you think를 포함한 간접의문문을 이용할 것
2. 7단어의 완전한 문장으로 쓸 것

A Look! That's Eddie, isn't it?
B Yeah, right.
A 넌 그가 어딜 가고 있다고 생각하니?
B I think he is going to the gym. He practices basketball on Fridays.

→ _____

01 다음 〈보기〉의 밑줄 친 that과 쓰임이 같은 것은?

> 보기 People know _that_ fast food is not healthy.

① She is the student _that_ is good at soccer.
② I don't think _that_ she prefers coffee to tea.
③ The tourists _that_ he met there were very kind.
④ I visited the fancy restaurant _that_ I saw on TV.
⑤ That's the boy _that_ goes to the same school as me.

02 다음 중 빈칸에 접속사 that을 쓸 수 없는 문장의 개수는?

> ⓐ It is certain _____ he can handle this job.
> ⓑ Do you agree _____ dogs make nice pets?
> ⓒ He said _____ his left arm was broken yesterday.
> ⓓ Have you heard the rumor _____ there are treasures on the island?
> ⓔ You should not ask _____ he knows the truth or not.

① 1개 ② 2개 ③ 3개 ④ 4개 ⑤ 5개

03 다음 빈칸에 알맞은 말이 순서대로 바르게 짝지어진 것은?

> • Danny noticed _____ something was going on.
> • It's up to you _____ or not you succeed in life.
> • The good news is _____ the exact answer has recently been found!

① that – if – that ② that – whether – that
③ that – if – what ④ whether – that – that
⑤ if – what – whether

04 다음 밑줄 친 부분의 쓰임이 나머지 넷과 _다른_ 것은?

① If you want to leave, let's go now.
② You will surely succeed _if_ you try hard.
③ If you need more information, visit our website.
④ You don't need to do so _if_ you don't want to.
⑤ I don't remember _if_ I took my medicine or not.

05 다음 중 어법상 옳은 문장끼리 묶은 것은?

> ⓐ He asked me if I knew the lady.
> ⓑ I'm not sure what does she do for a living.
> ⓒ I don't know if or not Mr. Lee is married.
> ⓓ He won't care whether or not you are late.
> ⓔ Do you guess when she will come back?

① ⓐ, ⓓ   ② ⓑ, ⓒ   ③ ⓒ, ⓔ
④ ⓐ, ⓒ, ⓓ ⑤ ⓑ, ⓓ, ⓔ

06 다음 중 밑줄 친 부분을 if로 바꿔 쓸 수 _없는_ 것을 _모두_ 고르면?

① _Whether_ he comes or not is not my business.
② I wondered _whether_ I could reach the finish line.
③ I'm not sure _whether_ she was serious or not.
④ It is unclear to me _whether_ or not she likes it.
⑤ I don't know _whether_ it will snow this Christmas.

07 다음 문장 중 어법상 옳은 것은?

① Who do you know did take my bag?
② I want to know how did they escape from the prison.
③ What do you suppose she is hiding from us?
④ Do you think why he gave up his dream?
⑤ I called him to ask that he could attend the meeting.

대표유형 04 통합형   출제율 20%

08 다음 우리말과 같도록 괄호 안의 어구를 바르게 배열하시오. (단, 필요 없는 한 단어는 <u>제외</u>할 것)

> 그는 전에 그 배우를 봤던 것을 기억했다.
> (seen, before, that, had, he, the actor, whether)
> → He remembered _____
> _____.

09 다음 괄호 안의 단어를 바르게 배열하시오. (단, 알맞은 접속사를 <u>추가</u>할 것)

> I learned (are, the fact, not, spiders, insects)
> → I learned _____.

[신유형]

10 다음 문장의 적절한 위치에 if 또는 whether를 넣어 문장을 다시 쓴 다음, 우리말로 해석하시오.

> You agree with me or not does not matter.
> → _____
> _____ (해석)

11 다음 두 문장을 한 문장으로 바꿔 쓸 때 빈칸에 알맞은 말을 쓰시오.

> Do you believe me? It is your own concern.
> → _____ _____ _____
> _____ _____ is your own concern.
> → It is your own concern _____
> _____ _____ or not.
> → It is your own concern _____
> _____ _____ me.

[12-13] 다음 두 문장을 간접의문문을 이용하여 한 문장으로 바꿔 쓰시오.

12

> I have no idea. + Where did I put my bag?
> → _____

13

> Would you mind telling me? + Do you recognize this man?
> → _____
> _____

14 다음 중 어법상 <u>어색한</u> 부분이 있는 문장을 <u>두 개</u> 골라 기호를 쓰고 바르게 고치시오.

> ⓐ It's not surprising that the detective caught the thief.
> ⓑ I'm not sure that there will be any seats left on the train.
> ⓒ She asked me how far is it to the subway station.
> ⓓ Can you tell me when the first animated film was created?
> ⓔ Which team do you believe will win the tournament?

(1) ____: _____ → _____
(2) ____: _____ → _____

15 괄호 안의 어구를 이용하여 다음 우리말을 영어로 옮기시오.

> 너는 내가 거기에 도착하는 데 시간이 얼마나 걸릴 것이라고 생각하니?
> (think, it, take, will, get there, how long, me)
> → _____
> _____

01 다음 중 빈칸에 들어갈 말이 나머지 넷과 <u>다른</u> 것은?

① I can come at once _____ necessary.

② Have you decided _____ you'll take the job?

③ I wonder _____ the weather will be like tomorrow.

④ I don't know _____ what I'm saying makes any sense.

⑤ He couldn't tell _____ Jennifer was laughing or crying.

02 다음 두 문장을 한 문장으로 바꾼 것 중 옳은 문장의 개수로 알맞은 것은?

ⓐ I'm not sure. + Did she keep her word?
→ I'm not sure if or not she kept her word.

ⓑ Do you think? + Which is the proper method?
→ Which do you think is the proper method?

ⓒ I wonder. + Will he write me back?
→ I wonder whether he will write me back.

ⓓ No one knows for sure. + Why did dinosaurs become extinct?
→ No one knows for sure why dinosaurs became extinct.

① 없음　② 1개　③ 2개　④ 3개　⑤ 4개

03 다음 중 어법상 <u>어색한</u> 문장을 <u>모두</u> 고르면?

① The waiter realized whether he had made a mistake.

② Whether she will get back in time is doubtful.

③ It is obvious if he wants to quit working.

④ Many scientists support the idea that climate change is real.

⑤ I want to know whether the plane will be delayed or not.

04 다음 〈조건〉에 맞게 빈칸에 알맞은 질문을 쓰시오.

[조건] 1. do you guess를 포함한 간접의문문을 이용할 것
2. 7단어의 완전한 문장으로 쓸 것

A What a tall girl! _____
B I guess she is about 180cm tall.

05 다음 대화를 읽고, 어법상 <u>어색한</u> 부분을 <u>두 군데</u> 찾아 바르게 고쳐 쓰시오.

A Suji, you look so gloomy. Tell me what is the problem.
B I'm worried about my friend, Monica. I think she's unhappy. She's usually social, but she's been really quiet lately.
A Has she told you why she's unhappy?
B No. I'm not sure that I should ask her why or not.
A I think you should ask her why.

(1) _____ → _____
(2) _____ → _____

06 다음은 Jake와 Lisa가 현재 하고 있는 일과 앞으로 하게 될 일을 나타낸 표이다. 표를 보고 빈칸에 알맞은 질문을 완전한 문장으로 쓰시오. (단, do you know와 do you think를 각각 <u>두 번씩</u> 사용할 것)

Name	Doing now	Doing after
Jake	read a book	eat dinner
Lisa	watch TV	study English

A (1) _____ now?
B Yes, I do. She is watching TV.
A (2) _____ now?
B Yes, I do. He is reading a book.
A (3) _____ after watching TV?
B I think she will study English.
A (4) _____ after reading a book?
B I think he will eat dinner.

01
a It is clear which the music is going to be a big hit.

b It is clear that the music is going to be a big hit.

02
a Do you know the fact that more types of bees live in cities?

b Do you know the fact what more types of bees live in cities?

03
a An old lady stopped and asked me if I needed any help.

b An old lady stopped and asked me that I needed any help.

04
a The question is whether Ms. Baker will attend the ceremony.

b The question is if Ms. Baker will attend the ceremony.

05
a Whether it will rain or not tomorrow is important to me.

b If it will rain or not tomorrow is important to me.

06
a The police have not decided if or not they should arrest him.

b The police have not decided whether or not they should arrest him.

07
a Can you tell me where can I claim my baggage?

b Can you tell me where I can claim my baggage?

08
a Who do you think will be selected to lead the committee?

b Do you think who will be selected to lead the committee?

유형별 기출 적용 빈도

유형 O1   시간·이유의 접속사   25%

유형 O2   조건·양보의 접속사   25%

유형 O3   목적·결과의 접속사   25%

유형 O4   통합형   25%

>> 출제 포인트
다양한 의미를 갖는 접속사의 쓰임과 전치사(구)와 접속사의 구별, 문장 전환 등이 자주 출제된다.

>> 정답률 100% Tip
1 시간과 조건의 부사절에서 현재 시제로 미래를 나타내는 것에 주의
2 「접속사+주어+동사」 vs. 「전치사+명사(구)」

Grammar Point

Point ①   시간·이유의 접속사

시간	when	~할 때, ~하면	since	~한 이래로, ~ 이후로
	while	~하는 동안	once	일단 ~하면
	as	~하면서, ~할 때	every time	~할 때마다
	until	~할 때까지	as soon as	~하자마자(on -ing)
이유	because, as, since		~ 때문에, ~이므로	

주의 (1) because of 뒤에는 명사(구)를 쓴다.
　　 (2) while은 '~인 반면'이라는 뜻으로 대조를 나타내기도 한다.

Point ②   조건·양보의 접속사

조건	if	만약 ~한다면	unless	만약 ~하지 않으면 (= if ~ not)
	in case (that)		~할 경우에는(= in case of + 명사(구))	
양보	though, although, even though		비록 ~이지만, ~에도 불구하고 (= despite [in spite of] + 명사(구))	

주의 시간과 조건의 부사절에서는 미래를 나타낼 때 현재 시제를 쓴다.
　　 If it is rainy tomorrow, I'll stay home.

Point ③   목적·결과의 접속사

목적	so that ~ can*	~하기 위해, ~하도록
	in order that ~ can*	= in order + to부정사 / so as + to부정사
결과	so ~ that	매우 ~해서 …하다
	so ~ that ... can	매우 ~해서 …할 수 있다 (= ~ enough + to부정사)
	so ~ that ... can't	너무 ~해서 …할 수 없다 (= too ~ to부정사)

주의 목적을 나타낼 때 can 대신 may, will 등도 쓸 수 있다.

✅ 바로 체크

01   Did anyone call (while / if) I was away?

02   I'll tell her the truth when I (see / will see) her tomorrow.

03   Brandon couldn't arrive on time (because / because of) he missed the bus.

04   (Even though / Since) it was freezing, we didn't go out.

05   My house is comfortable (in spite of / though) it is small.

06   (If / Unless) you wear a coat, you'll feel cold.

07   The backpack was so expensive (since / that) I couldn't buy it.

08   I got up early (so / such) that I could catch the first train.

대표유형 01 시간·이유의 접속사   출제율 25%

01 다음 두 문장의 빈칸에 공통으로 알맞은 것은?

> • We can't buy the computer _____ we have no money.
> • She hasn't seen any snow _____ she moved to Bangkok.

① while   ② since   ③ once
④ until   ⑤ though

02 다음 문장의 빈칸에 들어갈 말로 알맞은 것은?

> _____ you leave the office, you must turn off the heater.

① So   ② Though   ③ Because of
④ Until   ⑤ When

03 다음 중 밑줄 친 부분의 의미가 〈보기〉와 같은 것은?

> 보기   I like to study <u>as</u> I listen to pop music.

① Do <u>as</u> I say!
② He used to be <u>as</u> tall as me.
③ <u>As</u> I was tired, I soon fell asleep.
④ We watched the game <u>as</u> we chatted.
⑤ She worked <u>as</u> a flight attendant when she was young.

04 다음 우리말에 맞게 빈칸에 알맞은 말을 쓰시오.

> Tim은 그 소식을 듣자마자 서둘러 집으로 되돌아왔다.
> → _____ _____ _____ he heard the news, Tim hurried back to his house.

05 다음 두 문장이 같은 뜻이 되도록 빈칸에 알맞은 것은?

> Nancy had nothing special to do, so she took a walk.
> = Nancy took a walk _____ she had nothing special to do.

① after   ② until   ③ while
④ when   ⑤ because

06 다음 대화의 빈칸에 들어갈 말이 바르게 짝지어진 것은?

> **A** What do you usually do _____ you're free?
> **B** I usually go to the library _____ I love to read.

① though – when   ② when – while
③ because – when   ④ when – because
⑤ because – though

07 다음 우리말에 맞게 괄호 안의 단어들을 바르게 배열하시오.

> 그는 그녀가 말을 끝마칠 때까지 기다렸다.
> → He waited _____.
>   (had, she, finished, until, speaking)

08 다음 밑줄 친 부분의 형태로 알맞은 것은?

> Jack will not leave the classroom until he <u>solve</u> the math problem.

① solves   ② solved   ③ is solving
④ will solve   ⑤ has solved

09 다음 중 밑줄 친 부분의 쓰임이 나머지 넷과 다른 것은?

① Please text me <u>when</u> you arrive.

② Do you know <u>when</u> the show starts?

③ It started to rain <u>when</u> we left the house.

④ He usually doesn't answer <u>when</u> he is busy.

⑤ Jenny wants to be an engineer <u>when</u> she grows up.

대표유형 02 조건·양보의 접속사   출제율 25%

10 다음 두 문장이 같은 뜻이 되도록 빈칸에 알맞은 것은?

> If he doesn't show up in ten minutes, we'll just leave.
>
> = _____ he shows up in ten minutes, we'll just leave.

① Since   ② Unless   ③ As soon as

④ While   ⑤ Even though

---

11 다음 빈칸에 들어갈 말로 가장 알맞은 것은?

> _____ we lost the game, we were proud of ourselves.

① As   ② Once   ③ When

④ Because   ⑤ Though

---

12 다음 중 밑줄 친 부분의 쓰임이 나머지 넷과 다른 것은?

① Call me <u>if</u> it doesn't work.

② I'll help you <u>if</u> you help me.

③ I wonder <u>if</u> I can stay three days longer.

④ We'll go on a picnic <u>if</u> it is fine tomorrow.

⑤ You will get good grades <u>if</u> you study harder.

---

13 다음 문장에서 어법상 어색한 부분을 찾아 바르게 고쳐 쓰시오.

> Ted will be very surprised if he will hear the news.

---

14 다음 두 문장이 같은 뜻이 되도록 빈칸에 알맞은 말을 한 단어로 쓰시오.

> I told my sister not to wear my clothes, but she wore them and went out.
>
> = _____ I told my sister not to wear my clothes, she wore them and went out.

---

15 다음 두 문장을 한 문장으로 바꿔 쓸 때 빈칸에 알맞은 말을 쓰시오.

> Chris has lived in Korea for ten years. He can't speak Korean.
>
> → _____ _____ he has lived in Korea for ten years, Chris can't speak Korean.

---

16 다음 빈칸에 알맞은 것을 모두 고르면?

> You will cut yourself with the knife _____ _____.

① if you will be careful

② if you are not careful

③ unless you are careful

④ if you won't be careful

⑤ unless you will be careful

대표유형 03 목적·결과의 접속사   출제율 25%

17 다음 빈칸에 들어갈 말이 바르게 짝지어진 것은?

> He was _____ nervous _____ he couldn't say a word.

① so – that   ② so – because

③ too – that   ④ very – if

⑤ such – that

---

18 다음 빈칸에 공통으로 알맞은 말을 쓰시오.

- The street was _____ crowded that we could hardly move.
- We went shopping _____ as to buy some camping gear.

19 다음 두 문장을 한 문장으로 바르게 나타낸 것은?

It was very dark. So I couldn't see anything.

① It was very dark that I could see anything.
② It was dark so that I couldn't see anything.
③ It was so dark that I can see anything.
④ It was so dark that I couldn't see anything.
⑤ It was too dark that I couldn't see anything.

20 다음 우리말에 맞게 빈칸에 들어갈 말로 알맞은 것은?

나는 배가 몹시 고파서 그 피자를 모두 다 먹었다.
→ I was _____.

① so hungry that I ate all of the pizza
② so hungry to eat all of the pizza
③ too hungry to eat all of the pizza
④ hungry enough that I ate all of the pizza
⑤ so hungry that I couldn't eat all of the pizza

21 다음 우리말과 같도록 빈칸에 알맞은 말을 쓰시오.

나는 햇빛으로부터 눈을 보호하기 위해 선글라스를 꼈다.
→ I put on my sunglasses _____ _____ I could protect my eyes from the sun.

[22-23] 다음 두 문장의 의미가 같도록 빈칸에 알맞은 말을 쓰시오.

22

Our team practiced hard in order to win the championship.
= Our team practiced hard _____ _____ we could win the championship.

23

She felt too sad to sing at that moment.
= She felt _____ sad _____ she _____ sing at that moment.

24 다음 괄호 안에서 알맞은 것끼리 바르게 짝지어진 것은?

- The game was canceled (because of / because) it rained heavily.
- (Though / Despite) the pain in my legs, I finished the race.
- We found a boat (while / during) we were playing on the beach.

① because of – Despite – while
② because – Despite – while
③ because of – Though – while
④ because – Despite – during
⑤ because of – Though – during

25 다음 〈보기〉에서 알맞은 접속사를 골라 빈칸에 쓰시오.

보기   if   when   so that

(1) I feel nervous _____ I make a speech.
(2) She won't be upset _____ you don't lie.

대표유형 01   시간·이유의 접속사   출제율 25%

01 다음 중 밑줄 친 부분의 의미가 나머지 넷과 <u>다른</u> 것은?

① Regina loves sports <u>while</u> her sister prefers to read a book.
② Glen took a lot of pictures <u>while</u> he traveled.
③ I texted Mom <u>while</u> I was waiting for the bus.
④ <u>While</u> we were watching the movie, we ate popcorn.
⑤ <u>While</u> you were out, she was trying to reach you on the phone.

02 다음 문장 중 어법상 <u>어색한</u> 것은?

① I prefer this jacket because it is cheaper.
② As soon as I arrive home, I wash my hands.
③ We called 911 since my dad passed out.
④ She sat in the seat quietly while the flight.
⑤ He grew up in his grandparents' house when he was a child.

대표유형 03   목적·결과의 접속사   출제율 25%

03 다음 빈칸에 that이 들어갈 수 <u>없는</u> 것은?

① Jake was so upset _____ he could hardly breathe.
② The actor wore a mask so _____ no one could recognize him.
③ He came to this island so _____ take a rest.
④ The car was so expensive _____ they decided not to buy it.
⑤ Marilyn walked so fast _____ I couldn't catch up with her.

---

04 다음 우리말을 영어로 옮길 때 빈칸에 알맞은 것을 <u>모두</u> 고르면?

> 커피가 너무 뜨거워서 나는 마실 수가 없었다.
> → The coffee was _____.

① too hot for me to drink
② so hot that I couldn't drink it
③ too hot that I couldn't drink it
④ such hot that I couldn't drink
⑤ hot enough for me to drink

05 다음 밑줄 친 부분과 의미가 같은 것을 <u>모두</u> 고르면?

> She put an ad in the paper <u>to find a new roommate</u>.

① in order to find a new roommate
② once she found a new roommate
③ that she has found a new roommate
④ so that she could find a new roommate
⑤ such that she could find a new roommate

대표유형 04   통합형   출제율 25%

06 다음 빈칸에 들어갈 말이 바르게 짝지어진 것은?

> • He saw something strange _____ he was walking.
> • You will get a speeding ticket _____ you slow down.

① while – if   ② during – if
③ while – in case   ④ during – unless
⑤ while – unless

07 다음 중 밑줄 친 부분의 쓰임이 <u>어색한</u> 것은?

① <u>Unless</u> you start now, you'll miss the train.
② <u>Even though</u> they are twins, they look nothing alike.
③ <u>When</u> I hate to do this job, I must finish it.
④ <u>As</u> he was sick, he was absent from school.
⑤ He has been interested in flowers <u>since</u> he was a little boy.

대표유형 02   조건·양보의 접속사   출제율 25%

08 다음 우리말을 영어로 옮긴 문장에서 <u>어색한 부분</u>을 찾아 바르게 고쳐 쓰시오.

> 네가 그에게 사과하지 않으면 그는 너에게 화를 낼 거야.
> → He will get angry at you unless you don't apologize to him.

09 다음 문장과 의미가 통하도록 알맞은 접속사를 사용하여 문장을 완성하시오. (단, 과거 시제로 쓸 것)

> Despite the rain, we enjoyed our holiday.
> → _____, we enjoyed our holiday.

≫ 실전 Tip despite / in spite of는 '~에도 불구하고'라는 의미의 전치사로 명사(구)와 함께 쓰인다.

대표유형 04   통합형   출제율 25%

10 〈보기〉에서 알맞은 접속사를 찾아 빈칸에 쓰시오. (단, 한 번씩만 쓸 것)

> 보기   while   as soon as   so that

(1) Some plants need a lot of water _____ others live in very dry areas.
(2) The theater doors were closed _____ the latecomers could not disturb the show.
(3) _____ I stepped on the wet floor, I slipped and fell.

[11-12] 다음 두 문장이 같은 뜻이 되도록 빈칸에 알맞은 말을 쓰시오.

11

> She had to stay in bed because she was ill.

= She had to stay in bed _____ _____ her illness.

12

> I searched all over for the receipt in order to exchange the running shoes.

= I searched all over for the receipt _____ _____ _____ _____ _____ the running shoes.

13 다음 대화의 내용에 맞게 문장을 완성하시오.

> A How was the movie, Janet?
> B I fell asleep because the movie was too boring.

→ The movie was so _____ _____ Janet fell asleep.

14 다음 문장을 밑줄 친 접속사의 뜻에 유의하여 해석하시오.

(1) <u>As</u> we entered the theater, the movie had already started.
→ _____
(2) <u>As</u> she grew older, she became wiser.
→ _____
(3) <u>As</u> it was getting dark, we hurried to the bus stop.
→ _____

15 괄호 안의 단어를 이용하여 다음 문장과 의미가 통하는 문장을 쓰시오.

> Tony was healthy enough to leave the hospital.

→ _____
_____ (so, that, can)

대표유형 01, 02 시간·이유의 접속사 / 조건·양보의 접속사 출제율 25%

01 다음 중 밑줄 친 부분의 의미가 나머지 넷과 다른 것은?

① I was late for school <u>since</u> I got up late.

② <u>Since</u> he worked all day, he was very tired.

③ It has been a year <u>since</u> I became a vet.

④ The girl didn't ride a roller coaster <u>since</u> she was afraid of heights.

⑤ <u>Since</u> he lost money, he couldn't buy some of the books.

02 다음 빈칸에 공통으로 들어갈 말로 가장 알맞은 것은?

> • _____ she was asleep, thieves broke in and stole her jewelry.
>
> • The "thumbs-up" sign means "excellent" in the United States _____ it is used as an insult in some parts of Africa.

① As [as]　　　　② When [when]

③ While [while]　④ Because [because]

⑤ Although [although]

03 다음 문장 중 어법상 어색한 것을 두 개 고르면?

① Nobody was in the office when I arrived.

② We attended the meeting even though the snow.

③ Until the man spoke, I hadn't realized he was Korean.

④ If it will be sunny tomorrow, I'll go hiking.

⑤ I love my brother though he is sometimes annoying.

04 다음 중 빈칸에 because가 들어갈 수 없는 것은?

① He hates himself _____ the mistake he made.

② We were delayed _____ there was an accident.

③ I didn't know where to go _____ everything looked different.

④ She walked carefully _____ the streets were covered in ice.

⑤ Henry got so excited _____ he got an autograph of his favorite star.

대표유형 03 목적·결과의 접속사 출제율 25%

05 다음 밑줄 친 부분 중 '목적'을 의미하는 것을 모두 고르면?

① The wind was so strong <u>that my hat was blown away</u>.

② I lowered my voice <u>so Becky couldn't hear</u>.

③ Jasmine will renew her passport <u>so that she can travel overseas</u>.

④ The news was so shocking <u>that he almost passed out</u>.

⑤ It was strange <u>for Diana to wake up so early</u>.

06 다음 문장과 의미가 다른 것은?

> They wanted to see the sunrise, so they started the hike before dawn.

① They started the hike before dawn so that they could see the sunrise.

② As they saw the sunrise, they started the hike before dawn.

③ They started the hike before dawn in order to see the sunrise.

④ To see the sunrise, they started the hike before dawn.

⑤ They started the hike before dawn so as to see the sunrise.

07 다음 우리말을 바르게 영작한 것을 모두 고르면?

> 그 경기장은 매우 넓어서 50,000명 이상을 수용할 수 있다.

① The stadium is so large that it can hold more than 50,000 people.

② The stadium is such large in order to hold more than 50,000 people.

③ The stadium is too large so that it can hold more than 50,000 people.

④ The stadium is too large to hold more than 50,000 people.

⑤ The stadium is large enough to hold more than 50,000 people.

대표유형 01, 02 시간·이유의 접속사/조건·양보의 접속사 출제율 25%

08 다음 두 문장을 접속사 when을 사용하여 한 문장으로 쓰시오. (단, 부사절을 앞에 쓸 것)

> I will meet Suji this Sunday. I'll remind her to call you.

→ _____

09 다음 우리말에 맞게 괄호 안의 단어를 바르게 배열하시오. (단, 한 단어는 제외할 것)

> 나는 저녁 식사 준비를 하다가 화상을 입었다.
> → I _____.
> (during, was, myself, dinner, I, burned, preparing, while)

10 다음 밑줄 친 우리말에 맞게 괄호 안의 단어를 바르게 배열하시오.

> A Have you seen Monica recently?
> B 나는 지난 토요일에 그녀와 점심을 먹은 후로 그녀를 못 봤어. (I, I, seen, since, had, with her, her, haven't, lunch)

→ _____
last Saturday.

11 다음 문장 중 어법상 어색한 것을 두 개 골라 기호를 쓴 뒤, 바르게 고치시오.

> ⓐ Miranda waved at me as she was getting off the bus.
> ⓑ If the machine will stop working, please contact customer service.
> ⓒ The beach is crowded with many tourists because its beauty.

(1) _____ : _____ → _____
(2) _____ : _____ → _____

신유형

12 〈조건〉에 맞게 우리말을 두 개의 문장으로 영작하시오.

> [조건] 1. 접속사를 사용할 것
> 2. agree with, our proposal, can, make a contract를 이용할 것
> 3. 부사절을 앞에 쓸 것

> 그녀가 우리의 제안에 동의하지 않으면 우리는 계약을 할 수 없다.
> → _____
> _____
> → _____
> _____

대표유형 03 목적·결과의 접속사 출제율 25%

13 다음 문장을 괄호 안의 표현을 이용하여 바꿔 쓰시오.

> She turned on the lantern and we could see much better.
> → _____
> _____ (so that)

14 괄호 안의 단어를 이용하여 주어진 문장과 의미가 통하는 문장을 2개 쓰시오.

> The plane couldn't land because the fog was very thick.
> → _____
> _____ (so, that)
> → _____
> _____ (too, to)

15 다음 우리말을 괄호 안의 표현을 활용하여 영작하시오.

> 그 여행 가방은 매우 커서 많은 것들을 담을 수 있다.
> (that, the trunk, things, lots of, so, big, hold)

→ _____

01 다음 중 빈칸에 한 번도 들어가지 <u>않는</u> 것은? (단, 대·소 문자 무시)

> ⓐ Things did not remain the same _____ time passed.
>
> ⓑ _____ there is no clear evidence, most people think he is guilty.
>
> ⓒ We were unable to eat in their restaurant _____ it was fully booked.
>
> ⓓ _____ food is stored properly, it can become spoiled with germs.

① as ② since ③ so that ④ unless ⑤ though

02 알맞은 접속사를 사용하여 두 문장을 한 문장으로 바꿔 쓰시오. (단, 부사절을 앞에 쓸 것)

> I was a stranger. He treated me in a friendly way.

→ _____

_____

03 다음 중 짝지어진 두 문장의 의미가 서로 <u>다른</u> 것은?

① I was so full that I couldn't eat the dessert.
  = I was too full to eat the dessert.

② Unless you have a student ID card, you can't enter the library.
  = If you don't have a student ID card, you can't enter the library.

③ I wrote down his name so that I would not forget it.
  = I wrote down his name in order not to forget it.

④ As soon as he heard the song, he started humming.
  = On hearing the song, he started humming.

⑤ Although the traffic was heavy, we could arrive on time.
  = In case the traffic was heavy, we could arrive on time.

04 다음 문장 중 어법상 옳은 것끼리 묶은 것은?

> ⓐ Ten years have passed since he left.
>
> ⓑ The bus was getting delayed because the argument between the driver and Jack.
>
> ⓒ I left early so that I could avoid the traffic jam.
>
> ⓓ Although the fact that he had been warned many times, he was late again.
>
> ⓔ The pearls are fake even though they look real.
>
> ⓕ As soon as I'll know the result, I'll let you know.

① ⓐ, ⓒ, ⓔ   ② ⓐ, ⓓ, ⓔ   ③ ⓑ, ⓒ, ⓓ
④ ⓑ, ⓓ, ⓕ   ⑤ ⓒ, ⓔ, ⓕ

05 다음 우리말을 〈조건〉에 맞게 영어로 옮기시오.

> [조건] 1. so, messy, decide, clean it up을 활용할 것
>
>   2. 12단어의 완전한 문장으로 쓸 것

> 내 방이 매우 지저분해서 나는 그곳을 청소하기로 결심했다.
>
> → _____

06 [A], [B]에서 서로 어울리는 말을 하나씩 골라 문장을 완성하시오. (단, 중복 사용 불가)

[A] • when   • though   • so that

[B] • I heard the thunder
   • I can keep myself warm
   • the alarm clock rang many times

(1) I'll take some blankets _____

_____ .

(2) He didn't wake up _____

_____ .

(3) I was frightened _____

_____ .

01
a They got upset because the noisy neighbors.

b They got upset because of the noisy neighbors.

02
a Some people eat fish and meat until others are vegetarians.

b Some people eat fish and meat while others are vegetarians.

03
a It has been five years since she began writing novels.

b It has been five years when she began writing novels.

04
a If he does not do this, it will be a missed opportunity.

b If he will not do this, it will be a missed opportunity.

05
a Instead of taking a taxi, we walked there in order to we can save money.

b Instead of taking a taxi, we walked there so that we could save money.

06
a You don't need to change the poster design unless you want to.

b You don't need to change the poster design though you want to.

07
a Despite he was broke, he refused to get a job.

b Although he was broke, he refused to get a job.

08
a This land is so dry that crops don't grow well.

b This land is too dry for crops not to grow well.

유형별 기출 적용 빈도

유형 01 예시·결과를 나타내는 접속부사	25%	
유형 02 역접·첨가를 나타내는 접속부사	20%	
유형 03 기타 접속부사	25%	
유형 04 통합형	30%	

≫ 출제 포인트
예시, 결과, 역접, 첨가를 나타내는 접속부사의 의미와 쓰임을 묻는 문제가 자주 출제된다.

≫ 정답률 100% Tip
접속부사의 앞뒤에 오는 문장 간의 관계를 파악하여 알맞은 접속부사 고르기

Grammar Point

Point 1 예시·결과를 나타내는 접속부사

예시	for example[instance](예를 들면)
결과	as a result(결과적으로, 그 결과), therefore(그러므로), thus(따라서)

Too much sunlight can cause a lot of problems. For example, it can cause skin cancer.

His novel was a success. As a result, it was made into a movie.

Point 2 역접·첨가를 나타내는 접속부사

역접	however(그러나), though(하지만), yet(하지만), instead(그 대신에), on the other hand(한편으로는, 반면에)
첨가	also(또한), in addition(게다가), besides(게다가), furthermore(더욱이), moreover(더욱이)

Everybody liked Nicole's idea. I had a different idea, though.

The food was delicious. In addition, the service was great.

Point 3 기타 접속부사

대조	in contrast(대조적으로)
요약	in brief(요컨대, 간단히 말해), in conclusion(결론적으로)
재진술	in other words(다시 말해서)
양보	nevertheless, yet, still(그럼에도 불구하고)
기타	otherwise(그렇지 않으면), above all, first of all, most of all(무엇보다도, 우선), finally, at last, in the end(마침내, 결국), in fact(사실은)

She didn't have enough time to practice. Nevertheless, her performance was great.

You'd better take a raincoat. Otherwise, you'll get wet.

✅ 바로 체크

01 Susan tries to save water. (In addition / For example), she takes a shorter shower.

02 Elizabeth started to jog every morning. (However / As a result), she lost 3kg in a week.

03 Lily had a high fever. (Therefore / However), she went to work.

04 Exercise can keep you healthy. (Instead / In addition), it can help you sleep better at night.

05 Jake must be smart. (Still / Otherwise), he wouldn't have got into college.

06 It is important to use your time well. (Above all / Otherwise), make a study plan.

07 Jina is tall. (On the other hand / In other words), her sister is short.

대표유형 01 예시 · 결과를 나타내는 접속부사   출제율 25%

01 다음 빈칸에 들어갈 말로 알맞은 것은?

> Some animals have amazing talents. _____, ants can carry up to 50 times their own body weight.

① However
② Therefore
③ For example
④ In contrast
⑤ On the other hand

02 다음 밑줄 친 부분과 바꿔 쓸 수 있는 것은?

> Most of the evidence was destroyed in the fire. Thus it would be almost impossible to prove her guilty.

① Instead
② Moreover
③ Otherwise
④ Therefore
⑤ Nevertheless

03 다음 글의 빈칸에 알맞은 말을 모두 고르면?

> Some English words came from other languages. _____, the word cafe came from French.

① In addition
② For instance
③ For example
④ As a result
⑤ On the other hand

04 다음 빈칸에 들어갈 말로 가장 알맞은 것은?

> You're just 16 years old. _____, you can't vote.

① For example
② However
③ In brief
④ Therefore
⑤ In addition

05 다음 글의 밑줄 친 부분과 바꿔 쓸 수 있는 접속부사를 세 단어로 쓰시오.

> About 30 years ago, it wasn't easy to own a car because cars were very expensive. Therefore, only the rich could buy them.

_____ _____ _____

06 다음 글의 밑줄 친 ① ~ ⑤ 중 의미상 어색한 것은?

> Rules are ① important in any group. There are many rules ② around us. ③ Without them, people can't ④ get along with others, and there will be a lot of problems. ⑤ However, people have to follow the rules in their group.

07 다음 빈칸에 들어갈 말이 순서대로 바르게 짝지어진 것은?

> • I didn't study hard. _____, I didn't get a good grade.
> • Tommy likes to help people. _____, when he sees someone carrying something heavy, he always gives him or her a hand.

① However – In addition
② Instead – For example
③ Otherwise – As a result
④ Therefore – For instance
⑤ Thus – On the other hand

08 다음 글에서 의미상 어색한 부분을 찾아 바르게 고치시오.

> We can protect the environment in our daily life. Otherwise, we can ride a bike instead of a car.

대표유형 02 역접·첨가를 나타내는 접속부사   출제율 20%

09 다음 빈칸에 들어갈 말로 알맞은 것은?

> George really likes dogs. _____, his mother doesn't allow him to raise a dog.

① However   ② Therefore   ③ Otherwise
④ Besides   ⑤ For example

10 다음 글의 밑줄 친 부분과 바꿔 쓸 수 있는 것은?

> There is a boy I like in my class. His name is Taeho. He is very tall and handsome. In addition, he is kind and smart. I want to be friends with him.

① Instead   ② However   ③ Besides
④ In brief   ⑤ First of all

11 다음 빈칸에 들어갈 말로 알맞은 것은?

> Living in a cold climate can be hard for some people. _____, there are many fun activities to enjoy that they can't do in a warm climate.

① For instance   ② In addition
③ As a result   ④ In other words
⑤ On the other hand

12 다음 우리말과 같은 뜻이 되도록 빈칸에 들어갈 알맞은 말을 주어진 철자로 시작하여 쓰시오.

> 나는 방 청소를 해야 해서 너와 함께 외출할 수가 없어. 게다가 나는 개도 산책시켜야 해.
> → I can't go out with you because I have to clean my room. I_____ a_____, I have to walk the dog.

13 다음 빈칸에 들어갈 말로 알맞은 것을 <u>모두</u> 고르면?

> Most children want a lot of friends. For some kids, _____, one or two friends could be enough.

① yet   ② however   ③ thus
④ in short   ⑤ for example

14 다음 빈칸에 들어갈 말이 순서대로 바르게 짝지어진 것은?

> • Our team lost. It was a great game, _____.
> • He didn't reply. _____, he turned around and left the room.

① though – Instead
② therefore – Moreover
③ for instance – In brief
④ instead – Nevertheless
⑤ otherwise – As a result

15 다음 빈칸에 들어가기에 <u>어색한</u> 것을 <u>모두</u> 고르면?

> I don't want to go swimming today. I'm so tired. _____, it is freezing out there.

① Besides   ② However   ③ Furthermore
④ Thus   ⑤ In addition

16 다음 중 〈보기〉의 밑줄 친 <u>Yet</u>과 쓰임이 같은 것은?

> 보기   Brian got up late and traffic was heavy. <u>Yet</u> he arrived at work on time.

① Haven't you been to London <u>yet</u>?
② We have heard nothing from Jennifer <u>yet</u>.
③ Have you finished your breakfast <u>yet</u>?
④ I didn't receive an e-mail from Ms. Thompson <u>yet</u>.
⑤ I've known Yunmo for only a few years, <u>yet</u> he's my best friend.

17 다음 글의 밑줄 친 부분을 문맥에 맞게 바르게 고치시오. (단, 주어진 철자로 시작할 것)

Joseph sings and dances well. <u>However,</u> he can play the violin very well.

→ M_____

대표유형 03 기타 접속부사 출제율 25%

18 다음 빈칸에 들어갈 말로 알맞은 것은?

You need to work harder. _____, you'll fail the test.

① However ② Instead
③ Above all ④ Otherwise
⑤ Nevertheless

19 다음 우리말과 같도록 빈칸에 들어갈 말로 알맞은 것은?

무엇보다도, 그 여행은 많은 나의 생각을 변화시켰다.
→ _____, the trip changed a lot of my thinking.

① At last ② Above all
③ In contrast ④ For example
⑤ In conclusion

20 다음 빈칸에 들어가기에 <u>어색한</u> 것을 <u>모두</u> 고르면?

Sarah received more than 10 gifts for her birthday. _____, she was not happy.

① Still ② Yet
③ Nevertheless ④ Besides
⑤ For instance

21 다음 빈칸에 알맞은 말을 주어진 철자로 시작하여 쓰시오.

I have a twin brother. He is very talkative and active. I_____ c_____, I am quiet and shy.

[22-23] 다음 빈칸에 들어갈 말로 알맞은 것을 고르시오.

22

I e-mailed Barbara a week ago and I've waited for her reply ever since. _____, I got an e-mail from her today.

① At last ② Instead ③ Besides
④ In contrast ⑤ Otherwise

23

The boss asked her to leave the company. _____, she was fired.

① First of all ② In addition
③ In contrast ④ In other words
⑤ On the other hand

24 다음 글의 밑줄 친 부분과 바꿔 쓸 수 있는 것은?

It's very cold outside. Put your coat on, <u>or</u> you'll get a cold.

① otherwise ② however
③ in short ④ in other words
⑤ on the other hand

25 다음 우리말을 영어로 바꿀 때 <u>어색한</u> 부분을 바르게 고쳐 쓰시오. (단, 주어진 철자로 시작할 것)

비가 세차게 오기 시작했다. 그럼에도 불구하고 아무도 경기장을 떠나지 않았다.
→ It started to rain hard. Furthermore, no one left the stadium.

_____ → N_____

대표유형 01, 02 예시·결과 / 역접·첨가를 나타내는 접속부사 　출제율 25%

01 다음 빈칸에 들어갈 말로 알맞은 것을 <u>모두</u> 고르면?

> Before you travel abroad, you should check your passport and apply for any necessary visas. _____, you'd better learn about the customs, culture, and etiquette of the country you will visit.

① However
② Besides
③ For example
④ In addition
⑤ As a result

02 다음 빈칸에 들어갈 말로 알맞은 것은?

> There have been many leaders in history who have tried to rule the entire world. _____, Alexander the Great wanted to conquer the whole world with his great ambition.

① Therefore
② However
③ In short
④ In contrast
⑤ For example

03 다음 빈칸에 들어갈 말이 순서대로 바르게 짝지어진 것은?

> • Julia didn't like the cap that she bought online. _____, she decided to exchange it for another one.
> • I wanted to see a scary movie. _____, all of my friends wanted to see an action movie.

① However – In addition
② Instead – For example
③ Otherwise – Above all
④ Therefore – However
⑤ Thus – As a result

04 다음 글의 밑줄 친 ① ~ ⑤ 중 <u>어색한</u> 것은?

> My dad ① spends a lot of time ② taking care of the garden. ③ On the other hand, our house has ④ the finest garden ⑤ in town and he is really proud of it.

대표유형 03 기타 접속부사 　출제율 25%

05 다음 밑줄 친 부분과 바꿔 쓸 수 있는 것은?

> Tammy didn't give up and kept running. <u>At last</u>, she took first place in the marathon.

① At least
② In contrast
③ In brief
④ First of all
⑤ In the end

06 다음 밑줄 친 부분의 우리말 뜻이 <u>잘못</u> 짝지어진 것은?

① <u>First of all</u>, I fed the baby. Then I made myself a sandwich. (= 우선)
② It is a long letter, but <u>in brief</u> he says, "No." (= 간단히 말하면)
③ What you said was true. It was, <u>nevertheless</u>, a little unkind. (= 결론적으로)
④ I know the actress really well. <u>In fact</u>, I had dinner with her last week. (= 사실은)
⑤ We were thinking about going to Switzerland, but <u>in the end</u> we went to Austria. (= 결국은)

07 다음 빈칸에 들어갈 말로 알맞은 것은?

> You'd better hurry up. _____, you'll miss the subway and be late for the meeting.

① Otherwise
② Furthermore
③ In contrast
④ For example
⑤ On the other hand

대표유형 04　통합형　　　　　　　　　　출제율 30%

08 다음 글에서 의미상 어색한 부분을 찾아 바르게 고치시오.

> To save energy, you should not use electricity when it is unnecessary. However, turn off your monitor if you're not using it.

09 다음 두 문장이 같은 의미가 되도록 빈칸에 알맞은 말을 주어진 철자로 시작하여 쓰시오.

> Oranges contain a lot of vitamin C; besides, they taste really great.
> = Oranges contain a lot of vitamin C; i_____ a_____, they taste really great.

10 다음 글의 빈칸에 들어갈 알맞은 말을 세 단어로 쓰시오.

> The subway system in Seoul is very well-organized, so you can go anywhere you want. _____ _____ _____,(그 결과) visitors to Seoul usually travel by subway.

11 다음 우리말과 같은 뜻이 되도록 빈칸에 알맞은 말을 주어진 철자로 시작하여 쓰시오.

> 나는 학교 버스를 놓쳤다. 하지만 Jenny의 엄마께서 나를 학교까지 태워 주셨다.
> → I missed the school bus. Jenny's mom gave me a ride to the school, t_____.

12 다음 우리말을 영어로 옮긴 문장에서 어색한 부분을 찾아 바르게 고쳐 쓰시오.

> 치과에 가라. 그렇지 않으면 너의 치통은 더 악화될 것이다.
> → Go see a dentist. Moreover, your toothache will get worse.

13 다음 우리말과 같은 뜻이 되도록 빈칸에 알맞은 말을 주어진 철자로 시작하여 쓰시오.

> 우리는 오랫동안 계속해서 이야기를 나누었다. 마침내 우리는 결론에 도달했다.
> → We talked and talked for a long time. F_____, we've reached the conclusion.
> = We talked and talked for a long time. A_____ l_____, we've reached the conclusion.
> = We talked and talked for a long time. I_____ t_____ e_____, we've reached the conclusion.

14 다음 문장을 글의 흐름에 맞게 바르게 배열하시오.

> (A) However, I couldn't agree with them. I got the worst score.
> (B) Yura, Jinho and I were discussing the exam.
> (C) Yura and Jinho said it was still easier, compared to the last one.

_____ – _____ – _____

신유형
15 다음 영영풀이에 해당하는 접속부사를 주어진 철자로 시작하여 쓰시오.

> *adv.* used to introduce the logical result of something that has just been mentioned

> The singer can't sing very well. T_____, it's not surprising that she was chosen as the Worst Singer of the Year.

대표유형 01, 02 | 예시·결과 / 역접·첨가를 나타내는 접속부사 | 출제율 25%

01 다음 빈칸에 들어갈 말로 알맞은 것은?

> Positive thinking will lead us to success in life. _____, negative thinking will lead us to failure.

① As a result
② In conclusion
③ First of all
④ For instance
⑤ On the other hand

02 다음 문장에 이어질 말을 흐름에 맞게 배열한 것은?

> Last weekend my friends and I tried to fly to New York because we wanted to see our favorite band perform there.
> (A) As a result, all flights were canceled.
> (B) Therefore, we had to sleep at the airport overnight.
> (C) However, storms passed through the region.
> (D) In addition, all of the hotels near the airport were full.

① (A)–(C)–(B)–(D)
② (B)–(C)–(D)–(A)
③ (B)–(D)–(A)–(C)
④ (C)–(A)–(B)–(D)
⑤ (C)–(A)–(D)–(B)

03 다음 빈칸에 However[however]가 들어가기에 어색한 것은?

① Sharon has never been to Spain. _____, she's fluent in Spanish.
② We have a growing population. _____, the demand for food is increasing.
③ Losing at games doesn't matter to some people. Other people, _____, can't stand it.
④ Alex laughed loudly to draw people's attention. _____, no one cared about him.
⑤ The war between the two countries ended. _____, the peace did not last long.

04 다음 문장에 이어질 말로 가장 알맞은 것은?

> Mike and Judy had eaten nothing all day.

① Therefore, they were very hungry.
② In brief, they had a delicious breakfast.
③ However, they couldn't go a step further.
④ In other words, they ate three meals a day.
⑤ For example, they tried to eat healthy food.

대표유형 04 | 통합형 | 출제율 30%

05 다음 밑줄 친 부분과 바꿔 쓸 수 있는 것은?

> Edward is a very smart club leader. <u>Yet</u> most club members don't support him.

① Therefore
② Finally
③ Besides
④ Furthermore
⑤ Nevertheless

06 다음 빈칸에 알맞은 말이 순서대로 짝지어진 것은?

> • Annie is good at science and math. She's not very good at art, _____.
> • People were worrying that the rain would not stop. _____, it stopped on the fifth day.

① instead – In addition
② in brief – As a result
③ as a result – Still
④ though – At last
⑤ above all – In fact

07 〈보기〉의 밑줄 친 Still과 같은 의미로 쓰인 것은?

> 보기 I hadn't seen David for 20 years. <u>Still</u>, I recognized him immediately when I saw him.

① <u>Still</u> waters run deep.
② I woke up and felt like I was <u>still</u> dreaming.
③ Some people think paper books are <u>still</u> better than e-books.
④ It's important to stay <u>still</u> while the MRI scan is running.
⑤ He'll probably say, "No." <u>Still</u>, it's worth asking.

08 다음 우리말과 같은 뜻이 되도록 빈칸에 알맞은 말을 쓰시오.

> 다시 말해서, 건강을 위해 할 가장 중요한 일은 규칙적으로 운동하는 것이다.
> → _____ _____ _____ , the most important thing to do for good health is exercising regularly.

[09-10] 다음 글의 빈칸에 알맞은 말을 주어진 철자로 시작하여 쓰시오.

09
> Some gestures can mean different things in different cultures. F_____ i_____, the OK gesture means money in some countries.

10
> Jessica has few friends to help her. I_____ c_____, Peter has a lot of friends to help him.

11 다음 두 문장이 같은 의미가 되도록 바꿔 쓸 때 <u>어색한</u> 부분을 찾아 바르게 고쳐 쓰시오.

> The program is very easy and simple, so you can learn fast.
> → The program is very easy and simple, and yet, you can learn fast.

12 다음 문장의 밑줄 친 부분이 의미하는 바를 한 단어로 바꿔 쓰시오.

> We hope the weather gets better. <u>If it doesn't get better</u>, we'll have to cancel the picnic.
> → We hope the weather gets better. _____ , we'll have to cancel the picnic.

13 다음 두 문장이 같은 의미가 되도록 빈칸에 알맞은 말을 쓰시오.

> The part-time job wasn't very satisfying. It was well-paying, though.
> = The part-time job wasn't very satisfying. _____ _____ _____ _____ , it was well-paying.

신유형
14 다음 영영풀이에 해당하는 접속부사를 주어진 철자로 시작하여 쓰시오.

> *adv.* used to introduce information that adds to or supports what has previously been said

> Traveling by plane is tiring. M_____ , it is generally expensive.

15 〈보기〉에서 알맞은 접속부사를 골라 두 문장을 다시 쓰시오. (단, 접속부사는 문장의 맨 앞에 쓰고 두 문장으로 쓸 것)

> 보기 nevertheless   besides   as a result

> The school was old and badly heated. It was too far from their house.
> → _____
> _____

01 다음 빈칸에 알맞은 말이 순서대로 짝지어진 것은?

- His essay was badly organized. _____, it had some brilliant ideas.
- Peter had energy and enthusiasm. _____ he has a sense of humor.
- The violin is not easy to play. _____, it is one of the most difficult musical instruments.

① Furthermore – Besides – In fact
② Therefore – Otherwise – In contrast
③ Nevertheless – Besides – In fact
④ Therefore – Above all – At last
⑤ Nevertheless – Otherwise – In contrast

02 다음 빈칸에 공통으로 들어갈 말로 알맞은 것은?

- There's a possibility that he'll recover _____ the doctors can't say for sure.
- Maria and I were close friends in high school. I haven't seen her for ages, _____.

① besides   ② however   ③ nevertheles
④ finally   ⑤ though

03 다음 중 밑줄 친 부분의 쓰임이 어색한 것끼리 묶은 것은?

ⓐ The power was out in the whole office building. For example, they could not get any work done.
ⓑ Tropical storms are common in the Philippines. In conclusion, they are rare in Canada.
ⓒ I thought that I had made a right decision. Still, I felt guilty about what happened.
ⓓ His parents lent him some money. Otherwise, he couldn't have afforded the car.
ⓔ Books and clothes were all over the floor. In other words, Joe's room was a mess.

① ⓐ, ⓑ   ② ⓐ, ⓔ   ③ ⓐ, ⓑ, ⓓ
④ ⓑ, ⓒ, ⓓ   ⑤ ⓒ, ⓓ, ⓔ

04 〈보기〉에서 알맞은 접속부사를 골라 두 문장을 다시 쓰시오. (단, 접속부사는 문장의 맨 앞에 쓰고 두 문장으로 쓸 것)

보기   for instance   moreover   nevertheless

(1) She got lost. Her car broke down.
→ _____
_____

(2) They thought that the plan sounded risky. They were willing to try.
→ _____
_____

(3) There are some foods that dogs cannot have. Chocolate is harmful to dogs.
→ _____
_____

05 〈보기〉에서 알맞은 접속부사를 골라 빈칸에 각각 쓰시오. (단, 중복 사용 불가)

보기   as a result   also
       for example   however

Most people are familiar with air, water, and land pollution. _____, few people know that light pollution is as serious as other forms of pollution. According to one survey, about 80% of the world's population lives under skies that are not dark enough at night. _____, people often suffer from disturbed sleep, which makes them feel tired all through the day. Wildlife is threatened by light pollution, too. _____, millions of birds that migrate at night become confused by the light coming from the windows of tall buildings and end up dying after hitting buildings. _____, many baby sea turtles die because artificial light draws them away from the ocean.

01
a   The sun was shining, yet it was quite cold.

b   The sun was shining, besides it was quite cold.

02
a   We couldn't raise funds on time. Nevertheless, we gave up the project.

b   We couldn't raise funds on time. Therefore, we gave up the project.

03
a   These sneakers are expensive. Besides, they are too small.

b   These sneakers are expensive. However, they are too small.

04
a   I tried to keep calm. Nevertheless, my heart wouldn't stop beating.

b   I tried to keep calm. As a result, my heart wouldn't stop beating.

05
a   Nate wants to be a B-boy. In brief, his parents won't allow him to dance.

b   Nate wants to be a B-boy. His parents won't allow him to dance, though.

06
a   Mike tried to solve the problem, but he couldn't. In the end, he decided to ask Paul for help.

b   Mike tried to solve the problem, but he couldn't. For instance, he decided to ask Paul for help.

07
a   You have to go now, thus you'll be late for the club meeting.

b   You have to go now, otherwise you'll be late for the club meeting.

08
a   A big earthquake happened. As a result, the village was destroyed.

b   A big earthquake happened. Nevertheless, the village was destroyed.

유형별 기출 적용 빈도

유형 01 원급 비교   **40%**

유형 02 비교급 비교   **60%**

≫ 출제 포인트

원급 비교와 비교급 비교의 여러 가지 형태를 묻는 문제가 많이 출제되고, 비교급 강조에 관한 문제도 자주 출제된다.

≫ 정답률 100% Tip

1 「A ~ not as[so]+원급+as B」
  = 「A ~ less+원급+than B」
  = 「B ~ 비교급+than A」

Grammar Point

Point 1 원급 비교

as+형용사/부사의 원급+as	~만큼 …한/하게
as+원급+as possible = as+원급+as+주어+can[could]	가능한 한 ~한/하게
배수사+as+원급+as (*배수사: half, twice, three times 등)	… 배만큼 ~한/하게

Health is as important as money.

He runs as fast as possible. (= He runs as fast as he can.)

Is the full moon twice as bright as the half moon?

주의 「배수사+as+원급+as」는 「배수사+비교급+than」으로 쓸 수 있는데, 이때 twice와 half는 쓸 수 없다.

Point 2 비교급 비교

형용사/부사의 비교급+than	~보다 더 …한/하게
less+원급+than	~보다 덜 …한/하게
비교급+and+비교급	점점 더 ~한
the+비교급 ~, the+비교급 …	~할수록 더 …하다
the+비교급+of the two	둘 중에서 더 ~한

주의 원급은 앞에 very를 써서 강조하고, 비교급은 앞에 much, far, still, a lot, even 등을 써서 강조한다.

Rachel is four years older than me.

He is less kind than his brother.

He is much taller than you.

The cows ate more and more grass.

The more you try, the more you get.

= As you try more, you get more.

This table is the cheaper of the two.

✅ 바로 체크

01 Julie is as (tall / taller) as Tom.

02 I ate as much as I (can / could).

03 This car is (two / twice) as expensive as that car.

04 Baseball is as popular (as / than) soccer.

05 My new bag is (big / bigger) than my old one.

06 He is less (wise / wiser) than me.

07 It looks (much / less) more delicious than mine.

08 The faster, (better / the better).

09 I moved closer (and / than) closer to the cat.

10 The lower prices are, (more / the more) people like them.

대표유형 01 원급 비교   출제율 40%

01 다음 우리말을 영어로 바르게 옮긴 것은?

> 과학은 수학만큼 어렵다.

① Science is difficult as math.
② Science is as difficult as math.
③ Science is not as difficult as math.
④ Math is more difficult than science.
⑤ Math is as more difficult as science.

02 다음 빈칸에 들어갈 말로 알맞은 것은?

> Chris is not as _____ as Joseph.

① slower   ② taller
③ hungry   ④ older
⑤ more handsome

03 다음 빈칸에 공통으로 알맞은 것은?

> • I let my son play as much _____ he wants.
> • Ed is as friendly _____ his brother.

① than   ② as   ③ then
④ so   ⑤ and

04 다음 중 밑줄 친 부분이 어법상 어색한 것은?

① He cooks as well as his wife.
② I am not as tired as my sister.
③ This pen is as light as a feather.
④ Is this as more important as that?
⑤ The book was not as interesting as I expected.

05 다음 우리말과 같도록 빈칸에 알맞은 말을 쓰시오.

> 저 노트북은 내 노트북만큼 비싸다. (expensive)
> → That laptop is _____ my laptop.

06 다음 밑줄 친 부분을 어법에 맞게 고쳐 쓰시오.

> Sally wants a dog as <u>cuter</u> as mine.

07 다음 우리말을 영어로 바르게 옮긴 것은?

> 날씨가 전처럼 덥지는 않다.

① The weather is not so hot so before.
② The weather is not as hot so before.
③ The weather is not hot as before.
④ The weather is not so hot as before.
⑤ The weather is not so hotter as before.

08 다음 밑줄 친 부분과 바꿔 쓸 수 있는 것은?

> Please reply as soon <u>as possible</u>.

① as you did   ② as you are
③ as you can   ④ as you do
⑤ as she can

09 다음 우리말과 같도록 할 때 빈칸에 알맞은 것은? (2개)

> 이 책상은 내 것보다 두 배 더 크다.
> → This desk is _____ as large as mine.

① two   ② twice   ③ second
④ half   ⑤ two times

10 다음 문장에서 어법상 <u>어색한</u> 부분을 찾아 바르게 고쳐 쓰시오.

> Speak as quiet as possible in the library.

11 다음 괄호 안의 단어를 바르게 배열한 것은?

> Raise your arms (can, as, you, as, high).

① you can as high as
② as can high as you
③ as you can high as
④ as you can as high
⑤ as high as you can

대표유형 02 비교급 비교　　　　　　　출제율 60%

12 다음 빈칸에 들어갈 말로 알맞은 것은?

> Her gift is _____ to me than anything else.

① valuable　　　　② happiest
③ expensive　　　④ useless
⑤ more special

13 다음 문장에서 어법상 <u>어색한</u> 부분을 찾아 바르게 고쳐 쓰시오.

> His new album is popularer than the previous one.

---

14 다음 문장 중 어법상 <u>어색한</u> 것은?

① We got very busier.
② She is lazier than before.
③ He is less generous than her.
④ This tool is more helpful than that one.
⑤ The movie is more boring than the book.

15 다음 빈칸에 공통으로 알맞은 말을 주어진 철자로 시작하여 쓰시오.

> • Tim is m_____ creative than Sam.
> • I have m_____ books than him.

16 다음 그림을 보고, <보기>를 참고하여 문장을 완성하시오.

Judy　Annie　Monica

> 보기　Monica is shorter than Judy.

(1) Judy is _____ Annie.

(2) Annie is _____ Monica.

17 다음 빈칸에 들어갈 말로 어색한 것은?

> The _____, the better.

① happier　　② sooner　　③ more
④ slow　　　⑤ less

18 다음 빈칸에 공통으로 알맞은 말을 쓰시오. (단, 대·소문자 무시)

> • _____ more you have, _____ more you want.
> • He is _____ younger of the two.

19 다음 우리말을 영어로 바르게 옮긴 것은?

> 철은 나무보다 더 단단하다.

① Iron is hard than wood.
② Wood is harder than iron.
③ Iron is harder than wood.
④ Iron is harder as wood.
⑤ Iron is more hard than wood.

20 다음 두 문장의 의미가 같을 때 빈칸에 알맞은 말을 쓰시오.

> As you climb higher, it is colder.
> = The _____ you climb, the _____ it is.

21 다음 주어진 단어를 바르게 배열한 것은?

> stronger, Daniel, is, her, than, much

① Her is much stronger than Daniel.
② Daniel is stronger much than her.
③ Daniel is stronger than her much.
④ Her is stronger much than Daniel.
⑤ Daniel is much stronger than her.

22 다음 밑줄 친 부분을 어법에 맞게 고쳐 쓰시오.

> Samuel is <u>careful</u> than his rival.

23 다음 빈칸에 들어갈 말로 어색한 것은?

> Ben is _____ smarter than his sister.

① far   ② much   ③ very
④ even   ⑤ a lot

24 다음 우리말과 같도록 빈칸에 공통으로 알맞은 말을 쓰시오.

> 풍선이 점점 더 커지고 있다. (big)
> → The balloon is getting _____ and _____.

25 다음 괄호 안의 단어를 바르게 배열하여 문장을 완성하시오.

> The Earth is (larger, four, than, times) the moon.
> → The Earth is _____ the moon.

대표유형 01 원급 비교   출제율 40%

01 다음 대화의 빈칸에 알맞은 것은?

> **A** Is Ron _____ Harry?
> **B** Yes, they are the same age.

① so old as
② as old as
③ older than
④ less old than
⑤ not as old as

---

02 다음 대화의 밑줄 친 ① ~ ⑤ 중 어법상 어색한 것은?

> **A** Who is ① faster, Edward ② or Stephen?
> **B** Edward. Stephen is ③ not as ④ faster ⑤ as Edward.

---

03 다음 우리말을 영어로 바르게 옮긴 것은?

> 그녀의 책은 내 것보다 세 배 더 두껍다.

① Her book is three times as thick as me.
② Her book is three times as thicker as mine.
③ Her book is third times as thick as mine.
④ Her book is as third times thick as mine.
⑤ Her book is three times as thick as mine.

---

04 다음 빈칸에 들어갈 말로 알맞은 것은?

> Everyone wants to stay heathy _____ possible.

① as many as
② as soon as
③ as long as
④ as little as
⑤ as well as

대표유형 02 비교급 비교   출제율 60%

05 다음 글에서 밑줄 친 단어의 형태로 알맞은 것끼리 바르게 짝지은 것은?

> Rachel has a lovely sister. Her sister is two years <u>old</u> than her. She is much <u>tall</u> than Rachel.

① old – taller
② old – tall
③ older – taller
④ older – more tall
⑤ more old – taller

통합형

06 다음 문장과 의미가 가장 가까운 것은?

> Bob is more diligent than Teddy.

① Teddy is as diligent as Bob.
② Teddy is not as diligent as Bob.
③ Bob is not as diligent as Teddy.
④ Bob is less diligent than Teddy.
⑤ Teddy is twice as diligent as Bob.

---

07 다음 우리말을 영어로 바르게 옮긴 것은?

> 열심히 일할수록, 너는 더 많이 얻을 수 있다.

① You work harder, the more you can get.
② The hard you work, the more you can get.
③ The harder you work, you can get more.
④ The harder you work, more you can get.
⑤ The harder you work, the more you can get.

대표유형 01 원급 비교   출제율 40%

08 다음 두 문장이 같은 뜻이 되도록 할 때 빈칸에 알맞은 말을 쓰시오.

> Anne cried out to me as loudly as possible.
> = Anne cried out to me as loudly as _____ _____.

≫ 실전 Tip 주절의 동사 cried의 시제에 맞춰 과거형을 쓰는 것에 유의한다.

통합형

09 다음 두 문장이 의미가 통하도록 빈칸에 알맞은 말을 쓰시오.

> My brother's room is not as small as my room.
> → My room is _____ _____ my brother's room.

대표유형 02 비교급 비교   출제율 60%

10 다음 우리말과 같도록 괄호 안의 단어를 이용하여 빈칸에 알맞은 말을 쓰시오.

> 그는 나보다 더 조심스럽게 운전했다. (carefully)
> → He drove _____ _____ _____ _____.

11 괄호 안의 단어를 이용하여 빈칸에 공통으로 알맞은 말을 쓰시오.

> There are _____ and _____ tourists visiting Korea every year. (many)

12 다음 그림을 보고, 그림의 내용과 일치하도록 대화의 빈칸에 알맞은 말을 쓰시오.

> **A** Was the movie theater crowded?
> **B** No, it was _____ _____ _____ I had thought.

13 다음 문장과 의미가 통하도록 주어진 〈조건〉에 맞게 바꿔 쓰시오.

> As I earn more, I spend more.
> → _____ _____ I _____, _____ _____ I _____.

> [조건] 「the+비교급 ~, the+비교급 …」을 쓸 것

14 다음 우리말과 같도록 괄호 안의 표현을 바르게 배열하시오.

> 날씨가 작년 봄보다 훨씬 더 따뜻하다. (than, the weather, last, warmer, is, spring, much)
>
> → _____

15 다음 대화의 밑줄 친 ⓐ, ⓑ를 알맞은 형태로 고쳐 쓰시오.

> **A** Is this book ⓐ expensive than that one?
> **B** Yes, this is 20,000 won and that is only 3,000 won.
> **A** Oh, I see. That book is much ⓑ cheap than this one.

ⓐ _____   ⓑ _____

대표유형 01 원급 비교   출제율 40%

01 다음 대화가 자연스럽도록 빈칸에 알맞은 것은?

> **A** Ashley is honest. Is her sister honest, too?
> **B** Yes, _____ Ashley.

① her sister is as honest so
② her sister is so honest than
③ her sister is as honest as
④ her sister is not as honest as
⑤ her sister is as more honest than

02 다음 우리말을 영어로 옮긴 것 중 <u>어색한</u> 것은?

① 나는 너보다 두 배 많은 모자를 가지고 있다.
   → I have twice as many caps as you do.
② 그는 예전만큼 자주 극장에 가지 않는다.
   → He doesn't go to the movies as often as he used to.
③ 그것은 나무늘보처럼 느리게 움직였다.
   → It moved as slow as a sloth.
④ 일본은 러시아만큼 크지 않다.
   → Japan is less large than Russia.
⑤ 가능한 한 일찍 미래의 목표를 설정해라.
   → Set your future goals as early as can.

대표유형 02 비교급 비교   출제율 60%

03 다음 글의 빈칸에 알맞은 말을 순서대로 바르게 짝지은 것은?

> Leonard was a true friend. He helped me _____ than anybody did. When I called him, he always came to me _____ than anyone else.

① much – fast
② more – faster
③ much – faster
④ the more – faster
⑤ the more – the faster

04 다음 문장의 빈칸에 들어갈 말이 나머지 넷과 <u>다른</u> 것은?

① He got _____ better than before.
② I was _____ taller than my sister.
③ Jacob is _____ weaker than his brother.
④ Her daughter is _____ smart that people consider her a genius.
⑤ The station was _____ nearer than I had thought.

통합형
05 다음 중 어법상 <u>어색한</u> 문장의 개수는?

> ⓐ Who is the better of the two?
> ⓑ The more nervous you get, the many mistakes you make.
> ⓒ She doesn't speak Spanish so fluently as her brother.
> ⓓ This computer works two times slower than that one.

① 1개 ② 2개 ③ 3개 ④ 4개 ⑤ 없음

06 다음 빈칸에 들어갈 말로 알맞은 것은?

> Chris studied _____ and his grades became worse and worse.

① more and more
② harder and harder
③ less and less
④ less hard and hard
⑤ more and more hard

07 다음 중 밑줄 친 부분의 쓰임이 나머지 넷과 <u>다른</u> 것은?

① He needs <u>much</u> more help.
② Adam had <u>much</u> fun with his friends.
③ There is <u>much</u> difference between them.
④ You can make <u>much</u> money if you work hard.
⑤ Parents have to pay <u>much</u> attention to their children.

대표유형 01 원급 비교   출제율 40%

08 다음 우리말을 괄호 안의 표현을 이용하여 영작하시오.

> 내 가방은 네 것만큼 무겁지 않다.
> (my bag, as, heavy)
>
> → _____

09 다음 우리말에 맞게 괄호 안의 표현 중에서 필요 <u>없는</u> 단어를 제외한 나머지를 바르게 배열하시오.

> 시간은 금만큼 소중하다.
> (gold, more, precious, as, is, the, time, as)

→ _____

[10-11] 다음 문장과 의미가 통하도록 빈칸에 알맞은 말을 쓰시오.

10

> Art class is three times as long as music class.

→ Art class is _____ _____ _____
_____ music class.

11

> I will call you as soon as possible.

→ I will call you _____ _____ _____
_____ _____ .

대표유형 02 비교급 비교   출제율 60%

12 다음 대화의 밑줄 친 우리말을 괄호 안의 단어를 이용하여 영작하시오.

> **A** Who is more intelligent, Peter or Matt?
> **B** <u>Peter가 Matt보다 훨씬 더 총명해.</u> (much)

→ _____

13 다음 두 문장이 같은 의미가 되도록 빈칸에 알맞은 말을 쓰시오.

> He is three years younger than me.
> = I am _____ him.

신유형

[14-15] 다음 〈보기〉를 참고하여 주어진 대답에 알맞은 질문을 쓰시오.

> 보기   **A** Is he more friendly than before?
> **B** Yes, he is more friendly than before.

14

> **A** _____
> **B** No, she is not more cheerful than her brother.

15

> **A** _____
> **B** Yes, he cooks better than his wife.

01 다음 중 밑줄 친 부분의 쓰임이 나머지 넷과 <u>다른</u> 것은?

① Do you need <u>more</u> water?
② Ellie has <u>more</u> than enough.
③ He has <u>more</u> experience than me.
④ I had to spend <u>more</u> time fixing the machine.
⑤ We bought <u>more</u> bread than we needed.

신유형
02 다음 중 어법상 어색한 부분을 찾아 바르게 고친 것은?

> ⓐ They became much and much excited.
> ⓑ The population of India is as twice large as that of your country.
> ⓒ She hurried to the office as quickly as she can.

① ⓐ much and much → many and many
② ⓐ much and much excited → more excited and more excited
③ ⓑ as twice large as → as two times large as
④ ⓑ that of your country → your country
⑤ ⓒ can → could

03 다음 우리말을 〈조건〉에 맞게 영작하시오.

> 나이가 들수록, 너는 더 현명해질 것이다.

> [조건] **1.** old, get, wise, become을 사용할 것
> **2.** 9단어의 완전한 문장으로 쓸 것

→ _____

04 다음 중 빈칸에 들어갈 말로 알맞은 것을 <u>모두</u> 고르면?

> Thanks to man-made satellites, the world is becoming a _____ place.

① even smaller   ② a lot smaller
③ still smaller   ④ very much smaller
⑤ much smaller

05 다음 표를 보고, 대화의 빈칸을 각각 완성하시오. (단, 완전한 문장으로 쓸 것)

	Height	Weight	Score
Aaron	170cm	58kg	84
Lisa	168cm	54kg	95
Edward	174cm	64kg	92

> **A** Who is taller, Aaron or Edward?
> **B** (1) _____
> **A** Who is heavier, Lisa or Edward?
> **B** (2) _____
> **A** Who got a higher score, Aaron or Lisa?
> **B** (3) _____

06 다음 〈보기〉와 같이 자신과 다른 친구를 비교하는 문장을 다섯 개 쓰시오.

> 보기 • I am as tall as Bora.
> • Inho has more books than me.

(1) _____
(2) _____
(3) _____
(4) _____
(5) _____

01
a　The new machine is not so useful as the old one.

b　The new machine is not so useful than the old one.

02
a　You should walk as fast as you do.

b　You should walk as fast as you can.

03
a　This box is three times heavy than that one.

b　This box is three times as heavy as that one.

04
a　Steve is more generous than his brother.

b　Steve is much generous than his brother.

05
a　This jacket is little comfortable than that coat.

b　This jacket is less comfortable than that coat.

06
a　This mountain is very higher than you think.

b　This mountain is much higher than you think.

07
a　The weather grew cold and cold.

b　The weather grew colder and colder.

08
a　The faster he drives, more nervous I become.

b　The faster he drives, the more nervous I become.

최상급 비교

유형별 기출 적용 빈도

유형 01   최상급 비교   40%

유형 02   원급과 비교급을 이용한 최상급 표현   60%

Grammar Point

Point 1   최상급 비교

최상급은 형용사나 부사의 원급에 -(e)st를 붙이거나 most를 써서 '가장 ~한'을 나타낸다.

the+최상급 ~+in+장소/집단	…에서 가장 ~한
the+최상급 ~+of+복수 명사	… 중에서 가장 ~한
one of the+최상급+복수 명사	가장 ~한 … 중 하나
the+최상급+명사(+that)+주어+ have ever+과거분사	지금까지 …한 것 중 가장 ~한

What is the most important thing in your life?
This building is the highest of all.
Michael is one of the most famous singers in the world.
Prague is the most beautiful city (that) I have ever seen.

Point 2   원급과 비교급을 이용한 최상급 표현

No (other)+명사 ~+as+원급+as	어떤 –도 …만큼 ~하지 않은
No (other)+명사 ~+비교급+than	어떤 –도 …보다 더 ~하지 않은
비교급+than any other+단수 명사	다른 어떤 …보다 더 ~한
비교급+than all the other+복수 명사	다른 모든 …보다 더 ~한

Seoul is the largest city in Korea.
= No other city is as large as Seoul in Korea.
= No other city is larger than Seoul in Korea.
= Seoul is larger than any other city in Korea.
= Seoul is larger than all the other cities in Korea.

주의 「There is nothing+비교급+than」: ~보다 더 …한 것은 없다
There is nothing more important than your health.
= Nothing is more important than your health.

바로 체크

01 He is the (taller / tallest) of all the students.

02 Sue is the prettiest girl (in / of) her class.

03 Nobody is as old (as / than) him.

04 Nobody is (smart / smarter) than me.

05 He is (faster / the fastest) than anybody else.

06 This is one of the best (park / parks) in Korea.

07 Bill is (richer / the richest) man that I have ever met.

08 Harry is the happiest (between / of) all.

09 (No / Any) other dancer is as unique as her.

10 Andy Warhol is one of the most well-known (artist / artists) in the world.

대표유형 01 최상급 비교   출제율 40%

01 다음 빈칸에 들어갈 말로 알맞은 것은?

> The science test was the most difficult _____ all the tests.

① to   ② for   ③ of   ④ in   ⑤ by

02 다음 우리말과 같도록 밑줄 친 단어의 형태를 바르게 고치시오.

> 이것은 내가 지금까지 맛본 것 중 가장 신 것이다.
> → This is the <u>sour</u> thing that I have ever tasted.

03 다음 빈칸에 알맞은 말을 바르게 짝지은 것은?

> • She is the eldest daughter _____ her family.
> • That is the most expensive chair _____ all.

① on – of   ② of – with   ③ of – on
④ in – of   ⑤ in – with

04 다음 그림을 보고, 〈보기〉와 같이 최상급을 이용한 문장을 완성하시오.

Sam   Paul   Greg
(13세, 52kg) (14세, 54kg) (13세, 60kg)

| 보기 | Sam is the shortest of the three. |

(1) Paul is _____ .
(2) Greg is _____ .

05 다음 우리말과 같도록 빈칸에 알맞은 말을 쓰시오.

> 그는 그의 생애 최악의 결정을 했다.
> → He made _____ _____ decision of his life.

06 다음 밑줄 친 부분 중 어법상 어색한 것은?

① What do you like <u>most</u>?
② Sam is <u>the oldest</u> of the six.
③ She has <u>the most beautiful</u> smile.
④ The largest city <u>in Canada</u> is Toronto.
⑤ He is one of the <u>greatest scientist</u> of all time.

≫ 실전 Tip 부사의 최상급은 the를 쓰지 않는다.

07 다음 중 표의 내용과 일치하지 <u>않는</u> 것은?

제품명	KN-1	KN-2	KN-3
가격	$20	$30	$40
인기도	★★	★★★	★

① KN-1 is the most cheapest of the three.
② KN-2 is the least popular of the three.
③ KN-3 is the most expensive of the three.
④ KN-3 is twice as expensive as KN-1.
⑤ KN-2 is cheaper than KN-3.

08 다음 우리말과 같도록 괄호 안의 표현을 이용하여 빈칸에 알맞은 말을 쓰시오.

> 이것은 내가 읽은 최고의 소설이다. (good, read)
> → This is _____ _____ novel that I _____ ever _____ .

09 다음 빈칸에 들어갈 말로 어색한 것은?

> Skydiving is the most _____ experience that I have ever had.

① extreme　　② wonderful　　③ best
④ fantastic　　⑤ exciting

10 다음 중 빈칸에 들어갈 말이 나머지 넷과 다른 것은?
(단, 대·소문자는 무시)

① _____ of them are Europeans.
② This is the _____ interesting movie.
③ I visited the _____ beautiful lake there.
④ I think love is _____ important than money.
⑤ He is the _____ friendly person in this town.

11 다음 우리말과 같도록 할 때 빈칸에 알맞은 것은?

> 그는 모든 학생들 중에서 가장 어리다.
> → He is the _____.

① youngest of all the student
② youngest of all the students
③ most young of all the students
④ youngest in all the students
⑤ youngest in all the student

대표유형 02　원급과 비교급을 이용한 최상급 표현　　출제율 60%

12 다음 두 문장의 의미가 같도록 할 때 빈칸에 알맞은 것은?

> Nothing here is as light as this bag.
> = This bag is the _____ one here.

① light　　② lighter　　③ lightest
④ heavy　　⑤ heaviest

[13-14] 다음 두 문장의 의미가 같도록 빈칸에 알맞은 말을 쓰시오.

13

> Randy is the strongest player on the team.
> = No player on the team is _____ _____ Randy.

14

> Mt. Everest is the highest mountain in the world.
> = No mountain in the world is _____ _____ Mt. Everest.

15 다음 빈칸에 공통으로 들어갈 말로 알맞은 것은? (단, 대·소문자 무시)

> There is _____ more valuable than happiness.
> = _____ is more valuable than happiness.

① no　　② much　　③ one
④ not all　　⑤ nothing

16 다음 두 문장의 의미가 같도록 빈칸에 알맞은 것끼리 짝지어진 것은?

> Nobody can sing _____ than Julia.
> = Nobody can sing as _____ as Julia.

① well – good　　② better – well
③ better – good　　④ more – well
⑤ more – good

17 다음 단어를 바르게 배열하여 문장을 완성하시오.

> is, brave, as, nobody, as

→ _____ him.

[18-19] 다음 우리말을 영어로 옮길 때 빈칸에 알맞은 것을 고르시오.

18
> 어떤 것도 게임하는 것만큼 흥미롭지 않다.
> → Nothing is _____.

① interesting as playing games
② interesting than playing games
③ less interesting than playing games
④ most interesting than playing games
⑤ as interesting as playing games

19
> 물리학은 다른 어떤 과목보다 더 어렵다.
> → Physics is _____.

① most difficult subject
② more difficult than any other subject
③ more difficult than any other subjects
④ more difficult than all the other subject
⑤ the most difficult than any other subject

20 다음 두 문장의 의미가 같도록 할 때 빈칸에 알맞은 것은?

> Nick is the wisest man in his family.
> = No one in his family is _____ Nick.

① wise than
② wise as
③ as wiser as
④ as wise as
⑤ not as wise as

21 다음 문장 중 어법상 어색한 것은?

① Nobody can't speak English as fluently as I.
② Nothing is as useful as this app.
③ No one has as many books as he does.
④ You are the most important person to me.
⑤ He is the best writer that I've ever known.

22 다음 빈칸에 알맞은 말을 바르게 짝지은 것은?

> • No _____ star is as large as the sun.
> • Luke plays the drums better than _____ other drummer.

① other – all
② one – all
③ other – any
④ thing – any
⑤ one – any

신유형
23 다음 우리말을 영어로 옮길 때 ⓐ~ⓔ에 들어갈 말이 바르게 짝지어진 것은?

> 그녀에게 요리하는 것보다 더 쉬운 것은 없다.
> → There ___ⓐ___ ___ⓑ___ ___ⓒ___ ___ⓓ___ ___ⓔ___ for her.

① ⓐ be
② ⓑ no
③ ⓒ easier
④ ⓓ as
⑤ ⓔ cook

24 다음 단어들로 문장을 만들 때 네 번째로 오는 것은?

① bullying
② worse
③ nothing
④ than
⑤ is

25 다음 우리말과 같도록 괄호 안의 단어를 바르게 배열하여 문장을 완성하시오.

> Ted는 다른 어떤 소년보다 더 높이 점프한다.
> (other, any, higher, boy, than)

→ Ted jumps _____.

대표유형 01 최상급 비교 　　　　　　　　출제율 40%

01 다음 문장 중 어법상 <u>어색한</u> 것은?

① Brian works hardest in his office.
② I like music best of all the subjects.
③ The Pacific is the deepest ocean in the world.
④ February is the shortest of the months.
⑤ One of the most beautiful countries are Spain.

>> 실전 Tip 부사의 최상급 앞에는 the를 쓰지 않는다.

02 다음 대화의 빈칸에 들어갈 말로 알맞은 것은?

A Who is the kindest girl in your class?
B _____

① Linda is kinder girl in my class.
② Linda is the kindest girls in my class.
③ Linda is as kind as girl in my class.
④ Linda is the most kind girl in my class.
⑤ Linda is the kindest girl in my class.

03 다음 글의 빈칸에 알맞은 것을 바르게 짝지은 것은?

Sue is the _____ friend that I have ever had. She always does her _____ in everything. I am proud of her as a friend.

① greater – better　　② greater – best
③ greatest – better　　④ greatest – best
⑤ great – best

대표유형 02 원급과 비교급을 이용한 최상급 표현 　　출제율 60%

04 다음 문장 중 어법상 <u>어색한</u> 것을 <u>두 개</u> 고르면?

① No is more precious than my family.
② Nobody can dance better than you.
③ No other man can run faster than him.
④ Venus is brighter than any other planets.
⑤ No one in my class is as wise as Jina.

05 다음 빈칸에 알맞은 말을 바르게 짝지은 것은?

• The ostrich is bigger than all the other _____.
• No other _____ is as long as the Nile in the world.
• Everyone was tired, but I was the most tired _____ all.

① birds – river – of　　② birds – rivers – of
③ birds – river – in　　④ bird – rivers – in
⑤ bird – river – of

신유형

06 다음 우리말과 같도록 괄호 안의 말을 배열할 때, 두 번째와 여섯 번째 오는 말이 바르게 짝지어진 것은?

세계에서 그 어떤 산도 에베레스트 산보다 높지 않다.
→ (in the world, than, other, is, mountain, higher, no) Mt. Everest.

① is – than　　② mountain – higher
③ other – higher　　④ no – in the world
⑤ in the world – than

07 다음 중 〈보기〉의 문장과 바꿔 쓸 수 <u>없는</u> 것은?

보기　*Spago* is the best restaurant in town.

① No other restaurant is as good as *Spago* in town.
② *Spago* is one of the best restaurants in town.
③ No other restaurant is better than *Spago* in town.
④ *Spago* is better than any other restaurant in town.
⑤ *Spago* is better than all the other restaurants in town.

대표유형 01 최상급 비교   출제율 40%

08 다음 대화가 자연스럽도록 밑줄 친 부분을 알맞은 형태로 고쳐 쓰시오.

> **A** Is that book the (1)thick one in this library?
> **B** No, this book is (2)thick than that one.
> **A** Oh, I see.

(1) _____   (2) _____

09 다음 우리말과 같도록 괄호 안의 단어를 이용하여 문장을 완성하시오.

> Ron은 그의 학교에서 가장 재미있는 선생님 중 한 명이다. (funny)

→ Ron is _____ in his school.

10 다음 상황에서 할 수 있는 말을 문장에 쓰인 표현과 최상급을 사용하여 완성하시오.

> You have just watched a movie, and it was really frightening.

→ This is _____ _____ _____ _____ that I've ever _____ .

11 다음 두 문장의 의미가 같도록 괄호 안의 지시대로 문장을 다시 쓰시오.

> No other month of the year is hotter than August. (최상급 사용)
> = August is _____ .

[12-13] 다음 두 문장의 의미가 같도록 빈칸에 알맞은 말을 쓰시오.

12

> Taylor is the wittiest of all the students.
> = _____ _____ is _____ _____ as Taylor.

13

> Soccer is the most popular sport in the UK.
> = _____ _____ in the UK is _____ _____ than soccer.

[14-15] 다음 문장에서 어법상 어색한 부분을 찾아 바르게 고쳐 쓰시오.

14

> No other islands is as small as this island.

_____ → _____

15

> Sandy is more diligent than all the other worker in the company.

_____ → _____

대표유형 01 최상급 비교 출제율 40%

01 다음 문장 중 어법상 옳은 것을 <u>모두</u> 고르면?

① Anne has the more pets in this town.
② He is the diligentest boy in his class.
③ Eric is the smartest man of all my friend.
④ I met the most famous actor in Korea.
⑤ This is the weirdest story I've ever heard.

02 다음 글의 빈칸에 알맞은 말을 바르게 짝지은 것은?

> Sandra was there when he needed her
> _____. So he thanked her for that for all
> his life. That was the _____ time of his
> life. After he lost her, he could never be
> happy again.

① more – best
② best – most
③ most – more
④ more – more
⑤ most – best

대표유형 02 원급과 비교급을 이용한 최상급 표현 출제율 60%

03 다음 문장과 바꿔 쓸 수 있는 것을 <u>모두</u> 고르면?

> Nothing is more precious than freedom.

① Freedom is as precious as it.
② Freedom is more precious than it.
③ Nothing is as precious as freedom.
④ Nothing is not so precious as freedom.
⑤ There is nothing more precious than freedom.

04 다음 중 어법상 <u>어색한</u> 문장의 개수는?

> ⓐ This is the rarest item I have ever had.
> ⓑ Dr. White has more patients than all the other doctor in the hospital.
> ⓒ Nothing is as real as a dream.
> ⓓ The cobra is one of the most dangerous snake.

① 1개　② 2개　③ 3개　④ 4개　⑤ 없음

---

05 다음 밑줄 친 부분을 바르게 고치지 <u>않은</u> 것은?

① Areca Palm is better at cleaning the air than <u>all the plant</u>. (→ all the other plant)
② Russia is <u>as large as</u> all the other countries. (→ larger than)
③ Amy is cuter than any <u>other girls</u> in her class. (→ other girl)
④ <u>No other dish are</u> more yummy than the pasta in this restaurant. (→ No other dish is)
⑤ Mike plays <u>the best</u> anyone else on his team. (→ better than)

06 다음 짝지어진 두 문장의 뜻이 서로 <u>다른</u> 것은?

① • No other season is colder than winter.
　• No other season is as cold as winter.
② • Jack is the laziest classmate.
　• No other classmate is as lazy as Jack.
③ • He is much cleverer than others at school.
　• He is cleverer than all the other students at school.
④ • Nothing is more beautiful than a smile.
　• There is nothing more beautiful than a smile.
⑤ • No other desert is larger than the Sahara.
　• The Sahara is larger than any other desert.

07 다음 문장 중 나머지 넷과 의미가 <u>다른</u> 것은?

① No student in my class is as humorous as Dean.
② Dean is more humorous than all the other students in my class.
③ Dean is the least humorous student in my class.
④ Dean is more humorous than any other student in my class.
⑤ No student in my class is more humorous than Dean.

대표유형 01 최상급 비교   출제율 40%

08 다음 우리말을 괄호 안의 단어를 이용하여 8단어로 영작하시오.

> 오늘은 내 인생에서 가장 행복한 날이다.
> (today, happy)
> → _____

09 다음 우리말과 같도록 주어진 표현 중에서 필요 없는 한 단어를 제외한 나머지를 바르게 배열하여 문장을 완성하시오.

> 그는 내가 만나본 사람 중 가장 예의 바른 사람이다.
> (the, ever, polite, have, more, person, most, met)

→ He is _____ that
    I _____ .

대표유형 02 원급과 비교급을 이용한 최상급 표현   출제율 60%

10 다음 문장과 의미가 같도록 괄호 안의 지시대로 문장을 바꿔 쓰시오.

> I think an aurora is the most amazing thing. (원급을 이용한 최상급 문장으로)
> → I think nothing _____ .

11 주어진 〈조건〉에 맞게 빈칸에 알맞은 말을 써 넣어 대화를 완성하시오.

> **A** What is (A) _____ thing in your life?
> **B** Friendship is (B) _____ thing.

> [조건] **1.** (A)에 최상급을 쓸 것
>   **2.** (B)에 비교급을 이용한 최상급 표현을 쓸 것
>   **3.** (A), (B)에 important를 활용할 것

신유형

[12-13] 다음 〈보기〉와 같이 주어진 대답을 참고하여 알맞은 질문을 쓰시오.

> 보기 **A** Is she the best cook?
>   **B** Yes, nobody can cook better than her.

12

> **A** _____
> **B** Yes, nobody can sing better than him.

>> 실전 Tip 부사의 최상급과 「형용사의 최상급＋명사」의 두 가지 형태로 최상급을 나타낼 수 있다.

13

> **A** _____
> **B** Yes, nothing is more necessary for them than water.

14 다음 우리말과 같도록 괄호 안의 단어를 바르게 배열하여 문장을 완성하시오.

> 아무것도 이 노래만큼 그녀를 기쁘게 할 수는 없다.
> (nothing, please, her, as, this, can, song, as, much)
> → _____

15 다음 글의 밑줄 친 우리말을 괄호 안의 표현을 이용하여 영작하시오.

> Harry is the most popular in his school. <u>그는 학교에서 다른 어떤 소년보다 더 친절하다.</u> (kind, at school) That's why everybody likes him.

→ _____

01 다음 글의 빈칸에 들어갈 알맞은 말을 바르게 짝지은 것은?

> I got the ___ⓐ___ news from the doctor. That was the most ___ⓑ___ thing that ___ⓒ___ to me.

	ⓐ	ⓑ	ⓒ
①	best	terrible	happens
②	best	beautiful	will ever happen
③	most	least	has ever happened
④	worst	useless	happens
⑤	worst	miserable	had ever happened

02 다음 문장 중 어법상 어색한 것을 바르게 짝지은 것은?

> ⓐ No other mountain in Korea is as high as Mt. Halla.
> ⓑ This is one of my most favorite TV reality show.
> ⓒ His photo is the most impressive than any other photo in the museum.
> ⓓ No other bridge in America was longer than the Golden Gate Bridge until 1964.

① ⓐ, ⓑ   ② ⓑ, ⓒ   ③ ⓐ, ⓒ
④ ⓒ, ⓓ   ⑤ ⓑ, ⓓ

03 다음 우리말을 주어진 〈조건〉에 맞게 영작하시오.

> 스마트폰(smartphone)보다 더 편리한 것은 없다.

> [조건] 1. 비교급을 사용할 것
>   2. nothing으로 시작하는 7단어의 완전한 문장으로 쓸 것

→ _____

04 다음 표의 내용과 일치하도록 대화의 빈칸에 알맞은 말을 쓰시오. (단, 완전한 문장으로 쓸 것)

	IQ	Height	Age
Sumin	149	157cm	15
Minsu	138	177cm	16
Dongho	142	172cm	14

> **A** Who is the smartest of the three?
> **B** (1) _____
> **A** Who is the tallest of the three?
> **B** (2) _____
> **A** Who is the youngest of the three?
> **B** (3) _____

05 다음 문장에서 어법상 어색한 부분을 바르게 고친 것은?

> ⓐ Most countries ⓑ in Africa ⓒ have suffered ⓓ the worse drought ⓔ since 2010.

① ⓐ → Almost countries
② ⓑ → on Africa
③ ⓒ → have been suffered
④ ⓓ → the worst drought
⑤ ⓔ → for 2010

06 다음 〈보기〉와 같이 자신의 가장 뛰어난 점 다섯 개를 최상급을 이용하여 쓰시오.

> 보기   • I am the smartest person in my class.
>   • I know the most poems in my family.

(1) _____
(2) _____
(3) _____
(4) _____
(5) _____

01
a   Russel is the wisest one of his friend.

b   Russel is the wisest one of his friends.

02
a   Paris is one of the most beautiful cities in the world.

b   Paris is one in the most beautiful cities in the world.

03
a   This is the most fantastic scenery that I saw.

b   This is the most fantastic scenery that I've ever seen.

04
a   Nothing is more difficult as dealing with people.

b   Nothing is more difficult than dealing with people.

05
a   No composer is as famous as Mozart.

b   No composer is as famous than Mozart.

06
a   This painting is more unique than all the other painting.

b   This painting is more unique than all the other paintings.

07
a   Ron's report was more creative than any other's report.

b   Ron's report was more creative than any other's reports.

08
a   It is one of the longest river in this country.

b   It is one of the longest rivers in this country.

유형별 기출 적용 빈도

유형 01 가정법 과거 **35%**

유형 02 I wish 가정법 과거 **25%**

유형 03 as if 가정법 과거 **15%**

유형 04 without 가정법 과거 **10%**

유형 05 통합형 **15%**

Grammar Point

Point ① 가정법 과거

> If+주어+동사의 과거형/were ~, 주어+조동사의 과거형+동사원형 ....

'(만약) ~한다면, …할 텐데'라는 의미로 현재 사실과 반대되거나 실제로 일어날 가능성이 거의 없는 일을 가정할 때 쓴다.

If I were you, I would tell her the truth.

주의 가정법 과거 문장에서 if절의 동사가 be동사일 경우 주어의 인칭이나 수에 관계없이 주로 were를 쓴다.

Point ② I wish / as if 가정법 과거

> I wish+주어+동사의 과거형/were ....

'~라면 좋을 텐데'라는 의미로 이루기 힘든 현재의 소망이나 현실에 대한 아쉬움을 나타낸다.

I wish I had a brother. → (I'm sorry that I don't have a brother.)

> as if+주어+동사의 과거형/were ....

'마치 ~인 것처럼'이라는 의미로 주절과 같은 시점의 사실과 반대되는 상황을 가정할 때 쓴다.

He looks as if he were a model. → (In fact, he is not a model.)

Point ③ without 가정법 과거

> Without+명사(구), 주어+조동사의 과거형+동사원형 ....

'만약 ~이 없다면', '만약 ~이 아니라면'이라는 의미로 현재 있는 것이 없다고 가정할 때 쓴다. Without 대신 But for나 If it were not for로 바꿔 쓸 수 있다.

Without[But for] my advice, he would fail.

= If it were not for my advice, he would fail.

✅ 바로 체크

01 If I had money, I (can / could) buy a new backpack.

02 If I (travel / traveled) to England, I would visit London.

03 I wish I (were / did) good at dancing.

04 I wish he (does not / did not) spend all his time playing games.

05 Mom treats me as if I (am / were) a baby.

06 The man talked as if he (is / were) a teacher.

07 Without your help, I (would fail / failed) the test.

08 If it (were / were not) for the Internet, it would be very inconvenient.

STEP 1 만만한 **기초** 유형으로 다져라

대표유형 01 가정법 과거 출제율 35%

01 다음 빈칸에 들어갈 말로 알맞은 것은?

> If I had a ticket, I _____ to the concert.

① go
② will go
③ went
④ could go
⑤ gone

02 괄호 안의 단어를 알맞은 형태로 고쳐 쓰시오.

> If I _____ free, I would visit you. (be)

03 다음 빈칸에 들어갈 말로 알맞은 것은?

> If I _____ the lottery, I would build a hospital for sick children.

① win
② won
③ will win
④ would win
⑤ have won

04 다음 우리말을 영어로 바르게 옮긴 것은?

> 비가 내리고 있지 않으면 나는 소풍을 갈 수 있을 텐데.

① If it was not raining, I can go on a picnic.
② If it were not raining, I could go on a picnic.
③ If it been not raining, I could go on a picnic.
④ If it were not raining, I went on a picnic.
⑤ If it not were raining, I could go on a picnic.

05 다음 우리말과 같도록 괄호 안의 단어를 바르게 배열하여 문장을 완성하시오. (단, if절을 앞에 쓸 것)

> 내가 그의 주소를 알면 그에게 선물을 보낼 텐데.
> (address, would, a gift, send, him, his, knew, I, I, if)
>
> → _____

06 다음 빈칸에 들어갈 말이 바르게 짝지어진 것은?

> Lucy is very busy with work. If she _____ time, she _____ on a vacation.

① has – went
② has – would go
③ had – will go
④ had – would go
⑤ have – will go

07 다음 문장과 의미가 같은 것은?

> As I am not a computer expert, I can't help you.

① If I am a computer expert, I can't help you.
② If I were a computer expert, I can help you.
③ If I were a computer expert, I could help you.
④ If I was not a computer expert, I couldn't help you.
⑤ If I were not a computer expert, I could help you.

08 다음 두 문장의 의미가 같도록 빈칸에 알맞은 말을 쓰시오.

> If I had the book, I could lend it to you.
> = As I _____ the book, I _____ lend it to you.

대표유형 02 I wish 가정법 과거 출제율 25%

09 다음 빈칸에 들어갈 말로 알맞은 것은?

> I'm really shy and quiet. I wish I _____ more outgoing.

① am
② be
③ were
④ have been
⑤ had been

10 다음 두 문장의 의미가 같도록 할 때 빈칸에 알맞은 것은?

> I'm sorry that I can't play the guitar like you.
> = I wish I _____ the guitar like you.

① play   ② played   ③ can be play
④ will play   ⑤ could play

11 다음 우리말과 같도록 빈칸에 알맞은 말을 쓰시오.

> 네가 여기에 나와 함께 있으면 좋을 텐데.
> → I wish _____ _____ here with me.

12 다음 빈칸에 들어갈 말로 알맞은 것은?

> I'm not good at speaking French. I wish I
> _____ French very well.

① speak   ② spoke
③ spoken   ④ have spoken
⑤ had spoken

13 다음 우리말을 영어로 바르게 옮긴 것은?

> 내게 자동차를 살 만큼 충분한 돈이 있다면 좋을 텐데.

① I wished I had enough money to buy a car.
② I wished I have enough money to buy a car.
③ I wish I have enough money to buy a car.
④ I wish I would had enough money to buy a car.
⑤ I wish I had enough money to buy a car.

14 다음 두 문장의 의미가 같도록 빈칸에 알맞은 말을 쓰시오.

> I wish I had a true friend.
> = I'm sorry that I _____ _____ a true friend.

대표유형 03 as if 가정법 과거   출제율 15%

15 다음 두 문장의 의미가 같도록 할 때 빈칸에 알맞은 것은?

> Eddie isn't our captain, but he acts like our captain.
> = Eddie acts _____ he were our captain.

① as   ② as if   ③ that
④ even if   ⑤ even though

16 다음 우리말을 영어로 옮길 때 빈칸에 알맞은 것은?

> 그들은 마치 부자인 것처럼 돈을 쓴다.
> → They spend money _____.

① as if they are rich
② as if they were rich
③ as if they have been rich
④ as if they had been rich
⑤ as if they have to be rich

17 다음 빈칸에 들어갈 말로 알맞은 것은?

> This chair is made of plastic. But it looks as if it _____ made of stone.

① be   ② is   ③ were
④ been   ⑤ has been

18 다음 글에서 어법상 어색한 부분을 찾아 바르게 고쳐 쓰시오.

> Max doesn't know everything. But he talks as if he knows everything.

_____ → _____

19 다음 문장이 의미하는 바로 가장 알맞은 것은?

> Peter acted as if he enjoyed his new life.

① In fact, Peter didn't enjoy his new life.
② In fact, Peter enjoyed his new life.
③ Peter will finally enjoy his new life.
④ Peter has enjoyed his new life so far.
⑤ Peter didn't say that he enjoyed his new life.

대표유형 04 without 가정법 과거   출제율 10%

20 다음 빈칸에 들어갈 말로 알맞은 것을 모두 고르면?

> _____ the sun, nothing could live on Earth.

① As   ② Like   ③ Without
④ But for   ⑤ Thanks to

21 다음 우리말을 영어로 나타낼 때 빈칸에 들어갈 말이 순서대로 바르게 짝지어진 것은?

> 만약 중력이 없다면, 우리는 공중에 뜰 텐데.
> → _____ gravity, we _____ up into the air.

① Without – floated
② But for – has float
③ Without – will have floated
④ If it is not for – will float
⑤ If it were not for – would float

22 다음 두 문장의 의미가 같도록 빈칸에 알맞은 말을 쓰시오.

> Without music, life would be boring.
> = If it _____ _____ _____ music, life would be boring.

대표유형 05 통합형   출제율 15%

23 다음 중 밑줄 친 부분이 어법상 어색한 것은?

① I wish I <u>have</u> straight hair.
② If he <u>scored</u> one more goal, he would win.
③ Helen stood there as if she <u>were</u> a statue.
④ Without her care, the dog <u>would</u> die.
⑤ If Jack <u>didn't watch</u> TV so much, he would have more time to read.

24 다음 빈칸에 들어갈 know의 형태가 나머지 넷과 <u>다른</u> 것은?

① I wish I _____ his secret.
② If I _____ his number, I could call him right away.
③ If they _____ the truth, they would not forgive me.
④ If you _____ the answer, you will win 100 dollars.
⑤ Jeremy talks as if he _____ my sister. In fact, he doesn't know her.

25 두 문장의 의미가 같도록 빈칸에 알맞은 말을 쓰시오.

(1) As I don't like seafood, I don't go to his restaurant often.
    → If I _____ seafood, I would go to his restaurant often.

(2) I'm sorry that I don't own a yacht.
    → I wish I _____ a yacht.

(3) In fact, I was sitting next to Clara. But she ignored me.
    → Clara ignored me as if I _____ next to her.

대표유형 01   가정법 과거   출제율 35%

01 다음 두 문장이 같은 의미가 되도록 빈칸에 들어갈 말이 순서대로 바르게 짝지어진 것은?

> As I don't get more pocket money, I can't buy a new cell phone.
> → If I _____ more pocket money, I _____ buy a new cell phone.

① get – can't   ② will get – can
③ got – could   ④ got – couldn't
⑤ gotten – could

02 다음 대화의 빈칸에 들어갈 말로 가장 알맞은 것은?

> **A** I think that dress looks nice.
> **B** _____ It's too expensive.

① If I am you, I would buy it.
② If I am you, I won't buy it.
③ If I are you, I wouldn't buy it.
④ If I were you, I would buy it.
⑤ If I were you, I wouldn't buy it.

03 다음 중 직설법을 가정법으로 잘못 바꾼 것은?

① As I don't know the answer, I can't tell you.
 → If I knew the answer, I could tell you.
② As I am not strong enough, I won't try the marathon.
 → If I were strong enough, I would try the marathon.
③ As I have a headache, I can't go to the party.
 → If I don't have a headache, I could go to the party.
④ As it is so late, I won't play in the pool.
 → If it were not so late, I would play in the pool.
⑤ As she doesn't study hard, she won't pass the test.
 → If she studied hard, she would pass the test.

04 다음 문장 중 어법상 <u>어색한</u> 것은?

① If it rains tomorrow, the baseball game will be canceled.
② If I have a cat, I would take good care of it.
③ If I were taller, I'd be better at basketball.
④ If I didn't have to do my homework, I could join you.
⑤ What would you do if you picked up a wallet with a lot of money?

대표유형 02, 03   I wish 가정법 과거 / as if 가정법 과거   출제율 25%

05 다음 빈칸에 공통으로 들어갈 말로 알맞은 것은?

> • I wish it _____ Christmas every day.
> • Mr. Lee talks as if he _____ my boss.

① is   ② were   ③ be   ④ are   ⑤ has been

06 다음 밑줄 친 부분을 바르게 고쳐 쓴 것끼리 짝지은 것은?

> Rachel doesn't love Alex, but she acts as if she <u>love</u> him. I wish Alex <u>know</u> the truth.

① loved – knew   ② love – knew
③ loves – known   ④ loved – knows
⑤ has loved – had known

07 다음 두 문장의 의미가 서로 <u>다른</u> 것은?

① I wish I were rich and famous.
 = I'm sorry that I'm not rich and famous.
② I wish I had time to travel.
 = I'm sorry that I don't have time to travel.
③ I wish it would stop raining.
 = I'm sorry that it won't stop raining.
④ Helen acts as if she had a daughter.
 = In fact, Helen doesn't have a daughter.
⑤ Kelly talked as if she were not responsible for the accident.
 = In fact, Kelly was not responsible for the accident.

대표유형 01 가정법 과거   출제율 35%

08 다음 두 문장이 같은 의미가 되도록 빈칸에 알맞은 말을 쓰시오.

> As Stuart is not in Korea, I can't invite him to my wedding.

→ If Stuart _____,

   I _____.

09 다음 우리말을 〈조건〉에 맞게 영작하시오.

> [조건] **1.** 가정법 과거 문장을 쓰되, if절을 앞에 쓸 것
>   **2.** have a million dollars, can, build를 활용할 것

> 내게 백만 달러가 있다면, 나는 새 집을 지을 수 있을 텐데.

→ _____

대표유형 02 I wish 가정법 과거   출제율 25%

10 다음 두 문장이 같은 의미가 되도록 빈칸에 알맞은 말을 쓰시오.

> I'm sorry I don't live near the beach.
> = I wish _____.

신유형

11 다음 내용이 자연스럽도록 빈칸에 알맞은 말을 쓰시오.

> I can't travel alone because I'm too young. I wish I _____ _____ enough to travel alone.

대표유형 03 as if 가정법 과거   출제율 15%

12 다음 두 문장이 같은 의미가 되도록 빈칸에 알맞은 말을 쓰시오.

> Kevin is not an adult, but he behaves like an adult.
> = Kevin behaves _____ _____ he were an adult.

13 주어진 문장과 같은 의미가 되도록 as if 가정법 과거를 이용하여 문장을 완성하시오.

(1) In fact, the man is interested in money.

   → The man talks _____

   _____.

(2) In fact, the baby did not understand what his mom said.

   → The baby smiled _____

   _____.

대표유형 04 without 가정법 과거   출제율 10%

14 다음 두 문장이 같은 의미가 되도록 주어진 말로 시작하여 쓰시오.

> Without my bad cold, I could go swimming.
> = If it _____,
>   I could go swimming.

15 다음 우리말에 맞게 빈칸에 알맞은 말을 쓰시오.

> 부모님이 안 계신다면, 나는 지금의 내가 아닐 것이다.
> → _____ my parents, I would not be what I am today.
> → _____ my parents, I would not be what I am today.
> → If it _____ _____ _____ my parents, I would not be what I am today.

대표유형 01 가정법 과거 출제율 35%

01 다음 문장 중 어법상 <u>어색한</u> 것은?

① You wouldn't be sick if you ate healthy food.
② If my back were not aching, I could play badminton.
③ If I met my favorite actor, I would ask him for an autograph.
④ How would you feel if your best friend talked behind your back?
⑤ If there are fewer cars, there would be less pollution.

02 다음 두 문장이 같은 의미가 되도록 빈칸에 알맞은 것은?

As he is not dressed up, he is not allowed to enter the conference room.
→ If he _____ dressed up, he _____ allowed to enter the conference room.

① was – won't be　　② were – would be
③ was – wouldn't be　　④ has been – would be
⑤ were – won't have been

대표유형 02 I wish 가정법 과거 출제율 25%

03 다음 문장이 의미하는 바로 가장 알맞은 것은?

I'm sorry I can't go back to my country.

① I wish I will go back to my country.
② I wish I can go back to my country.
③ I wish I could go back to my country.
④ I wish I can't go back to my country.
⑤ I wish I could have gone back to my country.

04 다음 글에 이어질 말로 가장 알맞은 것은?

It is hot outside. I don't like working outside when it is hot.

① I wish it were hot outside.
② I wish I worked outside.
③ I wish I didn't work outside.
④ I wished I don't work inside.
⑤ I wished it were not hot inside.

대표유형 05 통합형 출제율 15%

05 다음 두 문장의 의미가 같은 것을 <u>모두</u> 고르면?

① Without dreams, my life would be empty.
= But for dreams, my life would be empty.
② In fact, he was not a doctor.
= He talked as if he were not a doctor.
③ If it were warm, we would go camping.
= As it was not warm, we didn't go camping.
④ I wish I didn't have to study for tomorrow's exam now.
= I'm sorry that I have to study for tomorrow's exam now.
⑤ If I didn't work full-time, I could exercise more.
= As I worked full-time, I couldn't exercise more.

06 다음 중 빈칸에 들어갈 be동사의 형태가 나머지 넷과 <u>다른</u> 것은?

① I wish he _____ my boyfriend.
② If there _____ any problem, I'll let you know.
③ What would you do if you _____ in my place?
④ He treated me as if I _____ a complete fool.
⑤ If it _____ not for your help, he would not succeed.

07 다음 중 어법상 옳은 것끼리 묶은 것은?

ⓐ If I were not busy, I will pick you up at the airport.
ⓑ Jerome acts as if he did everything by himself.
ⓒ What would happen if the moon disappears?
ⓓ She used to say, "I wish I were 10 years younger."
ⓔ Without his mustache, no one could recognize him.

① ⓐ, ⓑ　　② ⓒ, ⓓ　　③ ⓐ, ⓓ, ⓔ
④ ⓑ, ⓒ, ⓓ　　⑤ ⓑ, ⓓ, ⓔ

대표유형 01 가정법 과거 · 출제율 35%

08 다음 문장을 괄호 안의 지시대로 바꿔 쓰시오.

> As she is afraid of heights, she can't go to the top of the Eiffel Tower. (가정법으로)

→ _____

_____

09 다음 우리말을 〈조건〉에 맞게 영작하시오.

> [조건] **1.** 가정법 과거를 이용하되, if절을 앞에 쓸 것
> **2.** 주어진 표현을 활용하여 15단어로 쓸 것

> 의사들이 모든 질병에 대한 치료법을 발견한다면, 사람들은 지금보다 훨씬 더 오래 살 텐데.

→ _____

_____ (if, find, a cure for
all diseases, will, much, than)

대표유형 02 I wish 가정법 과거 · 출제율 25%

10 다음 문장을 I wish 가정법을 이용하여 바꿔 쓰시오.

> I'm sorry that I have so much homework tonight.

→ I wish _____.

11 Victor의 소망을 나타낸 메모를 보고, 〈보기〉와 같이 문장을 완성하시오.

> **My Wish List:** get an A in math class
> (1) be popular with girls
> (2) have a chance to meet my favorite singer

> 보기 I wish I got an A in math class.

(1) I wish _____.
(2) I wish _____.

대표유형 05 통합형 · 출제율 15%

12 다음 글의 내용이 자연스럽도록 빈칸에 알맞은 말을 쓰시오.

(1) Maria is not wearing a raincoat, so she gets wet. If _____
she _____ get wet.
(2) Edward talks as if _____.
In fact, he knows me.

13 다음 우리말에 맞게 〈보기〉에서 알맞은 말을 두 개씩 골라 문장을 완성하시오. (단, 필요시 형태를 바꿀 것)

> 보기 as if   if   agree with   it

(1) 그는 마치 그녀에게 동의하는 것처럼 보였다.
→ He looked _____.
(2) Emily가 없다면 우리는 절대 우승하지 못할 텐데.
→ _____, we could never win.

14 다음 두 문장이 같은 의미가 되도록 빈칸에 알맞은 말을 쓰시오.

(1) In fact, Mr. Watson is not rich.
→ Mr. Watson acts as if _____.
(2) As it doesn't snow, we can't go skiing.
→ If _____.
(3) I'm sorry our school uniforms don't look cool.
→ I wish _____.

15 다음 글에서 어법상 어색한 부분을 모두 찾아 바르게 고치시오.

> Semi is Korean, and she has never been to America. Surprisingly, however, she speaks English fluently as if she is American. Semi's brother is not good at English, and he always says, "I wish I speak English like my sister."

_____

01 다음 우리말을 영어로 옮긴 문장 중 어법상 알맞은 것끼리 묶은 것은?

ⓐ 휴가 시즌이 더 길면 좋을 텐데.
→ I wish the holiday season would last longer.
ⓑ 교통 소음이 없다면, 나는 이 도시를 정말 좋아할 텐데.
→ If it weren't for the traffic noise, I would love this city.
ⓒ 나는 구름을 만질 수 있을 것 같은 기분이다.
→ I feel as if I can touch the clouds.
ⓓ 만약 내게 초능력이 있다면, 나는 어려움에 처한 사람을 도울 수 있을 텐데.
→ If I have superpowers, I could help people in need.
ⓔ 만약 우리 할머니께서 살아 계신다면, 나를 자랑스러워 하실 텐데.
→ If my grandma has been alive, she would be proud of me.

① ⓐ, ⓑ
② ⓐ, ⓒ
③ ⓑ, ⓓ
④ ⓐ, ⓑ, ⓔ
⑤ ⓒ, ⓓ, ⓔ

02 다음 짝지어진 두 문장의 의미가 서로 <u>다른</u> 것은?

① If Andy were brave enough, he could ask Sandra out.
→ As Andy is not brave enough, he can't ask Sandra out.
② She talked as if she cared about him.
→ In fact, she didn't care about him.
③ I wish I understood what my dog is trying to tell me.
→ I'm sorry that I don't understand what my dog is trying to tell me.
④ If it didn't rain a lot, I would drive to the office.
→ It rained a lot, so I didn't drive to the office.
⑤ Without insects, there would be far fewer animals and plants.
→ If it were not for insects, there would be far fewer animals and plants.

03 다음 우리말과 같도록 괄호 안의 표현을 이용하여 영작하시오.

(1)
그들은 그녀가 마치 어린아이인 것처럼 그녀를 대한다. (treat, as if, child)
→ _____

(2)
네가 더 조심스럽게 운전한다면 좋을 텐데.
(wish, drive, carefully)
→ _____

04 다음 글의 내용이 자연스럽도록 빈칸에 알맞은 말을 쓰시오.

I'm not smart and I don't know the answer to the question. I'm sorry about that. I wish
I _____ and _____
_____.

05 다음 우리말을 괄호 안의 표현을 이용하여 영작하시오. (단, 가정법 과거로 나타낼 것)

내가 부유하고 충분한 시간이 있다면, 나는 세계 여행을 할 텐데.
(rich, enough, travel around)
→ _____
_____

06 다음 질문에 대한 대답을 알맞게 완성하시오.

The Internet makes our life convenient. What would our life be like without the Internet?
→ If _____ the Internet, our life _____ convenient.

최종 선택 QUIZ

어법상 옳은 문장에
✔ 표시하세요.

01
  a   If he had more time, he learned English after work.

  b   If he had more time, he could learn English after work.

02
  a   I would be happy if my parents allowed me to play outside.

  b   I will be happy if my parents allowed me to play outside.

03
  a   I wish the prince knew who had saved him.

  b   I wish the prince knows who had saved him.

04
  a   I wish it is not snowing right now.

  b   I wish it were not snowing right now.

05
  a   James looks as if he saw a monster.

  b   James looks as if he sees a monster.

06
  a   Evelyn talks as if she is a queen.

  b   Evelyn talks as if she were a queen.

07
  a   But the navigation system, we couldn't find the restaurant.

  b   Without the navigation system, we couldn't find the restaurant.

08
  a   If it were for my pet, I would be sad.

  b   If it were not for my pet, I would be sad.

유형별 기출 적용 빈도

- 유형 01 가정법 과거완료 — 35%
- 유형 02 혼합 가정법 — 15%
- 유형 03 I wish / as if 가정법 과거완료 — 25%
- 유형 04 without 가정법 과거완료 — 10%
- 유형 05 통합형 — 15%

>> 출제 포인트
가정법 과거완료의 조건절이나 주절의 동사의 형태를 묻는 문제가 많이 출제되고, 가정법 문장과 직설법 문장의 전환 문제도 자주 출제된다.

>> 정답률 100% Tip
I wish / as if 다음에는 가정법 과거와 가정법 과거완료가 모두 쓰일 수 있으므로 우리말 의미에 주의해서 시제를 판단하기

Grammar Point

Point 1 가정법 과거완료

If+주어+had+과거분사 ~, 주어+조동사의 과거형+have+과거분사 ....

'(만약) ~했다면, …했을 텐데'라는 의미로 과거 사실과 반대되는 일을 가정한다.
If I had been rich, I could have bought the car.

Point 2 혼합 가정법

If+주어+had+과거분사 ~, 주어+조동사의 과거형+동사원형 ....

'(만약) ~했다면, …할 텐데'라는 의미로 과거에 실현되지 못한 일이 현재까지 영향을 줄 때 사용하며 if절에는 가정법 과거완료를, 주절에는 가정법 과거를 쓴다.
If Angela had left earlier, she would be here now.

Point 3 I wish / as if 가정법 과거완료

I wish+주어+had+과거분사 .... (~했더라면 좋을 텐데)

I wish 가정법 과거완료는 과거에 이루지 못한 일에 대한 아쉬움을 나타낸다.
I wish you had come. (→ I'm sorry that you didn't come.)

as if+주어+had+과거분사 .... (마치 ~이었던 것처럼)

as if 가정법 과거완료는 주절보다 앞선 시점의 사실과 반대되는 상황을 가정한다.
He talks as if he had known her. (→ In fact, he didn't know her.)

Point 4 without 가정법 과거완료

Without+명사(구), 주어+조동사의 과거형+have+과거분사 ....

'~이 없었다면, …했을 것이다'라는 의미로 과거에 있었던 것이 없었다고 가정한다.
Without[But for] my advice, he would have failed.
= If it had not been for my advice, he would have failed.

✅ 바로 체크

01 If it had been fine, we (would go / would have gone) hiking.

02 He could have been on time if he (caught / had caught) the subway.

03 I wish I (had accepted / have accepted) your suggestion.

04 I wish you (studied / had studied) with me last weekend.

05 It looked as if there (had been / been) an accident.

06 She talks as if she (had met / has met) the actor.

07 If it (were not / had not been) for his help, I could not have finished the job.

08 If I had gone to bed earlier, I (wouldn't be / wouldn't have been) tired now.

대표유형 01 가정법 과거완료   출제율 35%

01 다음 빈칸에 들어갈 말로 알맞은 것은?

> If I _____ the alarm clock, I wouldn't have been late for school this morning.

① hear   ② heard   ③ have heard
④ had heard   ⑤ have had heard

02 다음 밑줄 친 부분을 알맞은 형태로 고쳐 쓰시오.

> If I <u>know</u> her address, I could have sent her a letter.

03 다음 문장의 내용과 일치하도록 둘 중 알맞은 것에 동그라미 하시오.

> If Judy had told Kevin that the game was canceled, he wouldn't have gone to the stadium.

(1) Judy (told, didn't tell) Kevin that the game was canceled.
(2) Kevin (went, didn't go) to the stadium.

04 다음 두 문장이 같은 의미가 되도록 빈칸에 들어갈 말이 바르게 짝지어진 것은?

> If I had been hungry, I would have eaten the soup.
> = As I _____ hungry, I _____ the soup.

① am – will eat
② was – didn't eat
③ was – ate
④ wasn't – didn't eat
⑤ wasn't – would eat

05 다음 우리말과 같도록 괄호 안의 단어를 이용하여 빈칸에 알맞은 말을 쓰시오.

> 네가 나를 돕지 않았더라면 나는 성공하지 못했을 텐데.
> → If you _____ _____ me, I couldn't have succeeded. (help)

06 다음 우리말을 영어로 바르게 옮긴 것은?

> 내가 더 빨리 달렸더라면, 나는 우승할 수 있었을 텐데.

① If I ran faster, I could have won.
② If I had run faster, I could have won.
③ If I had run faster, I can have won.
④ If I have run faster, I could win.
⑤ If I have run faster, I could have won.

07 다음 우리말과 같도록 괄호 안의 표현을 바르게 배열하시오.

> 내가 숙제를 했었더라면 나는 벌을 받지 않았을 텐데. (have, punished, wouldn't, been, done, I had)
> → If I _____ my homework, _____
> _____.

08 다음 문장을 가정법으로 바꿔 쓸 때 빈칸에 알맞은 말을 쓰시오. (단, 조동사는 will을 활용할 것)

> As Andrew didn't pay attention to his teacher, he didn't understand what she said.
> → If Andrew _____ attention to his teacher, he _____ what she said.

09 다음 밑줄 친 부분 중 어법상 어색한 것은?

① If she <u>had left</u> a message, I would have called her.

② If Robert worked harder, he <u>could finish</u> the work.

③ If I had known she was a vegetarian, I <u>wouldn't have cooked</u> steak.

④ If I <u>were</u> stronger, I would carry the furniture for you.

⑤ If she <u>were not</u> sick, she could have attended the meeting.

대표유형 02 혼합 가정법 출제율 15%

10 다음 두 문장이 같은 의미가 되도록 빈칸에 들어갈 말이 바르게 짝지어진 것은?

> As it snowed last night, the road is slippery today.
> → If it _____ last night, the road _____ slippery today.

① didn't snow – wouldn't be

② hadn't snowed – wouldn't be

③ didn't have snowed – wouldn't be

④ hadn't snowed – wouldn't have been

⑤ hasn't snowed – wouldn't be

11 다음 빈칸에 들어갈 말로 알맞은 것은?

> Mia sprained her ankle last weekend, so she can't go skating today. If she hadn't sprained her ankle, she _____ skating with her friends now.

① will be   ② would be

③ will have been   ④ would have been

⑤ would had been

12 다음 우리말에 맞게 괄호 안의 단어를 이용하여 알맞은 말을 쓰시오.

> 네가 의사의 조언을 들었더라면, 지금 건강할 텐데.
> → If you _____ the doctor's advice, you _____ healthy now. (take, will)

대표유형 03 I wish / as if 가정법 과거완료 출제율 25%

13 다음 우리말과 같도록 빈칸에 알맞은 말을 쓰시오.

> 네가 좀 더 조심했더라면 좋았을 텐데.
> → I wish you _____ _____ more careful.

14 다음 문장 중 의미가 나머지 넷과 <u>다른</u> 것은?

① I'm sorry that I ate too much.

② I shouldn't have eaten too much.

③ I wish I had not eaten too much.

④ I must have eaten too much.

⑤ I regret that I ate too much.

15 다음 빈칸에 들어갈 말로 알맞은 것은?

> Fred has never been to London, but he talks as if he _____ London.

① visits   ② visited

③ is visiting   ④ has visited

⑤ had visited

[16-17] 다음 두 문장의 의미가 같도록 빈칸에 알맞은 말을 쓰시오.

16

> I wish I had learned how to drive a car.
> = I'm sorry that I _____ _____ how to drive a car.

17

> Matt acts as if he had been a professional golfer.
> = In fact, he _____ a professional golfer.

18 다음 빈칸에 들어갈 말로 가장 알맞은 것은?

> He talks as if he had read her novel. In fact, he _____ it.

① read
② didn't read
③ doesn't read
④ would have read
⑤ has read

[19-20] 다음 우리말을 영어로 옮길 때 빈칸에 알맞은 것을 고르시오.

19
> 내가 공부를 더 열심히 했더라면 좋을 텐데.
> → I wish _____.

① I studied harder
② I have studied harder
③ I had studied harder
④ I have had studied harder
⑤ I had been studied harder

20
> 그녀는 마치 아무 일도 없었던 것처럼 행동한다.
> → She behaves _____.

① as if nothing happened
② as if nothing had happened
③ as if nothing has happened
④ as if nothing had been happened
⑤ as if nothing has had happened

대표유형 04 without 가정법 과거완료   출제율 10%

21 다음 밑줄 친 부분과 바꿔 쓸 수 있는 것은?

> <u>Without</u> Mr. Brown's help, I couldn't have accomplished my goals.

① But for
② But
③ Like
④ As if
⑤ Thanks to

22 다음 두 문장의 의미가 같도록 빈칸에 알맞은 말을 쓰시오.

> But for the accident, I would have been world champion.
> = If _____ the accident, I would have been world champion.

23 다음 우리말에 맞게 괄호 안의 단어를 이용하여 문장을 완성하시오.

> 지도가 없었다면 우리는 그 궁전을 찾지 못했을 것이다.

→ _____ the map, we _____ _____
_____ the palace. (can, find)

대표유형 05 통합형   출제율 15%

24 다음 밑줄 친 부분이 어법상 옳은 것은?

① If I were not busy, I <u>could have helped</u> you now.
② If we <u>had traveled</u> by bus, we would have saved money.
③ I wish I <u>have gone</u> to his birthday party yesterday.
④ If he <u>drove</u> more slowly, he wouldn't have crashed the car.
⑤ If you joined us, you <u>could have seen</u> the most wonderful show in the world.

25 다음 빈칸에 들어갈 have의 형태가 나머지 넷과 다른 것은?

① I really love cats. I wish I _____ one.
② I wish I _____ brought my umbrella.
③ If I _____ more time, I could have gone sightseeing.
④ He talked as if he _____ been famous when he was young.
⑤ If I _____ a good memory, I could do a better job at my work.

대표유형 01 가정법 과거완료   출제율 35%

01 다음 문장과 의미가 같은 것은?

> If I had taken a taxi, I could have come earlier.

① As I didn't take a taxi, I couldn't come earlier.

② As I didn't take a taxi, I could come earlier.

③ As I have taken a taxi, I can't come earlier.

④ As I took a taxi, I could come earlier.

⑤ As I don't take a taxi, I can't come earlier.

[02-03] 다음 빈칸에 들어갈 말이 순서대로 바르게 짝지어진 것을 고르시오.

02

> I didn't feel well yesterday. If I _____ well, I would _____ to the movie.

① felt – go   ② has felt – go

③ has felt – gone   ④ had felt – had gone

⑤ had felt – have gone

03

> I skipped classes often, so I didn't pass the test. If I _____ classes often, I _____ the test.

① skipped – will have passed

② had skipped – would pass

③ didn't skip – will have pass

④ hadn't skipped – would have passed

⑤ haven't skipped – would have passed

04 다음 문장 중 어법상 옳은 것의 개수는?

> ⓐ If I had eaten a sandwich, I wouldn't be hungry now.
>
> ⓑ If Anderson had been more careful, he wouldn't have spilled the milk.
>
> ⓒ If you apologized to Helen, she would have forgiven you.
>
> ⓓ They would have enjoyed the trip more if it hasn't rained yesterday.

① 1개   ② 2개   ③ 3개   ④ 4개   ⑤ 없음

대표유형 03 I wish / as if 가정법 과거완료   출제율 25%

05 다음 빈칸에 들어갈 말로 알맞은 것은?

> The French restaurant is full, so Alice will have to wait for a long time. She whispers, "_____"

① I wish I made a reservation in advance.

② I wish I have made a reservation in advance.

③ I wish I had made a reservation in advance.

④ I wish I had been made a reservation in advance.

⑤ I wish I will have made a reservation in advance.

06 다음 문장의 의미로 가장 알맞은 것은?

> Peter keeps talking as if he had won a gold medal.

① Peter will win a gold medal.

② In fact, Peter didn't win a gold medal.

③ In fact, Peter won a gold medal.

④ Peter has won a gold medal many times.

⑤ Peter is not interested in winning a gold medal.

07 다음 중 직설법을 가정법으로 <u>잘못</u> 바꾼 것을 <u>모두</u> 고르면?

① I regret that I changed my mind.

   → I wish I didn't change my mind.

② As I didn't see the sign, I didn't stop.

   → If I had seen the sign, I would have stopped.

③ As you didn't follow the rules, you are in trouble now.

   → If you had followed the rules, you wouldn't be in trouble now.

④ I'm sorry that I didn't take my camera with me.

   → I wish I had taken my camera with me.

⑤ As I yelled at him, we quarreled.

   → If I hadn't yelled at him, we wouldn't had quarreled.

대표유형 01　가정법 과거완료　출제율 35%

08 다음 우리말에 맞게 괄호 안의 단어를 이용하여 문장을 완성하시오.

기차를 놓쳤더라면 나는 모임에 늦었을 텐데.

→ If I _____ the train, I _____
_____ for the meeting. (miss, will be)

09 다음 주어진 문장을 가정법으로 바꿔 쓰시오. (단, if절을 앞에 쓸 것)

Ruth didn't buy the dress because it was not on sale.

→ _____
_____

10 다음 글에서 어법상 어색한 부분을 모두 찾아 바르게 고치시오.

I haven't finished the English essay yet. If I stayed up late last night, I probably would finish it.

대표유형 03　I wish / as if 가정법 과거완료　출제율 25%

11 다음 문장을 I wish 가정법을 이용하여 바꿔 쓰시오.

I'm sorry I drank so much coffee last night.

→ _____

[12-13] 괄호 안의 표현을 이용하여 문장을 알맞게 완성하시오.

12

I didn't prepare well for the interview, and I didn't get a job. _____
better for the interview. (I wish)

13

Jasmine talked _____ the accident. In fact, she hadn't seen it. (as if)

대표유형 04　without 가정법 과거완료　출제율 10%

14 다음 우리말과 같도록 괄호 안의 단어를 이용하여 빈칸에 알맞은 말을 쓰시오.

나의 삼촌의 도움이 없었다면 나는 대학을 졸업하지 못했을 것이다. (graduate)
→ _____ my uncle's help, I _____
_____ _____ from university.

15 다음 우리말에 맞게 괄호 안의 표현을 바르게 배열하시오. (단, if절을 앞에 쓸 것)

너의 조언이 없었더라면 나는 그 일에 지원하지 못했을 텐데. (wouldn't, been, not, applied, it, had, your advice, for, if, the job, I, have, for)

→ _____
_____

대표유형 01 가정법 과거완료   출제율 35%

01 다음 글의 빈칸에 알맞은 말끼리 짝지어진 것은?

> My bike was broken, so I had to take a bus this morning. If my bike _____, I _____ a bus.

① hadn't broken – wouldn't have taken
② didn't broken – would have taken
③ haven't broken – would haven't taken
④ could have broken – had taken
⑤ would have broken – hadn't taken

02 다음 문장에서 어법상 어색한 부분을 바르게 고친 것은?

> If I hadn't illegally parked in a handicapped spot, I wouldn't have be fined.

① hadn't → hasn't   ② parked → parking
③ wouldn't → would   ④ have → had
⑤ be → been

대표유형 02 혼합 가정법   출제율 15%

03 다음 빈칸에 들어갈 말이 순서대로 바르게 짝지어진 것은?

> If we _____ the trip before we left, we _____ in this mess now.

① had planned – wouldn't be
② had planned – wouldn't have been
③ have planned – wouldn't be
④ have planned – wouldn't has been
⑤ have has planned – hadn't been

04 다음 문장 중 어법상 어색한 것은?

① If you had taken a nap, you would have felt better now.
② If he hadn't lied to me, we would still be good friends.
③ If I hadn't eaten dessert, I wouldn't be so full now.
④ If they had called the store, they would have known it was closed.
⑤ If you had read this book yesterday, you would understand what I'm saying.

대표유형 05 통합형   출제율 15%

05 다음 문장 중 어법상 옳은 것의 개수는?

> ⓐ I wish you had taught me how to cook.
> ⓑ Melanie bought clothes as if she had a lot of money.
> ⓒ If his speech hadn't been so boring, I wouldn't have fallen asleep.
> ⓓ If the ambulance had arrived sooner, she would still be alive.

① 1개   ② 2개   ③ 3개   ④ 4개   ⑤ 없음

06 다음 문장 중 나머지 넷과 의미가 다른 것은?

① If Lucy didn't help me, I would give up my dreams.
② As Lucy helped me, I didn't give up my dreams.
③ But for Lucy's help, I would have given up my dreams.
④ If Lucy hadn't helped me, I would have given up my dreams.
⑤ If it had not been for Lucy's help, I would have given up my dreams.

07 다음 직설법을 가정법으로 고친 문장 중 옳은 것을 모두 고르면?

① I regret that I forgot Mom's birthday.
   → I wish I didn't forget Mom's birthday.
② In fact, Jonathan has never met Suji before.
   → Jonathan acts as if he had never met Suji before.
③ I'm sorry that he didn't stay with us longer.
   → I wish he had stayed with us longer.
④ As I didn't know the truth, I blamed her.
   → If I had known the truth, I wouldn't have blamed her.
⑤ As she had a car accident, she is in the hospital now.
   → If she hadn't had a car accident, she wouldn't have been in the hospital now.

대표유형 01 가정법 과거완료 출제율 35%

08 다음 두 문장을 if를 이용하여 한 문장으로 바꿔 쓰시오.

> I didn't know Alex was such a terrible driver. I'm sorry now that I lent him my car.
>
> → _____
>
> _____

09 괄호 안의 표현을 이용하여 다음 우리말을 영작하시오.

> 그녀에게 더 많은 돈이 있었더라면, 그녀는 식당을 개업했을 텐데. (have, will, open a restaurant)

→ _____

_____

10 다음 상황을 읽고, Olivia가 엄마에게 할 말을 〈조건〉에 맞게 쓰시오.

> Last weekend, Olivia went to the beach with her friends. But she forgot to bring her swimsuit, so she couldn't swim. When she came back, her mom asked her if she had swum in the sea. What would she probably say to her mom?

> [조건] 1. 가정법을 이용하여 10단어로 쓸 것
> 2. if, bring, can, swim을 이용할 것

→ _____

대표유형 03 I wish/as if 가정법 과거완료 출제율 25%

11 다음 문장과 같은 뜻이 되도록 I wish 가정법을 이용하여 바꿔 쓰시오.

> I shouldn't have spent so much money on the car.
>
> → _____

12 다음 문장과 같은 의미의 문장을 쓰시오.

(1) I wish I hadn't thrown away the receipt.

→ _____

(2) Laura pretended as if she had come up with the idea first.

→ _____

13 다음 우리말을 가정법을 이용하여 주어진 단어 수에 맞게 영작하시오.

(1) 네가 이 영화를 봤더라면 좋을 텐데. (7단어)

→ _____

(2) 그녀는 마치 그 소식을 못 들었던 것처럼 말했다. (9단어)

→ _____

대표유형 05 통합협 출제율 15%

14 다음 문장을 괄호 안의 지시대로 바꿔 쓰시오.

(1) I'm sorry my dad didn't let me go to the concert.

→ _____

(I wish 가정법을 이용하여)

(2) The shop owner didn't catch him stealing the jewelry, so he wasn't arrested.

→ _____

_____

(if절을 이용하여)

15 다음 각 문장의 밑줄 친 부분을 어법상 알맞게 고치시오. (단, 어법상 옳은 경우에는 '없음'이라고 쓸 것)

(1) If it <u>rains</u> enough last year, they would have gathered a good harvest. → _____

(2) If Justin hadn't invested all his savings, he <u>wouldn't be</u> broke now. → _____

(3) How stupid I was to send such a letter! I wish I <u>didn't send</u> it. → _____

(4) If it <u>weren't</u> for her care, the patient couldn't have survived. → _____

01 다음 빈칸 중 had been이 들어가기에 <u>어색한</u> 것은?

① I wish I _____ there with you.

② Barbara talks as if she _____ a celebrity.

③ If it _____ for a lifeboat, I would have drowned.

④ If I _____ invited, I would have gone to their housewarming party.

⑤ If it _____ sunny, they would have enjoyed dinner in the garden.

02 다음 대화의 내용이 자연스럽도록 빈칸에 알맞은 말을 쓰시오. (단, as if를 이용할 것)

> **A** Do you know who wrote the paper?
> **B** Yes, I do. Jack wrote it.
> **A** Really? I thought Tom wrote the paper. He acts _____.

03 다음 두 문장의 의미가 서로 <u>다른</u> 것의 개수는?

> ⓐ If I had had free time, I could have traveled more.
>   = As I didn't have free time, I couldn't travel more.
> ⓑ If he hadn't had his hat off, I wouldn't have recognized him.
>   = As he had his hat off, I was not able to recognize him.
> ⓒ I wish I had handed in my essay on time.
>   = I'm sorry that I didn't hand in my essay on time.
> ⓓ If the war hadn't broken out, they would still have homes.
>   = As the war broke out, they don't have homes anymore.
> ⓔ But for the wind, the fire wouldn't have spread so fast.
>   = If it hadn't been for the wind, the fire wouldn't have spread so fast.

① 1개　② 2개　③ 3개　④ 4개　⑤ 없음

04 다음 각 인물의 행동과 결과를 진술한 문장을 〈보기〉와 같이 가정법을 이용하여 바꿔 쓰시오.

Yuna	I didn't clean my room, so my mom was angry.
Jaeho	I overslept this morning, so I couldn't see the sunrise.
Doran	I didn't put the eggs back in the fridge, so they went bad.

> 보기 **Yuna** If I had cleaned my room, my mom wouldn't have been angry.

(1) **Jaeho** _____

_____

(2) **Doran** _____

_____

05 괄호 안에 주어진 표현을 이용하여 우리말을 영작하시오.

(1) Lisa는 중국에 가봤던 것처럼 말했다.

→ _____

(talk, as if)

(2) 안전벨트가 없었다면, 그 운전자는 다쳤을 것이다. (without, the seat belt, hurt)

→ _____

(3) 내가 네게 전화하는 것을 잊지 않았더라면 좋을 텐데. (wish, forget, call)

→ _____

06 다음 글에서 어법상 <u>어색한</u> 부분을 <u>모두</u> 찾아 바르게 고치시오.

> My toothache started a few days ago. Mom told me to go to the dentist right away, but I ignored her advice. Now my tooth aches so badly that I can't stand it any longer. If I went to the dentist earlier, the situation wouldn't be so bad now. I wish I didn't ignore my mom's advice.

_____

01

a If I didn't miss the plane, I could have attended his wedding.

b If I hadn't missed the plane, I could have attended his wedding.

02

a If Jim had asked her politely, she wouldn't had refused his offer.

b If Jim had asked her politely, she wouldn't have refused his offer.

03

a If I had practiced enough, I would have a driver's license now.

b If I had practiced enough, I would have had a driver's license now.

04

a I wish I were at the flower festival last week.

b I wish I had been at the flower festival last week.

05

a Kevin acts as if he didn't understand. (← In fact, he understood.)

b Kevin acts as if he hadn't understood. (← In fact, he understood.)

06

a She talked as if she had been a movie star when she was young.

b She talked as if she has been a movie star when she was young.

07

a Without Robin's goal, we would lose the game yesterday.

b Without Robin's goal, we would have lost the game yesterday.

08

a If it were not for the stove, I would have frozen to death.

b If it had not been for the stove, I would have frozen to death.

유형별 기출 적용 빈도

유형 01 수 일치   55%

유형 02 시제 일치   45%

≫ 출제 포인트

특정 어구들이 주어로 쓰일 때 수의 일치를 묻는 문제는 혼동하기 쉬워 단골로 출제된다. 시제 일치뿐만 아니라 시제 일치 예외의 경우도 반드시 알아둔다.

≫ 정답률 100% Tip
1 「the number of+복수 명사」는 단수이고, 「a number of+복수 명사」는 복수인 것에 주의
2 '불변의 진리와 속담'은 항상 현재 시제, '역사적 사실'은 항상 과거 시제

Grammar Point

Point 1 수 일치

주어가 단수이면 단수 동사를 쓰고, 복수이면 복수 동사를 쓴다.

단수 취급	every / each+명사	every class, each box
	-thing, -one, -body	nothing, someone
	(복수형의) 나라, 작품, 학문 이름	the Philippines, politics
	시간, 거리, 금액, 무게, 온도	ten years, ten dollars
	동명사구, to부정사구, 명사절	what I want to do
	「A and B」가 하나의 개념일 때	curry and rice (카레라이스)
	one of+복수 명사	one of my friends
	the number of+복수 명사 (~의 수)	the number of visitors
복수 취급	a number of+복수 명사 (많은 ~)	a number of people
	both (A and B)	both a dog and a cat
	the+형용사 (~한 사람들)	the rich(= rich people)
	쌍으로 된 명사	socks, glasses, scissors

주의 양을 나타내는 표현에서는 of 뒤에 오는 명사에 수를 일치시킨다.

「all, some, most, half, the rest, 분수, 퍼센트+of+단수 명사」: 단수 취급

「all, some, most, half, the rest, 분수, 퍼센트+of+복수 명사」: 복수 취급

Point 2 시제 일치

주절의 시제에 종속절의 시제를 일치시킨다.

(1) **시제 일치**: 주절이 현재 시제이면 종속절에 모든 시제를 쓸 수 있고, 주절이 과거 시제이면 종속절에 과거, 과거완료를 쓴다.

(2) **시제 일치의 예외**: 주절의 시제와 상관없이 경우에 따라 다르다.

   ① 불변의 진리, 속담, 현재의 사실이나 습관은 현재 시제로 쓴다.

   ② 과거의 역사적 사실이나 사건은 과거 시제를 쓴다.

   ③ 가정법이 쓰인 종속절, 비교 구문 등은 주절에 영향 받지 않는다.

✅ 바로 체크

01 Every dog (has / have) his day.

02 Mathematics (is / are) interesting.

03 The blind (needs / need) a guide dog to walk around.

04 A number of renowned scholars (is / are) filing into the event hall.

05 Ten years (is / are) not a short time.

06 Both Julia and her sister (are / is) middle school students.

07 Jonathan said he (has studied / had studied) English hard.

08 I knew that Mt. Halla (is / was) higher than Mt. Seorak.

대표유형 01 수 일치   출제율 55%

01 다음 빈칸에 알맞은 be동사가 순서대로 바르게 짝지어진 것은?

> · When we got there yesterday, a number of people _____ waiting in line.
> · At that time, the number of students _____ 50 for each class.

① was – was   ② was – were
③ were – was   ④ are – were
⑤ are – was

02 다음 대화의 빈칸에 알맞은 말을 쓰시오.

> **A** What's your favorite food?
> **B** Curry and rice _____ one of my favorite foods.

03 다음 밑줄 친 부분이 어법상 자연스러운 것은?

① Every person <u>have</u> a talent.
② Everyone <u>know</u> the answer.
③ Economics <u>are</u> difficult for me.
④ One of my friends <u>sing</u> very well.
⑤ Three years <u>is</u> a long time to wait.

[04-05] 다음 문장에서 어법상 어색한 부분을 찾아 바르게 고치시오.

04

> There was a fire in the building last night, but thankfully nobody were hurt.

_____ → _____

05

> The Netherlands are located in Western Europe.

_____ → _____

06 다음 빈칸에 공통으로 들어갈 말로 알맞은 것은?

> · Ten kilometers _____ a long distance for the child to walk.
> · Two thousand dollars _____ a lot of money to my family.

① is   ② are   ③ make
④ have   ⑤ takes

≫ 실전 Tip 시간·거리·금액·무게를 나타내는 명사구를 하나의 단위로 볼 때는 단수 취급을 하지만, 하나하나 세는 의미일 때는 복수 취급을 한다.
e.g. Two years have passed since I entered middle school.

07 다음 빈칸에 들어갈 말이 순서대로 바르게 짝지어진 것은?

> Three-fourths of the spectators _____ high school students and the rest of them _____ middle school students.

① was – was   ② were – were
③ was – were   ④ were – was
⑤ are – was

08 다음 문장 중 어법상 알맞은 것은?

① Most of the book is wet.
② I think the rich is getting richer.
③ Your new glasses looks good on you.
④ Every boy in my class like computer games.
⑤ These days the number of new-born babies are decreasing.

09 주어진 우리말과 같도록 괄호 안의 단어를 활용하여 문장을 완성하시오.

> 매일 영자 신문을 읽는 것은 당신의 영어를 향상시키는 것을 돕는다. (help, improve)

→ Reading English newspapers every day

_____.

10 다음 괄호 안에서 어법상 알맞은 것끼리 짝지어진 것은?

- (Each / All) of us has a name.
- (The / A) number of children are playing in the pool.
- Bread and butter (are / is) my favorite breakfast.

① All – A – are   ② Each – A – is
③ All – The – is   ④ Each – The – are
⑤ All – A – is

11 주어진 우리말을 괄호 안의 단어를 활용하여 영어로 옮길 때, 빈칸에 들어갈 말로 알맞은 것은?

거의 모든 학생들이 더 좋은 성적을 얻기를 원한다.
(want, get)
→ Almost every student ＿＿＿＿＿＿＿.

① want to get better grades
② want getting better grades
③ wants to get better grades
④ wants getting better grades
⑤ wants to be getting better grades

12 다음 빈칸에 be동사의 알맞은 형태를 쓰시오.
(단, 현재 시제로 쓸 것)

- Helping other people ＿＿＿＿ a valuable thing.
- What he wants now ＿＿＿＿ some rest.

13 다음 문장 중 빈칸에 is가 들어갈 수 <u>없는</u> 것은?
① One of my favorite hobbies ＿＿＿ reading.
② All the furniture in the shop ＿＿＿ antique.
③ Nothing ＿＿＿ more important than health.
④ Two hours ＿＿＿ enough to finish the report.
⑤ Half of the cars in the parking lot ＿＿＿ silver.

14 다음 빈칸에 들어갈 말로 알맞은 것을 <u>모두</u> 고르면?

John suddenly realized that ＿＿＿＿＿＿.

① Lilly has gone to Japan
② he hasn't worn a helmet
③ he forgot to bring his camera
④ he had already read the book
⑤ his father will go on a business trip

[15-16] 다음 밑줄 친 부분을 어법상 바르게 고쳐 쓰시오.

15

He says he <u>went</u> to the museum next Friday.

→ ＿＿＿＿＿＿＿

16

We knew that light <u>traveled</u> faster than sound.

→ ＿＿＿＿＿＿＿

[17-18] 다음 문장의 빈칸에 들어갈 말로 알맞은 것을 고르시오.

17

When Ann went to the shop, she ＿＿＿＿ a pair of red shoes.

① buys   ② bought
③ was buying   ④ will buy
⑤ had bought

18

I learned that water ＿＿＿＿ of hydrogen and oxygen.

① consists   ② consisted
③ will consist   ④ has consisted
⑤ had consisted

≫ 실전 Tip 불변의 진리, 속담·격언, 현재의 사실이나 습관 등은 주절의 시제와 상관없이 현재 시제로 쓴다.

19 다음 빈칸에 알맞은 be동사의 형태가 나머지 넷과 <u>다른</u> 것은?

① I wish she _____ my girlfriend.
② I'm sure they _____ sick yesterday.
③ I heard the tickets _____ sold out.
④ Didn't you say that honesty _____ the best policy?
⑤ If I _____ you, I would accept her offer.

20 다음 문장의 밑줄 친 동사를 과거형으로 바꾸어 쓴 문장으로 알맞은 것은?

> I <u>know</u> Mark is sick in bed.

① I knew Mark is sick in bed.
② I knew Mark was sick in bed.
③ I knew Mark has been sick in bed.
④ I knew Mark had been sick in bed.
⑤ I knew Mark would be sick in bed.

21 다음 문장의 빈칸에 들어갈 말로 <u>어색한</u> 것은?

> I thought that Kate _____ for you.

① was waiting   ② waited
③ had waited   ④ has waited
⑤ would wait

22 다음 우리말에 맞도록 괄호 안에 주어진 동사의 알맞은 형태를 쓰시오.

> 나는 어제 네가 나에게 왜 거짓말을 했는지 궁금하다.
> (lie)

→ I wonder why you _____ to me yesterday.

23 다음 빈칸에 들어갈 말로 알맞은 것끼리 순서대로 짝지어진 것은?

> • Jina said that she always _____ up at 7 a.m.
> • The child answered that twelve plus three _____ fifteen.
> • Do you know who first discovered that the Earth _____ round?

① gets – is – is   ② gets – is – was
③ gets – was – is   ④ got – is – was
⑤ got – was – was

신유형

24 다음 문장에서 어법상 <u>어색한</u> 부분을 바르게 고친 것은?

> Michael thought that he can express himself through songs.

① that → if   ② that → what
③ can → could   ④ himself → him
⑤ songs → song

25 다음 밑줄 친 부분이 어법상 <u>어색한</u> 것은?

① I believe he <u>will win</u> first prize.
② Rachel said she <u>is going</u> there to meet her friend.
③ The teacher taught the students that the sun <u>rises</u> in the east.
④ She wanted to go home because she <u>had</u> a headache.
⑤ They think Isabella <u>is</u> the most beautiful girl of the three.

대표유형 01 수 일치 출제율 55%

01 다음 문장의 빈칸에 들어갈 수 <u>없는</u> 것은?

> _____ are over there.

① Your socks
② Most of the hats
③ Both of them
④ All of the money
⑤ A number of birds

02 다음 빈칸에 is를 쓸 수 <u>없는</u> 문장의 개수는?

> ⓐ Having real friends _____ important.
> ⓑ *Romeo and Juliet* _____ a tragedy.
> ⓒ The United States _____ a melting pot of cultures.
> ⓓ Fifty percent of the books on the shelf _____ novels.

① 1개   ② 2개   ③ 3개   ④ 4개   ⑤ 없음

03 다음 우리말을 영어로 바르게 나타낸 것은?

> 우리 동아리의 회원 수는 열 명이다.

① A number of members in our club is ten.
② A number of members in our club are ten.
③ The number of members in our club is ten.
④ The number of members in our club are ten.
⑤ The number of members in our club was ten.

04 다음 문장 중 어법상 알맞은 것은?

① Do you know how politics affect our lives?
② The scissors on the table looks sharp.
③ The violin and the cello differs in size.
④ There is a number of flowers in this park.
⑤ Each of you needs to answer the question.

대표유형 02 시제 일치 출제율 45%

05 다음 문장 중 어법상 <u>어색한</u> 것은?

① I believe that Ellen liked me.
② We learned that oil was lighter than water.
③ The doctor told him that he is addicted to alcohol.
④ Luke knew that he had made a mistake.
⑤ She noticed that her son wasn't listening to her.

통합형

06 다음 밑줄 친 단어의 형태로 알맞은 것은?

> I thought sixty dollars <u>be</u> a reasonable price for this jacket.

① is   ② are   ③ was
④ were   ⑤ being

07 밑줄 친 주절의 시제를 과거로 바꿔 쓴 문장 중 어법상 <u>어색한</u> 것은?

① Jim <u>thinks</u> that the painting is beautiful.
　→ Jim thought that the painting was beautiful.
② He <u>says</u> he has already read the book.
　→ He said he had already read the book.
③ She <u>asks</u> me why I didn't come to the party.
　→ She asked me why I hadn't come to the party.
④ The teacher <u>tells</u> us that the Second World War ended in 1945.
　→ The teacher told us that the Second World War had ended in 1945.
⑤ He <u>says</u> he will go to Hawaii to visit his grandmother.
　→ He said he would go to Hawaii to visit his grandmother.

대표유형 01 수 일치　　　출제율 55%

08 다음 우리말과 일치하도록 어법상 <u>어색한</u> 부분을 바르게 고쳐 쓰시오.

> 참가자들 중 절반은 프로그램을 즐기는 것처럼 보인다.
> → Half of the participants seems to enjoy the program.

→ _____

신유형

09 다음 우리말과 같도록 주어진 표현들을 바르게 배열하시오.

(1)
> 벌의 수가 수년 동안 감소하고 있다.
> (for years, bees, declining, of, has, the number, been)

→ _____

(2)
> 6시간에서 8시간의 수면은 여러분의 몸에 좋다. (of, good for, six to eight hours, your body, is, sleep)

→ _____

10 어법상 <u>어색한</u> 부분을 찾아 문장을 바르게 고쳐 쓰시오.

> Two-fifths of Julia's income are spent on clothes.

→ _____

대표유형 02 시제 일치　　　출제율 45%

11 다음 괄호 안의 동사를 활용하여 빈칸에 알맞은 말을 <u>모두</u> 쓰시오.

> I thought she _____(solve) the problem.

→ _____

[12-13] 다음 문장에서 주절의 시제를 과거로 바꿀 때, 빈칸에 알맞은 말을 쓰시오.

12
> The coach knows that we did our best to win the game.

→ The coach knew that we _____ our best to win the game.

13
> I think that Chris and Edwin have gone to the same middle school.

→ I thought that Chris and Edwin _____ to the same middle school.

14 다음 문장에서 어법상 <u>어색한</u> 부분을 찾아 바르게 고치시오.

> The history teacher told us that the French Revolution had broken out in 1789.

_____ → _____

15 자연스러운 문장이 되도록 밑줄 친 동사의 알맞은 형태를 <u>모두</u> 쓰시오.

> He knew that he <u>make</u> the right choice.

→ _____

---

01 다음 빈칸에 들어갈 말이 순서대로 바르게 짝지어진 것은?

> • The rest of the sandwich _____ thrown away.
> • All individuals _____ equal before the law.
> • Do you know where a needle and thread _____?

① were – are – are   ② were – is – is

③ was – are – are   ④ was – are – is

⑤ was – is – is

» 실전 Tip 「A and B」가 하나의 사물이나 사람을 나타낼 때는 단수 취급한다. e.g. a teacher and poet(교사이자 시인인 한 사람) a teacher and a poet(교사 한 사람과 시인 한 사람)

02 다음 문장에서 어법상 어색한 부분을 바르게 고친 것은?

① The car which he drives are mine.
 (drives → drove)

② Not only you but also your sister is brave.
 (is → are)

③ The number of stars are shining in the sky.
 (The → A)

④ An actor and singer was singing on the stage. (was → were)

⑤ Three quarters of the Earth's surface is covered with water. (is → are)

03 다음 문장 중 어법상 어색한 것을 모두 고르면?

① Most of the colleagues I work with is very friendly.

② To experience many things are important for you.

③ Every boy and girl was enjoying the field trip.

④ Either she or I have the wrong answer.

⑤ Five years have already passed since my father passed away.

» 실전 Tip every는 A and B로 연결되어도 단수 취급한다.

04 다음 문장 중 어법상 알맞은 것끼리 짝지어진 것은?

> ⓐ Your new shoes look expensive.
> ⓑ Remembering people's names are not easy for me.
> ⓒ The elderly is an important part of our society.
> ⓓ Is two thousand dollars a month a livable salary?

① ⓐ, ⓑ   ② ⓐ, ⓒ   ③ ⓑ, ⓒ

④ ⓑ, ⓓ   ⑤ ⓐ, ⓓ

---

05 다음 문장의 빈칸에 들어갈 수 없는 것은?

> I was thankful that _____.

① she was safe   ② we have met

③ I could find him   ④ you were with me

⑤ he had been rescued

06 다음 우리말과 같도록 할 때 빈칸에 알맞은 말끼리 짝지어진 것은?

> 우리는 한글이 1446년에 발명된 것을 안다.
> → We _____ Hangeul _____ in 1446.

① know – was invented   ② knew – invented

③ know – is invented   ④ knew – invents

⑤ know – invents

07 다음 문장 중 어법상 어색한 것은?

① Emma says she will be busy tomorrow.

② He thought I would be perfect for the job.

③ Everybody said that Seho is a hardworking student.

④ I thought two heads were better than one.

⑤ Mr. Kim knows I have been sick for a week.

대표유형 01 수 일치   출제율 55%

08 주어진 표현을 이용하여 우리말을 영작하시오.

> 수학은 내가 가장 좋아하는 과목이다.
> (mathematics, favorite, subject)

→ _____

09 다음 〈보기〉에서 알맞은 표현을 골라 문장을 완성하시오.

> 보기
> • two-thirds of the students
> • some of the books
> • the rest of the money

(1) _____ is yours.
(2) _____ enjoy playing computer games.

10 다음 우리말과 같도록 〈보기〉에서 알맞은 표현을 골라 활용하여 쓰시오. (단, 중복 사용 가능)

> 보기   tourists   be   visit   number   elephants

(1) 많은 관광객들이 매년 한국을 방문한다.
 → _____ Korea every year.
(2) 코끼리의 수가 빠르게 감소하고 있다.
 → _____ decreasing rapidly.

대표유형 02 시제 일치   출제율 45%

11 다음 밑줄 친 부분을 바르게 고쳐 쓰시오.

> ⓐ He thinks the group had dinner soon.
> ⓑ He learned that water froze at 0℃.
> ⓒ She said that she will go to Busan next month.
> ⓓ Did you tell her that you miss the last bus?

ⓐ → _____   ⓑ → _____
ⓒ → _____   ⓓ → _____

[12-14] 밑줄 친 주절의 시제를 바꿔 문장을 쓸 때 빈칸에 알맞은 말을 쓰시오.

12

> We guess that the police did not find the missing boy.

→ We guessed that _____
_____.

>> 실전 Tip 주절의 시제가 현재에서 과거로 바뀔 때, 종속절의 시제 변화: 현재 → 과거, 현재완료 → 과거완료, 과거 → 과거완료, will → would

13

> He asked me whether she had arrived.

→ He asks me _____.

14

> We know that the sun sets in the west.

→ We knew that _____.

15 다음 중 어법상 어색한 문장을 두 개 골라 기호를 쓰고, 바르게 고쳐 쓰시오.

> ⓐ She asked me if I have fed the puppies.
> ⓑ I thought she went to bed at 10 p.m. every night.
> ⓒ My mother realized she had left her keys in the car.
> ⓓ Do you remember that I gave the book to you?
> ⓔ The teacher said we would go on a field trip to City Hall the next morning.

(1) _____ : _____ → _____
(2) _____ : _____ → _____

01 다음 중 어법상 옳은 문장의 개수는?

> ⓐ Where is my gloves?
> ⓑ A watch and a jewel were stolen.
> ⓒ Each of my friends has a cell phone.
> ⓓ Statistics are a branch of mathematics.
> ⓔ A number of big matches were held in this stadium.

① 1개　　　② 2개　　　③ 3개
④ 4개　　　⑤ 5개

02 다음 문장 중 어법상 알맞은 것은?

① Half of the fruit in the box are rotton.
② David said that he likes me much.
③ I told the boy that two and two made four.
④ She realized that she had made a terrible mistake.
⑤ The history book says Columbus discovers America in 1492.

03 다음 괄호 안의 동사를 빈칸에 알맞은 형태로 쓸 때, 시제가 나머지 넷과 **다른** 것은?

① It is said that practice_____ perfect. (make)
② My brother said that his old bike _____ to be fixed. (need)
③ The foreigner didn't know that Korea _____ four seasons. (have)
④ The child knew that France _____ much bigger than Korea. (be)
⑤ We learned that swallows _____ south for the winter. (fly)

04 다음 표는 학생의 교복 착용에 관한 설문 조사 결과이다. 표의 내용과 일치하도록 〈조건〉에 맞게 문장을 완성하시오.

총 학생 수	30명
찬성하는 학생 수	6명
반대하는 학생 수	15명
기타 의견	9명

> [조건] number, one-fifth, half를 이용할 것

(1) _____ _____ _____ the students in the class _____ thirty.
(2) _____ - _____ _____ _____ _____ _____ for school uniforms.
(3) _____ _____ _____ _____ _____ against school uniforms.

05 다음 대화에서 동사의 형태가 어법상 <u>어색한</u> 것을 <u>모두</u> 찾아 바르게 고쳐 쓰시오.

> **A** Here is the dessert menus, sir. Which would you like for dessert, ice cream or cake?
> **B** Either are fine with me.
> **A** My restaurant is famous for its ice cream sundae.
> **B** OK, I took it.

06 다음 〈조건〉에 맞게 우리말을 영작하시오.

> 나는 모든 사람들이 교통 법규를 지켜야 한다고 생각한다.

> [조건] 1. 7단어로 쓸 것
> 　　　 2. person, have to, follow를 활용할 것

→ _____ traffic rules.

최종 선택 QUIZ

어법상 옳은 문장에
✔ 표시하세요.

01
a Every cloud has a silver lining.

b Every cloud have a silver lining.

02
a The Philippines consists of more than 7,000 islands.

b The Philippines consist of more than 7,000 islands.

03
a A number of scholars attended the meeting.

b The number of scholars attended the meeting.

04
a The rest of the passengers was rescued.

b The rest of the passengers were rescued.

05
a Slow and steady wins the race.

b Slow and steady win the race.

06
a David said that he will open another restaurant next month

b David said that he would open another restaurant next month.

07
a I couldn't believe that he has done volunteer work for years.

b I couldn't believe that he had done volunteer work for years.

08
a Galileo found out that the Earth revolves around the sun.

b Galileo found out that the Earth revolved around the sun.

유형별 기출 적용 빈도

유형		빈도
유형 01	화법 전환	25%
유형 02	강조	35%
유형 03	도치	25%
유형 04	통합형	15%

>> **출제 포인트**
화법 전환, 「It is[was] ~ that」 강조 구문, 부정어, 부사구 등이 도치될 때 어순을 묻는 문제가 자주 출제된다.

>> **정답률 100% Tip**
1 「It ~ that ...」 강조 구문과 「It(가주어) ~ that(진주어) ...」 구문 구별하기
2 「so[neither]+동사+주어」에서 동사는 앞서 쓰인 동사의 종류에 맞추어 써야 함

Grammar Point

Point ① 화법 전환

	동사 전환	주절과 피전달문 연결	대명사, 부사(구) 일치
평서문	say → say say to → tell	접속사 that으로 연결	this → that here → there
의문문	say (to) → ask	의문사나 if[whether]로 연결	now → then ago → before
명령문	say (to) → tell, order, advise, ask, warn 등	• 긍정명령문 → to부정사 • 부정명령문 → not+to 부정사	today → that day tomorrow → the next[following] day

Jenny said to me, "You look great today." 〈직접 화법〉
→ Jenny told me that I looked great that day. 〈간접 화법〉

Point ② 강조

동사를 강조할 때는 주어의 인칭과 수, 시제를 맞추어 「do[does/did]+동사원형」의 형태로 쓴다. 주어나 목적어, 부사(구) 등을 강조할 때는 강조하고자 하는 말을 It is[was]와 that 사이에 넣어 「It is[was] ~ that ....」의 형태로 쓴다.
Annie did promise to come here yesterday. 〈동사 강조〉
It was Eric that[who] played computer games. 〈주어 강조〉

Point ③ 도치

• 장소 · 방향을 나타내는 부사(구) 도치: 「부사(구)+동사+주어」
• 부정어 도치: 「부정어+조동사/do동사+주어+동사」 또는 「부정어+be동사+주어」
• 「so[neither/nor]+동사+주어」: ~도 또한 그렇다[아니다]
Down came a shower. 〈방향의 부사 강조〉 *cf.* Down it came. 〈부사+대명사 주어+동사〉
Never have I seen her since then. 〈부정어 강조〉
I'm hungry. – So am I. (= I'm hungry, too.)
I don't like math. – Neither[Nor] do I. (= I don't like math, either.)

✅ **바로 체크**

01 Sarah (said / told) me that she was so tired.

02 I asked Susan how (she was / was she).

03 Mother asked me (if / that) I was hungry.

04 The teacher told the students (don't / not to) run in the classroom.

05 Billy does (want / wants) to marry Judy.

06 It was Mark (which / that) broke the window with his ball.

07 Little (I dreamed / did I dream) that I would pass the test.

08 I can't believe that our team lost the game. – (So / Neither) can I.

대표유형 01 화법 전환   출제율 25%

01 주어진 문장을 다음과 같이 바꿔 쓸 때 빈칸에 알맞은 것은?

> Mike said, "I am busy now."
> → Mike said that _____.

① I was busy now   ② I was busy then
③ he is busy now   ④ he was busy now
⑤ he was busy then

02 주어진 문장을 다음과 같이 바꿔 쓸 때 빈칸에 알맞은 말을 모두 고르면?

> Liz said to me, "Can you help me with my math homework?"
> → Liz asked me _____ I could help her with her math homework.

① if   ② and   ③ what
④ that   ⑤ whether

03 주어진 문장을 다음과 같이 바꿔 쓸 때 빈칸에 알맞은 말이 순서대로 짝지어진 것은?

> The foreigner said to me, "Where is the nearest bookstore?"
> → The foreigner _____ me _____ the nearest bookstore was.

① said – if   ② said – where
③ asked – if   ④ asked – that
⑤ asked – where

04 주어진 문장을 다음과 같이 바꿔 쓸 때 빈칸에 알맞은 것은?

> Mother said to Ryan, "Be careful while crossing the street."
> → Mother told Ryan _____ careful while crossing the street.

① be   ② being   ③ been
④ to be   ⑤ to being

[05-06] 주어진 문장을 다음과 같이 바꿔 쓸 때 빈칸에 알맞은 말을 쓰시오.

05

> Julie said to me, "I will go to the amusement park on the weekend."
> → Julie _____ me _____ _____ _____ go to the amusement park on the weekend.

06

> Dad said to me, "Don't eat junk food."
> → Dad told me _____ _____ _____ junk food.

07 다음 문장에서 어법상 어색한 부분을 찾아 바르게 고쳐 쓰시오.

> The teacher asked students whether was the report going well.

_____ → _____

08 다음 중 화법 전환이 잘못된 것은?

① He said, "I can't remember your name."
  → He said that he couldn't remember my name.
② Greg said to me, "I will prepare for the exam today."
  → Greg told me that he would prepare for the exam that day.
③ Jim said to me, "Do you know Bill's address?"
  → Jim asked me that I knew Bill's address.
④ She said to John, "Where are you from?"
  → She asked John where he was from.
⑤ The teacher said to her, "Don't give up your dream."
  → The teacher told her not to give up her dream.

대표유형 02 강조   출제율 35%

09 다음 밑줄 친 말을 강조하여 다시 쓸 때 빈칸에 알맞은 말을 쓰시오.

> Helen <u>worries</u> about her mom's health.
> → Helen _____ about her mom's health.

10 다음 중 밑줄 친 부분의 쓰임이 〈보기〉와 같은 것은?

> 보기 I <u>do</u> think she's right.

① It will <u>do</u>.
② I <u>do</u> not like horror movies.
③ We <u>do</u> love to go to the amusement park.
④ <u>Do</u> your homework first, George.
⑤ When <u>do</u> you leave for Chicago?

11 다음 문장 중 어법상 어색한 것을 <u>모두</u> 고르면?

① I do believe you.
② My sister does hates spiders.
③ I did see the accident.
④ Mia and Chris does know your secret.
⑤ You do look nice in that jacket.

[12-13] 다음 문장의 밑줄 친 부분을 강조하는 문장으로 바꿔 쓸 때 빈칸에 알맞은 말을 쓰시오.

12

> Martin <u>decided</u> to major in computer science in college.
> → Martin _____ _____ to major in computer science in college.

13

> Her family's generosity made a great impact on young Mother Teresa's life.
> → _____ _____ her family's generosity _____ made a great impact on young Mother Teresa's life.

14 다음 밑줄 친 부분을 강조하여 문장을 다시 쓰시오.

> The accident changed my plan.

→ _____

15 다음 문장의 밑줄 친 부분을 강조하여 다시 쓴 것 중 <u>어색한</u> 것은?

① Sumi left for Busan <u>yesterday</u>.
 → It was yesterday that Sumi left for Busan.
② I lost <u>Eva's book</u> on the bus.
 → It was Eva's book that I lost on the bus.
③ We met Dorothy <u>in the park</u>.
 → It was in the park that we met Dorothy.
④ <u>Minho</u> likes to draw cartoons.
 → It is Minho that likes to draw cartoons.
⑤ Mary <u>watched</u> the soccer game in the living room.
 → It was watched that Mary did the soccer game in the living room.

16 다음 밑줄 친 부분 중 쓰임이 나머지 넷과 <u>다른</u> 것은?

① It was John <u>that</u> I met last Friday.
② It is your happiness <u>that</u> matters most.
③ It was a sweater <u>that</u> I bought at the shop.
④ It is important <u>that</u> you should do your best.
⑤ It was in 1929 <u>that</u> the first Oscar ceremony took place.

대표유형 03 도치   출제율 25%

17 주어진 문장을 다음과 같이 바꿔 쓸 때 빈칸에 알맞은 것은?

> The bus comes here.
> → Here _____.

① the bus comes
② does the bus come
③ come the bus
④ comes the bus
⑤ the bus does come

18 다음 빈칸에 들어갈 말로 알맞은 것은?

> Andy lives in New York, and so _____ Nancy.

① do ② does ③ did ④ is ⑤ was

19 다음 대화의 밑줄 친 ⓐ와 ⓑ 대신 쓸 수 있는 말이 순서대로 짝지어진 것은?

> • **A** I've been to Australia.
>   **B** ⓐ I've been to Australia, too.
> • **A** I don't like science.
>   **B** ⓑ I don't like science, either.

① So do I. – So am I.
② So have I. – Neither am I.
③ So have I. – Neither do I.
④ Neither am I. – Neither do I.
⑤ Neither have I. – So do I.

20 다음 문장에서 어법상 어색한 부분을 찾아 바르게 고쳐 쓰시오.

> I enjoyed fishing, and so she did.

_____ → _____

21 다음 문장을 주어진 말로 시작하여 바꿔 쓰시오.

> Two little boys were in the back seat of the car.
> → In the back seat of the car _____
>   _____.

22 다음 밑줄 친 부분을 강조하여 도치시킨 문장으로 알맞은 것은?

> Joseph was <u>never</u> kind to his classmates.

① Never Joseph was kind to his classmates.
② Never Joseph wasn't kind to his classmates.
③ Never was Joseph kind to his classmates.
④ Never wasn't Joseph kind to his classmates.
⑤ Never does Joseph be kind to his classmates.

23 다음 밑줄 친 부분을 강조하는 문장으로 바꿔 쓸 때 빈칸에 알맞은 말을 쓰시오.

> We stayed <u>not a single day</u> in the hotel.
> → _____ a single day _____
>   _____ in the hotel.

≫ 실전 Tip 동사가 일반동사이면 주어 앞에 do[does/did]를 써야 한다.

24 다음 짝지어진 대화 중 어색한 것은?

① I am hungry and tired. – So do I.
② I saw Brendan yesterday. – So did I.
③ Mike can play the piano. – So can I.
④ I don't like vegetables. – Neither do I.
⑤ I won't go there again. – Neither will I.

≫ 실전 Tip 「so[neither/nor]+동사+주어」를 쓸 때 동사는 앞서 쓰인 동사의 종류에 맞추어 써야 한다.

25 다음 밑줄 친 부분 중 어법상 어색한 것을 모두 고르면?

① Mary passed the test, and <u>so did I</u>.
② <u>Seldom does my mother wear</u> jewelry these days.
③ Sue doesn't like to travel alone, and <u>so does Anne</u>.
④ <u>Nowhere in the world is there</u> a place like home.
⑤ <u>Hardly we talked</u> to each other during those two hours.

대표유형 01 화법 전환   출제율 25%

01 주어진 문장을 다음과 같이 바꿔 쓸 때 빈칸에 알맞은 말이 순서대로 짝지어진 것은?

> The doctor said to Mr. James, "Don't have too much caffeine."
> → The doctor _____ Mr. James _____ too much caffeine.

① said – to not have ② advised – not to have
③ told – to not have ④ said – not having
⑤ advised – don't to have

02 다음 글의 밑줄 친 ①~⑤ 중 어법상 어색한 것은?

> ① On my way to school, an old lady ② was carrying heavy luggage. I asked her ③ that I ④ could help her. She ⑤ said with a smile, "Oh, thanks a lot."

대표유형 02 강조   출제율 35%

03 다음 우리말을 영어로 옮길 때 빈칸에 알맞은 것은?

> Jonathan은 정말로 네가 낫기를 바란다.
> → Jonathan _____ that you'll get well.

① does hope ② does hopes ③ do hope
④ do hopes ⑤ did hopes

04 다음 중 밑줄 친 부분의 쓰임이 나머지 넷과 다른 것은?

① She did study very hard.
② I do want to meet her in person.
③ Jason did the dishes after dinner.
④ We do agree with your opinion.
⑤ Our family did have a good time in Sydney.

05 다음 문장의 밑줄 친 부분을 강조하여 다시 쓴 것 중 올바른 것은?

① My mother makes her own clothes.
  → My mother does makes her own clothes.
② I believed what you said to me.
  → I do believe what you said to me.
③ John's strong will made him succeed.
  → It is John's strong will that made him succeed.
④ Alexander Graham Bell invented the telephone.
  → It was the telephone who Alexander Graham Bell invented.
⑤ Nancy met her friends in front of the theater.
  → It was in front of the theater that Nancy met her friends.

대표유형 04 통합형   출제율 15%

06 다음 문장 중 어법상 어색한 것은?

① In front of the door stood a tall man.
② The coach told the players to do their best.
③ Little did Sophia realize the danger she was in.
④ Jim is good at singing, and so does Mike.
⑤ It was the action movie that Edward watched with Mark.

07 다음 중 빈칸에 들어갈 말이 나머지 넷과 다른 것은?

① Tim asked Jenny _____ he could borrow her science notebook.
② Billy told Cathy _____ he was glad to see her.
③ It was her smartphone _____ Annie was looking for.
④ It was at that moment _____ I realized my mistake.
⑤ Charles said _____ he didn't mean to hurt my feelings.

대표유형 01 화법 전환 출제율 25%

08 다음 문장을 간접 화법으로 바꿔 쓰시오.

> Lisa said, "I will go hiking tomorrow."

→ _____

09 다음 문장을 간접 화법으로 바꿀 때, 빈칸에 알맞은 말을 쓰시오.

(1)
> I said to her, "How did you spend your holiday?"

→ I asked her _____.

(2)
> The guide said to us, "Don't feed the animals in the zoo."

→ The guide told _____.

10 다음 대화의 내용에 맞게 문장을 완성하시오.

> **Brad** Have you ever visited Korea?
> **Ellen** No, I haven't.

→ Brad asked Ellen _____
  Korea. Ellen said that _____.

대표유형 02 강조 출제율 35%

11 다음 문장의 밑줄 친 부분을 강조하여 문장을 다시 쓰시오.

(1) I told him the truth.
  → _____

(2) Jack wants to buy a new laptop.
  → _____

12 〈조건〉에 맞게 다음 우리말을 영작하시오.

> [조건] 괄호 안의 표현을 사용하되, 필요 없는 2개는 제외할 것

> Steve가 내게 전화를 했던 것은 바로 어젯밤이었다.
> (me, is, that, Steve, was, it, called, who, last night)

→ _____

대표유형 03 도치 출제율 25%

13 다음 문장을 주어진 말로 시작하여 다시 쓰시오.

> I never dreamed of winning the first prize.

→ Never _____.

14 다음 두 문장이 같은 뜻이 되도록 빈칸에 알맞은 말을 쓰시오.

(1) Susie felt guilty, and so did I.
  = Susie felt guilty, and I _____ _____,
  _____.

(2) Kate can't drive a car, and neither can her brother.
  = Kate can't drive a car, and her brother
  _____ _____ _____ _____,
  _____.

15 다음 우리말과 같은 뜻이 되도록 빈칸에 알맞은 말을 쓰시오.

> Sue는 입학시험에 합격하지 못했고, Amy도 역시 합격하지 못했다.
> → Sue didn't pass the entrance exam, and
> _____ _____ _____.

대표유형 02, 03 강조/도치 출제율 35%

01 다음 대화의 빈칸에 들어갈 말이 순서대로 바르게 짝지어진 것은?

> **A** Why didn't Sam come to your birthday party?
> **B** He _____. It was Kevin _____ didn't come.

① did come – that
② did came – who
③ do came – who
④ does come – who
⑤ does came – that

02 다음 중 밑줄 친 부분의 쓰임이 나머지 넷과 다른 것은?

① It was Miranda that scored the last goal.
② It was a ring that he held in his hand.
③ It was at the Italian restaurant that she first met him.
④ It was shocking that he left without saying anything.
⑤ It is in winter that most tourists gather here.

03 다음 우리말을 영어로 옮길 때 빈칸에 알맞은 것은?

> 그는 동아리 모임에 제시간에 오는 적이 거의 없다.
> → _____ to the club meeting on time.

① Hardly he doesn't come
② Hardly comes he
③ Hardly he does come
④ Hardly does he come
⑤ Hardly does he comes

>> 실전 Tip hardly, rarely, seldom, scarcely 등은 부정의 의미를 포함하고 있으므로 not과 함께 쓰지 않는다.

04 다음 문장의 밑줄 친 부분을 강조하여 문장 앞으로 보낼 때, 주어와 동사의 자리에 변화가 없는 것을 모두 고르면?

① It is here.
② He goes there.
③ An old castle stood over the hill.
④ I did not stay there last night.
⑤ The bird flew away.

대표유형 04 통합형 출제율 15%

05 다음 문장 중 어법상 어색한 것을 모두 고르면?

① The lifeguard warned us to not swim so far from shore.
② Under the tree were there a lot of people.
③ It was last Christmas that I sent him a special gift.
④ He didn't believe the fact, and neither did I.
⑤ Rarely he had seen such a beautiful moon.

06 다음 우리말을 영어로 바르게 옮긴 문장을 모두 고르면?

① Peter는 어제 정말로 Sally를 만나고 싶었다.
  → Peter did wanted to see Sally yesterday.
② 그녀는 James에게 늦지 말라고 말했다.
  → She told James not being late.
③ 엄마는 내게 숙제를 끝냈는지 물어보셨다.
  → Mom asked me if I had finished my homework.
④ Martin에게는 큰 개가 있고, Kate도 역시 그렇다.
  → Martin has a big dog, and so Kate has.
⑤ 통조림을 발명한 사람은 바로 Napoleon이었다.
  → It was Napoleon who invented canned food.

07 다음 중 어법상 어색한 문장의 개수는?

> ⓐ Annie asked her mom what time it was.
> ⓑ Not a word did my father say.
> ⓒ It was in the library that I saw Megan.
> ⓓ I haven't heard of this song, neither did my friends.
> ⓔ Mickey did turn off the stove before leaving the house.

① 1개 ② 2개 ③ 3개 ④ 4개 ⑤ 5개

대표유형 01 화법 전환　　　　　　　　출제율 25%

08 다음 문장을 괄호 안의 단어를 이용하여 간접 화법으로 바꿔 쓰시오.

> He said to her, "Don't park your car here."

→ _____ (order)

09 다음 대화를 간접 화법으로 바꿀 때, 빈칸에 알맞은 말을 쓰시오.

> **Sam** Can you take care of my dog while I'm away?
> **Julie** Sure, I can. When are you coming back?

→ Sam asked Julie _____
_____. Julie said that she
could and asked _____.

대표유형 02, 03 강조 / 도치　　　　　　　출제율 35%

10 다음 괄호 안의 단어를 이용하여 우리말을 영작하시오.

> 그 의사는 그녀를 살리기 위해 정말 노력했다. (do, try, save)

→ _____

11 〈조건〉에 맞게 대화의 빈칸에 알맞은 대답을 쓰시오.

> [조건] **1.** 괄호 안의 말을 강조하여 완전한 문장으로 답할 것
> **2.** 「It ~ that」 구문을 이용할 것

A Who was attacked by the lion?
B _____
(the zookeeper)

12 다음 우리말의 밑줄 친 부분이 강조되도록 괄호 안의 단어를 바르게 배열하시오.

> 나는 그런 이상한 이야기를 들은 적이 <u>결코 없다</u>.
> (have, such a, story, never, I, heard, strange)

→ _____

13 다음 두 문장이 같은 의미가 되도록 빈칸에 알맞은 말을 쓰시오. (단, so나 neither를 이용할 것)

(1) I forgot to bring an umbrella, and my sister forgot to bring one, too.
　　→ I forgot to bring an umbrella, and
　　_____.

(2) Olivia has never ridden a horse, and Max has never ridden a horse, either.
　　→ Olivia has never ridden a horse, and
　　_____.

대표유형 04 통합형　　　　　　　　　　출제율 15%

14 다음 중 어법상 어색한 문장을 2개 찾아 기호를 쓰고 바르게 고쳐 쓰시오.

> ⓐ Rarely they eat any kind of fish.
> ⓑ Emma is from England, and so are we.
> ⓒ Alex doesn't want to go to the beach, and neither doesn't Steve.
> ⓓ It was on Friday night that the shop was broken into.

(1) _____ : _____ → _____
(2) _____ : _____ → _____

15 다음 문장을 괄호 안의 지시대로 바꿔 쓰시오.

(1) He said to Mary, "Do you want to get a refund?" (간접 화법을 이용하여)
　　→ _____

(2) She told me that she had moved there a year before. (직접 화법을 이용하여)
　　→ _____

(3) He took the medicine after dinner. (동사를 강조하여)
　　→ _____

(4) His films have seldom received positive reviews. (부정어를 강조하여)
　　→ _____

01 다음 빈칸에 들어갈 말이 나머지 넷과 <u>다른</u> 것은?

① I am not the only child. – _____ am I.
② I went to bed early last night. – _____ did I.
③ I can't solve this problem. – _____ can I.
④ I don't like action movies. – _____ do I.
⑤ I have never been to America. – _____ have I.

02 다음 문장을 밑줄 친 부분을 강조하여 바꿔 쓸 때 어법상 <u>어색한</u> 것끼리 묶은 것은?

ⓐ Mr. Brown <u>made</u> a chocolate cake for us.
 → Mr. Brown did made a chocolate cake for us.
ⓑ Minho bought <u>a new bike</u> at the shop.
 → It was a new bike that Minho bought at the shop.
ⓒ A police officer stood <u>at the bus stop</u>.
 → At the bus stop stood a police officer.
ⓓ John <u>little</u> imagined that he would become an idol.
 → Little imagined John that he would become an idol.

① ⓐ, ⓑ ② ⓐ, ⓓ ③ ⓐ, ⓒ, ⓓ
④ ⓑ, ⓒ, ⓓ ⑤ ⓐ, ⓑ, ⓒ, ⓓ

03 다음 문장을 괄호 안의 단어를 이용하여 간접 화법으로 바꿔 쓰시오.

(1) She said to me, "Keep the door locked."
(2) They said to him, "How long have you been waiting here?"
(3) Sally said to Jack, "Can you give me a ride home tomorrow?"

(1) _____ (warn)
(2) _____
 (ask)
(3) _____
 _____ (ask)

04 다음 짝지어진 대화 중 <u>어색한</u> 것을 <u>모두</u> 고르면?

① A Will you join the band?
 B I won't join it, and neither Sam will.
② A You should have apologized to Eric.
 B But I did apologize to him.
③ A Who was it that wrote this poem?
 B It was Nicolas who wrote the poem.
④ A Hardly I can believe that this can ever happen.
 B Nor can I.
⑤ A What did the doctor say?
 B She advised me not to use my right hand for a while.

05 다음은 세 학생의 좋아하는 과목과 싫어하는 과목을 나타낸 표이다. 표의 내용에 맞게 빈칸에 알맞은 말을 쓰시오. (단, so나 neither를 이용할 것)

Name	Likes	Dislikes
Eva	history, P.E.	math, science
Paul	math, history	French, P.E.
Lydia	math, French	science, P.E.

(1) Eva likes history, and _____ _____
 _____.
(2) Paul doesn't like P.E., and _____
 _____.

06 다음 밑줄 친 부분을 강조하는 문장으로 바꿔 쓰시오.

<u>Diana</u>	<u>found</u>	<u>a cat</u>	<u>under the car</u>	<u>yesterday</u>.
(1)	(2)	(3)	(4)	(5)

(1) _____
 _____
(2) _____
 _____
(3) _____
 _____
(4) _____
 _____
(5) _____
 _____

01
a I love to read fantasy novels. – So do I.

b I love to read fantasy novels. – So am I.

02
a The clerk asked me what color of shirt would I like to buy.

b The clerk asked me what color of shirt I would like to buy.

03
a The tour guide told us not to take pictures in the gallery.

b The tour guide told us don't take pictures in the gallery.

04
a Patrick did remember what he saw last night.

b Patrick did remembered what he saw last night.

05
a Never does Nick realize that Judy is preparing a surprise party for him.

b Never Nick realizes that Judy is preparing a surprise party for him.

06
a It was in her backpack that Chloe found her passport.

b It was in her backpack which Chloe found her passport.

07
a John didn't pass the driving test, and neither didn't David.

b John didn't pass the driving test, and neither did David.

08
a Hardly Mr. Thompson has time to exercise every day.

b Hardly does Mr. Thompson have time to exercise every day.

memo

1

미래를 바꾸는
긍정의 한 마디

저는 미래가 어떻게 전개될지는 모르지만,
누가 그 미래를 결정하는지는 압니다.

오프라 윈프리(Oprah Winfrey)

오프라 윈프리는 불우한 어린 시절을 겪었지만 좌절하지 않고 열심히 노력하여
세계에서 가장 유명한 TV 토크쇼의 진행자가 되었어요.
오프라 윈프리의 성공기를 오프라이즘(Oprahism)이라 부른다고 해요.
오프라이즘이란 '인생의 성공 여부는
온전히 개인에게 달려있다'라는 뜻이랍니다.

인생의 꽃길은 다른 사람이 아닌, 오직 '나'만이 만들 수 있어요.

문제 Q

바로 푸는 문법

1460제

LEVEL

3

ANSWERS

CHUNJAE
EDUCATION, INC.

문제

바로 푸는 문법

UNIT 01 5형식

✅ 바로 체크
p. 8

01 a fool	02 happy	03 swim	04 to help
05 clean	06 busy	07 to go	08 boring
09 singing	10 repaired		

STEP 1 · 만만한 기초
pp. 9 – 11

01 ①　　02 ⑤　　03 ③　　04 fascinating　　05 leader
06 ③　　07 ③　　08 in　　09 in → at　　10 ③　　11 ⑤
12 to keep　　13 ③　　14 My parents want me to be a
scientist.　　15 ③　　16 gave → to give　　17 not to play
18 ⑤　　19 I saw him cross the street.　　20 ①
21 stolen　　22 ③　　23 He had his car washed.　　24 ④
25 ①

01 find와 make의 목적격보어로 형용사가 알맞다.

02 make의 목적격보어로 부사는 올 수 없다.

03 ③ keep의 목적격보어로 부사는 올 수 없으므로 부사 cleanly는 형용사 clean으로 써야 한다.

04 주제가 '흥미로운' 것이므로 find의 목적격보어로 형용사 fascinating이 알맞다.

05 elect의 목적격보어로는 명사가 올 수 있으므로 lead를 leader로 고쳐 써야 한다.

06 ③은 「동사 + 간접목적어 + 직접목적어」의 4형식 문장이고, 나머지는 모두 「동사 + 목적어 + 목적격보어」의 5형식 문장이다.

07 「get + 목적어 + in trouble」은 '~을 곤경에 처하게 하다'의 의미로 in big trouble은 get의 목적격보어이다.

08 in good shape는 목적격보어로 쓰인 전치사구로 '건강한 상태로'의 의미이다.

09 make oneself at home은 '자신의 집에 있는 것처럼 편히 쉬다'의 의미로 여기서의 at home은 make의 목적격보어이다.

10 tell은 목적격보어로 to부정사를 취한다.

11 help는 목적격보어로 동사원형과 to부정사를 둘 다 취한다.

12 ask는 목적격보어로 to부정사를 취하는 동사이므로 to keep을 써야 한다.

13 ask, tell, want는 목적격보어로 to부정사를 취하고 help는 to부정사와 동사원형 둘 다 취하는데, make는 목적격보어로 동사원형을 취한다.

14 「주어 + want + 목적어 + 목적격보어(to부정사)」의 어순으로 배열해야 한다.

15 allow는 목적격보어로 to부정사를 취하고, let은 동사원형을 취한다.

16 advise는 목적격보어로 to부정사를 취하므로 gave를 to give로 고쳐 써야 한다.

17 ask는 목적격보어로 to부정사를 취하는데, to부정사의 부정은 to부정사 앞에 not을 쓴다.

18 지각동사 hear는 목적어와 목적격보어의 관계가 능동일 때 목적격보어로 동사원형이나 현재분사를 취한다.

19 「주어 + 지각동사 see + 목적어 + 목적격보어(동사원형)」의 어순으로 배열한다.

20 사역동사 make는 목적격보어로 동사원형이나 과거분사를 취하는데, 목적어와 목적격보어의 관계가 능동이므로 동사원형 fix가 알맞다.

21 have의 목적어와 목적격보어의 관계가 수동이므로 과거분사 stolen을 써야 한다.

22 leave의 목적어와 목적격보어의 관계가 능동이므로 현재분사 waiting을 써야 한다.

23 「have + 목적어 + 과거분사」는 '~되도록 하다, ~을 당하다'를 의미한다.

24 지각동사 listen to의 목적어와 목적격보어의 관계가 수동의 의미이므로 과거분사 played가 목적격보어로 와야 하고, 동사 find의 목적어와 목적격보어의 관계는 능동의 의미이므로 현재분사 sleeping이 목적격보어로 알맞다.

25 목적어인 my name과 목적격보어가 수동의 관계이므로 과거분사 called로 써야 한다.

STEP 2 · 오답률 40~60% 문제
pp. 12 – 13

01 ④　　02 ③　　03 ①　　04 ②　　05 ①　　06 ⑤
07 ⑤　　08 read → to read　　09 play[playing]　　10 you
to do　　11 closing → closed　　12 He kept me waiting
for an hour.　　13 (1) I had my computer repaired.　　(2) He
saw her take[taking] a walk.　　14 washed　　15 cried →
cry[crying]

01 ④ find는 목적격보어로 형용사를 쓰므로 동사 excite는 형용사 exciting으로 써야 한다.

02 find의 목적격보어로 형용사 easy, make의 목적격보어로 형용사 angry가 알맞다.

03 ①은 「동사 + 간접목적어 + 직접목적어」의 4형식 문장이고, 나머지는 모두 「동사 + 목적어 + 목적격보어」의 5형식 문장이다.

04 ask는 목적격보어로 to부정사를, make는 동사원형을 취한다.

05 let은 목적격보어로 동사원형을 쓰고, allow는 to부정사를 쓴다.

06 ① cried → cry[crying] ② to sleep → sleeping ③ go → to go ④ to swim → swim

07 advise는 목적격보어로 to부정사를 취하므로 to play가 알맞다.

08 동사 ask는 목적격보어로 to부정사를 취한다.

09 지각동사 see의 목적격보어로 동사원형 또는 현재분사를 써야 한다.

10 want의 목적어로 you를 쓰고, want는 목적격보어로 to부정사를 취하는 동사이므로 to do를 써야 한다.

11 목적어 the door와 목적격보어의 관계가 수동이므로 과거분사 closed를 써야 한다.

12 '~를 기다리게 하다'는 「keep + 목적어 + waiting」으로 표현한다.

13 (1) have의 목적어와 목적격보어의 관계가 수동이므로 과거분사 repaired를 써서 문장을 완성한다.

(2) 지각동사 see의 목적어와 목적격보어의 관계가 능동이므로 목적격보어로 동사원형 또는 현재분사를 쓸 수 있다.

14 have의 목적어 the dog와 목적격보어의 관계가 수동이므로 과거분사 washed로 써야 한다.

15 지각동사 hear의 목적어 her baby와 목적격보어의 관계가 능동이므로 목적격보어로 동사원형 cry 또는 현재분사 crying을 써야 한다.

13 find의 목적어 an old man과 목적격보어의 관계가 능동이므로 lived를 현재분사 living으로 고쳐야 한다.

14 동사 feel의 목적어 her hair와 목적격보어의 관계가 수동이므로 과거분사 touched를 써서 문장을 완성한다.

15 '~가 재미있다는 것을 알다'는 「find + 목적어 + interesting」으로 표현할 수 있고, '~가 …에 흥미를 갖게 만들다'는 「make + 목적어 + interested in」으로 표현할 수 있다.

STEP 3 · 오답률 60~80%문제
pp. 14 – 15

01 ②　02 ⑤　03 ②, ⑤　04 ③　05 ③　06 ③, ⑤
07 ⑤　08 sadly → sad, to cry → cry　09 brush, to brush　10 me not to listen　11 to move → move, safety → safe　12 Ted tried to get his album released.
13 lived → living　14 Caren felt her hair touched by someone.　15 I found the history movie (was) interesting. And the movie made me (become) interested in history.

01 목적격보어로 부사는 쓸 수 없고 형용사를 써야 한다.
① cleanly → clean ③ sadly → sad ④ thoughtfully → thoughtful ⑤ comfortably → comfortable

02 ⑤는 '그의 부모님은 그에게 책상을 만들어주셨다.'라는 의미로 「주어 + 동사 + 간접목적어 + 직접목적어」의 4형식 문장이다. 나머지는 모두 「주어 + make+목적어 + 목적격보어」의 5형식 문장이다.

03 주어진 문장과 ②, ⑤의 밑줄 친 부분은 5형식 문장에 쓰인 목적격보어이다. ①은 4형식의 직접목적어, ③, ④는 3형식의 부사(구)이다.

04 ① surprising → surprised ② going → go ④ joined → to join ⑤ bored → boring

05 find의 목적격보어로 형용사를 쓰고, 부사는 쓸 수 없으므로 prudently는 알맞지 않다.

06 지각동사 watch의 목적격보어로는 동사원형과 현재분사를 둘 다 쓸 수 있다.

07 allow는 목적격보어로 to부정사를 취하는 동사이다.

08 make는 목적격보어로 부사가 아닌 형용사를 취하므로 sadly가 아니라 sad가 되어야 한다. 또한 make는 5형식 문장에서 목적격보어로 동사원형을 취하므로 to cry가 아니라 cry가 되어야 한다.

09 사역동사 have의 목적어와 목적격보어의 관계가 능동의 의미이므로 동사원형 brush를 써야 하고, 동사 get의 목적격보어로 to부정사 to brush를 써야 한다.

10 5형식 동사 tell의 목적어로 me, 목적격보어로 to부정사 to listen이 오는데, to부정사의 부정은 not to listen으로 쓴다.

11 사역동사 let은 목적격보어로 동사원형을 취하고, help는 목적격보어로 to부정사 또는 동사원형을 취한다. keep은 목적격보어로 형용사를 취한다.

12 get의 목적어 his album과 목적격보어의 관계가 수동이므로 과거분사 released를 목적격보어로 써야 한다. '~하려고 노력하다'는 「try + to부정사」로 표현한다.

STEP 4 · 실력 완성 테스트

01 ② angrily → angry, ③ study → to study　02 ③
03 Mom[My mom] made me clean my room and told my sister to do her homework.　04 to having my room lock → to have my room locked　05 The news made them surprised. But it didn't sound surprising to me.　06 (1) He[John] kept Jane[her] waiting (for two hours).　(2) He[John] made Jane[her] (feel) miserable.

01 ② make의 목적격보어로는 부사가 아닌 형용사가 와야 한다.
③ 동사 tell의 목적격보어는 to부정사 형태로 쓴다.

02 네 번째 문장의 to dance는 dance 또는 dancing, 마지막 문장의 set은 to set이 되어야 올바른 문장이 된다.

03 사역동사 make의 목적격보어로 동사원형을 쓰고, 시제가 과거이므로 「made + 목적어 + 목적격보어(동사원형)」 형태로 쓴다. '~에게 …을 하라고 말하다'는 tell을 사용해서 시제가 과거이므로 「told + 목적어 + 목적격보어(to부정사)」 구문으로 쓴다.

04 advise의 목적격보어는 to부정사 형태로 써야 하고, have의 목적어와 목적격보어의 관계가 수동이므로 목적격보어로 과거분사 locked를 써야 한다. have my room locked는 '내 방 문을 잠기게 하다'의 의미이다.

05 '~을 …하게 만들다'는 「make + 목적어 + 목적격보어」 구문을 사용하는데 주어가 The news이고 목적어 them이 사람이므로 목적격보어로는 surprising이 아니라 surprised를 써야 한다. '~하게 들리다'는 「sound + 형용사」 구문을 사용하는데 주어가 the news이므로 주격보어로 surprising이 알맞다.

06 '~를 기다리게 하다'는 「keep + 목적어 + waiting」 구문을 사용하고, '~를 비참하게 (느끼게) 만들다'는 「make + 목적어 + (feel +) miserable」 구문을 사용한다.

최종 선택 QUIZ

01 a　02 a　03 b　04 b　05 a　06 b　07 a　08 a

2 · UNIT 01

UNIT 02 완료 시제

✔️바로 체크   p. 18

01 yet   02 has known   03 already   04 went
05 had talked   06 had lost   07 had   08 will have known   09 has been working

STEP 1 · 만만한 기초 pp. 19 – 21

01 ③   02 has lived   03 ①   04 have been
05 ①   06 Have you ever watched the movie before?
07 ③   08 has gone   09 ④   10 have played   11 ①
12 ②   13 had lost   14 ④   15 I had kept my old book   16 had   17 ④   18 ⑤   19 have → had
20 ③   21 will have finished   22 have taken → will have taken   23 ③   24 ⑤   25 been

01 ③ 명백한 과거를 나타내는 부사구는 현재완료 시제와 함께 쓸 수 없다. (have visited → visited)

02 민수가 어려서부터 지금까지 계속 이곳에서 살고 있는 것이므로 현재완료 시제를 써야 한다.

03 〈보기〉와 ①은 현재완료의 용법 중 완료이다. ②, ⑤ 경험 ③ 결과 ④ 계속

04 상대방의 질문이 현재완료 시제이므로, 이에 대한 대답도 현재완료로 해야 한다.

05 ① '친구의 집에 여러 번 가 본 적이 있다'는 경험의 의미이므로 has been으로 써야 한다.

06 경험을 물을 때는 현재완료를 써서 「Have you ever + 과거분사 ...?」로 표현한다.

07 ③은 경험을 나타내고 나머지는 모두 현재완료의 계속 용법이다.

08 '스페인에 가서 현재 여기에 없다'라는 의미이므로 현재완료의 결과를 나타내는 has gone이 알맞다.

09 '너는 벌써 이 책을 읽었니?'라는 의미이므로 부사 already가 알맞다. 나머지는 모두 현재완료 시제와 같이 쓸 수 없는 표현이다.

10 현재완료의 계속 용법이므로 have played로 써야 한다.

11 〈보기〉와 ①은 과거완료의 용법 중 계속이다. ② 결과 ③ 완료 ④, ⑤ 대과거

12 ① 과거 이전의 사건이므로 had gone을 써야 한다. ③ 책을 남긴 것이 먼저이고 발견한 것이 나중이므로, had found 대신 found를 써야 한다. ④ '현재까지(until now)'라는 표현에 어울리도록 현재완료 시제 has lived를 써야 한다. ⑤ 3인칭 복수 주어인 they 뒤에는 have나 had를 써서 현재완료나 과거완료를 나타낸다.

13 과거 이전에 시계를 잃어버려서 그때 시계가 없었던 것이므로 과거완료 had lost를 써야 한다.

14 ④ 내가 거기 갔을 때 그녀가 이미 도착한 것이므로 과거완료를 써서 had already arrived로 고쳐야 한다.

15 과거에 새 책을 사기 전부터 갖고 있던 책이므로 과거완료 시제를 써서 문장을 완성한다.

16 과거완료는 「had + 과거분사」 형태로 쓴다.

17 과거보다 더 이전부터 과거까지의 일을 나타내므로 과거완료 시제 had had를 써야 한다.

18 과거보다 이전 시점부터 과거까지의 일이므로 과거완료 had been이 알맞다.

19 과거보다 먼저 일어난 일을 나타낼 때는 과거완료 시제를 사용해야 하므로 had reached로 써야 한다.

20 미래 시점을 나타내는 '다음 달이면 3주 동안 토론토에 있게 된다'는 의미이므로 미래완료 시제가 알맞다.

21 미래의 어느 시점까지 완료되는 일을 나타내므로 미래완료 시제 will have finished를 써야 한다.

22 미래의 어느 시점에 영향을 미칠 일을 나타내므로 미래완료 시제 will have taken을 써야 한다.

23 현재완료 진행의 의문문이므로 ③은 been talking이 되어야 한다.

24 과거 이전부터 '오랫동안 달리고 있던 중이었다'는 의미이므로 과거완료 진행시제가 알맞다.

25 현재완료 진행은 「have[has] been + 현재분사」를 써서 나타낸다.

STEP 2 · 오답률 40~60% 문제 pp. 22 – 23

01 ④   02 ④   03 ⑤   04 ②   05 ⑤   06 ③
07 ②   08 I have seen this play.   09 Alice had been sick for a long time until she got better.   10 had swum → have swum   11 have been interested, have been making
12 will have gone   13 had been dancing   14 has been looking for   15 will work → will have worked

01 ① 현재완료와 특정 시점을 나타내는 의문사 when은 함께 쓸 수 없다. ② 과거의 시점을 나타내는 ago는 현재완료와 함께 쓸 수 없다. ③ Kelly는 3인칭 단수이므로 「has + 과거분사」로 현재완료형을 나타내야 한다. ⑤ 현재까지 영향을 미치는 사건에 대해서는 과거완료가 아닌 현재완료를 써야 한다. (had lost → have lost)

02 과거부터 현재까지 계속되는 일을 나타내므로 현재완료 시제를 써야 한다.

03 〈보기〉와 ⑤는 현재완료의 계속 용법이다. ①, ④ 경험 ② 완료 ③ 결과

04 표를 산 것이 표를 잃어버린 것보다 더 먼저 일어난 일이므로 첫 번째 빈칸에는 과거동사 lost가, 두 번째 빈칸에는 과거완료 had bought가 알맞다.

05 내가 역에 도착한 것보다 기차가 떠난 것이 더 먼저 일어난 일이므로 과거완료 시제를 써야 한다.

06 첫 번째 문장은 과거를 나타내는 부사 ago가 있으므로 과거시제 had가 알맞고, 두 번째 문장은 since와 함께 쓰이는 현재완료 시제가 알맞다.

07 첫 번째 문장은 주절이 과거시제이므로 종속절은 과거완료 시제가 알맞고, 두 번째 문장은 과거부터 현재까지 계속되는 일을 나타내므로 현재완료 시제가 알맞다.

08 경험을 나타내는 현재완료 시제 have seen을 사용하여 문장을 완성한다.

09 Alice가 아픈 것이 나은 것보다 더 먼저 일어난 일이므로 과거완료 시제 had been sick을 써서 문장을 완성한다.

10 과거에 수영을 시작해서 현재도 하고 있으므로 계속의 의미를 나타내는 현재완료 시제 have swum을 써야 한다.

11 과거부터 현재까지 계속되는 행동이나 상태를 나타내는 현재완료는 「have[has] + 과거분사」, 현재완료 진행시제는 「have[has] been + 현재분사」의 형태로 나타낸다.

12 미래의 어느 시점에 영향을 미칠 상태를 나타내므로 미래완료 시제 will have gone을 써야 한다.

13 과거 기준 시점 이전에 시작된 일이 과거 기준 시점까지 계속 진행되고 있는 상태이므로 과거완료 진행시제 had been dancing을 써야 한다.

14 과거에 시작된 일이 현재에도 계속 진행되고 있으므로 현재완료 진행시제를 써야 한다.

15 미래의 어느 시점까지 계속되는 상태를 나타내므로 미래완료 시제 will have worked로 고쳐야 한다.

STEP 3 · 오답률 60~80%문제　　　　　pp. 24 – 25

```
01 ④    02 ②    03 ④    04 ⑤    05 ④    06 ⑤
07 ④    08 She paints → She has painted    09 a robber
had broken into    10 will have been    11 I have thought
about it seriously.    12 I have been playing computer
games    13 Dave had been waiting for her    14 has
been snowing → had been snowing    15 had been lying
→ has been lying
```

01 첫 번째 문장은 by then으로 보아 미래완료를 써야 함을 알 수 있고, 두 번째 문장은 의미상 현재완료의 계속 용법을 써야 한다.

02 ②는 「will have + 과거분사」의 미래완료이므로 have가 들어가고, 나머지는 모두 과거완료에 쓰는 had가 들어가야 한다.

03 ① I forgot what you had done yesterday. ② has left → had left ③ fell → had fallen ⑤ seen → had seen

04 ⑤는 현재완료의 계속 용법으로 How long have you been in this town?으로 묻는 것이 적절하다.

05 '박물관에 갔다'는 의미의 현재완료 결과 용법을 쓰는 것이 알맞다.

06 미래의 어느 시점에 완료되는 일을 나타내므로 미래완료 시제가 알맞다.

07 첫 번째 문장은 집에 갔던 과거 시점 이전에 가족들이 벌써 식사를 끝마친 것이므로 과거완료 시제가 알맞고, 두 번째 문장은 내년에 17살이 되는 것이므로 미래시제가 알맞다.

08 과거부터 현재까지 계속되는 상황을 나타내므로 현재완료 시제를 써야 한다.

09 그녀가 경찰에 전화한 것보다 도둑이 침입한 것이 더 먼저 일어난 일이므로 과거완료 시제를 써야 한다.

10 미래의 어느 시점까지 계속되는 일을 나타내므로 미래완료 시제 will have been을 써야 한다.

11 현재완료로 질문한 경우, 대답 역시 현재완료로 해야 한다.

12 과거에 시작한 행동이 현재까지 계속적으로 이어지고 있으므로 현재완료 진행시제를 써서 표현할 수 있다.

13 과거 이전에 시작된 일이 과거의 어느 시점까지 계속 진행되고 있으므로 「had been + 현재분사」 형태의 과거완료 진행시제를 써야 한다.

14 과거의 기준 시점 이전에 발생한 일이 과거의 기준 시점까지 계속되는 일을 나타내므로 과거완료 진행시제를 써야 한다.

15 과거에 시작하여 현재까지 계속 진행되는 일을 나타내므로 현재완료 진행시제를 써야 한다.

STEP 4 · 실력 완성 테스트　　　　　p. 26

```
01 Did you hear, I didn't, have watched TV    02 ③
03 (1) He has played basketball for a[one] year.  (2) He
has learned Chinese for four months.  (3) He has played
the piano for two years.    04 What had he done? / He
had played baseball.    05 (1) She has been making a
cake for three hours. (2) He has been cleaning his room for
two hours.    06 She will have lost weight by this winter.
```

01 just now는 과거를 나타내는 부사구로 과거 시제와 함께 써야 하고, 2시부터 계속 TV를 보고 있었다고 했으므로 현재완료 시제로 써야 한다.

02 ⓐ have been → was ⓒ have been played → have been playing ⓓ has finished → will have finished

03 표를 보면 각각의 학생들이 얼마 동안 해당 과목을 배워왔는지를 알 수 있다. 이에 대해 묻는 현재완료 질문에 현재완료로 답해야 한다.

04 그림을 보면 야구를 했었다는 것을 알 수 있으므로, 내용에 맞게 과거완료 질문과 대답을 완성한다.

05 (1) 주어인 3인칭 단수 she에 맞게 has been making을 사용하여 문장을 완성한다.
(2) 주어인 3인칭 단수 he에 맞게 has been cleaning을 사용하여 문장을 완성한다.

06 미래의 어느 시점까지 완료될 일을 나타내므로 미래완료 시제를 사용하여 문장을 완성한다.

최종 선택 QUIZ　　　　　p. 27

```
01 b   02 a   03 b   04 b   05 a   06 b   07 a   08 b
```

✅ 바로 체크   p. 28

01 do   02 had better not   03 than   04 used to

05 used to   06 must   07 may   08 cannot

09 shouldn't

STEP 1 · 만만한 기초   pp. 29 – 31

01 ③   02 ④   03 ⑤   04 ②   05 ①   06 You had better slow down because the road is slippery.

07 would rather stay   08 ④   09 ③   10 ④

11 ⑤   12 am used → used   13 used to be a hospital

14 ②   15 ②   16 ③   17 must have been

18 ③   19 ②   20 ④   21 ②   22 ⑤   23 ⑤

24 came → come   25 must have practiced

01 'B하느니 차라리 A하겠다'는 의미의 「would rather A than B」, '~하는 것이 낫다'는 의미의 had better가 알맞다.

02 'B하느니 차라리 A하겠다'는 would rather A than B로 쓴다.

03 ⑤ had better의 부정은 had better not으로 쓴다.

04 '~하는 것이 좋겠다'는 의미의 조동사 had better를 사용하고, '지금 당장'은 right now로 표현한다.

05 「would rather A than B」 구문에서 A와 B에는 동사원형이 온다.

06 '속도를 줄이다'는 slow down으로, '~하는 것이 좋겠다'는 「had better+동사원형」으로 표현한다.

07 'B하느니 차라리 A하겠다'라는 의미의 would rather A than B를 써야 한다.

08 '과거에는 좋아했지만 지금은 좋아하지 않는다'는 내용이므로 빈칸에는 used to가 알맞다.

09 과거의 습관을 나타내는 「used to+동사원형」은 「would+동사원형」으로 바꿔 쓸 수 있다.

10 〈보기〉와 ④의 would는 '~하곤 했다'의 의미로 과거의 습관을 나타낸다.

11 「used to+동사원형」은 '~하곤 했다, ~이었다'라는 의미로 과거의 습관이나 상태를 나타내고, 「be used to+동사원형」은 '~하는 데 쓰이다'라는 의미이다.

12 과거에 동생과 방을 함께 썼다는 내용이 자연스러우므로 「used to+동사원형」을 써야 한다.

13 There used to be ~는 '(지금은 없으나) 예전에 ~이 있었다'는 의미를 나타낸다.

14 「used to+동사원형」은 과거의 습관이나 상태를 나타내고, 「be used to+동명사」는 '~에 익숙하다'를 의미한다.

15 창문을 깨지 않았을 것이라는 내용이므로 '~했을 리가 없다'는 의미의 cannot have p.p.가 알맞다.

16 ① feel → felt ② be → been ④ ate → eaten ⑤ has → have

17 Tom이 결석한 이유로 Tom이 아팠을 것이라고 하는 것이 자연스럽다. 과거에 대한 추측이고 must가 주어졌으므로 빈칸은 must have p.p.의 형태로 쓰면 된다. be동사의 과거분사는 been이다.

18 운동선수가 레드카드를 받아 경기장 밖에 있는 것으로 보아 공정한 경기를 펼치지 않았을 것이다. 즉 과거의 일에 대한 부정적인 확신을 나타내므로 '~했을 리가 없다'는 의미의 cannot have p.p.를 사용해서 표현한다.

19 허락과 과거에 대한 추측을 나타낼 수 있는 조동사 may가 알맞다.

20 기차를 놓친 것에 대한 후회이므로 '~했어야 했다'는 의미의 should have p.p.의 형태가 알맞다.

21 과거에 하지 못한 일에 대한 유감은 '~했어야 했다'는 의미의 should have p.p.로 표현한다.

22 '~할 수도 있었을 텐데'라는 의미는 could have p.p.로 표현한다.

23 과거에 한 일에 대한 후회이므로 should not have p.p.를 써야 한다.

24 '~했을지도 모른다'라는 의미는 could have p.p. 형태로 나타내므로 came을 과거분사형 come으로 고쳐야 한다.

25 경연 대회에서 우승을 했으므로 연습을 많이 했을 것이라는 확신이 자연스럽다. 따라서 '~했음에 틀림없다'는 의미의 must have p.p.를 써야 한다.

STEP 2 · 오답률 40~60% 문제   pp. 32 – 33

01 ②   02 ⑤   03 ②   04 ①   05 ③   06 ④

07 ⑤   08 would → used to   09 would play

10 cannot have been   11 should have called

12 must have rained   13 may[might] have happened

14 must → should   15 ⓒ: joined → join

01 You had better not go out too often.이 되어야 하므로 not이 정답이다.

02 'B하느니 차라리 A하겠다'라는 의미는 would rather A than B로 쓴다.

03 ① taking → take ③ to get → get ④ don't had better → had better not ⑤ plays → play

04 문맥상 '~하는 것이 좋다'는 의미의 조동사 had better를 쓰는 것이 알맞다.

05 과거의 일에 대한 확실한 추측이므로 must have p.p.가 알맞다.

06 과거의 습관을 나타내는 「would+동사원형」, '어렸을 때'를 의미하는 when I was young이 알맞다.

07 과거의 상태를 나타내므로 used to를 써야 한다.

08 would는 과거의 상태를 나타낼 수 없으므로 used to로 고쳐야 한다.

09 과거의 습관을 나타내므로 「would+동사원형」으로 쓴다.

10 과거의 일에 대한 부정적인 추측이므로 '~이었을 리가 없다'는 의미의 cannot have p.p.로 쓴다.

11 밑줄 친 부분은 엄마에게 전화를 하지 않은 것에 대한 후회이므로 should have p.p.로 써야 한다.

12 과거의 일에 대한 강한 추측은 must have p.p.로 표현한다.

13 과거에 대한 불확실한 추측은 may[might] have p.p.로 표현한다.

14 과거의 일에 대한 후회가 오는 것이 문맥상 자연스러우므로 must have p.p.를 should have p.p.로 고쳐야 한다.

15 ⓒ would rather 다음에는 동사원형이 와야 하므로 joined를 join으로 고쳐야 한다.

13 대화의 흐름상 'Mike가 아팠을 리가 없다'는 내용이 되어야 하므로 Mike must ~는 Mike cannot ~이 되어야 한다. 과거의 일에 대한 부정적인 강한 추측은 cannot have p.p.로 표현한다.

14 돈을 현명하게 쓰지 못한 것을 후회하는 내용이므로 should not have p.p.를 사용하여 바꿔 쓸 수 있다.

15 문맥상 '~이었을 리가 없다'는 내용이 되어야 하므로 cannot have p.p.를 써야 한다.

STEP 3 · 오답률 60~80%문제
pp. 34 – 35

> **01** ④   **02** ⑤   **03** ③   **04** ①   **05** ④   **06** ②, ③
> **07** ⑤   **08** ① → used to be   **09** used to not → used not to 또는 didn't use(d) to   **10** There would → There used to, coming → come, chatted → chat   **11** cannot → should
> **12** must[may / might] have gone   **13** Mike must have been sick. → Mike cannot have been sick.   **14** I should not have spent the money foolishly.   **15** cannot have been

01 '~하지 않는 게 좋다'라는 의미의 had better not을 쓰는 것이 적절하다.

02 과식을 멈추라고 조언하는 내용이므로 must, have to, should, ought to, had better 등을 쓸 수 있다. 「be able to + 동사원형」은 '~할 수 있다'는 의미로 가능이나 능력을 나타낸다.

03 would rather의 부정은 would rather not으로 쓴다.

04 문맥상 '~하는 것이 좋겠다'라는 의미의 had better가 알맞다.

05 '~하는 것이 좋겠다'라는 의미의 충고는 「had better + 동사원형」, '과거에 ~했으나 지금은 그렇지 않다'는 의미는 「used to + 동사원형」, 'B하느니 차라리 A하겠다'는 의미는 would rather A than B를 쓴다.

06 '~하곤 했다'라는 의미의 과거의 습관은 used to 또는 would로 나타낸다.

07 '~했을지도 모른다'라는 의미의 과거의 일에 대한 불확실한 추측을 나타내는 may[might] have p.p.가 알맞다. 부정문이므로 may[might] have p.p.의 부정형인 may[might] not have p.p.로 써야 한다.

08 ① 과거의 상태를 나타내는 말이므로 would는 쓸 수 없고 used to be로 써야 한다. ⑤ be used to ~는 '~에 익숙하다'는 의미로 자연스럽다.

09 used to의 부정은 used not to 또는 didn't use(d) to로 쓴다.

10 '~에 있었지만 지금은 없다'는 의미의 과거의 상태는 there used to be로 표현하고, used to 다음에는 동사원형이 온다. chatted는 meet와 함께 조동사 would에 걸리는 말이므로 동사원형으로 써야 한다.

11 과거에 하지 않은 일에 대한 후회를 나타내므로 should have p.p.를 써야 한다.

12 가게에 들어간 Jack이 가게 안에 없는 것으로 보아 뒷문을 통해 가게 밖으로 나갔음이 틀림없다 또는 나갔을지도 모른다는 내용이 되도록 must[may / might] have p.p.를 사용하여 표현한다.

STEP 4 · 실력 완성 테스트
p. 36

> **01** I must have put down the address wrong.   **02** There would → There used to, I am used to climbing → I used to climb, reads → read   **03** You had better not smoke. / You had better stop smoking.   **04** ④   **05** She cannot have written the letter by herself.   **06** shouldn't[should not] have been late for the interview

01 「It is certain that + 주어 + 과거형 동사」는 과거 사실에 대한 확신을 나타내므로 must have p.p.로 바꿔 쓸 수 있다.

02 과거의 습관을 나타낼 때는 would와 used to 둘 다 쓸 수 있지만, 과거의 상태를 나타낼 때는 used to만 쓸 수 있다. 「be used to + 동명사」는 '~에 익숙하다'는 의미이므로 문맥상 '~하곤 했다'라는 의미의 used to climb이 알맞다. 조동사 would 뒤에는 동사원형인 read가 와야 한다.

03 충고할 때는 should (not), ought (not) to, had better (not) 등을 쓸 수 있는데, 주어진 어구에 had better가 있으므로 「had better (not) + 동사원형」을 사용하여 답해야 한다.

04 '(과거에) ~했었다'는 의미의 과거의 상태는 「used to + 동사원형」으로 표현하고, 과거의 일에 대한 확실한 추측은 must have p.p.로 표현하며, 과거에 하지 않은 일에 대한 후회는 should have p.p.로 나타낸다.

05 '~했을 리 없다'는 의미의 과거의 일에 대한 부정적인 확신은 cannot have p.p.로 나타낸다.

06 어제 인터뷰에 늦은 것에 대한 유감을 나타내야 하므로 shouldn't[should not] have p.p.로 표현해야 한다.

최종 선택 QUIZ
p. 37

> **01** a   **02** a   **03** b   **04** b   **05** a   **06** b   **07** b   **08** a

UNIT 04 to부정사 1

바로 체크
p. 38

01 보어   02 목적어   03 him   04 for   05 not to stay   06 to get   07 It   08 for me

STEP 1 · 만만한 기초
pp. 39 – 41

01 ④   02 ③   03 want to be[become]   04 ②
05 ⑤   06 They decided to go to the theater.   07 to be praised by her mom   08 to help[helping], to become
09 ③   10 not to reveal   11 wanted me not to read
12 ④   13 what to do   14 (1) where to put (2) when to watch   15 to choose which → which to choose   16 ③
17 ①   18 ⑤   19 I found it hard to understand her.
20 It is not safe to swim.   21 It is necessary to reduce food waste.   22 ②   23 ③   24 for him   25 It took three months for her to finish this sculpture.

01 ④ Relieve → To relieve[Relieving], 동사가 문장의 주어 자리에 올 때 「to+동사원형」 또는 동명사 형태로 쓴다. make up with: ~와 화해하다
02 빈칸에는 보어 역할을 하는 to부정사가 알맞다.
03 want는 목적어로 to부정사를 쓰는 동사이다.
04 〈보기〉와 ②는 보어로 쓰인 to부정사이다. ①, ③, ⑤는 목적어, ④는 주어로 쓰였다.
05 mind는 목적어로 동명사를 쓰는 동사이다.
06 decide는 목적어로 to부정사를 쓰는 동사이고, 과거 시제로 쓴다.
07 want는 목적어로 to부정사를 쓴다. 엄마에게 칭찬받기를 원한다는 수동의 의미이므로 「to+be+과거분사」의 형태로 쓴다.
08 like는 목적어로 to부정사와 동명사를 의미의 차이 없이 둘 다 쓸 수 있다. decide는 목적어로 to부정사를 쓴다.
09 to부정사의 부정은 to부정사 앞에 부정어를 쓴다.
10 to부정사의 부정은 부정어를 to부정사 바로 앞에 쓴다.
11 「want+목적어+not+to부정사」는 '(목적어)가 ~하지 않기를 원하다'라는 의미이다.
12 「의문사 how+to부정사」: ~하는 방법 / How about ~?: ~는 어때?
13 「의문사+주어+should+동사원형」은 「의문사+to부정사」로 바꿔 쓸 수 있다.
14 (1) B의 응답에 장소를 나타내는 말이 있으므로 where to put이 자연스럽다. (2) '언제 볼지'를 나타내는 when to watch를 쓴다.
15 '어느 것을 ~할지'라는 의미로 쓰인 「의문사 which+to부정사」이다.
16 careless는 '부주의한'이라는 뜻의 성격을 나타내는 형용사이므로 to부정사의 의미상 주어로 「of+목적격」을 쓴다.
17 to부정사가 주어일 때 가주어 it을 쓰고 to부정사는 뒤로 보낼 수 있다. 의미상 주어는 일반적으로 「for+목적격」을 쓴다.
18 important 뒤에는 의미상 주어로 「for+목적격」을 쓴다.

19 가목적어가 쓰인 5형식 문장으로, 「주어+동사+가목적어 it+목적격 보어(형용사/명사)+to부정사」 순으로 쓴다.
20 to부정사가 주어로 쓰일 때 주로 가주어 it을 주어 자리에 쓰고 to부정사(구)는 뒤에 쓴다.
21 to부정사가 주어일 때 가주어 it을 쓰고 to부정사는 뒤로 보낼 수 있다.
22 가목적어가 쓰인 5형식 문장으로, 가목적어 it은 동사와 목적격보어 사이에 쓴다.
23 「It+takes+사람+시간+to부정사」: ~가 …하는 데 시간이 걸리다
24 「It takes+사람+시간+to부정사」=「It takes+시간+for+목적격+to부정사」
25 「It takes+시간+for+목적격+to부정사」: ~가 …하는 데 시간이 걸리다

STEP 2 · 오답률 40~60% 문제
pp. 42 – 43

01 ⑤   02 ④   03 ③   04 ③   05 ④   06 ④
07 ①   08 it is difficult for me to learn English   09 (1) kind of him to help me with my homework (2) not easy for me to take care of my sister   10 It is important for you to learn how to manage stress.   11 for me, of him, her
12 It took me two hours to find a present for Dad. / It took two hours for me to find a present for Dad.   13 It will take her some time to decide[It will take some time for her to decide]   14 It will take me 30 minutes to get ready for the party.[It will take 30 minutes for me to get ready for the party.]   15 to take

01 ⑤ 5형식으로 사역동사 make는 목적격보어로 동사원형을 취한다. / make+목적어+동사원형: (목적어)가 ~하도록 만들다[시키다]
02 refuse, promise는 to부정사를 목적어로 쓰고, enjoy, practice는 동명사를 목적어로 쓰는 동사이다. ① going → to go ② calling → to call ③ to walk → walking ⑤ to paint → painting
03 ③은 부사적 용법(목적)이고, 나머지는 명사적 용법(①, ④ 목적어, ② 주어, ⑤ 보어)이다.
04 ③ to부정사의 부정은 to부정사 바로 앞에 부정어 not이나 never를 쓴다. (to not be → not to be)
05 to부정사의 부정은 to부정사 앞에 부정어를 쓴다.
06 ④ what to fix → how to fix / 「의문사 how+to부정사」: ~하는 방법, 어떻게 ~할지
07 ① 의문사 why 다음에는 to부정사를 쓰지 않는 것이 일반적이다. (→ I don't know why I should do it.)
08 「가주어(it)+동사 ~ 의미상 주어(for+목적격)+진주어(to부정사)」로 쓴다.
09 (1) kind는 성격을 나타내는 말이므로 to부정사의 의미상 주어로 「of+목적격」을 쓴다. (2) easy 뒤에는 「for+목적격」으로 의미상 주어를 나타낸다.
10 「가주어(it)+동사 ~ 의미상 주어(for+목적격)+진주어(to부정사)」 구문과 '~하는 방법'이라는 의미의 「how+to부정사」를 이용해야 한다. important 뒤에는 의미상 주어로 「for+목적격」을 쓴다.

11 to부정사의 의미상 주어는 주로 「for+목적격」으로 나타내고, 성격·태도를 나타내는 형용사 뒤에서는 「of+목적격」을 쓴다. 「동사+목적어+to부정사」의 형태에서는 목적어가 의미상 주어이다.

12 '~가 …하는 데 시간이 걸리다'라는 표현은 「It takes+사람+시간+to부정사」 또는 「It takes+시간+for+목적격+to부정사」로 나타낸다.

13 「It takes+사람+시간+to부정사」: ~가 …하는 데 시간이 걸리다 (= 「It takes+시간+for+목적격+to부정사」)

14 「It+takes+사람+시간+to부정사」 구문이나 「It takes+시간+for+목적격+to부정사」 구문으로 답한다.

15 「It+takes+사람+시간+to부정사」: ~가 …하는 데 시간이 걸리다 / 「allow+목적어+to부정사」: ~가 …하는 것을 허락하다 / 「want+to부정사」: ~하고 싶다

STEP 3 · 오답률 60~80% 문제
pp. 44 – 45

01 ④ 02 ② 03 ⑤ 04 ② 05 ② 06 ⑤
07 ③, ⑤ 08 They agreed to get along with each other.
09 leaving → to leave 10 (1) us not to make any noise
(2) us to turn off the lights and fans when we go[went] out
(3) us not to make a mess 11 not to go out alone at night 12 not to buy a new house 13 which way to go
14 I don't know how to fix[repair] my computer. 15 We haven't decided yet where to stay tonight. / We haven't decided yet where we should stay tonight.

01 ④ difficult 뒤에는 의미상 주어로 「for+목적격」을 쓴다. (of → for)

02 ② natural 뒤에는 의미상 주어로 「for+목적격」을 쓴다. 나머지는 모두 of가 알맞다.

03 5형식에서 to부정사가 목적어로 쓰일 때 가목적어 it을 목적어 자리에 쓰고 to부정사(구)는 뒤로 보낸다.

04 ②는 비인칭 주어이고, 나머지는 모두 가주어 it이다.

05 ② take a whole day her → take her a whole day 또는 take a whole day for her / 「It takes+사람+시간+to부정사」: ~가 …하는 데 시간이 걸리다 (= 「It takes+시간+for+목적격+to부정사」)

06 ⑤ arriving → to arrive / 「It takes+사람+시간+to부정사」: ~가 …하는 데 시간이 걸리다 (= 「It takes+시간+for+목적격+to부정사」)

07 '~가 …하는 데 시간이 걸리다'라는 표현은 「It takes+사람+시간+to부정사」 또는 「It takes+시간+for+목적격+to부정사」로 나타낸다.

08 agree는 목적어로 to부정사를 쓴다.

09 expect는 목적어로 to부정사를 쓰는 동사이다.

10 ask, want, order는 모두 to부정사를 목적격보어로 쓰는 동사이다. to부정사의 부정은 not을 to부정사 앞에 쓴다.

11 「tell+목적어+not+to부정사」는 '(목적어)에게 ~하지 말라고 말하다'라는 의미이다.

12 decide는 to부정사를 목적어로 쓰는 동사이다. '그들은 새 집을 사지 않기로 결정했다.'는 의미로 to부정사 앞에 not을 쓴다.

13 「의문사+주어+should+동사원형」=「의문사+to부정사」

14 '고치는 방법'은 「의문사 how+to부정사」를 이용하여 나타낸다.

15 「의문사+주어+should+동사원형」=「의문사+to부정사」 / 「의문사 where+to부정사」: 어디에서 ~할지

STEP 4 · 실력 완성 테스트
p. 46

01 ①, ⑤ 02 ③ 03 (1) how to use (2) which dress to wear 04 ⑤ 05 (1) careless of him to lose his passport (2) impossible for her to win the audition 06 It took her two hours to paint the picture. / It took two hours for her to paint the picture. 07 It took him 30 minutes [half an hour] to wash the car. / It took 30 minutes[half an hour] for him to wash the car.

01 ① to shake → shake[shaking], feel은 지각동사이며 목적격보어로 동사원형이나 현재분사를 쓴다. ⑤ '~가 …하는 데 시간이 걸리다'라는 표현은 「It takes+시간+for+목적격+to부정사」로 나타낸다.

02 ⓑ foolish는 의미상 주어로 「of+목적격」을 쓴다. ⓔ 「It is hard+for+목적격+to부정사 ~」의 어순으로 쓴다.

03 「의문사+to부정사」를 이용해서 대화를 완성한다. 「how+to부정사」: ~하는 방법 / 「which+명사+to부정사」: 어떤 ~을 …할지

04 ⓐ to how cook → how to cook / 「의문사 how+to부정사」: ~하는 방법, ⓒ 5형식으로 동사 found 뒤에 가목적어 it을 쓴다.

05 의미상의 주어를 나타낼 때 careless는 사람의 성격·태도를 나타내는 형용사이므로 「of+목적격」으로, impossible은 일반적인 형용사이므로 「for+목적격」으로 나타낸다.

06 Jane은 그림을 그리는 데 2시간이 걸렸다.

07 Steven이 세차를 하는 데 30분이 걸렸다.

최종 선택 QUIZ
p. 47

01 b 02 a 03 b 04 a 05 a 06 a 07 b 08 a

UNIT 05 to부정사 2

바로 체크   p. 48

01 형용사적 용법   02 부사적 용법   03 결과   04 의지
05 enough to   06 too, to   07 to tell   08 to have loved

STEP 1 · 만만한 기초   pp. 49 – 51

01 ③   02 They have a lot of children to look after.
03 something cold to drink   04 ①   05 ④   06 ③
07 ②   08 ⑤   09 ③   10 ⑤   11 to receive her invitation   12 in order to[so as to] watch   13 ②
14 He did his best not to lose the game.   15 too, to
16 ⑤   17 too tight, to wear   18 warm enough, to relax   19 ②   20 ①   21 ⑤   22 ②   23 ④
24 (1) It seems, cares (2) It seemed, had lost   25 You seemed to be surprised.

01 to부정사는 '~할, ~하는'이라는 의미로 쓰여 명사 뒤에서 명사를 꾸며준다. to부정사의 수식을 받는 명사 house가 전치사 in의 목적어이므로 to live 다음에 in을 써야 한다.

02 to부정사가 형용사적 용법으로 쓰일 때는 명사를 뒤에서 수식한다.

03 「something + 형용사 + to부정사」의 어순으로 써야 한다.

04 〈보기〉와 ①은 앞의 명사를 꾸며주는 형용사적 용법이다. ② 명사적 용법(진주어) ③ 부사적 용법(목적) ④ 부사적 용법(결과) ⑤ 부사적 용법(형용사 수식)

05 ④는 부사적 용법(판단의 근거)이고, 나머지는 모두 형용사적 용법이다.

06 「be + to부정사」 구문으로 의무(~해야 한다)를 나타낼 수 있다.

07 예정을 나타내는 「be + to부정사」이므로, be going to를 이용하여 바꿔 쓸 수 있다.

08 〈보기〉와 ⑤는 의무(~해야 한다)를 나타낸다. ① 예정 ② 운명 ③ 가능 ④ 의지

09 '~하기 위해서'라는 뜻의 목적을 나타내는 부사적 용법의 to부정사가 알맞다.

10 ⑤는 감정의 원인을 나타내고, 나머지는 모두 목적을 나타낸다.

11 '~해서'라는 의미의 감정의 원인을 나타내는 to부정사를 써야 한다.

12 목적을 나타내는 to부정사는 in order to 또는 so as to와 바꿔 쓸 수 있다.

13 〈보기〉와 ②는 부사적 용법 중 결과의 의미로 쓰였다. ① 부사적 용법 (감정의 원인) ③ 부사적 용법(형용사 수식) ④ 부사적 용법(목적) ⑤ 부사적 용법(판단의 근거)

14 to부정사의 부정은 to부정사 앞에 not을 쓴다.

15 「too + 형용사/부사 + to부정사」: …하기에 너무 ~한/하게

16 「형용사/부사 + enough + to부정사」: …할 만큼 충분히 ~한/하게

17 「so + 형용사/부사 + that + 주어 + can't + 동사원형」은 「too + 형용사/부사(+ for + 목적격) + to부정사」로 바꿔 쓸 수 있다.

18 「so + 형용사/부사 + that + 주어 + can」은 「형용사/부사 + enough (+ for + 목적격) + to부정사」로 바꿔 쓸 수 있다.

19 ②「형용사 + enough + to부정사」 구문으로 enough는 형용사 다음에 써야 한다. → good enough

20 「so + 형용사/부사 + that + 주어 + can't + 동사원형」은 「too + 형용사/부사(+ for + 목적격) + to부정사」로 바꿔 쓸 수 있다.

21 「형용사/부사 + enough + to부정사」: …할 만큼 충분히 ~한/하게

22 seem to는 '~인 것 같다'라는 의미이며, to부정사와 본동사의 시제가 같으므로 단순부정사로 쓴다.

23 to부정사의 행위가 본동사의 시제보다 이전에 일어났을 때는 「주어 + seem(s) to + have + p.p.」로 나타낸다.

24 (1) 단순부정사가 쓰였으므로 본동사의 시제와 to부정사의 시제가 같다는 것을 알 수 있다.
(2) 완료부정사가 쓰였으므로 that절의 시제는 주절의 시제보다 앞선 과거완료로 써야 한다.

25 to부정사와 본동사의 시제가 같으므로 단순부정사로 쓴다.

STEP 2 · 오답률 40~60% 문제   pp. 52 – 53

01 ①   02 ⑤   03 ②, ⑤   04 ④   05 ②
06 ②   07 ⑤   08 I need something sweet to eat.
09 (1) I need a chair to sit on. (2) I need a fork to eat with.
10 kept a diary to improve her writing skills   11 The boys were excited to see the ocean.   12 too late to see
13 My brother is strong enough to move that heavy table.
14 to have been   15 seemed that the kids were satisfied

01 ①은 형용사적 용법으로 쓰였고 나머지는 모두 부사적 용법이다. ② 감정의 원인 ③ 목적 ④ 판단의 근거 ⑤ 형용사 수식

02 to부정사의 수식을 받는 명사 toy가 전치사 with의 목적어이므로 to play with가 알맞다. / '회복하기 위해'라는 의미가 되도록 목적을 나타내는 to부정사를 쓴다.

03 ② 사역동사 make는 목적격보어로 동사원형이 와야 하므로 빈칸에 to를 쓸 수 없다. ⑤ 빈칸 다음에 동명사가 쓰였으므로 for가 들어가는 것이 알맞다.

04 〈보기〉와 ④는 감정의 원인을 나타내는 부사적 용법으로 쓰였다. ① 형용사적 용법 ② 형용사 수식 ③ 목적 ⑤ 결과

05 ⓑ 명사 pen이 전치사 with의 목적어이므로 to부정사 다음에 with를 써야 한다. to write → to write with ⓓ 「-thing + 형용사 + to부정사」의 어순으로 써야 한다. important something → something important

06 ② 「be + to부정사」가 '~해야 한다'라는 의미로 쓰였으므로 You shouldn't feed the animals in the zoo.로 바꿔 쓸 수 있다. don't have to는 '~할 필요가 없다'라는 의미이다.

07 ⑤는 '~할 작정이다'라는 의미로 쓰였고, 나머지는 모두 '~할 예정이다'라는 의미이다.

08 「-thing + 형용사 + to부정사」의 어순으로 써야 한다.

09 '의자에 앉다'는 sit on a chair, '포크로 먹다'는 eat with a fork이므로 to부정사 다음에 각각 전치사 on과 with를 써야 한다.

10 '글쓰기 실력을 향상시키기 위해'라는 목적의 의미를 나타내는 부사적 용법의 to부정사를 쓴다.

11 감정을 나타내는 형용사 뒤에 to부정사를 써서 감정의 원인을 나타낸다.

12 「so + 형용사/부사 + that + 주어 + can't ....」는 「too + 형용사/부사 + to부정사」로 바꿔 쓸 수 있다.

13 「형용사/부사 + enough + to부정사」: …할 만큼 충분히 ~한/하게

14 to부정사의 시제가 본동사의 시제보다 이전에 일어난 일이므로 완료부정사인 「to + have + p.p.」를 써야 한다.

15 「주어 + seem(s) + to부정사」는 「It seems that + 주어 + 동사」로 바꿔 쓸 수 있고, 단순부정사이므로 that절의 동사도 과거 시제로 쓴다.

11 감정을 나타내는 형용사 다음에 to부정사를 써서 감정의 원인을 나타낸다.

12 목적을 나타내는 to부정사를 이용한다.

13 '강의가 너무 혼란스러워서 Cathy는 강의를 이해할 수 없었다'라는 내용이 되도록 「too + 형용사/부사(+ for + 목적격)+ to부정사」 또는 「so + 형용사/부사 + that + 주어 + can't + 동사원형」 구문을 쓴다. that절의 목적어인 it을 빠뜨리지 않도록 유의한다.

14 「형용사/부사 + enough + to부정사」: …할 만큼 충분히 ~한/하게

15 「too + 형용사/부사(+ for + 목적격)+ to부정사」와 「so + 형용사/부사 + that + 주어 + can't + 동사원형」 구문을 이용한다. that절의 목적어인 it을 빠뜨리지 않도록 유의한다.

STEP 3 · 오답률 60~80%문제
pp. 54 – 55

01 ②, ⑤　02 ①　03 ②　04 ③　05 ③　06 ④
07 ④　08 anything interesting to write about　09 (1) is to visit (2) are not to touch　10 turned down the volume in order not to wake the baby　11 was disappointed to fail the audition　12 Kevin wrote everything down (in order / so as) to memorize it fast.　13 too confusing for Cathy to understand, so confusing that Cathy couldn't understand it　14 She was lucky enough to avoid the crash.　15 The soup is too salty for me to eat. / The soup is so salty that I can't eat it.

01 ② to live → to live with ⑤ to not make → not to make

02 ⓐ, ⓒ는 목적을 나타내는 to부정사이므로 in order to와 바꿔 쓸 수 있다. ⓑ 감정의 원인 ⓓ 형용사 수식 ⓔ 결과

03 ② '퀴즈쇼에 참가할 만큼 똑똑하다'라는 의미가 되도록 Olivia is smart enough to take part in the quiz show.라고 하는 것이 자연스럽다.

04 ③ → for her, to부정사의 의미상 주어는 「for + 목적격」으로 나타내야 한다.

05 ③은 '비록 바빴지만 나는 가까스로 모임에 참석할 수 있었다.'라는 뜻이고, 나머지는 모두 '나는 너무 바빠서 모임에 참석할 수 없었다.'라는 뜻이다.

06 to부정사가 본동사와 같은 시제일 경우에는 단순부정사를, to부정사가 본동사보다 앞선 시제일 경우에는 완료부정사를 쓴다.

07 to부정사가 본동사보다 앞선 시제일 경우에는 완료부정사(「to + have + p.p.」)를 쓴다.

08 「-thing + 형용사 + to부정사」의 어순으로 쓰고, to부정사 다음에 전치사 about을 써야 한다.

09 「be + to부정사」를 이용해서 예정, 의무 등의 의미를 나타낼 수 있다.

10 「in order not to + 동사원형」: ~하지 않도록(= 「so as not to + 동사원형」)

STEP 4 · 실력 완성 테스트
p. 56

01 ①　02 ②　03 ③　04 (1) I want some friends to play soccer with. (2) I was shocked to find the room empty.　05 (1) The noise is too loud for the boy to concentrate on studying. (2) The sofa is comfortable enough for the girl to sleep on.　06 It seems that it rained last night. / It seems to have rained last night.

01 ⓒ, ⓓ: 형용사적 용법 ⓔ: 부사적 용법(감정의 원인)

02 ⓐ to write → to write with ⓑ hot something → something hot ⓔ to having → to have

03 to부정사가 본동사와 같은 시제일 경우에는 단순부정사를, to부정사가 본동사보다 앞선 시제일 경우에는 완료부정사를 쓴다. ③은 같은 의미가 되려면 It seems that he is hiding something.으로 써야 한다.

04 (1) to부정사가 명사 friends를 수식하므로 명사 뒤에 쓰고, 전치사를 생략하지 않도록 유의한다.
(2) 감정을 나타내는 형용사 뒤에 to부정사를 쓴다.

05 (1) 「too ~ to부정사」는 '…하기에 너무 ~한/하게'라는 의미이다.
(2) 「형용사/부사 + enough + to부정사」는 '…할 만큼 충분히 ~한/하게'라는 의미이다.

06 「It seems that + 주어 + 동사」나 「주어 + seem(s) + to부정사」 형태로 쓸 수 있다. that절의 동사가 본동사보다 앞선 시제를 나타내므로 완료부정사 형태로 써야 한다.

최종 선택 QUIZ
p. 57

01 b　02 b　03 a　04 a　05 a　06 b　07 a　08 b

UNIT 06 동명사

p. 58

바로 체크

01 Being 02 writing 03 not keeping 04 her
05 not having answered 06 opening 07 to call
08 seeing

STEP 1 · 만만한 기초

pp. 59 – 61

01 ④ 02 ④, ⑤ 03 Talking 04 ⑤ 05 lose → losing
06 ③ 07 ① 08 ② 09 ⑤ 10 ⑤
11 (1) solving (2) solving 12 ③ 13 ② 14 I hate
my little brother's using my stuff. 15 ③ 16 ①
17 ② 18 ② 19 ③ 20 (1) to avoid (2) eating
21 ④ 22 to bring 23 ② 24 ③ 25 to make →
making

---

01 be동사 뒤의 보어 자리에 쓸 수 있는 것은 동명사 또는 to부정사이다.
02 enjoy는 동명사를 목적어로 쓰는 동사이다.
03 주어 자리이므로 동명사의 형태로 써야 한다.
04 〈보기〉와 ⑤는 보어로 쓰인 동명사이고 ①, ②는 동사의 목적어, ③은 주어, ④는 전치사의 목적어로 쓰인 동명사이다.
05 전치사의 목적어 자리에 동사를 써야 할 경우 동명사의 형태로 쓴다.
06 동명사의 부정은 「not[never]＋동명사」의 형태로 쓴다.
07 ① '새로운 사람들을 만나는 것'이라는 의미가 되도록 주어를 동명사 또는 to부정사로 고쳐야 한다. Meet → Meeting[To meet]
08 〈보기〉와 ②는 동명사이고 나머지는 모두 현재분사이다.
09 ⑤는 동명사이고 나머지는 모두 현재분사이다.
10 〈보기〉와 ①~④는 현재분사이고 ⑤는 동명사이다.
11 (1) 동사의 목적어로 쓰인 동명사를 써야 한다.
   (2) 진행형을 만드는 현재분사를 써야 한다.
12 동명사의 의미상 주어는 동명사 앞에 소유격 또는 목적격을 써서 나타낸다.
13 동명사가 문장의 시제보다 앞선 일을 나타낼 때는 「having＋p.p.」로 쓴다.
14 동명사의 의미상 주어는 동명사 앞에 쓴다.
15 enjoy는 목적어로 동명사를 쓰는 동사이고 나머지는 모두 목적어로 to부정사를 쓰는 동사이다.
16 mind와 finish는 목적어로 동명사를 쓰는 동사이고 agree는 목적어로 to부정사를 쓰는 동사이다.
17 keep은 목적어로 동명사를 쓰는 동사이고 나머지는 모두 목적어로 동명사와 to부정사 둘 다 쓸 수 있다.
18 과거에 있었던 일을 기억할 것이라는 내용이 되어야 하므로 동명사가 와야 한다.
19 manage는 목적어로 to부정사를 쓰는 동사이므로 to escape로 고쳐야 한다. 「manage to＋동사원형」: 가까스로 ~하다, 그럭저럭 ~하다

---

20 try가 to부정사와 함께 쓰이면 '~하기 위해 노력하다'라는 의미이다. avoid는 목적어로 동명사를 쓰는 동사이다.
21 의미의 차이 없이 동명사와 to부정사 둘 다 목적어로 쓰는 동사는 like, hate, begin, start, prefer, continue 등이 있다.
22 '수영복을 가져올 것을 잊었다'라는 의미가 되도록 to부정사를 쓰는 것이 적절하다.
23 ① to go → going ③ to visit → to visiting ④ to clean → cleaning ⑤ ask → asking
24 주어진 표현을 바르게 배열하면 It is no use blaming him.이다.
25 「have difficulty (in)＋동명사」: ~하는 데 어려움을 겪다

STEP 2 · 오답률 40~60% 문제

pp. 62 – 63

01 ④ 02 ③ 03 ② 04 ① 05 ① 06 ⑤
07 ④ 08 ①, ③ 09 listening to pop music 10 to
turn off 11 to buy → buying 12 (1) ⓐ → Chris gave
up playing the guitar. (2) ⓑ → I expect to be back in an
hour. 13 riding, joining, getting up 14 She is used to
traveling alone. 15 is worth watching twice

---

01 전치사 뒤에는 명사 또는 동명사가 와야 한다.
02 동명사(구) 주어는 단수로 취급한다.
03 ②는 '~하고 있는 중이다'의 의미로 쓰인 현재분사이고, 나머지는 모두 동명사이다.
04 ① 전치사의 목적어 자리에 동사를 써야 할 경우 동명사의 형태로 쓴다. shop → shopping
05 동명사의 의미상 주어는 동명사 앞에 소유격 또는 목적격을 써서 나타내고, mind는 목적어로 동명사를 쓰는 동사이다.
06 ⑤ 동명사가 문장의 시제보다 앞선 일을 나타낼 때는 「having＋p.p.」로 쓴다. → The player is ashamed of having made a mistake.
07 ① to fix → fixing 또는 to be fixed ② to take → taking ③ to travel → traveling ⑤ attending → to attend
08 ② locking → to lock ④ to meet → meeting ⑤ to fight → fighting
09 enjoy는 목적어로 동명사를 쓰는 동사이다.
10 집에서 나가기 전에 TV를 끄는 것을 잊지 말라는 의미이므로 '(앞으로) ~할 것을 잊다'라는 의미의 「forget＋to부정사」 형태가 알맞다.
11 '돈을 아끼기 위해 필요 없는 물건을 사는 것을 멈추어야 한다'라는 의미가 되도록 stop 다음에 동명사를 써야 한다.
12 give up은 목적어로 동명사를 써야 하고, expect는 목적어로 to부정사를 써야 한다.
13 「make a point of＋동명사」: ~하는 것을 규칙으로 하다, 「How about＋동명사 ~?」: ~하는 게 어때?, 「have difficulty (in)＋동명사」: ~하는 데 어려움이 있다
14 「be used to＋동명사」: ~하는 데 익숙하다
15 「be worth＋동명사」: ~할 만한 가치가 있다

> **01** ②   **02** ④   **03** ②   **04** ①   **05** ①   **06** ③
> **07** ④   **08** donate → donating   **09** (1) to pay (2) spending (3) to inform   **10** Using plastic bags is harmful
> **11** (1) Mike's dream is becoming[being] a famous writer. (2) His plan for this year is writing a fantasy novel.
> **12** Most people are afraid of not getting a job.   **13** She hates someone's[someone] talking behind her back.
> **14** (1) her telling a lie   (2) his[him] being successful
> **15** The boy regrets not having studied harder.

01 ① writing → to write ③ finding → to find ④ to sell → selling ⑤ to ring → ringing

02 ④ '담배 피우는 것을 멈추다'라는 의미이므로 smoking으로 고쳐야 한다. 「stop + 동명사」: ~하는 것을 멈추다

03 Tim은 사고를 목격한 것을 부인했다는 내용이 되어야 알맞다. deny는 동명사를 목적어로 쓰는 동사이다.

04 어법상 옳은 것은 ⓑ이다. ⓐ to drink → drinking ⓒ taking → to take ⓓ turning → to turn

05 look forward to 다음에는 명사(구) 또는 동명사(구)가 온다.

06 laugh → laughing, 「cannot help -ing」: ~하지 않을 수 없다

07 「used to + 동사원형」은 '~하곤 했다'라는 의미로 과거의 습관을 나타내고, 「be used to + 동명사」는 '~하는 데 익숙하다'라는 의미이다.

08 consider는 동명사를 목적어로 쓰는 동사이다.

09 「forget+to부정사」: (앞으로) ~할 것을 잊다, 「remember + 동명사」: (과거에) ~한 것을 기억하다, 「regret + to부정사」: ~하게 되어 유감이다

10 주어 역할을 하는 동명사구를 쓰고 단수 동사를 쓴다.

11 보어 역할을 하는 동명사를 이용하여 문장을 완성한다.

12 전치사의 목적어로 동명사가 와야 하고, not은 동명사 앞에 쓴다.

13 동명사의 의미상 주어는 동명사 앞에 소유격 또는 목적격을 써서 나타낸다.

14 (1) 동명사의 의미상의 주어인 소유격 her를 쓰고 다음에 동명사를 쓴다.
(2) 동명사의 의미상의 주어인 소유격 his 또는 목적격 him을 쓰고 다음에 동명사를 쓴다.

15 열심히 공부하지 않았던 것이 후회하는 시점보다 더 이전의 일이므로 「having + p.p.」를 쓰고 not은 동명사 앞에 쓴다.

> **01** ②   **02** ③, ⑤   **03** ①   **04** His poor eyesight kept him from becoming a pilot.   **05** (1) avoid eating ice cream (2) I recommend drinking (3) forget to take medicine   **06** (1) stop listening to the radio (2) minds sharing his room with Tom

01 동명사: ⓐ treating, ⓑ buying, ⓔ Guiding / 현재분사: ⓒ shaking, ⓓ sitting, ⓕ learning

02 ① read → reading ② to eat → eating ④ to control → (in) controlling

03 ⓐ → I'm sure of their not attending the party.
ⓑ → The woman admitted having stolen the car.

04 「keep … from -ing」: …가 ~하지 못하게 막다

05 (1), (2) avoid와 recommend는 목적어로 동명사를 쓰는 동사이다. (3) 「forget + to부정사」: (앞으로) ~할 것을 잊다

06 (1) Ben이 라디오를 끄겠다고 했으므로 '라디오 듣는 것을 그만둘 것이다'라는 의미의 문장이 되어야 한다. 「stop + 동명사」: ~하는 것을 그만두다
(2) Steve는 혼자 방을 쓰고 싶다고 했으므로 'Tom과 방을 함께 쓰는 것을 꺼린다'라는 의미가 되어야 하며 mind는 목적어로 동명사를 쓴다.

> **01** b   **02** a   **03** a   **04** b   **05** a   **06** b   **07** a   **08** b

✓ 바로 체크
p. 68

01 crying 02 broken 03 dancing 04 called
05 built 06 reading 07 exciting 08 interested
09 동명사 10 현재분사

STEP 1 · 만만한 기초
pp. 69 – 71

01 ⑤ 02 ③ 03 ① 04 buzz → buzzing, make → making 05 painted, paint 06 ④ 07 ① 08 ③
09 steal → stolen 10 The man standing by the car
11 presented 12 ① 13 (1) chopped (2) boiling
14 I heard the song sung by a famous rock band. 15 ②
16 breaking → broken 17 ④ 18 running 19 ④
20 ② 21 ④ 22 satisfying, satisfied 23 exciting, excited 24 ⑤ 25 ②

01 첫 번째 빈칸: 바닥이 '덮여진' 것이므로 수동의 의미를 지닌 과거분사가 알맞다. 두 번째 빈칸: 새들이 '노래하는' 것이므로 능동의 의미를 지닌 현재분사가 알맞다.

02 책이 프랑스어로 '쓰여진' 것이므로 수동의 과거분사가 알맞다.

03 창문이 '닫힌' 것이므로 수동의 과거분사가 알맞다.

04 buzz는 bee를 수식하는 능동의 현재분사로, make는 진행형의 현재분사로 고쳐야 한다.

05 사역동사 have가 쓰인 5형식 문장에서 목적어와 목적격보어의 관계가 수동이면 과거분사를, 능동이면 동사원형을 쓴다.

06 ④ 여자가 경찰에 의해 '잡힌' 것이므로 수동의 의미를 지닌 과거분사 (caught)로 써야 한다.

07 ① 지각동사가 있는 5형식 문장이고 목적어와 목적격보어가 능동의 관계이므로 현재분사인 shaking 또는 동사원형 shake가 알맞다.

08 ③의 과거분사는 명사를 수식하는 한정적 용법으로 쓰였다. 나머지는 모두 주어 또는 목적어의 상태나 동작을 보충·설명하는 서술적 용법으로 쓰였다.

09 「사역동사(have) + 목적어 + 목적격보어」의 5형식 문장으로 목적어와 목적격 보어가 수동 관계이므로 목적격보어는 과거분사로 쓴다.

10 분사(standing)가 다른 수식어와 함께 쓰였으므로 명사 뒤에 써야 한다.

11 아이디어가 '제시되는' 것이므로 과거분사가 알맞다.

12 현재완료 의문문은 「Have[Has] + 주어 + 과거분사 ~?」의 형태이고, '잃어버린 짐'은 과거분사를 이용하여 lost luggage로 나타낸다.

13 명사와의 관계가 능동이면 현재분사를 쓰고 수동이면 과거분사를 쓴다.

14 지각동사가 있는 5형식 문장이고, 목적어와 목적격보어의 관계가 수동이므로 song 다음에 과거분사(sung)로 이어준다.

15 ② 여자가 '응시하는' 것은 현재분사인 staring이 알맞고, 사진들은 런던에서 '찍힌' 것이므로 과거분사 taken이 알맞다.

16 마음이 '상처 받은' 것이므로 breaking 대신 과거분사 broken으로 써야 한다.

17 ④는 명사 list의 용도, 목적을 나타내는 동명사이고, 〈보기〉와 나머지는 모두 명사의 동작이나 상태를 설명하는 현재분사이다.

18 첫 번째는 명사의 용도를 나타내는 동명사인 running이, 두 번째는 동작을 나타내는 현재분사 running이 알맞다.

19 첫 번째는 동사 enjoy의 목적어로 동명사가 알맞고, 두 번째는 명사를 뒤에서 수식하는 현재분사가 알맞다.

20 ②는 명사(machine)의 용도, 목적을 나타내는 동명사이고, 나머지는 모두 명사를 꾸며 주는 현재분사이다.

21 첫 번째 문장은 주어가 혼란스러움을 느끼게 하는 원인이므로 현재분사로, 두 번째 문장은 주어가 혼란스러운 감정을 느끼는 주체이므로 과거분사로 써야 한다.

22 첫 번째는 주어가 만족을 느끼게 하는 원인이므로 현재분사로, 두 번째는 주어가 만족되지 않은 감정을 느끼는 주체이므로 과거분사로 써야 한다.

23 첫 번째는 쇼가 흥분시키는 원인이므로 현재분사로, 두 번째는 아이들이 흥미를 느끼는 주체이므로 과거분사로 써야 한다.

24 ⑤ 주어가 감정의 원인이 되는 것이므로 현재분사인 challenging으로 고쳐야 한다.

25 ② 팀이 우승했다는 소식은 감정의 원인이 되는 것이므로 현재분사인 surprising으로 고쳐야 한다.

STEP 2 · 오답률 40~60% 문제
pp. 72 – 73

01 ②, ⑤ 02 ③ 03 ② 04 ② 05 ③ 06 ④
07 ③ 08 looking for a sleeping bag 09 ⓑ: connected → connecting 10 We saw a castle made of ice.
11 (1) leaving (2) invited (3) damaged 12 (1) wear → wearing (2) played → playing 13 (1) impressed (2) amazing 14 boring, boring 15 (1) depressing (2) amused

01 ② '삶은 달걀'이므로 과거분사 boiled로 쓴다. ⑤ 명사와의 관계가 능동이면 현재분사를 써야 하므로 driving이 알맞다.

02 첫 번째 빈칸에는 능동·진행의 의미를 갖는 현재분사가 알맞고, 두 번째 빈칸에는 이름이 '불리는' 것이므로 수동의 과거분사가 알맞다.

03 차는 '주차된' 것이므로 과거분사가 알맞고, 남자는 '누워 있는' 것이므로 현재분사가 알맞다.

04 분사가 수식어구와 함께 쓰일 때는 명사 뒤에서 명사를 수식한다.

05 '~로 가득하다'는 be filled with를 이용하고, '타버린' 토스트는 과거분사 burnt를 이용하여 나타낸다.

06 〈보기〉는 명사(girl)를 꾸며 주는 현재분사이다. ④의 smoking은 명사의 목적이나 용도로 쓰인 동명사이고, 나머지는 모두 현재분사이다.

07 ③은 보어로 쓰인 동명사로 '~하는 것'이라는 의미이고 나머지는 모두 현재분사이다.

08 be동사가 있으므로 현재분사로 진행형을 나타낸다. 명사의 목적이나 용도를 나타낼 때는 동명사 형태가 와야 하므로 침낭은 a sleeping bag으로 쓴다.

09 ⓑ '두 섬을 연결하는 다리'라는 능동의 의미로 connected를 현재분사로 고친다.

10 얼음으로 '만들어진' 성이므로 과거분사 made를 이용한다.

11 (1) 그들은 뉴질랜드로 떠나는 비행기에 탑승했다.
(2) 파티에 초대된 대부분의 사람은 그의 오랜 친구들이었다.
(3) 저희는 파손된 제품에 대해 전액 환불을 해 드릴 것입니다.

12 '파란색 드레스를 입고 있는 소녀가 모차르트를 연주하고 있다.'라는 의미가 되도록 wear와 played를 현재분사로 고쳐야 한다.

13 주어가 감정의 원인이 될 때 현재분사를 쓰고 주어가 감정을 느끼는 주체일 때는 과거분사를 쓴다.

14 boring person은 '지루한 사람'이라는 의미이다.

15 주어가 감정의 원인이 될 때 현재분사를 쓰고 주어가 감정을 느끼는 대상일 때는 과거분사를 쓴다.

STEP 3 · 오답률 60~80%문제

pp. 74 – 75

01 ① **02** ③, ⑤ **03** ①, ⑤ **04** ② **05** ③
06 ③ **07** ①, ③ **08** studying bacteria made a new discovery **09** (1) pull → pulled (2) eat → eaten
10 She likes the songs composed by the Beatles.
11 Trees blown down by the wind blocked the road.
12 was disappointing, was disappointed **13** fascinating, interesting **14** (1) exhausting (2) embarrassed (3) frightened **15** ⓐ: tired → tiring ⓑ: boring → bored

01 'Green씨에게 속한 몇 가지 물건들이 옷장 안에서 발견되었을 때 모두가 놀랐다.'라는 의미이다. Everyone은 놀란 감정을 느끼게 된 주체이므로 과거분사를 쓰고, '~에게 속해 있'이라는 의미를 나타내기 위해서 현재분사 belonging을 쓰며, 수동태는 「be동사 + 과거분사」로 나타낸다.

02 ③ 영화가 흥미를 느끼게 하는 원인이므로 현재분사 interesting으로 고쳐야 한다. ⑤ All of us는 감동을 느낀 주체이므로 과거분사 moved로 고쳐야 한다.

03 ① → scratching ⑤ → throwing

04 ① slept → sleep[sleeping] ③ frustrated → frustrating
④ interesting → interested ⑤ crossed → crossing

05 Adele의 목소리가 놀라움을 유발하는 원인이므로 amazed를 amazing으로 고쳐야 한다.

06 ③은 동명사로 '~하는 것'으로 해석하고 나머지는 모두 현재분사이다. 「be used to + 동명사」: ~하는데 익숙하다

07 ①과 ③은 현재분사이고 나머지는 모두 동명사이다.

08 분사가 수식어구와 함께 쓰일 때는 명사 뒤에 쓴다. 진행의 의미가 되도록 study를 현재분사로 바꾼다.

09 목적어와 목적격보어의 관계가 수동이므로 pull은 과거분사인 pulled로 써야 하고, 현재완료 시제 문장에서 have 다음에 과거분사를 써야 한다.

10 수동의 의미이므로 compose를 과거분사로 바꿔 써야 한다.

11 바람에 의해 '쓰러진' 나무들이라는 의미가 되도록 과거분사를 써야 한다.

12 첫 번째 문장: 결과가 '실망을 주는' 것이므로 능동의 현재분사가 알맞다. 두 번째 문장: 가족이 '실망을 하게 된' 것이므로 수동의 과거분사가 알맞다.

13 주어가 감정의 원인이 될 때 현재분사를 쓴다.

14 (1) 주어가 '힘들게 하는 원인'이므로 현재분사가 알맞다. (2), (3) 주어가 '감정(당황함, 두려움)을 느끼는 대상'이므로 과거분사가 알맞다.

15 ⓐ는 주어가 '피곤함을 느끼게 하는' 것이므로 tired를 현재분사인 tiring으로 고쳐야 한다. ⓑ는 주어가 '지루함을 느끼는' 것이므로 boring을 과거분사인 bored로 고쳐야 한다.

STEP 4 · 실력 완성 테스트

p. 76

01 (1) 현재분사: ⓐ, ⓒ, ⓔ (2) 동명사: ⓑ, ⓓ, ⓕ **02** ①, ④
03 ② **04** A puppy run over by a truck was taken to the animal hospital. **05** amazed → amazing, pleasing → pleased, excited → exciting **06** (1) wearing an orange sweater is walking his dog (2) sitting on the bench is talking on the phone (3) surrounded by children is making a balloon teddy bear

01 현재분사는 명사 앞에서 명사의 동작이나 상태를 나타내거나 진행 시제로 쓰인다.

02 ① frozen → freezing ④ relaxed → relaxing

03 ⓑ tear → torn ⓓ frustrating → frustrated
ⓔ shocked → shocking

04 주어는 a puppy이고, 강아지가 '트럭에 치인 것'이므로 수동의 과거분사를 활용하여 run over by a truck으로 표현하며, 본동사는 수동태를 이용한다.

05 주어가 감정의 원인이 될 때 현재분사를 쓰고 주어가 감정을 느끼게 되는 주체일 때는 과거분사를 쓴다.

06 분사가 수식어구와 함께 쓰일 때는 명사를 뒤에서 수식한다.

최종 선택 QUIZ

p. 77

01 a **02** a **03** a **04** a **05** b **06** b **07** a **08** b

UNIT 08 분사구문

✔ 바로 체크   p. 78

01 Seeing	02 Left	03 Having eaten	04 shaking
05 broken	06 Being	07 It being	08 Not being

STEP 1 · 만만한 기초   pp. 79 – 81

01 ③   02 ②, ③   03 listening   04 Living
05 Feeling frightened   06 Not having   07 ⑤   08 ①
09 ①   10 Being poor   11 (1) If you go upstairs (2) As he didn't feel hungry   12 Andy was taking a shower, whistling to himself.   13 Being → There being
14 Having locked   15 ②   16 (Being) Written in old English   17 ⑤   18 ④   19 ⑤   20 ⑤   21 Judging from my experience   22 ①   23 with the kettle boiling
24 ④   25 ①, ⑤

01 부사절과 주절의 주어가 같으므로 접속사와 주어를 없애고 동사를 현재분사로 바꿔 분사구문으로 만든다. 부사절이 진행형일 경우 being은 쓰지 않고 현재분사인 -ing만 남긴다.

02 '피곤했기 때문에'라는 의미가 되도록 부사절(As I was tired) 또는 분사구문(Being tired)으로 쓸 수 있다.

03 동시에 진행되는 동작을 나타낼 때 분사구문을 사용할 수 있다.

04 부사절과 주절의 주어가 같으므로 접속사와 주어를 생략한 뒤 동사 live를 현재분사 living으로 바꾼다.

05 부사절과 주절의 주어가 같으므로 접속사와 주어를 생략한 뒤 동사 felt를 현재분사 feeling으로 바꾼다.

06 분사구문의 부정은 분사 앞에 not을 쓴다.

07 ⑤ 분사구문의 부정은 분사 앞에 not을 써야 한다. Knowing not → Not knowing

08 첫 번째 빈칸: '웹 사이트를 방문한다면, 더 많은 정보를 얻을 수 있다.'라는 의미가 되도록 조건의 접속사 If를 쓴다. 두 번째 빈칸: '한국에 머무르는 동안, 머드 축제를 경험했다.'라는 의미가 되도록 접속사 While을 쓴다.

09 ①은 조건을 나타내는 분사구문이고 나머지는 모두 이유를 나타내는 분사구문이다.

10 Because they were poor에서 접속사와 주어를 생략하고 be동사를 현재분사인 being으로 바꿔 쓴다.

11 (1) '위층에 올라간다면, 지배인을 만날 수 있을 것이다.'라는 의미가 되도록 조건의 접속사 if를 쓴다. (2) '배가 고프지 않아서 저녁을 먹지 않았다.'라는 의미가 되도록 이유를 나타내는 접속사 as를 쓴다.

12 동시동작을 나타내는 분사구문이다.

13 부사절과 주절의 주어가 다르므로 주어를 생략하지 않고 남겨둬야 하고, 이를 독립분사구문이라고 한다.

14 부사절의 시제가 주절의 시제보다 앞선 경우이므로 완료 분사구문인 「having + 과거분사」로 쓴다.

15 첫 번째 문장: 연설을 끝낸 것이 출구 쪽으로 향한 것보다 먼저 일어난 일이므로 완료 분사구문으로 나타낸다. 두 번째 문장: 수동태의 분사구문으로 Being seen ~으로 시작하는데, Being은 생략할 수 있다.

16 부사절과 주절의 주어가 같으므로 접속사와 주어를 생략한 뒤, 동사 was를 분사로 바꾸면 Being written in old English가 되고, 이때 Being은 생략할 수 있다.

17 ⑤ 한국 역사를 공부한 것이 먼저 일어난 일이므로 완료 분사구문으로 나타내야 한다. Studied → Having studied

18 frankly speaking: 솔직히 말하면(= honestly)

19 generally speaking: 일반적으로 말하면

20 strictly speaking: 엄밀히 말하면, speaking of: ~ 이야기가 나와서 말인데

21 judging from: ~로 판단하건대

22 「with + 명사(구) + 분사」의 형태로 나타낼 수 있는데, 눈이 '감기는' 것은 수동이므로 과거분사를 쓴다.

23 「with + 명사(구) + 분사」에서 명사(구)와 분사의 관계가 능동이므로 현재분사를 쓴다.

24 ① turning → turned ② covering → covered ③ wagged → wagging ⑤ blown → blowing

25 ① closing → closed ⑤ slept → sleeping

STEP 2 · 오답률 40~60%문제   pp. 82 – 83

01 ①   02 ③   03 ⑤   04 ④   05 ②   06 ③, ④
07 ⑤   08 Waiting for the bus   09 Not having eaten for two days   10 injuring → injured   11 (1) Frankly speaking (2) Speaking of (3) Judging from
12 Considering his age   13 followed → following
14 with her legs crossed   15 with his arms folded

01 첫 번째 빈칸: As he looked for his missing dog를 분사구문으로 고친 것으로 접속사와 주어를 생략하고, 동사 looked를 현재분사로 바꾼다. 두 번째 빈칸: As we were surprised by the lightning and thunder를 분사구문으로 고친 것으로 Being surprised ~로 시작하는데, 이때 Being은 생략할 수 있다.

02 동시동작을 나타내는 분사구문이다.

03 '네가 말한 것을 인정한다'와 '나는 그것을 아직도 믿지 않는다'라는 내용은 서로 상반되므로 빈칸에는 양보를 나타내는 접속사가 알맞다.

04 부사절의 시제가 주절보다 앞선 시제이므로 완료 분사구문인 「having + 과거분사」의 형태로 쓰고 not은 having 앞에 쓴다.

05 분사구문과 주절의 주어가 서로 다르기 때문에 주어 It을 생략하지 않고 분사 앞에 써야 한다. (→ As it was cold, we couldn't go swimming.)

06 ① → Writing a letter to Julia ② → Not having a ticket ⑤ → (Having been) Born and raised in France

07 ⑤ 수동태의 분사구문으로 Not being invited to the party로 고쳐야 한다.

08 부사절이 진행형이면 being은 쓰지 않고 -ing만 남긴다.

09 부사절의 시제가 주절보다 앞선 경우이므로 완료 분사구문인 「having + 과거분사」의 형태로 쓰고, not은 having 앞에 쓴다.

10 차 사고로 '부상을 당한' 것이므로 수동태의 분사구문인 「being / having been + 과거분사」를 이용해야 한다. 이때 being과 having been은 생략할 수 있다.

11 frankly speaking: 솔직히 말하면, speaking of: ~ 이야기가 나와서 말인데, judging from: ~로 판단하건대

12 considering: ~을 고려하면

13 '개가 그녀의 뒤를 따라가고 있는 채로'라는 의미로 명사구와 분사의 관계가 능동이므로 followed를 following으로 고친다.

14 동시동작의 의미를 나타내는 「with + 명사(구) + 분사」를 이용해야 한다. '그녀의 다리를 꼰 채로'라는 의미로 명사구와 분사의 관계가 수동이므로 과거분사 crossed를 쓴다.

15 「with + 명사(구) + 분사」 구문에서 his arms와 fold와의 관계는 수동이므로 과거분사 folded를 쓴다.

11 (1) 분사구문의 시제가 주절보다 앞선 경우이므로 「having + 과거분사」로 고친다. (2) 수동태의 분사구문이므로 「being + 과거분사」로 쓰고, 이때 being은 생략이 가능하다.

12 '세차를 한 것'이 '쇼핑을 간 것'보다 더 이전에 일어난 일이므로 '세차한 후에'를 완료 분사구문인 「having + 과거분사」로 나타낸다.

13 부사절은 「접속사 + 주어 + 동사」의 어순으로 쓴다. 분사구문은 부정의 의미를 나타내야 하므로 not을 맨 앞에 쓰고 동사 want의 현재분사 wanting을 쓴다.

14 「with + 명사(구) + 분사」 구문에서 명사(구)와 분사의 관계가 능동이면 현재분사를 쓰고, 수동이면 과거분사를 쓴다.

15 '~한 채로'의 의미는 「with + 명사(구) + 분사」로 쓰고, the safety belt와 fasten의 관계는 수동이므로 fastened로 써야 한다.

STEP 3 · 오답률 60~80% 문제

pp. 84 – 85

01 ①, ④　02 ③　03 ①　04 ④　05 ③　06 ④
07 Not having slept　08 (Having been) Arrested and sent to jail　09 The score being equal　10 Realizing her mistake　11 (1) Lost → Having lost (2) Annoy → (Being) Annoyed　12 Having washed my car, I went shopping.
13 (부사절) As[Because/Since] I didn't want to miss the bus, I ran to the bus stop. (분사구문) Not wanting to miss the bus, I ran to the bus stop.　14 (1) his sister knitting beside him (2) her eyes filled with tears of joy　15 with the safety belt fastened

01 ② → Spilling coffee on the carpet ③ → (Being) Lost in thought ⑤ → Having seen the movie before

02 '비록 시인으로 널리 알려졌지만, 그는 성공적인 소설을 썼다.'라는 의미가 되도록 과거분사 Known이 되어야 한다. 수동태의 분사구문으로 Known 앞에는 Being이 생략되어 있다.

03 ⓐ 부사절과 주절의 주어가 서로 다르므로 생략할 수 없다. ⓑ 완료 분사구문으로 Having은 생략할 수 없다.

04 ④ '경고를 받았음에도, 그는 여전히 수업에 지각한다.'라는 의미로 Though he was warned before로 바꾸는 것이 알맞다.

05 첫 번째 빈칸: 비는 '쏟아지는' 것이므로 pouring이 알맞다. 두 번째 빈칸: 수동태의 분사구문 (Being) Left이다. 세 번째 빈칸: 커튼은 '쳐진' 것이므로 drawn이 알맞다.

06 ⓐ 부사절과 주절의 주어가 다르므로 부사절의 주어를 생략하지 않고 분사 앞에 남겨두어야 한다. Being → There being

07 '지금 피곤한 것'보다 '어젯밤에 잠을 못 잔 것'이 더 이전의 시제이므로 완료 분사구문을 써야 하고, not은 having 앞에 써야 한다.

08 수동태의 분사구문에서 having been은 생략할 수 있다.

09 부사절과 주절의 주어가 다르므로 분사 앞에 주어를 남겨 둔다.

10 접속사와 주어를 생략하고 동사 realized는 현재분사 realizing으로 바꿔 쓴다.

STEP 4 · 실력 완성 테스트

p. 86

01 ④　02 ②　03 ①, ③　04 (1) is running, watching (2) is running, with her eyes fixed　05 (1) (Being) Watered regularly, the plant will last long. (2) Slipping on the ice, he hurt his leg. (3) Having nothing left to do, I took a nap for a while.　06 (1) Never having been abroad before (2) with his hands tied behind his back

01 ④는 수동태 완료 분사구문이므로 been이 들어가야 하고 나머지는 모두 being이 알맞다.

02 ⓑ Spent → Having spent ⓒ Considered → Considering ⓓ Having not → Not having

03 ① 부사절과 주절의 주어가 다를 때 주어를 생략하지 않고 분사 앞에 남겨둔다. → It being sunny ③ 수동태의 분사구문이므로 Asked로 고친다.

04 (1) 동시동작을 나타내는 분사구문으로 쓴다. (2) '그녀의 눈을 고정시킨 채로'라는 의미가 되도록 fix의 과거분사를 쓴다.

05 (1) 조건의 의미를 나타내는 분사구문으로 바꾼다. (= If the plant is watered regularly, it will last long.) (2) 시간의 의미를 나타내는 분사구문으로 바꾼다. (= When he slipped on the ice, he hurt his leg.) (3) 이유를 나타내는 분사구문으로 바꾼다. (= As[Because/Since] I had nothing left to do, I took a nap for a while.)

06 (1) never를 맨 앞에 쓴 후 완료 분사구문인 「having + 과거분사」를 쓴다. (2) 「with + 명사(구) + 분사」의 어순으로 쓰고, 명사구와 분사의 관계가 수동이므로 tied로 고쳐 쓴다.

최종 선택 QUIZ

p. 87

01 b　02 b　03 b　04 a　05 b　06 a　07 a　08 b

UNIT 09 수동태 1

✓ 바로 체크
p. 88

01 broke 02 was written 03 him 04 were painted
05 is being fixed 06 has been fed 07 will be played
08 should not be opened 09 will disappear 10 has

STEP 1 · 만만한 기초
pp. 89 – 91

01 ③ 02 ② 03 ③ 04 ⑤ 05 ④ 06 was
built by my parents 07 are worn by many students
08 was arrested by the police 09 were not broken by
her 10 Were the flowers bought by him? 11 It was
invented by King Sejong. 12 (1) is helped (2) are baked
(3) are washed 13 ③ 14 ④ 15 can be seen
16 will be invited to the party by them 17 ③, ⑤ 18 ⑤
19 The 2022 FIFA World Cup will be held in Qatar.
20 has been written by the students 21 ⑤ 22 paid
→ be paid 23 be hurted → been hurt 24 ②, ⑤
25 ⑤

01 능동태를 수동태로 바꿀 때 시제가 과거이므로 능동태의 동사를 「was + 과거분사」로 바꾸고, 능동태의 주어를 「by + 행위자」의 형태로 바꾼다.

02 편지(The letter)는 행위의 주체가 아닌 대상이 되므로 수동태 문장이 되어야 한다. 주어(The letter)가 3인칭 단수이고 과거를 나타내는 부사구가 쓰였으므로 과거 시제 수동태 was written이 알맞다.

03 ③ 박물관은 동작의 대상이 되는 것이므로 첫 번째 빈칸은 과거 시제 수동태로 나타내야 하고, 관광객들은 행위를 하는 주체이므로 두 번째 빈칸은 현재 시제 능동태로 나타내야 한다.

04 ⑤ 동사의 행위를 당하는 대상이 주어이므로 수동태로 나타내야 한다. → was given

05 ④ The paintings가 복수이므로 was를 were로 고쳐야 한다.

06 주어가 동작의 대상이 될 때 수동태를 사용한다. 수동태의 기본 형태는 「be동사 + 과거분사(+ by + 행위자)」이다.

07 능동태를 수동태로 바꿀 때는 능동태의 목적어를 수동태의 주어로 쓴 다음 「be동사 + 과거분사(+ by + 행위자)」로 나타낸다. 시제가 현재이고 주어가 복수이므로 be동사는 are를 쓴다. wear의 과거분사는 worn이다.

08 시제가 과거이고 주어가 3인칭 단수이므로 be동사는 was를 쓴다.

09 시제가 과거이고 주어가 복수이므로 be동사는 were를 쓰고 행위자인 she는 목적격 her로 고친다. 수동태의 부정은 be동사 뒤에 not을 쓴다.

10 의미상 수동태의 의문문 문장이 되어야 한다. 구입한 시점이 과거이고, 주어 the flowers가 복수이므로 be동사는 were가 알맞다.

11 수동태 문장에서 동사는 「be동사 + 과거분사」, 행위자는 「by + 행위자」로 쓴다.

12 그림을 보면 엄마는 아빠의 도움을 받고 있고, Tom은 쿠키를 굽고 있으며, Sally는 설거지를 하고 있다. 각 행동을 수동태 「be동사 + 과거분사」로 나타낸다.

13 미래 시제 수동태는 「will be + 과거분사」로 나타낸다.

14 진행형 수동태는 「be동사 + being + 과거분사」로 나타낸다.

15 주어인 *Mona Lisa*는 '보는 대상'이므로 수동태가 되어야 한다. 조동사가 쓰인 수동태는 「조동사 + be + 과거분사」 형태로 쓴다.

16 미래 시제 수동태는 「will be + 과거분사」의 형태로 쓴다.

17 ③ 조동사가 쓰인 수동태의 의문문은 「조동사 + 주어 + be + 과거분사 ~?」의 형태이다. (kept → be kept) ⑤ 현재완료형이 쓰인 수동태가 알맞고, 형태는 「has + been + 과거분사」가 되어야 한다. (has used → has been used)

18 첫 번째 문장이 과거 진행형의 능동태이고 목적어 the hall이 단수이므로 수동태에서는 진행형 수동태의 형태인 「be동사(was) + being + 과거분사」가 알맞다.

19 의미상 행위(개최)의 대상인 FIFA 월드컵이 주어이므로 수동태 구문을 써야 하며, 2022년이므로 미래 시제(will be + 과거분사)로 표현한다.

20 주어진 문장은 현재완료 시제이고, 목적어를 주어로 하는 문장으로 바꿔야 하므로 완료형 수동태로 표현한다. 주어가 3인칭 단수이므로 완료형 수동태의 형태는 「has + been + 과거분사」이다.

21 ① been → be ② is → be ③ understand → understood ④ be → being

22 조동사가 쓰인 수동태는 「조동사 + be + 과거분사」의 형태로 쓴다.

23 주어가 3인칭 단수인 현재완료형 수동태의 형태는 「has + been + 과거분사」이다. 동사 hurt의 과거분사형은 hurt이다.

24 목적어가 없는 자동사인 happen과 소유를 나타내는 타동사인 have는 수동태로 쓰지 않는다.

25 목적어가 없는 자동사인 remain, weigh, belong, arrive는 수동태로 쓰지 않는다. ⑤의 빈칸에는 was가 들어가서 과거 시제의 수동태 형태를 취해야 의미가 자연스럽다.

STEP 2 · 오답률 40~60% 문제
pp. 92 – 93

01 ① 02 ① 03 ⑤ 04 ③ 05 ③ 06 ①
07 ⑤ 08 was blocked by the fallen trees 09 food
will be made by robots 10 Their presents are being
wrapped by the clerk. 11 Halloween has been celebrated
by many children. 12 has been stolen by a thief
13 (1) shot (2) watching (3) was carried (4) was caught
14 (1) will be happened → will happen (2) was suddenly
appeared → suddenly appeared 15 • 바꿀 수 있는 문장:
(2), (5) / • 바꿀 수 없는 문장: (1), (3), (4)

01 부가의문문에 didn't가 쓰였으므로 첫 번째 빈칸에는 능동태 일반동사의 과거형이 들어가야 하고, 두 번째 빈칸 앞에 쓰인 주어는 동작의 대상이 되기 때문에 과거 시제 수동태로 나타내야 한다.

02 행위자를 나타내는 by its owner로 보아 수동태 문장이므로 과거진행형은 쓸 수 없다.

03 ④ '바오밥 나무는 사막에서 발견된다'라는 의미로 수동태로 나타내야 하며 find의 과거분사는 found로 고쳐야 한다. → are found

04 ③은 주어가 동작을 하는 주체이므로 능동태로 써야 한다.
was composed → composed

05 미래 시제 수동태는 「will be + 과거분사」로 나타낸다.

06 ② must not be forgotten ③ is being tested ④ has been raised 또는 was raised ⑤ will be shown으로 써야 한다.

07 ⑤ 「be동사 + being + 과거분사」 형태의 진행형 수동태로 고쳐야 하므로 spread의 과거분사 spread가 되어야 한다. spreading → spread

08 능동태를 수동태로 바꿀 때 시제가 과거 시제이고 주어가 3인칭 단수이므로 「was + 과거분사」로 바꾸고, 능동태의 주어는 「by + 행위자」의 형태로 쓴다.

09 미래 시제 수동태는 「will be + 과거분사」로 나타낸다.

10 진행형 수동태의 형태는 「be동사 + being + 과거분사」이다.

11 능동태의 목적어가 수동태에서는 주어가 되므로 3인칭 단수의 현재완료형 수동태인 「has been + 과거분사」의 형태로 쓴다.

12 '보석이 도둑에게 도난당했다'라는 의미의 문장이 되어야 하고, have를 이용해야 하므로 현재완료 수동태로 나타내야 한다. steal의 과거분사형은 stolen이다.

13 (1) shoot의 과거분사는 shot이다. (2) 능동태 문장이고 과거진행형이 되어야 자연스럽다. (3) 집으로 '옮겨진' 것이므로 과거 시제 수동태로 나타내야 한다. (4) 군인에게 '잡힌' 것이므로 과거 시제 수동태로 나타내야 한다.

14 목적어가 없는 자동사인 happen과 appear는 수동태로 쓰지 않는다.

15 상태를 나타내는 타동사 fit와 resemble, 목적어를 취하지 않는 자동사 occur는 수동태로 쓰지 않는다.

03 '어두워진 후에는 창문을 닫아 두어라, 그렇지 않으면 너는 모기에 물릴 것이다'라는 의미가 되어야 자연스러우므로 미래 시제 수동태가 알맞다.

04 마지막 문장은 '안경다리가 나중에 덧붙여졌다'는 의미이므로 수동태 문장이 되어야 한다. 「be동사 + 과거분사」의 수동태 형태에 맞춰 쓰되, 주어 arms가 복수이고 시제는 과거임에 유의한다.

05 Jim이 차에 '치였다'라는 의미가 되도록 수동태로 표현해야 하며, luckily(다행히)라는 표현으로 짐작해 볼 때 '심하게 다치지 않았다'는 의미가 되어야 한다. 마지막 빈칸에는 지금 '치료를 받는 중이다'라는 의미가 되도록 진행형 수동태가 쓰여야 한다.

06 ③ → will be spent

07 ① are → be ⑤ be → been

08 조동사가 있는 수동태는 「조동사 + be + 과거분사」로 나타낸다.

09 두 번째 문장은 끝에 행위자를 나타내는 by the housekeeper로 보아 수동태이다. 첫 번째 문장은 미래 시제 완료형이므로 빈칸은 미래 시제 완료형 수동태인 「will have + been + 과거분사」로 나타낸다.

10 진행형 수동태를 의문문으로 쓸 때 「be동사 + 주어 + being + 과거분사 ~?」로 나타낸다.

11 조동사가 쓰인 수동태: 「조동사 + be + 과거분사」, 완료형 수동태: 「have[has/had/will have] + been + 과거분사」, 진행형 수동태: 「be동사 + being + 과거분사」

12 우리가 경기장에 도착한 것보다 경기가 취소된 것이 먼저 일어난 일이므로 과거완료형의 수동태 형태인 「had + been + 과거분사」로 나타낸다.

13 미래 시제 수동태는 「will be + 과거분사」로 나타낸다.

14 현재진행형 수동태의 형태는 「be동사 + being + 과거분사」로 나타낸다. water는 동사로 쓰이면 '물을 주다'의 의미이다.

15 목적어가 없는 자동사인 remain은 수동태로 쓰지 않는다.

STEP 3 · 오답률 60~80% 문제　　　　pp. 94 – 95

> **01** ③　　**02** ④　　**03** ②　　**04** ⑤　　**05** ③　　**06** ③
> **07** ①, ⑤　　**08** Wild animals should be protected by us.
> **09** will have been mopped　　**10** Are the victims being taken to hospital by the ambulance? 또는 Are the victims being taken by the ambulance to hospital?　　**11** be, been, being　　**12** had been canceled　　**13** (1) The city will be hit by a huge earthquake. (2) The winner's name will be announced by the show host.　　**14** (1) are being watered (2) is being played　　**15** will be remained → will remain

01 ① can bought → can be bought ② were put → put ④ has adopted → has been adopted 또는 was adopted ⑤ will be preparing → will be prepared

02 ④ 주어가 동작의 주체이므로 능동태로 써야 하며 현재완료 진행형을 이용하여 making이 되어야 한다. 나머지는 모두 수동태에 쓰이는 과거분사 made가 알맞다.

STEP 4 · 실력 완성 테스트　　　　p. 96

> **01** ①　　**02** ①　　**03** ②, ④　　**04** should not[shouldn't] be touched　　**05** was seemed → seemed, she left → she was left　　**06** (1) is being cleaned by Andy (2) will be fed by Andy (3) is being moved by Jean (4) will be returned by Jean

01 ⓐ was hiding → was hidden ⓑ will deliver → will be delivered ⓒ seen → be seen ⓓ had copied → had been copied ⓔ introduced → was introduced

02 ⓒ been 삭제 또는 Was → Has ⓓ has invented → was invented ⓔ is resembled by → resembles

03 ② 진행형 수동태는 「be동사 + being + 과거분사」로 쓴다. (been → being) ④ 조동사가 있는 수동태의 의문문은 「조동사 + 주어 + be + 과거분사 ~?」로 나타낸다. (delivered → be delivered)

04 안내판과 주어진 단어로 보아 조동사가 쓰인 수동태 형태인 「조동사 + be + 과거분사」로 표현하고, 조동사가 있는 수동태의 부정은 조동사 다음에 not을 쓴다.

05 목적어가 없는 자동사인 seem은 수동태로 쓰지 않고, '그녀가 홀로 남겨지는 것'이므로 left는 수동태 was left로 써야 한다.

진행형 수동태는 「be동사＋being＋과거분사」로 나타내고, 미래 시제 수동태는 「will be＋과거분사」로 나타낸다.

최종 선택 **QUIZ** p. 97

01 a	02 a	03 b	04 b	05 a	06 a	07 b	08 a

UNIT 10 수동태 2

✓ 바로 체크 p. 98

01 was handed, were handed to　**02** for　**03** to drive away　**04** were, singing　**05** was turned on　**06** in　**07** It, He, to be

---

STEP 1 · 만만한 기초 pp. 99 – 101

01 were given flowers, were given to　**02** ①, ⑤
03 ②　**04** ③　**05** ①　**06** ③, ⑤　**07** were made for me by my mother　**08** An interesting book was bought for me by Mom.　**09** weren't taught English, wasn't taught to us　**10** ②, ④　**11** to speak　**12** ③, ④　**13** A man was seen jumping over a wall by a police officer.　**14** was painted green　**15** were made to stand　**16** ①, ④　**17** ⑤　**18** ①　**19** His house was broken into by two men.　**20** (1) in (2) of (3) for (4) with　**21** ④　**22** ①, ③　**23** ①　**24** ②　**25** is said to be

01 주어진 문장은 4형식 문장으로 간접목적어(the winners)와 직접목적어(flowers)를 주어로 하여 두 종류의 수동태를 만들 수 있다. 직접목적어가 주어일 때는 간접목적어 앞에 전치사를 써야 하고, give는 전치사 to를 쓰는 동사이다.

02 4형식 문장은 수동태로 바꿀 때 간접목적어와 직접목적어를 모두 주어로 쓸 수 있다. 동사 teach는 직접목적어를 주어로 할 때 간접목적어 앞에 전치사 to를 쓴다.

03 4형식 문장에서 직접목적어를 주어로 하여 수동태로 바꿀 때, ask는 간접목적어 앞에 전치사 of를 쓰는 동사이다.

04 미래 시제의 부정문 수동태의 형태는 조동사 다음에 not을 써서 「won't be＋과거분사」의 형태로 표현한다. send는 수동태로 바꿀 때, 간접목적어 앞에 전치사 to를 쓰는 동사이다.

05 ① 동사 sell의 직접목적어를 주어로 할 때 간접목적어 앞에는 전치사 to를 써야 한다. for → to

06 4형식 문장에서 직접목적어를 수동태의 주어로 쓸 때 간접목적어 앞에 전치사 for를 쓸 수 있는 동사는 bake와 buy이다. sell, send, give는 전치사로 to를 쓰는 동사이다.

07 동사 make의 직접목적어를 주어로 할 때 간접목적어 앞에는 전치사 for를 써야 한다. 수동태의 주어가 복수이고, 시제가 과거임에 유의한다.

08 능동태 문장으로 고치면 Mom bought me an interesting book. 이 된다. 4형식 문장에서 buy는 직접목적어만 수동태의 주어로 쓰는 동사이므로 직접목적어를 주어로 해서 수동태 문장을 쓰고, 간접목적어 앞에는 전치사 for를 쓴다.

09 4형식 문장은 간접목적어와 직접목적어를 주어로 하는 두 가지 형태의 수동태 문장으로 바꿀 수 있다. teach는 직접목적어를 주어로 할 때 간접목적어 앞에 전치사 to를 쓰는 동사임에 유의한다.

10 ② 5형식 문장에서 목적격보어는 수동태의 주어가 될 수 없다. (→ She was considered a genius by everyone.) ④ 5형식 문장에서 지각동사의 목적격보어로 쓰인 동사원형은 수동태에서 to부정사로 바뀐다. (heard sing → heard to sing)

11 5형식 문장에서 사역동사 make의 목적격보어로 쓰인 동사원형은 수동태에서 to부정사로 써야 한다.

12 5형식 문장에서 지각동사의 목적격보어로 쓰인 동사원형은 수동태에서 to부정사로 바꾸고, 현재분사이면 그대로 동사 뒤에 현재분사를 쓴다.

13 5형식 문장을 수동태로 바꿀 때, 지각동사의 목적격보어로 쓰인 현재분사는 수동태에서도 동사 뒤에 그대로 쓴다.

14 5형식 문장을 수동태로 바꿀 때 목적격보어가 명사, 형용사, to부정사, 분사일 때는 목적격보어를 동사 뒤에 그대로 쓴다.

15 5형식 문장을 수동태로 바꿀 때 사역동사 make의 목적격보어인 동사원형은 to부정사로 바꿔야 한다.

16 ① 5형식 문장을 수동태로 바꿀 때 목적격보어가 명사일 때는 목적격보어를 그대로 쓴다. (to Kitty → Kitty) ④ 5형식 문장에서 사역동사 let, have는 수동태로 쓰지 않는다. 사역동사 make만 수동태로 쓴다. (let → made)

17 조동사가 쓰인 수동태는 「조동사＋be＋과거분사」로 쓰며, 동사구는 수동태로 바꿀 때 하나의 단어처럼 취급한다. take care of는 '~을 돌보다'의 의미이다.

18 ① '~을 놀리다'라는 의미의 동사구는 make fun of이므로 He was made fun of by his classmates.로 고쳐야 한다.

19 「동사＋전치사/부사」의 동사구는 수동태로 바꿀 때 하나의 단어처럼 취급한다.

20 be interested in: ~에 관심이 있다, be made of＋성질이 변하지 않는 재료: ~로 만들어지다, be known for: ~로 유명하다, be filled with: ~로 가득 차다

21 수동태의 행위자는 「by＋행위자」로 나타내지만, ④는 수동태로 쓸 때 be covered with로 쓴다.

22 ② → of, be made of＋성질이 변하지 않는 재료: ~로 만들어지다 ④ → at, be surprised at: ~에 놀라다 ⑤ → as, be known as: ~로 알려지다

23 목적어가 that절인 문장을 수동태로 바꿀 때에는 가주어 it을 사용하여 「It＋be동사＋과거분사＋that절」의 형태로 쓴다. 또는 that절의 주어를 수동태 문장의 주어로 하여 「that절의 주어＋be동사＋과거분사＋to부정사」의 형태로 쓸 수도 있다.

24 목적어가 that절인 문장은 수동태로 바꿀 때 가주어 it을 사용하여 「It＋be동사＋과거분사＋that절」로 쓰므로 빈칸에는 동사의 과거분사형이 와야 한다. (② → known)

25 that절의 주어를 수동태의 주어로 쓸 때에는 「that절의 주어＋be동사＋과거분사＋to부정사(that절의 동사)」의 형태로 쓴다.

STEP 2 · 오답률 40~60% 문제
pp. 102 – 103

01 ①, ⑤　　02 ②　　03 ②　　04 ④　　05 ③　　06 ①
07 ③　　08 They have been offered the job by Chris. / The job has been offered to them by Chris.　　09 He was considered a hero by us.　　10 We were made to do extra homework by the teacher.　　11 Both brunch and dinner will be made for you by a famous chef.　　12 I was asked to donate money by the man.　　13 with　　14 His performance was laughed at by most fans.　　15 was believed that the Earth was flat / was believed to be flat

01 4형식 문장은 수동태로 바꿀 때 간접목적어와 직접목적어를 모두 주어로 쓸 수 있다. 동사 bring의 직접목적어를 수동태의 주어로 쓸 때, 간접목적어 앞에 전치사 to를 쓴다.

02 4형식 능동태 문장인 ①을 3형식으로 바꾼 문장이 ③, 간접목적어가 주어인 수동태 문장이 ④, 직접목적어가 주어인 수동태 문장이 ⑤이다. ②는 'Ann이 Katie에게 핑크색 드레스를 주었다.'는 의미이다.

03 4형식 문장에서 직접목적어를 수동태의 주어로 쓸 때, 간접목적어 앞에 sell은 전치사 to를, cook은 for를 쓴다.

04 4형식 문장에서 직접목적어를 수동태의 주어로 쓸 때, 간접목적어 앞에 buy는 전치사 for를, ask는 of를 쓴다.

05 5형식 문장에서는 목적어만 수동태의 주어로 쓰인다. 사역동사 make의 목적격보어로 쓰인 동사원형은 수동태에서는 to부정사로 바꾼다.

06 ① 지각동사가 쓰인 5형식 문장을 수동태로 바꿀 때는 목적격보어인 동사원형을 to부정사로 바꾼다. (get → to get)

07 not은 to부정사에 대한 부정이므로 to부정사 앞에 써야 한다.

08 4형식 문장은 간접목적어와 직접목적어를 주어로 하여 두 종류의 수동태를 만들 수 있다. 직접목적어가 주어일 때는 간접목적어 앞에 전치사를 써야 하는데, 동사 offer는 전치사 to를 쓰는 동사이다.

09 5형식 문장에서 목적격보어는 수동태의 주어로 올 수 없으므로, 목적어인 him을 주어로 바꾸어야 한다. 목적격보어는 동사 뒤에 그대로 쓴다.

10 사역동사 make의 목적격보어로 쓰인 동사원형은 수동태에서 to부정사로 바뀐다.

11 동사 make는 직접목적어만 주어로 쓰며 간접목적어 앞에는 전치사 for를 써야 한다.

12 5형식 문장을 수동태로 바꿀 때 목적격보어가 명사, 형용사, to부정사, 분사일 때는 목적격보어를 동사 뒤에 그대로 쓴다.

13 be covered with: ~로 덮여 있다, be satisfied with: ~에 만족하다

14 laugh at은 '~을 비웃다'라는 의미의 동사구이므로 수동태로 바꿀 때 한 덩어리로 취급해 「be동사＋과거분사＋전치사」의 형태로 쓴다.

15 목적어가 that절인 문장은 수동태로 바꿀 때 that절을 목적어로 남기면서 가주어 it을 사용할 수 있으며, 이때 형태는 「It＋be동사＋과거분사＋that절」로 쓴다. 주어진 문장은 과거 시제이므로 believed는 was believed가 되어야 한다. 또는 that절의 주어를 문장의 주어로 쓰고 that절의 동사는 to부정사로 바꿔 쓴다.

STEP 3 · 오답률 60~80% 문제
pp. 104 – 105

01 ④　　02 ⑤　　03 ②　　04 ①, ④　　05 ③　　06 ①
07 ②, ⑤　　08 His parents allowed him to travel alone. / He was allowed to travel alone by his parents.　　09 James is encouraged to pass the test by her.　　10 Houses and cars were swept away by the flood.　　11 (1) made from (2) interested in (3) known to (4) satisfied with　　12 known as, been known for　　13 It is reported that the sailors are missing. / The sailors are reported to be missing.　　14 The man was made to stop the car by the police.　　15 It is said that air pollution is caused, is said to be caused by cars

01 동사 write는 직접목적어를 수동태의 주어로 쓸 때, 간접목적어 앞에 전치사 to를 쓴다.

02 4형식 문장에서 직접목적어를 수동태의 주어로 쓸 때, tell, teach, give, offer는 간접목적어 앞에 전치사 to를, buy는 for를 쓴다.

03 지각동사가 쓰인 5형식 문장에서는 목적어를 수동태 문장의 주어로 쓰고, 목적격보어로 쓰인 동사원형은 to부정사로 바꾼다.

04 ① sit → to sit ④ to a doctor → a doctor

05 ① of → for ② to chairman → chairman ④ A kite was made for me by my brother. ⑤ expected attract → expected to attract

06 ⓓ care by → care of by ⓔ participating → to participate

07 목적어가 that절인 문장의 수동태는 가주어 it을 사용하여 「It＋be동사＋과거분사＋that절」로 쓰거나 that절의 주어를 문장의 주어로 쓰고, that절의 동사는 to부정사로 바꿔 쓴다.

08 allow는 목적격보어로 to부정사를 쓰는 동사이다. 5형식 문장을 수동태로 바꿀 때 능동태의 목적어를 주어로 쓰고 동사를 「be동사＋과거분사」로 바꾼 다음, 목적격보어인 to부정사는 동사 뒤에 그대로 쓰면 된다.

09 5형식 문장을 수동태로 바꿀 때 목적격보어가 명사, 형용사, to부정사, 분사일 때는 목적격보어를 동사 뒤에 그대로 쓴다.

10 sweep away는 '~을 휩쓸다'라는 의미의 동사구이므로 수동태로 바꿀 때 한 덩어리로 취급해야 한다.

11 be made from + 성질이 변하는 재료: ~로 만들어지다, interested in: ~에 관심이 있다, be known to: ~에게 알려지다, be satisfied with: ~에 만족하다

12 be known as: ~로 알려지다, be known for: ~로 유명하다

13 목적어가 that절인 문장은 수동태로 바꿀 때 that절을 목적어로 남기면서 가주어 it을 사용할 수 있으며, 이때 형태는 「It＋be동사＋과거분사＋that절」로 쓴다. 또는 that절의 주어를 문장의 주어로 쓰고 that절의 동사는 to부정사로 바꿔 쓴다.

14 경찰관에 의해 차가 멈춰진 것이므로 수동태 문장을 써야 하고, 사역동사 make의 목적격보어인 동사원형을 수동태 문장에서는 to부정사로 바꾼다.

15 목적어가 that절인 문장을 수동태로 바꿀 때에는 1) that절을 목적어로 남기고 가주어 it을 사용하여 「It＋be동사＋과거분사＋that절」의 형태를 취하거나, 2) that절의 주어를 수동태 문장의 주어로 하여 「that절의 주어＋be동사＋과거분사＋to부정사」의 형태를 취하는 두 가지 방식이 있다.

01 ①　　02 ⑤　　03 ②　　04 The book is given to the woman by the man. / The woman is given the book by the man.　　05 were sent to, was made for, was asked of　　06 He made the waiter bring a cup of water. / The waiter was made to bring a cup of water by him.

01 능동태 문장인 ②를 3형식 문장으로 바꾼 것이 ③, 간접목적어를 주어로 해서 수동태로 바꾼 것이 ④, 직접목적어를 주어로 해서 수동태로 바꾼 것이 ⑤이다. 직접목적어를 주어로 할 때에는 간접목적어 앞에 전치사 to를 쓰는 것에 유의한다. ①은 '그는 경찰에게 진실을 말할 것이다.'는 의미이다.

02 ⓑ 5형식 문장을 수동태로 바꿀 때, 목적격보어는 수동태의 주어가 될 수 없다. ⓒ, ⓓ write와 buy가 쓰인 4형식 문장을 수동태로 바꿀 때는 간접목적어를 주어로 쓰지 않는다. ⓔ 사역동사 make가 쓰인 5형식 문장을 수동태로 바꿀 때, 목적격보어로 쓰인 동사원형은 to부정사로 바뀐다. (wash → to wash)

03 be made of＋성질이 변하지 않는 재료: ~으로 만들어지다, put off: ~을 미루다[연기하다], 목적어가 that절인 문장이 that절의 주어를 수동태의 주어로 할 때의 형태는 「that절의 주어＋be동사＋과거분사＋to부정사」이다.

04 4형식 문장은 각각 간접목적어와 직접목적어를 주어로 하여 두 가지 형태의 수동태로 만들 수 있는데, 직접목적어를 주어로 할 경우 give는 간접목적어 앞에 전치사 to를 쓰는 동사이다.

05 4형식 문장에서 직접목적어를 주어로 하여 수동태를 만들 때, 간접목적어 앞에 쓰는 전치사는 동사에 따라 다르다. send는 to를, make는 for를, ask는 of를 전치사로 취하는 동사이다.

06 사역동사 make는 목적격보어로 동사원형을 쓰는 동사이다. 사역동사 make가 쓰인 5형식 문장을 수동태로 바꾸면 목적격보어로 쓰인 동사원형이 to부정사로 바뀐다.

최종 선택 QUIZ　p. 107

01 a　02 b　03 a　04 a　05 a　06 b　07 b　08 b

UNIT 11 관계대명사 1

✔ 바로 체크　p. 108

01 who　　02 which　　03 whose　　04 which
05 whom　06 that　07 that　08 What　09 what

01 ①　　02 who　　03 which[that]　　04 ②　　05 whose
06 ⑤　　07 whose → which[that]　　08 ③　　09 who(m)[that]　　10 ⑤　　11 ②, ④　　12 ②　　13 ③　　14 ②
15 ①　　16 ④　　17 ⑤　　18 ②　　19 ②　　20 ③
21 ②　　22 what I want to see　　23 what　　24 ⑤
25 ④

01 선행사가 사람이고 관계사절에서 주어로 사용되었으므로 주격 관계대명사 who가 알맞다.

02 선행사가 the nun(수녀)으로 사람이고 관계사절에서 주어 역할을 하므로 알맞은 관계대명사는 who이다.

03 선행사가 decisions이고 관계대명사절에서 주어로 사용되었으므로 주격 관계대명사 which 또는 that을 쓴다.

04 선행사가 사물일 때의 목적격 관계대명사는 which, 선행사가 사람이고 소유의 의미일 때는 소유격 관계대명사 whose를 쓴다.

05 선행사인 The book이 관계대명사절에서 소유격으로 사용되었으므로 소유격 관계대명사 whose를 써야 한다.

06 첫 번째 빈칸에는 선행사가 the pride이고 관계대명사절에서 주어로 사용되었으므로 주격 관계대명사 which 또는 that이 알맞고, 두 번째 빈칸에는 선행사에 the only가 포함되었으므로 목적격 관계대명사 that이 와야 한다.

07 선행사가 our own feelings이고 관계사절에서 목적어 역할을 하므로 목적격 관계대명사 which 또는 that을 써야 한다.

08 선행사인 a monkey가 관계대명사절에서 소유격으로 사용되었으므로 소유격 관계대명사 whose가 알맞다.

09 선행사가 사람이고 관계사절에서 목적어 역할을 하므로 목적격 관계대명사 who(m) 또는 that을 써야 한다.

10 선행사인 my umbrella가 관대명사절에서 소유격으로 사용되었으므로 소유격 관계대명사 of which가 알맞다.

11 선행사 the backpack이 사물이고 관계사절에서 목적어 역할을 하므로 목적격 관계대명사 which나 that을 사용해야 한다.

12 선행사가 -thing인 경우, 관계대명사는 주로 that을 사용한다.

13 선행사가 사람으로 3인칭 단수이고, met로 보아 과거 시제이므로 「주격 관계대명사＋be동사」 who was가 생략되어 있다.

14 목적격 관계대명사는 생략할 수 있으나 ②처럼 전치사가 바로 앞에 있는 경우에는 생략할 수 없다. The woman (whom) Nick is talking to is Ms. Wilson.과 같이 전치사가 관계사절의 맨 뒤로 간 경우에는 whom을 생략할 수 있다.

15 ②, ③, ④, ⑤는 목적격 관계대명사이므로 생략할 수 있지만, ①은 주격 관계대명사이므로 생략할 수 없다.

16 선행사가 사물로 복수이고, 주어 역할을 하므로 「주격 관계대명사＋be동사」 which are가 생략되어 있다.

17 the sounds가 they heard의 목적어이므로 they heard 앞에 목적격 관계대명사 that이 생략되어 있다.

18 ② 창문(a window)이 '페인트칠된' 수동의 의미이므로 과거분사형 painted로 써야 한다. a window 다음에 「주격 관계대명사＋be동사」인 which[that] was가 생략되어 있다.

19 '~하는 것'이라는 의미로 선행사 the thing을 포함하는 관계대명사는 what이다.

20 ①, ②, ④, ⑤는 선행사를 포함하는 관계대명사로 '~하는 것'이라는 의미이고, ③은 의문사로 '무엇'이라는 의미이다.

21 '~하는 것'이라는 의미의 선행사를 포함하는 관계대명사 what이 알맞다.

22 관계대명사 what은 '~하는 것'이라는 의미로 빈칸에는 '내가 보고 싶은 것'이라는 말이 들어가야 하므로 what I want to see를 써야 한다.

23 '~하는 것'의 의미이므로 선행사를 포함하는 관계대명사 what으로 바꿔 쓸 수 있다.

24 '~하는 것'이라는 의미의 선행사를 포함하는 관계대명사 what을 써야 한다. 관계대명사 what은 문장에서 주어, 목적어, 보어 역할을 한다.

25 〈보기〉와 ④의 what은 관계대명사, ①, ②, ③ 의문사, ⑤ 의문형용사이다.

STEP 2 · 오답률 40~60% 문제 pp. 112 – 113

```
01 ③      02 ④      03 ②, ③     04 ①, ②, ⑤    05 ③
06 ③      07 ①      08 who is    09 The hat which my
father wears is very old.     10 My school which was built
30 years ago is still good.      11 what we need now
12 What I want     13 that → what     14 The situation is
different from what we expected.     15 what I am making
```

01 ①, ②, ④, ⑤는 선행사가 사람인 주격 관계대명사 who, ③은 선행사가 사물인 주격 관계대명사 which를 써야 한다.

02 선행사가 사람이고 소유격 역할을 해야 하므로 소유격 관계대명사 whose를 써야 한다.

03 선행사 the dog가 동물이므로 주격 관계대명사 which, that이 알맞다.

04 사람이 선행사인 목적격 관계대명사 who, whom, that을 쓸 수 있다.

05 첫 번째 빈칸에는 선행사가 사물이며 주어 역할을 하므로 주격 관계대명사 which, 두 번째 빈칸에는 선행사가 사물이며 목적어 역할을 하므로 목적격 관계대명사 which가 알맞다.

06 선행사 the picture가 사물이므로 주격 관계대명사는 which 또는 that을 쓰는데, 선행사가 단수이고 문맥상 그림을 그린 것은 과거이므로 be동사의 과거형 was가 알맞다.

07 A lot of books가 I read의 목적어이므로 I read 앞에 목적격 관계대명사 which[that]가 생략되어 있다.

08 「주격 관계대명사＋be동사＋분사」 구문에서 「주격 관계대명사＋be동사」는 생략할 수 있다.

09 The hat이 관계대명사절에서 목적어 역할을 하므로 목적격 관계대명사 which가 생략되었다.

10 선행사 My school 다음에 과거분사 built가 있는 것으로 보아 「주격 관계대명사＋be동사」 which was가 생략되어 있음을 알 수 있다.

11 the things that과 바꿔 쓸 수 있는 것은 선행사를 포함하는 관계대명사인 what이다.

12 '~하는 것'이라는 의미의 선행사를 포함하는 관계대명사 what을 이용해서 What I want라고 써야 한다.

13 선행사가 없으므로 '~하는 것'의 의미로 선행사를 포함하는 관계대명사인 what을 써야 한다.

14 '~하는 것'이라는 의미의 선행사를 포함하는 관계대명사 what을 써서 문장을 완성한다.

15 '~하는 것'이라는 의미의 선행사를 포함하는 관계대명사 what을 쓰고, 현재 '만들고 있는' 것이므로 현재진행형을 써야 한다.

STEP 3 · 오답률 60~80% 문제 pp. 114 – 115

```
01 ③, ④     02 ③     03 ①, ⑤     04 ②     05 ①, ②, ④
06 ③     07 ③     08 whose work → who[that] works
09 What[what]     10 She remembered the bag which[that]
she had left behind on a bus.     11 I saw an old man lying
on the bench.     12 The boy who(m)[that] you praised last
night was my little brother.     13 This is the house
which[that] he was born in.     14 Look at the boys who
are fighting in the street. / Look at the boys that are fighting
in the street. / Look at the boys fighting in the street.
15 My sister is reading a novel which[that] was written by
Hemingway.
```

01 빈칸 앞의 선행사가 모두 사물이고 관계사절에서 주어 역할을 하므로 주격 관계대명사 which 또는 that을 쓴다.

02 〈보기〉와 ③의 what은 선행사를 포함하는 관계대명사이다. ①, ②, ④ 의문사 ⑤ 의문형용사

03 두 번째 문장의 목적어 it을 생략하고 목적격 관계대명사 which 또는 that을 써서 선행사 a small plant에 연결해야 한다.

04 문장의 시제가 과거이므로 주격 관계대명사 다음에 오는 동사도 과거형이 적절하다.

05 선행사 the man을 수식하는 관계대명사절을 써야 한다. 선행사가 사람이므로 주격 관계대명사는 who[that], 시제가 과거이므로 be동사는 was를 쓴다. 이때, 분사 앞에 쓰인 「주격 관계대명사＋be동사」인 who[that] was는 생략할 수 있다.

06 ③ 선행사가 사물이고 뒤에 오는 the price로 보아 관계사절에서 소유격의 역할을 하므로 소유격 관계대명사 of which가 알맞다.

07 소유격 관계대명사 whose의 선행사가 a house이므로 Its windows로 받는 것이 적절하다.

08 선행사가 사람이고 관계사절에서 주어 역할을 하므로 주격 관계대명사 who 또는 that을 써야 한다. 또한 관계대명사절의 동사 work의 주어인 선행사 my neighbor가 3인칭 단수이고 주절의 시제가 현재 시제이므로 동사 work를 works로 써야 한다.

09 '~하는 것'이라는 의미의 선행사를 포함하는 관계대명사 what을 써야 한다. 관계대명사 what은 문장에서 주어, 목적어, 보어 역할을 한다.

10 '버스에 두고 내렸다'는 내용이 가방을 꾸며주므로 the bag을 선행사로 하고 첫 번째 문장을 관계대명사절로 쓴다. 사물이 선행사이고 목적어 역할을 하므로 목적격 관계대명사 which[that]를 써서 연결한다.

11 「주격 관계대명사＋be동사＋분사」 구문에서 「주격 관계대명사＋be동사」는 생략할 수 있다.

12 선행사 The boy 바로 다음에 목적격 관계대명사 who(m)[that]을 쓴다. 목적격 관계대명사는 생략할 수 있다.

13 the house가 관계대명사절에서 전치사 in의 목적어 역할을 하므로 목적격 관계대명사 which 또는 that이 생략되었다.

14 두 번째 문장은 첫 번째 문장의 the boys를 꾸며주므로 관계대명사 절로 만들어 선행사인 the boys 다음에 써 준다. 주격 관계대명사 who 대신 that을 쓸 수 있으며, 분사 앞에 쓰인 「주격 관계대명사+be동사」인 who[that] are는 생략할 수 있다.

15 선행사(a novel)가 사물이므로 주격 관계대명사 which[that]를 쓰며, 소설이 과거에 '쓰인' 것이므로 과거 시제 수동태(be동사의 과거형+p.p.)로 써야 한다.

STEP 4 · 실력 완성 테스트   p. 116

> **01** is a tool which[that] opens a bottle   **02** (1) who are playing basketball (2) which won the gold medal   **03** ⑤
> **04** (1) a person who[that] you know well and like (2) what connects one computer to another (3) something that you give to someone on a special day   **05** Do you know the student who[that] sent a text message to Sera?

01 병따개가 무엇인지를 주격 관계대명사 which[that]를 사용하여 설명해야 한다.

02 (1) 선행사(the boys)가 복수형이고 주어 역할을 하므로 주격 관계대명사 who를 쓰고, 현재 진행 중인 상황이므로 관계대명사절의 동사는 are playing으로 쓴다.
(2) 선행사가 농구팀(the basketball team)이므로 주격 관계대명사는 which, 금메달을 딴 것은 작년이므로 동사는 과거형 won으로 써야 한다.

03 ①, ②, ③, ④에는 관계대명사 what이 들어가야 하고, ⑤에는 명사절(주어 역할)을 이끄는 접속사 that이 들어가야 한다.

04 friend는 사람이므로 a person who[that], Internet과 gift는 사물인데, 인터넷은 기능을 설명하고 있으므로 '~하는 것'이라는 의미의 선행사를 포함하는 관계대명사 what, gift는 something 다음에 관계대명사 that을 사용하여 문장을 연결하는 것이 자연스럽다.

05 'Sera에게 문자 메시지를 보냈다(sent a text message to Sera)'는 것은 선행사인 학생(the student)을 설명하는 말이므로 주격 관계대명사 who[that] 다음에 쓴다.

최종 선택 QUIZ   p. 117

01 a   **02** b   **03** b   **04** a   **05** a   **06** a   **07** b   **08** a

UNIT 12   관계대명사 2

✔ 바로 체크   p. 118

01 in which   **02** with   **03** in which   **04** who
05 which   **06** which   **07** with whom   **08** whose
09 of which

STEP 1 · 만만한 기초   pp. 119 – 121

> **01** ④   **02** ③   **03** the dog to which the man threw a toy bone   **04** ⑤   **05** ②   **06** in which   **07** ⑤
> **08** at which   **09** ①   **10** which   **11** ①   **12** which
> **13** ②   **14** which doesn't fit any more   **15** who
> **16** ①   **17** which   **18** ③   **19** whose walls were broken   **20** ④   **21** who → whose   **22** ②   **23** of which   **24** ④   **25** whose

01 This is the reason. We have to build up our strength for this reason.의 두 문장이 관계대명사로 연결된 구조로, 관계대명사가 전치사 for의 목적어이다.

02 선행사 many ways가 전치사 in의 목적어이다.

03 개를 구체적으로 설명하고 있으므로 the dog를 선행사로 하고 「전치사+관계대명사」로 연결한다. 전치사 to는 관계사절의 끝에 올 수도 있다.

04 선행사가 (a lot of) money인데 남자는 그 돈으로(with the money) 소를 사고 싶어 하므로 money는 전치사 with의 목적어로 쓰였다. 따라서 「전치사+관계대명사」 with which가 알맞다.

05 선행사를 살펴보면 첫 번째 문장에서는 you live on the planet Earth, 두 번째 문장에서는 you walk on the wet sand at the beach, 세 번째 문장에서는 you lie down on the grass로, 모두 전치사 on의 목적어이므로 관계대명사 which 앞에 전치사 on을 써야 한다.

06 선행사 the blue blouse는 두 번째 문장 in the blue blouse에서 전치사 in의 목적어이다. 따라서 「전치사+관계대명사」 in which를 써야 한다.

07 ⑤ 동사 visit는 타동사로 전치사가 필요 없으므로 at을 삭제해야 한다. The museum (which) we visited in Italy was beautiful.에서 목적격 관계대명사 which는 생략할 수 있다.

08 She lost her bag at the store.이므로 선행사 the store는 전치사 at의 목적어이다. 따라서 of를 at으로 고쳐야 한다.

09 선행사 the woman이 사람이고 관계사절에서 주어가 생략되어 있으므로 주격 관계대명사 who를 써야 한다. 관계대명사절이 선행사를 보충 설명하는 구조이다.

10 앞 문장 전체를 선행사로 받는 계속적 용법의 관계대명사 which를 써야 한다.

11 관계대명사절이 선행사를 보충 설명하는 계속적 용법의 경우, 「접속사+대명사」로 쓸 수 있다. 여기서는 and he와 같은 의미이다.

12 첫 번째 문장에서는 선행사가 사물인 계속적 용법의 관계대명사 which, 두 번째 문장에서는 '어떤'이라는 의미의 의문형용사 which를 써야 한다.

13 문맥상 첫 번째 문장은 접속사 and로, 두 번째 문장은 but으로 연결할 수 있다.

14 선행사 a skirt를 보충 설명하므로 계속적 용법의 관계대명사 which를 써서 연결한다.

15 내 친구인 민호에 대한 보충 설명이므로, 계속적 용법의 관계대명사를 써야 한다. 빈칸 뒤에 동사가 이어지고 선행사는 사람이므로 주격 관계대명사 who를 써야 한다.

16 선행사 friends에 대해 보충 설명하는 「접속사+대명사」는 계속적 용

법의 관계대명사로 바꿔 쓸 수 있다. 선행사가 사람이고 주어 역할을 하므로 주격 관계대명사 who가 알맞다.

17 「접속사＋대명사」는 계속적 용법의 관계대명사로 바꿔 쓸 수 있다. 선행사(China)가 주어 역할을 하므로 주격 관계대명사 which를 써야 한다.

18 모델의 머리(the model's hair)가 빨간색이므로 소유격 관계대명사를 써야 한다.

19 '그 집의 벽'이 부서졌으므로 the house와 walls는 소유의 관계이다.

20 소년의 아버지(the boy's father)가 인기 있는 예술가이므로 소유격 관계대명사를 써야 한다.

21 선행사 a person과 language가 소유의 관계이므로 소유격 관계대명사 whose를 써야 한다.

22 소유격 관계대명사 whose 다음에는 명사가 바로 와서 선행사인 대학(a university)의 어떤 것에 대한 설명이 이어져야 하는데, ②는 명사가 바로 오지 않았으므로 빈칸에 들어갈 수 없다.

23 선행사 the classical music piece가 관계대명사절에서 소유격(the composer of the classical music piece)으로 사용되었으므로, 연결하는 관계대명사는 whose 또는 of which로 써야 한다.

24 셔츠의 단추가 빨간색이므로 소유격 관계대명사를 써야 한다.

25 선행사가 관계대명사절에서 각각 소유격(someone's hobby, the windows of the house)으로 사용되었으므로 소유격 관계대명사 whose를 써야 한다. 소유격 관계대명사 whose는 선행사가 사람이나 사물, 동물일 때 모두 쓸 수 있다.

STEP 2 · 오답률 40~60% 문제
pp. 122 – 123

01 ④   02 ③   03 ②   04 ①, ⑤   05 ①, ③, ④
06 ④   07 that → which   08 which made her
09 but he   10 and she   11 whose door   12 of which → whose   13 whose name was Bella   14 my neighbor whose son wants to be a designer   15 whose sister loves her pet cats

01 search for는 '~을 찾다'의 의미로 선행사 the opportunity는 전치사 for의 목적어이다. 따라서 for which가 알맞다.

02 전치사의 목적어로 쓰인 관계대명사 which이다. 첫 번째 문장에서는 We will have a party on the day.이고, 두 번째 문장에서는 Sena is leaning on the door.이므로 전치사 on을 각각 관계대명사 which 앞에 써야 한다.

03 the kings had lived ~ in the palace라는 의미로, the palace는 전치사 in의 목적어이므로 in which가 알맞다.

04 we keep children's wood blocks in the box라는 의미로, 선행사 the box가 전치사 in의 목적어이므로 in which로 써야 한다. 전치사 in은 관계사절의 맨 끝에 올 수도 있다.

05 선행사가 사물이므로 관계대명사는 which나 that을 쓴다. '~에 묵다'는 stay at이므로 전치사 at을 관계대명사의 앞이나 관계대명사절의 맨 뒤에 쓸 수 있다.

06 선행사 Taegwondo는 사물이므로 이를 보충 설명하는 관계대명사절을 이끄는 계속적 용법의 관계대명사로 which가 알맞다.

07 앞 문장 전체를 선행사로 하는 계속적 용법의 관계대명사 which를 써야 한다. that은 계속적 용법으로 쓸 수 없다.

08 앞 문장 전체를 받는 관계대명사 which(= and it)가 주어 역할을 하고 있다.

09 계속적 용법의 관계대명사 who는 문맥상 「접속사＋대명사」but he로 바꿔 쓸 수 있다.

10 계속적 용법의 관계대명사 who는 문맥상 「접속사＋대명사」and she로 바꿔 쓸 수 있다.

11 선행사 '건물(the building)'과 '문(door)'이 소유의 관계이므로 소유격 관계대명사 whose를 쓰고 다음에 door를 써야 한다.

12 선행사 her friend가 사람이므로 소유격 관계대명사 whose를 써야 한다. of which는 선행사가 사물이나 동물일 때 쓴다.

13 '공주(a princess)'와 '이름(name)'이 소유의 관계이므로 소유격 관계대명사 whose를 써야 한다.

14 선행사 my neighbor가 소유격(my neighbor's son)으로 사용되었으므로 소유격 관계대명사 whose를 쓰고 바로 다음에 son을 써야 한다.

15 선행사 a boy가 관계대명사절에서 소유격(the boy's sister)으로 사용되었으므로 소유격 관계대명사 whose를 쓰고 바로 다음에 sister를 써야 한다.

STEP 3 · 오답률 60~80% 문제
pp. 124 – 125

01 ④   02 ⑤   03 ③, ⑤   04 ①, ③   05 ②
06 ③   07 ⑤   08 which, of which, to which   09 (1) which was very scary (2) a stool on which   10 was holding a cat, whose eyes were green   11 are → is, what are → which is   12 whose tire   13 who invented the light bulb   14 which was made in Vietnam   15 two friends whose mothers are teachers

01 선행사가 사람이고 전치사의 목적어로 쓰였으므로 「전치사＋목적격 관계대명사」 with whom이 알맞다. get along with는 '~와 잘 지내다'의 의미이다.

02 선행사 a camera가 사물이고 전치사 with의 목적어로 쓰였으므로 with which가 알맞다.

03 선행사가 사람이고 전치사 with의 목적어로 쓰였으므로 목적격 관계대명사 whom을 전치사 다음에 써야 한다. 전치사 with는 관계대명사절의 맨 뒤에 올 수도 있다.

04 선행사가 사물이고 전치사 to의 목적어이므로 목적격 관계대명사 that과 which가 알맞다.

05 ② 선행사 a cousin이 관계대명사절에서 주어 역할을 하고 있으므로 주격 관계대명사 who를 써야 한다. whose → who

06 ①, ②, ④, ⑤는 주격 관계대명사 which, ③은 소유격 관계대명사 whose가 알맞다.

07 ①, ②, ③, ④는 소유격 관계대명사 whose, ⑤는 주격 관계대명사 who[that]가 알맞다.

08 첫 번째 빈칸에는 Ulsan을 선행사로 하는 계속적 용법의 주격 관계대명사 which가 알맞고, 두 번째 빈칸에는 선행사가 관계대명사절에서 소유격(the writer of the book)으로 사용되었으므로 소유격 관

계대명사 of which가 와야 한다. 세 번째 빈칸에는 The party를 선행사로 하며 전치사 to의 목적어 역할을 하는 「전치사＋목적격 관계대명사」 to which를 써야 한다.

09 (1) 선행사 a movie를 보충 설명하므로 계속적 용법의 관계대명사 which를 써야 한다.
(2) 선행사 a stool이 사물이고 두 번째 문장에서 전치사 on의 목적어이므로 「전치사＋관계대명사」 on which를 써서 연결해야 한다.

10 선행사(a cat)에 대한 보충 설명이므로 계속적 용법의 관계대명사로 바꿔 쓸 수 있다. 선행사와 the eyes가 소유의 관계이므로 소유격 관계대명사 whose를 쓴다.

11 첫 번째 문장의 주어는 one이므로 단수동사 is를 써야 하고, 앞 문장 전체를 받는 관계대명사는 which로 동사는 단수동사 is를 쓴다. what은 계속적 용법으로 쓸 수 없다.

12 남자가 보고 있는 차의 바퀴(the tire of his car)가 펑크가 났으므로 선행사 his car와 tire는 소유의 관계이다. 따라서 소유격 관계대명사 whose를 써야 한다. (= He is checking his car of which the tire is flat.)

13 선행사가 사람이므로 계속적 용법의 관계대명사 who를 써야 한다.

14 선행사를 보충 설명하는 계속적 용법의 관계대명사 which를 써야 한다.

15 친구의 어머니가 선생님이므로 소유격 관계대명사 whose를 쓰고, 선행사가 복수이므로 관계대명사절의 동사는 복수형 동사를 써야 한다.

STEP 4 · 실력 완성 테스트   p. 126

01 ④   **02** two daughters, who are famous reporters
03 (1) whose name is Martha (2) who(m)[that] I meet after school every day (3) who is good at telling funny stories
04 (1) who is talking to a foreigner now (2) which is good at jumping high (3) who work at a flower shop   **05** (1) The woman whose face is pale is my neighbor. (2) in which Jackson stayed for a long time 또는 which[that] Jackson stayed in for a long time (3) at which we drew pictures was very quiet 또는 which[that] we drew pictures at was very quiet

01 관계대명사의 계속적 용법은 선행사를 제한적으로 수식하지 않고 보충 설명하는 것이므로, (A)에서는 Harry의 삼촌이 둘인데 둘 다 작가임을 알 수 있다. (B)에서는 Harry의 삼촌이 모두 몇 명인지는 알 수 없으나 작가인 삼촌은 둘임을 알 수 있다.

02 Parker 씨에게는 딸이 두 명 있는데 두 사람 모두 기자이다. 따라서 두 딸을 보충 설명하는 계속적 용법의 관계대명사절을 써야 한다.

03 (1) '그녀의 이름'이므로 소유격 관계대명사 whose를 써야 한다.
(2) her가 meet의 목적어이므로 목적격 관계대명사 who(m)[that]를 써야 한다.
(3) I have a girlfriend 다음에 콤마(,)가 있는 것으로 보아 계속적 용법의 관계대명사 who를 써야 한다.

04 선행사가 (1)은 my classmate, (2)는 a dog, (3)은 his grandparents이며 모두 선행사를 보충 설명하는 계속적 용법으로

쓰였다. (1)에서는 '그가 지금 외국인에게 이야기하고 있는 것'이므로 현재진행형을 써서 표현한다.

05 (1) '얼굴이 창백한 여자는 나의 이웃이다.'라는 의미이므로 소유격 관계대명사절 whose face is pale이 the woman을 수식하는 구조가 되어야 한다.
(2), (3) 선행사가 in the room, at the park와 같이 전치사의 목적어로 쓰였으므로 「전치사＋목적격 관계대명사」 in which, at which로 써야 한다. 또는 which나 that을 쓰고 전치사를 관계사절의 맨 뒤로 보낼 수 있다.

최종 선택 QUIZ   p. 127

01 b   **02** b   **03** a   **04** a   **05** a   **06** b   **07** b   **08** b

UNIT 13 관계부사

✅ 바로 체크   p. 128

01 when   **02** where   **03** where   **04** why   **05** the way   **06** why   **07** on which   **08** where

STEP 1 · 만만한 기초   pp. 129 – 131

01 ②   **02** ⑤   **03** This is the restaurant where I had dinner yesterday.   **04** is the month when my school starts   **05** where   **06** ⑤   **07** where, in which
08 which → when[in which]   **09** ①   **10** ①   **11** ③
12 ⑤   **13** how   **14** ④   **15** The reason why
16 ①, ③   **17** why he refused to follow the directions
18 how he survived the car crash   **19** Her father asked the reason why she had lied to him.   **20** ④   **21** ②
22 ①   **23** when he will come   **24** ④   **25** ②

01 빈칸에는 접속사와 부사 역할을 하는 관계부사가 필요하며, 선행사가 the time으로 시간을 나타내므로 관계부사 when이 와야 한다.

02 첫 번째 빈칸은 선행사가 장소이므로 관계부사 where가 알맞고, 두 번째 빈칸은 선행사가 시간을 나타내므로 관계부사 when이 알맞다.

03 where는 관계부사로 선행사 the restaurant 바로 다음에 쓴다.

04 선행사가 the month로 시간을 나타내고 관계사절에 시간을 나타내는 부사구가 생략되어 있으므로 관계부사 when을 써서 연결한다.

05 빈칸 앞에 모두 장소를 나타내는 선행사가 있으므로 관계부사 where가 알맞다.

06 last Christmas는 시간을 나타내는 부사구이므로 관계부사 when을 사용한 문장이 적절하다.

07 The house는 장소를 나타내는 선행사이므로 관계부사 where 또는 「전치사 in + 관계대명사 which」로 써야 한다.

08 the year는 시간을 나타내는 선행사이므로 관계부사 when 또는 「전치사 in + 관계대명사 which」로 써야 한다.

09 첫 번째 빈칸은 의문사 When, 두 번째 빈칸은 관계부사 when이 알맞다.

10 ①은 시간을 나타내는 선행사 The month가 있으므로 관계부사 when을 써야 하고 나머지는 모두 장소를 나타내는 선행사와 함께 쓰이는 관계부사 where가 알맞다.

11 관계부사 where의 위치는 장소를 나타내는 선행사 the high school 다음이 알맞다.

12 선행사(the reason)가 이유를 나타내므로 관계부사 why가 알맞다.

13 첫 번째 빈칸은 '~하는 방법'이라는 의미의 「how + to부정사」가 알맞고, 두 번째 빈칸은 관계부사 how가 알맞다.

14 관계부사 why는 「전치사 + 관계대명사」의 형태인 for which와 바꿔 쓸 수 있다.

15 이유를 나타내는 선행사 The reason 다음에 관계부사 why를 써야 한다.

16 관계부사 how는 the way 또는 the way in which로 바꿔 쓸 수 있다.

17 the reason은 이유를 나타내는 선행사이므로 관계부사 why를 써야 한다.

18 the way는 방법을 나타내는 선행사이므로 관계부사 how를 써야 한다. 이때 선행사 the way는 생략해야 한다.

19 선행사 the reason은 관계부사 why 앞에 쓰며, 생략할 수 있다.

20 ① → the reason ② → the day 또는 the time ③ → when ⑤ → (the way)

21 빈칸 뒤에 there라는 장소를 나타내는 부사가 있으므로 where를 쓰는 것은 적절하지 않다.

22 ① 이유를 나타내는 말이 이어지므로 관계부사 why를 써야 한다.

23 「관계부사 when + 주어 + 동사」의 어순으로 쓴다. 선행사는 생략된 형태이다.

24 뒤에 관계부사 where가 있으므로 장소를 나타내는 선행사 the place가 알맞다.

25 ② 선행사 the way와 관계부사 how는 함께 쓸 수 없으므로 둘 중 하나만 써야 한다.

STEP 2 · 오답률 40~60% 문제　　pp. 132 – 133

> **01** ④　**02** ③　**03** ④　**04** ⑤　**05** ②　**06** ③
> **07** ④　**08** I will never forget the morning when we climbed up the old Mayan pyramid.　**09** a wonderful garden where you can take photographs of flowers
> **10** the way which → how 또는 the way (in which)　**11** for which most of the houses were damaged　**12** how
> **13** why he sent　**14** (1) the reason why I couldn't sleep (2) to visit a clinic where he can get some treatment for his snoring　**15** (1) ⓐ: where → which[that] (2) ⓒ: of which → for which 또는 why

01 첫 번째 빈칸은 선행사가 시간을 나타내므로 관계부사 when이 알맞고, 두 번째 빈칸은 선행사가 장소를 나타내므로 관계부사 where가 알맞다.

02 「장소의 선행사 + 관계부사 where + 주어 + 동사」의 어순이 되어야 한다.

03 ④는 관계대명사 which 또는 that이, 나머지는 모두 관계부사 when이 들어가야 한다. ④의 경우 관계사절에 부사구가 아니라 주어가 생략되어 있음에 유의한다.

04 관계부사 where는 장소를 나타내는 선행사 the stream 다음에 들어가야 한다.

05 관계부사 where를 「장소의 전치사 + 관계대명사」와 바꿔 쓸 수 있다.

06 문맥상 '부모님을 기쁘게 해드리는 방법'이라는 의미로 관계부사 how가 알맞다. / 절의 끝에 전치사 in이 있으므로 관계대명사 which[that]가 알맞다. / 선행사가 reasons이므로 관계부사 why가 알맞다.

07 ④ how는 방법을 나타내는 관계부사로 the way 또는 the way in which로 바꿔 쓸 수 있다.

08 the morning은 시간을 나타내는 선행사이므로 관계부사 when을 쓴다.

09 garden은 장소를 나타내는 선행사이므로 관계부사 where를 쓴다.

10 '~하는 방법'이라는 의미의 관계부사 how와 선행사 the way는 함께 쓸 수 없음에 유의한다.

11 관계부사 why는 「전치사 + 관계대명사」의 형태인 for which로 바꿔 쓸 수 있다.

12 첫 번째 빈칸은 '~하는 방법'이라는 의미의 「how + to부정사」, 두 번째 빈칸은 '사람들이 표를 구하는 방법'이라는 의미이므로 관계부사 how를 써야 한다.

13 여자는 왜 그가 이것을 보냈는지(why he sent this) 의아해하고 있다. 첫 번째 why는 관계부사, 두 번째 why는 간접의문문에 쓰인 의문사이다.

14 (1) 관계부사 why를 이용해야 한다. (2) 관계부사 where를 이용해야 한다.

15 ⓐ 주어 역할을 하는 주격 관계대명사가 필요한 문장이다. ⓒ 이유를 나타내는 선행사 the reasons 다음에 why 또는 for which가 알맞다.

STEP 3 · 오답률 60~80% 문제　　pp. 134 – 135

> **01** ④　**02** ①　**03** ①, ④　**04** ③　**05** ③　**06** ⑤
> **07** ②, ⑤　**08** The day on which my best friend moved to another school was the saddest of my life. / The day when my best friend moved to another school was the saddest of my life.　**09** My school is in the village in which my uncle was born. / My school is in the village where my uncle was born.　**10** Can you tell me the way[how] you studied Chinese?　**11** [모범 답] That's the reason (why) I keep a cat.　**12** [모범 답] I want to know the way[how] he arrived here.　**13** why I didn't visit you / I didn't know your address　**14** ⓐ: which → where 또는

in which (2) ⓑ: how → when 또는 on which　15 which →
when 또는 on which, the way how → the way (in which) 또는
how

01 ④에는 목적격 관계대명사 which[that]가 들어가고, 나머지 빈칸에
는 모두 관계부사 where가 들어간다.

02 주어진 말을 바르게 배열하면 The hotel where the president
stayed is located near the airport.이다.

03 장소의 관계부사 where는 선행사가 일반적인 the place일 때 생략
가능하다.

04 ③ 시간의 선행사이므로 관계부사 when을 써야 한다.

05 ⓔ spots는 장소를 나타내는 선행사이므로 관계부사 how를 where
로 고쳐야 한다.

06 ⑤ where → which 또는 that

07 ① → where[on which] ③ → which ④ → when[on which]

08 the day가 시간을 나타내는 선행사이므로 관계부사 when 또는 「전
치사＋관계대명사」의 형태인 on which로 쓸 수 있다.

09 장소를 나타내는 선행사 the village 다음에 관계부사 where 또는
「전치사＋관계대명사」의 형태인 in which로 쓸 수 있다.

10 선행사가 방법을 나타내므로 관계부사 how나 선행사 the way를 써
서 연결해야 한다. 이때, 선행사 the way와 관계부사 how는 함께
쓸 수 없다.

11 선행사가 '이유'이므로 관계부사 why를 써야 한다. 여기서 why는 생
략할 수 있다.

12 '~하는 방법'의 의미이므로 선행사 the way나 관계부사 how를 써야
한다.

13 선행사가 The reason이므로 관계부사는 why를 써야 한다.

14 ⓐ the parking lot은 장소를 나타내는 선행사이므로 관계부사
where를 쓰거나 「전치사＋관계대명사」의 형태로 쓴다. ⓑ day는 시
간을 나타내는 선행사이므로 관계부사 when을 쓰거나 「전치사＋관
계대명사」를 쓴다.

15 the day 다음에는 접속사와 부사 역할을 하는 시간의 관계부사
when이 알맞다. / the way와 how는 함께 쓰일 수 없고 둘 중 하나
를 생략해야 한다.

STEP 4 · 실력 완성 테스트　　　　　p. 136

01 ⑤　02 (1) why we go to the zoo (2) (the reason) why
we watched the movie　03 (1) [예시 답] Seoul is the city
where I was born. (2) [예시 답] My room is the place where I
usually study.　04 (1) I know how you feel. (2) That's
how he talks to people.　05 (1) where he grew up (2)
when he moved to Dallas (3) where he won first prize in
2018　06 (1) She forgot the day when she had to submit
her report. (2) I don't know the reason why he didn't show
up.

01 밑줄 친 부분은 어법상 모두 옳은 문장이다.

02 이유를 설명하는 것이므로 관계부사 why를 이용하여 답해야 한다.

03 장소에 관한 내용일 때는 관계부사 where를 이용하여 답한다.

04 관계부사 how를 사용하여 표현해야 한다. 관계부사 how를 쓸 때에
는 선행사 the way를 함께 쓰지 않는다.

05 (1)은 뉴욕이라는 장소이므로 관계부사 where, (2)는 1995년이라
는 시간이므로 관계부사 when, (3)은 the art festival이라는 행사
이므로 관계부사 where를 사용해서 표현해야 한다.

06 선행사가 the day, the reason, the place 등과 같이 일반적일 때
관계부사 또는 선행사 둘 중 하나를 생략할 수 있다.

최종 선택 QUIZ　　　　　p. 137

01 b　02 a　03 a　04 b　05 a　06 a　07 b　08 b

UNIT 14　복합 관계사

✔ 바로 체크　　　　　p. 138

01 Whoever　02 whatever　03 whichever　04 No
matter what　05 whenever　06 Wherever　07 No
matter how　08 wherever　09 However hot it is

STEP 1 · 만만한 기초　　　　　pp. 139 – 141

01 ②　　02 No matter what you suggest　03 ④
04 No matter what　　05 ②　　06 whatever
07 whoever　08 ③　　09 Whatever　　10 ③, ⑤
11 ⑤　　12 Whoever　　13 ①　　14 No matter how
15 ④　　16 However hard the problem may be　17 ④
18 No matter how high　　19 whenever　　20 ④
21 Whenever my father washes his car, it rains.　　22 ③
23 ③　　24 Wherever she goes, many people are waiting
to see her.　　25 ②

01 '누가 ~할지라도'라는 의미가 적절하므로 양보의 부사절을 이끄는 복
합 관계대명사 whoever가 와야 한다.

02 no matter what은 '~무엇이[을] ~할지라도'라는 의미로 다음에 「주
어＋동사」가 온다.

03 ④는 '무엇이[을] ~할지라도'라는 의미의 Whatever로 고쳐야 한다.

04 whatever가 양보의 부사절을 이끌어 '무엇이 ~할지라도'라는 의미
일 때는 no matter what으로 바꿔 쓸 수 있다.

05 '~하는 것은 무엇이든지'라는 의미이므로 복합 관계대명사 what-
ever(= anything that)가 알맞다.

UNIT 14 · 27

06 '무엇을 ~할지라도'라는 의미의 양보의 부사절을 이끄는 복합 관계대명사 whatever가 알맞다.

07 '~하는 누구든지'라는 의미의 명사절을 이끄는 복합 관계대명사 whoever가 알맞다.

08 선행사를 포함하여 '~인 사람은 누구나(= anyone who)'의 의미이므로 whoever가 알맞다.

09 no matter what은 '무엇을 ~할지라도'라는 양보의 의미로 복합 관계대명사 whatever와 바꿔 쓸 수 있다.

10 '~이 누구이든지(= no matter who)'라는 의미는 복합 관계대명사 whoever로 나타낸다. 「whoever + 주어 + 동사」가 양보의 부사절이므로 주절의 앞 또는 뒤에 놓일 수 있다.

11 동사 meets의 목적어로 쓰인 '누구를 ~한다 할지라도(= no matter whom)'라는 의미이므로 Whomever가 알맞다.

12 '누가 ~할지라도'라는 양보의 의미를 나타내고 있으므로 Whoever(= No matter who)로 써야 한다.

13 '아무리 ~할지라도'라는 의미는 「however + 형용사」로 나타내고, '~한 곳 어디에나'는 wherever로 쓴다.

14 '아무리 ~할지라도'는 no matter how 또는 however로 쓰고 바로 뒤에 형용사 또는 부사가 올 수 있다.

15 두 문장 모두 '~할 때마다'라는 의미이므로 복합 관계부사 Whenever가 알맞다.

16 「However + 형용사/부사 + 주어 + 동사」의 어순이다.

17 '~할 때마다'라는 의미이므로 복합 관계부사 whenever가 알맞다.

18 양보의 부사절을 이끄는 However는 No matter how로 바꿔 쓸 수 있다.

19 '~할 때는 언제든지'는 whenever(= at any time when)로 쓴다.

20 문맥상 '그가 어디에 가든지'가 되어야 하므로 wherever를 써야 한다.

21 whenever 다음에 「주어 + 동사」가 이어지는데, my father washes his car가 와야 의미상 자연스럽다. Whenever it rains, my father washes his car.가 되면 의미상 어색하다.

22 복합 관계부사 whenever는 시간의 부사절에서 '~할 때는 언제든지'의 의미로, at any time when으로 바꿔 쓸 수 있다.

23 '아무리 ~한다 할지라도(= no matter how)'의 의미인 however가 알맞다.

24 wherever는 '어디에[로] ~할지라도'라는 의미로 양보의 부사절을 이끈다.

25 문맥상 '~할 때는 언제든지'라는 의미의 복합 관계부사 whenever가 알맞다.

STEP 2 · 오답률 40~60% 문제　　　pp. 142 – 143

01 ①　02 ②　03 ④　04 ①　05 ①　06 ②
07 ③　08 I won't believe whatever you say.　09 No matter what　10 Whoever cheats on the test will be punished.　11 However late you get up, make sure to have breakfast.　12 Whenever　13 Whenever she sees me, she smiles.　14 wherever　15 No matter how

01 첫 번째 빈칸은 '도움이 필요한 누구든지'의 의미가 되어야 하므로 복합 관계대명사 whoever가, 두 번째 빈칸은 '네가 원하는 어느 것이든지'라는 의미가 되도록 복합 관계대명사 whichever가 와야 한다.

02 whatever는 양보의 부사절을 이끌어 '무엇을 ~할지라도(= no matter what)'의 의미로 쓰였다.

03 '~하는 사람은 누구나'의 의미를 갖는 Whoever가 알맞다.

04 '~하는 누구든지'의 의미를 나타내는 anyone who는 whoever로 바꿔 쓸 수 있다.

05 ① '아무리 ~할지라도'라는 의미이므로 「However + 형용사/부사 + 주어 + 동사」의 형태로 써야 한다.

06 문맥상 '~할 때마다'라는 의미가 적절하므로 Whenever를 써야 한다.

07 '어디를 ~하든지'는 복합 관계부사 wherever(= no matter where)로 써야 한다.

08 anything that은 '~하는 무엇이든지'라는 의미로 whatever로 바꿔 쓸 수 있다.

09 '네가 무엇을 하든지'라는 의미가 가장 자연스러우므로 No matter what(= Whatever)이 알맞다.

10 '~하는 누구든지'라는 의미의 whoever를 이용해서 영작한다. 복합 관계대명사가 주어이므로 단수 동사를 써야 한다.

11 복합 관계부사절은 However late you get up이고, 주절은 make sure to ~(반드시 ~해라)로 연결한다.

12 every time은 '~할 때마다'의 의미로 whenever와 바꿔 쓸 수 있다.

13 복합 관계부사 whenever 다음에 「주어 + 동사」가 온다.

14 '~하는 곳은 어디든지'의 의미인 to any place where는 장소의 부사절을 이끄는 복합 관계부사 wherever로 바꿔 쓸 수 있다.

15 '아무리 ~할지라도'라는 의미의 however는 no matter how로 바꿔 쓸 수 있다.

STEP 3 · 오답률 60~80% 문제　　　pp. 144 – 145

01 ①　02 ②, ⑤　03 ②, ④　04 ①, ③　05 ①
06 ①　07 ③, ④　08 which → whichever 또는 whatever
09 Whoever works hardest will be promoted next month.
10 Whatever you wear, you always look cool.　11 No matter where you go　12 ④ No matter what → No matter how[However]　13 However high the mountain is, he can climb to the top.　14 Whenever she is tired, she drinks a cup of coffee.　15 However rich they are, they always want more and more.

01 ⓒ anything whatever → whatever 또는 anything that
　ⓓ Whomever → Whoever

02 '누구를 ~하더라도'라는 의미의 양보의 부사절이므로 복합 관계대명사 Whomever(= No matter whom)가 알맞다.

03 '~하는 사람은 누구든지'의 의미로 주어로 쓰였으므로 복합 관계대명사 Whoever(= Anyone who)가 알맞다.

04 문맥상 '어느 스마트폰을 선택하더라도'의 의미가 적절하므로 복합 관계대명사 Whichever(= No matter which)가 알맞다.

05 '방문할 때는 언제든지'라는 의미가 적절하므로 시간을 나타내는 복합 관계부사 Whenever를 써야 한다.

06 ① nicely는 부사이므로 바로 앞에 올 수 있는 복합 관계사는 No matter what이 아니라 '아무리 ~하더라도'의 의미를 나타내는 No matter how(= However)이다.

07 '아무리 ~하더라도'라는 의미의 양보의 부사절을 이끄는 however는 「however + 형용사/부사 + 주어 + 동사」의 어순으로 쓴다. however는 no matter how로 바꿔 쓸 수 있다.

08 which를 '~하는 것은 무엇이든지(= anything that)'라는 의미의 whichever 또는 whatever로 고쳐야 한다. 선택의 범위가 한정되어 있을 때에는 whatever보다는 whichever를 쓰는 것이 적절하다.

09 '~하는 누구든지'라는 의미의 복합 관계대명사 whoever를 추가하여 문장을 완성해야 한다.

10 '무엇을 ~할지라도'라는 의미의 양보의 부사절을 이끄는 복합 관계대 명사 whatever를 쓰고, 「주어 + 동사」의 어순으로 쓴다.

11 '어디에 ~할지라도'의 의미이므로 No matter where를 이용해야 한 다. 복합 관계부사 Wherever와 바꿔 쓸 수 있다.

12 ④ No matter what 바로 다음에 형용사 small이 왔으므로 No matter what을 No matter how(= However)로 고쳐야 한다.

13 '아무리 ~일지라도'라는 의미이므로 복합 관계부사 however(= no matter how)를 이용한다. however 다음에는 형용사 high가 이어 진 다음 「주어 + 동사」를 쓴다.

14 '~할 때마다'의 의미이므로 복합 관계부사 Whenever를 써야 한다.

15 '아무리 ~일지라도'라는 의미이므로 복합 관계부사 However를 써 야 한다.

STEP 4 · 실력 완성 테스트　　　　　p. 146

01 ③　　**02** (1) you take, you can have it (2) sleepy he is, he goes to school on time　　**03** However windy it is, I will go swimming.　　**04** Whenever you want to talk with me, give me a call.　　**05** (1) [모범 답] I want to choose whoever is passionate and practices hard. (2) [모범 답] We are going to do whatever is necessary to help you. (3) [모범 답] I meet her whenever she wants to meet me.

01 ⓓ를 제외한 나머지는 모두 옳은 문장이다. ⓓ는 '어느 길로 가든지, 극장에 제시간에 도착하지 못할 것이다'라는 의미가 되도록 However를 Whichever[Whatever]로 쓰는 것이 알맞다.

02 (1) '무엇을 ~하더라도'라는 양보의 부사절을 이끄는 복합 관계대명 사 whatever에 「주어 + 동사」가 이어지는 구조이다.
　　(2) '아무리 ~일지라도'라는 의미의 양보의 부사절을 이끄는 「No matter how + 형용사 + 주어 + 동사」의 어순으로 배열한다.

03 「however + 형용사/부사 + 주어 + 동사」의 어순으로 써야 한다.

04 whenever 다음에 「주어 + 동사」가 이어지는데, want와 talk 두 개 의 동사가 있으므로 want to talk로 연결해야 한다.

05 (1) 복합 관계대명사 whoever가 '~하는 사람은 누구든지(= anyone who)'의 의미이므로 be동사와 practice를 3인칭 단수형으

로 써야 한다. (2) 복합 관계대명사 whatever가 관계사절에서 주어 역할을 하므로 다음에 단수 동사를 써야 한다. (3) 복합 관계부사 whenever 다음에는 「주어 + 동사」가 온다.

UNIT **15** 등위접속사 / 상관접속사

✔ 바로 체크　　　　　p. 148

01 or　**02** but　**03** so　**04** and　**05** or　**06** and
07 has　**08** nor　**09** are　**10** or

STEP 1 · 만만한 기초　　　　　pp. 149 – 151

01 ①　**02** ①　**03** ③　**04** silently　**05** ③　**06** ②
07 ④　**08** If you join us　**09** ⑤　**10** If you don't
listen　**11** Wear a swimming cap, or you can't get into
the pool.　**12** Don't be late, or you will not[won't]
13 ②　**14** as well as　**15** ①　**16** ②　**17** ①
18 ③　**19** ③　**20** ④　**21** both, and　**22** either
23 is not only cheap but also very useful　**24** I as well
as Wendy have to do the work.　**25** ④

01 첫 번째 빈칸은 의미상 서로 비슷한 내용의 단어를 연결하므로 접속 사 and가 알맞고, 두 번째 빈칸에는 둘 중 하나를 선택해야 하는 질 문이므로 or이 알맞다. 세 번째 빈칸은 앞뒤가 대조되는 내용이므로 but이 알맞다.

02 문맥상 '왜냐하면'이라는 뜻이 되어야 하므로 접속사 for가 알맞다.

03 ③ 앞뒤가 서로 대조되는 내용이므로 but이 알맞다.

04 등위접속사 and의 앞뒤로 동등한 문법 성분이 와야 하므로 부사로 고쳐야 한다.

05 등위접속사는 앞뒤로 동등한 문법 성분이 와야 한다. ① → healthy ② → shouting ④ → happiness ⑤ → (to) read

06 문맥상 '…해라, 그러면 ~할 것이다'라는 뜻이 되어야 하므로 「명령 문, and ~」가 알맞다.

07 첫 번째 문장은 문맥상 '…해라, 그러면 ~할 것이다'라는 뜻이 되어야 하므로 「명령문, and ~」가 알맞다. 두 번째 문장은 '…해라, 그렇지 않 으면 ~할 것이다'라는 뜻이 되어야 하므로 「명령문, or ~」가 알맞다.

08 「명령문, and ~」는 '…해라, 그러면 ~할 것이다'라는 뜻으로 if를 이 용하여 조건절로 나타낼 수 있다.

09 「명령문, and ~」는 '…해라, 그러면 ~할 것이다'라는 뜻이며 if를 써서 조건절로 나타낼 수 있다. if가 이끄는 조건절은 현재 시제로 미래의 의미를 나타낸다.

10 「명령문, or ~」는 '…해라, 그렇지 않으면 ~할 것이다'라는 뜻이며 「if … not, ~」으로 바꿔 쓸 수 있다.

11 unless가 쓰인 조건절은 「명령문, or ~」로 바꿔 쓸 수 있다.

12 '…해라, 그렇지 않으면 ~할 것이다'는 「명령문, or ~」를 써서 나타낼 수 있다.

13 ②에는 '…해라, 그렇지 않으면 ~할 것이다'라는 뜻이 되도록 or가 들어가야 하고, 나머지에는 and가 알맞다.

14 not only A but also B는 'A뿐만 아니라 B도'라는 의미의 상관접속사로 B as well as A로 바꿔 쓸 수 있다.

15 both A and B: A와 B 둘 다

16 either A or B: A 또는 B 둘 중 하나

17 not only A but (also) B: A뿐만 아니라 B도, not A but B: A가 아니라 B

18 feel이 감각동사이므로 뒤에 형용사 보어가 와야 하는데, both A and B에서 A와 B는 문법적으로 대등한 요소가 와야 하므로 둘 다 형용사가 알맞다.

19 neither A nor B: A도 B도 아닌

20 either A or B가 주어로 쓰일 때 B에 수를 일치시킨다.

21 both A and B: A와 B 둘 다

22 either A or B: A 또는 B 둘 중 하나

23 'A뿐만 아니라 B도 또한'은 not only A but also B로 나타낼 수 있으며 A와 B에는 문법적으로 대등한 요소가 온다.

24 not only A but also B는 B as well as A를 써서 바꿔 쓸 수 있으며 주어로 쓰일 때 B에 수를 일치시킨다.

25 ④ 상관접속사 neither A nor B가 주어로 쓰일 때 B에 수를 일치시키므로 are를 is로 고쳐야 한다.

STEP 2 · 오답률 40~60% 문제
pp. 152 – 153

01 ②	**02** ④	**03** ③	**04** ①	**05** ⑤	**06** ①

07 ③ **08** Wake up now, or you will miss the school bus.
09 don't stop → stop 또는 Unless → If **10** neither
11 (1) or → and (2) is → are **12** either eat out or order some food **13** Both Kate and Tim seem **14** Sam as well as I likes watching cartoon movies. **15** Neither Andy nor I was invited to her birthday party.

01 ② 'A와 B 둘 다'라는 의미의 both A and B는 복수 취급하므로 is를 are로 고쳐 써야 한다.

02 첫 번째 빈칸은 앞뒤의 내용이 대조를 이루므로 역접의 접속사 but이 알맞다. 두 번째 빈칸은 앞이 원인, 뒤가 결과에 해당하므로 접속사 so가 알맞다.

03 문맥상 'A뿐만 아니라 B도'라는 뜻을 나타내는 not only A but also B 구문이 되어야 하므로 ③의 and를 but으로 고쳐야 한다.

04 'A가 아니라 B'라는 뜻의 not A but B 구문을 써야 한다.

05 ⑤ not only A but also B: A뿐만 아니라 B도 ①, ②, ③ 「명령문, or

30 · UNIT 15

~」: …해라, 그렇지 않으면 ~할 것이다 ④ either A or B: A 또는 B 둘 중 하나

06 • either A or B: A 또는 B 둘 중 하나 • 빈칸 앞이 원인, 빈칸 뒤가 결과에 해당하므로 접속사 so가 알맞다. • 앞뒤의 내용이 대조를 이루므로 접속사 but이 알맞다.

07 ③ 'A도 B도 아닌'이라는 의미의 neither A nor B가 되어야 하므로 or를 nor로 고쳐야 한다.

08 「명령문, or ~」: …해라, 그렇지 않으면 ~할 것이다

09 unless에 이미 부정의 의미가 포함되어 있으므로 don't stop을 stop으로 고치거나 Unless를 「If … not, ~」으로 바꾼다.

10 neither A nor B: A도 B도 아닌

11 상관접속사 both A and B는 'A와 B 둘 다'라는 의미이고 주어로 쓰일 때 복수 취급한다.

12 either A or B: A 또는 B 둘 중 하나

13 상관접속사 both A and B는 'A와 B 둘 다'라는 의미이고 주어로 쓰일 때 복수 취급한다.

14 상관접속사 B as well as A는 'A뿐만 아니라 B도'라는 의미이고 주어로 쓰일 때 동사의 수는 B에 맞춘다.

15 neither A nor B 구문을 사용하고 동사의 수는 B에 맞춰 단수 동사를 쓴다. 과거시제 수동태는 「be동사의 과거형 + 과거분사」로 쓴다.

STEP 3 · 오답률 60~80% 문제
pp. 154 – 155

01 ④	**02** ⑤	**03** ①	**04** ②	**05** ②	**06** ④

07 ③ **08** you make a reservation in advance, you'll have to wait one hour or more **09** If you are not honest with him, Unless you are honest with him **10** not only, but also, as well as **11** visit → visiting **12** Chris as well as I enjoys watching horror movies and scaring people. **13** The actress is popular not only in Korea but also in many other countries. **14** Either Henry or his brother has spread the rumor. **15** Emilia was neither shocked nor disappointed by the news.

01 ① and → but ② or → for ③ and → or ⑤ to dance → dancing

02 Jean과 Alex 둘 다 호주에 가 본 적이 없다고 했다. neither A nor B: A도 B도 아닌

03 ⓒ doesn't eat → eats ⓓ so → but

04 ② 'A도 B도 아닌'이라는 뜻의 neither A nor B 구문이므로 빈칸에는 nor가 알맞다.

05 ② A as well as B는 A에 수를 일치시키므로 are를 is로 고쳐야 한다.

06 ④ unless는 '~하지 않으면'이라는 의미이다. 나머지는 모두 '너무 빨리 달리면 세부 사항을 놓칠 것이다'라는 의미이다.

07 ③에는 '…해라, 그렇지 않으면 ~할 것이다'라는 뜻이 되도록 or가 들어가야 알맞다. 나머지는 모두 and가 알맞다.

08 「명령문, or ~」는 '…해라, 그렇지 않으면 ~할 것이다'라는 의미로 접속사 unless가 이끄는 절이 포함된 문장으로 바꿔 쓸 수 있다.

09 「명령문, or ~」는 「If … not, ~」 또는 Unless가 이끄는 절을 포함한 문장으로 바꿔 쓸 수 있다.

10 'A뿐만 아니라 B도'라는 뜻을 나타내는 not only A but also B 구문으로 쓸 수 있으며, B as well as A 구문으로 바꿔 쓸 수 있다.

11 등위접속사 or가 「by -ing」 구문을 병렬구조로 연결하고 있는 형태이므로 visit를 동명사 visiting으로 고쳐야 한다.

12 A as well as B 구문을 사용하여 주어를 완성한다. A as well as B는 A에 수를 일치시키므로 동사는 3인칭 단수 현재형인 enjoys가 되어야 하며, 동사 enjoy는 동명사를 목적어로 취하므로 watching, scaring으로 써야 한다. 등위접속사 and가 enjoy의 목적어인 동명사구를 병렬구조로 연결한다.

13 not only A but also B: A뿐만 아니라 B도

14 either A or B: A 또는 B 둘 중 하나

15 neither A nor B: A도 B도 아닌

STEP 4 · 실력 완성 테스트　　　　　p. 156

01 ⑤　　**02** ①　　**03** Arrive on time, or you may not be allowed to take the test. / Unless you arrive on time, you may not be allowed to take the test.　　**04** ②, ④　　**05** I neither went to the fast food restaurant nor had a hamburger.　　**06** (1) Both, and, are (2) not only, but also (3) but Robert (4) Neither, nor

01 ⓐ or ⓑ and ⓒ nor ⓓ but

02 ⓑ speaks → speak ⓓ am → are ⓔ protect → (for) protection

03 「명령문, or ~」는 '…해라, 그렇지 않으면 ~할 것이다'라는 의미이고 unless절을 이용하여 바꿔 쓸 수 있다.

04 ② and → nor ④ and → but

05 상관접속사 neither A nor B를 사용하되, 시제가 과거이므로 동사는 과거형으로 써야 한다.

06 (1) Sophia와 Danny는 둘 다 캐나다인이다.
(2) Sophia는 영어뿐만 아니라 프랑스어도 할 수 있다.
(3) Danny가 아니라 Robert가 스페인어를 할 수 있다.
(4) Danny와 Robert 둘 다 프랑스어를 할 수 없다.

최종 선택 QUIZ　　　　　p. 157

01 a　**02** a　**03** b　**04** b　**05** a　**06** b　**07** b　**08** b

UNIT 16 명사절을 이끄는 접속사

✅ 바로 체크　　　　　p. 158

01 That　**02** that　**03** that　**04** It　**05** if[whether]
06 who he is　**07** that　**08** Whether　**09** whether
10 think

STEP 1 · 만만한 기초　　　　　pp. 159 – 161

01 ②　**02** ④　**03** ④　**04** ①　**05** that　**06** that he isn't interested in the movie　**07** ⑤　**08** what → that　**09** ④　**10** ②　**11** ④　**12** if Lucy will come to the party　**13** Whether　**14** ⑤　**15** If → Whether　**16** if[whether] he is telling a lie　**17** ⑤　**18** ②　**19** ④　**20** when she left　**21** if[whether] he will come　**22** the flowers sent → sent the flowers　**23** ②　**24** ①　**25** ③

01 첫 번째 빈칸에는 목적어 역할을 하는 명사절을 이끄는 접속사 that, 두 번째 빈칸에는 진주어인 명사절을 이끄는 접속사 that이 알맞다.

02 '내가 너에 대해서 들어 본 적이 없다는 것이 이상하다.'라는 뜻의 문장이 되어야 하므로 「It(가주어) ~ that절(진주어)」 구문이 알맞다.

03 ④는 주격 관계대명사이고 나머지는 모두 명사절을 이끄는 접속사이다.

04 ① 빈칸 다음에 불완전한 문장이 쓰였으므로 접속사 that을 쓸 수 없다. '~하는 것'이라는 의미의 관계대명사 what이 와야 한다.

05 빈칸에는 공통으로 명사절을 이끄는 접속사 that이 알맞다.

06 보어 역할을 하는 명사절이 되도록 접속사 that을 써서 배열한다. 접속사 that 뒤에는 「주어+동사」 형태의 절이 와야 한다.

07 〈보기〉와 ⑤는 보어 역할을 하는 명사절을 이끄는 접속사이다. ① 지시대명사 ② 목적격 관계대명사 ③ 지시형용사 ④ 주격 관계대명사

08 「It(가주어) ~ that절(진주어)」 구문이 되어야 하므로 what을 that으로 고쳐야 한다.

09 문맥상 '~인지 아닌지'라는 의미의 whether ~ or not이 알맞다.

10 '만일 ~라면'이라는 뜻으로 부사절을 이끌고, '~인지 아닌지'라는 뜻으로 명사절을 이끄는 접속사 if가 알맞다.

11 ④는 '만일 ~라면'이라는 뜻으로 조건의 부사절을 이끄는 접속사이고, 나머지는 모두 '~인지 아닌지'의 뜻으로 명사절을 이끄는 접속사이다.

12 접속사 if(~인지 아닌지)가 동사 wonder의 목적어 역할을 하는 명사절을 이끄는 형태로 써야 한다.

13 '~인지 아닌지'의 의미를 나타내고 주어 역할을 하는 명사절을 이끄는 접속사가 와야 하므로 Whether가 알맞다. if는 주어, 보어 역할을 하는 절을 이끌 수 없다.

14 ⑤에는 '~라는 것'의 의미로 명사절을 이끄는 접속사 that이 알맞다.

15 whether와 or not은 붙여 쓸 수 있지만, if와 or not은 붙여 쓰지 않는다. 또한 if는 주어로 쓰이는 절을 이끌 수 없다.

16 '~인지 아닌지'라는 의미로 목적어 역할을 하는 명사절을 이끄는 접속사 if나 whether를 써서 나타낼 수 있다.

17 ⑤ 간접의문문의 어순은 「의문사+주어+동사」이므로 why my sister was so angry로 고쳐야 한다.

18 의문사가 없는 의문문은 간접의문문으로 쓸 때 「if[whether]+주어+동사」의 어순으로 쓴다.

19 간접의문문에서 의문사 what이 주어이므로 뒤에 동사가 바로 이어진다. 의문사가 주어일 때는 단수 취급한다.

20 간접의문문의 어순은 「의문사+주어+동사」이다.

21 의문사가 없는 의문문은 간접의문문으로 쓸 때 「if[whether]+주어+동사」의 어순으로 쓴다.

22 간접의문문은 「의문사+주어+동사」의 어순으로 쓰며 의문사가 주어

로 쓰였으므로 「의문사 + 동사」의 어순으로 써야 한다. the flowers
는 주어가 아니라 목적어임에 유의한다.

23 ② 과거시제이므로 동사는 bought로 고쳐야 한다. buy → bought

24 주절의 동사가 think, believe, guess, suppose, imagine 등일
때는 의문사를 문장의 맨 앞에 쓴다.

25 ③ 주절의 동사가 think이므로 간접의문문의 의문사를 문장의 맨 앞
에 써야 한다. → How old do you think the dog is?

STEP 2 · 오답률 40~60% 문제   pp. 162 – 163

01 ⑤   02 ⑤   03 ③   04 ⑤   05 ③   06 ①, ④
07 ②   08 that   09 if → that   10 The fact that all
people are equal before the law is important.   11 ⓐ: If
→ Whether   12 if she will accept my proposal or not
13 Can you tell me how long she has been living here?
14 I wonder if[whether] John speaks French (or not).
15 Where do you think he is going?

01 첫 번째 빈칸에는 가주어 it과 함께 진주어절을 이끄는 접속사 that이,
두 번째 빈칸에는 동사의 목적어 역할을 하는 명사절을 이끄는 접속
사 that이 알맞다.

02 ⑤의 that은 목적격 관계대명사이고 나머지는 모두 접속사이다.

03 첫 번째 빈칸의 that은 동격절을 이끌고, 두 번째 빈칸의 that은 동사
의 목적어 역할을 하는 명사절을 이끈다.

04 ⑤ 「It(가주어) ~ that절(진주어)」 구문이 되어야 하므로 whether를
진주어절을 이끄는 접속사 that으로 고쳐야 한다.

05 ③의 if는 '만일 ~라면'의 뜻으로 조건의 부사절을 이끄는 접속사이고,
나머지는 모두 '~인지 아닌지'의 의미로 명사절을 이끄는 접속사이다.

06 의문사가 없는 의문문이 간접의문문이 될 때는 평서문의 어순으로 바
뀌고 앞에 접속사 if나 whether를 써서, 「if[whether] + 주어 + 동사」
의 형태가 된다.

07 ① → How often does she go jogging? ③ if or not → whether
or not 또는 if[whether] her story is true or not ④ what is your
name → what your name is ⑤ If → Whether

08 빈칸에는 모두 명사절을 이끄는 접속사 that이 들어가야 한다. 첫 번
째 that은 목적어 역할을 하고, 두 번째는 보어 역할을 한다.

09 '~라는 것'이라는 의미의 접속사 that을 써야 한다.

10 that절이 앞에 나오는 the fact와 동격을 이루는 구조로 쓴다.

11 ⓐ 접속사가 이끄는 명사절이 주어로 쓰인 문장으로, 접속사 if는 주
어 역할을 하는 명사절을 이끌 수 없으므로 whether를 써야 한다.

12 '~인지 아닌지'라는 뜻의 명사절을 이끄는 접속사 if를 쓴 다음 「주
어 + 동사 + 목적어」의 어순으로 문장을 완성한다.

13 의문사가 있는 간접의문문은 「의문사 + 주어 + 동사」의 어순이다.

14 의문사가 없는 간접의문문은 「if[whether] + 주어 + 동사」의 어순
이다.

15 간접의문문의 어순은 「의문사 + 주어 + 동사」이며 주절의 동사가
think, believe, guess, suppose, imagine 등일 때 의문사는 문
장의 맨 앞에 쓴다.

STEP 3 · 오답률 60~80% 문제   pp. 164 – 165

01 ②   02 ①   03 ②   04 ⑤   05 ①   06 ①, ④
07 ③   08 that he had seen the actor before   09 the
fact that spiders are not insects   10 Whether you agree
with me or not does not matter. / 네가 내게 동의하는지 아닌지
는 중요하지 않다.   11 Whether you believe me or not, if
[whether] you believe me, whether or not you believe
12 I have no idea where I put my bag.   13 Would you
mind telling me if[whether] you recognize this man?
14 (1) ⓑ: that → if[whether] (2) ⓒ: is it → it is   15 How
long do you think it will take me to get there?

01 〈보기〉와 ②의 that은 목적어 역할을 하는 명사절을 이끄는 접속사이
다. ①, ⑤는 주격 관계대명사이고 ③, ④는 목적격 관계대명사이다.

02 ⓔ 문장 맨 뒤의 or not으로 보아 빈칸에는 '~인지 아닌지'라는 뜻의
if나 whether가 와야 함을 알 수 있다.

03 • 목적어 역할을 하는 명사절을 이끄는 접속사 that이 알맞다. • 빈칸
바로 뒤에 or not이 이어지므로 '~인지 아닌지'의 의미를 나타내는
접속사 whether가 알맞다. • 보어 역할을 하는 명사절을 이끄는 접
속사 that이 알맞다.

04 ⑤는 '~인지 아닌지'의 뜻으로 명사절을 이끄는 접속사이고, 나머지는
모두 '만일 ~라면'이라는 뜻의 조건의 부사절을 이끄는 접속사이다.

05 ⓑ what does she do → what she does ⓒ if → whether 또는
or not을 삭제하거나 문장 맨 뒤로 이동 ⓔ → Do you guess
when → When do you guess

06 if는 주어로 쓰이는 절을 이끌 수 없으며 if or not으로 쓰지 않는다.

07 ① → Do you know who took my bag? ② how did they
escape → how they escaped ④ Do you think why → Why
do you think ⑤ that → if[whether]

08 '~라는 것'의 의미로 명사절을 이끄는 접속사 that을 사용하여 연결
하며 배우를 본 것은 기억하는 것보다 더 이전에 일어난 일이므로
that절의 시제는 과거완료로 나타낸다.

09 the fact 다음에 동격의 명사절을 이끄는 접속사 that을 사용하여 '~
라는 사실'이라는 의미를 나타낸다.

10 접속사가 이끄는 명사절이 주어로 쓰인 문장으로, 접속사 if는 주어
역할을 하는 명사절을 이끌 수 없으므로 whether를 써야 한다.

11 의문사가 없는 의문문을 간접의문문으로 쓸 때는 「if[whether] + 주
어 + 동사」로 나타낸다. whether는 주어, 보어, 목적어로 쓰이는 절
을 모두 이끌 수 있지만, if는 주어, 보어로 쓰이는 절을 이끌 수 없다.
또한 whether or not은 쓸 수 있지만 if는 바로 뒤에 or not을 쓸 수
없다.

12 의문사가 있는 간접의문문은 「의문사 + 주어 + 동사」의 어순이다.

13 의문사가 없는 간접의문문은 「if[whether] + 주어 + 동사」의 어순
이다.

14 ⓑ 의문이나 불확실을 나타내는 경우에는 '~인지 아닌지'의 의미인
접속사 if나 whether를 쓴다. ⓒ 간접의문문의 어순은 「의문사 + 주
어 + 동사」이다.

15 간접의문문의 주절의 동사가 think, believe, guess, suppose,
imagine 등일 때 의문사는 문장의 맨 앞에 쓴다.

01 ③   02 ④   03 ①, ③   04 How tall do you guess she is?   05 (1) is the problem → the problem is (2) that → if[whether]   06 (1) Do you know what Lisa is doing (2) Do you know what Jake is doing (3) What do you think Lisa will do (4) What do you think Jake will do

01 ③ 간접의문문이 포함된 문장으로 빈칸에는 의문사 what이 와야 하며, 나머지는 모두 접속사 if가 알맞다.

02 ④ if → whether 또는 or not을 삭제하거나 문장 맨 뒤로 이동

03 ① 내용상 '~라는 것'이라는 의미가 되어야 하므로 접속사 whether 대신 that을 써야 한다. ③ It이 가주어이므로 if 대신 진주어를 이끄는 접속사 that을 써야 한다.

04 간접의문문의 어순은 「의문사 + 주어 + 동사」이며 주절의 동사가 think, believe, guess, suppose, imagine 등일 때 의문사는 문장의 맨 앞에 쓴다.

05 (1) 간접의문문의 어순은 「의문사 + 주어 + 동사」이다.
    (2) '~인지 아닌지'를 의미하는 if 또는 whether가 알맞다.

06 간접의문문의 어순은 「의문사 + 주어 + 동사」이고, 주절의 동사가 think일 때 의문사는 문장의 맨 앞에 쓴다.

최종 선택 QUIZ   p. 167

01 b   02 a   03 a   04 a   05 a   06 b   07 b   08 a

UNIT 17   부사절을 이끄는 접속사

✅ 바로 체크   p. 168

01 while   02 see   03 because   04 Since
05 though   06 Unless   07 that   08 so

STEP 1 · 만만한 기초   pp. 169 – 171

01 ②   02 ⑤   03 ④   04 As soon as   05 ⑤
06 ④   07 until she had finished speaking   08 ①
09 ②   10 ②   11 ⑤   12 ③   13 will hear → hears   14 Though[Although]   15 Even though
16 ②, ③   17 ①   18 so   19 ④   20 ①   21 so that   22 so that   23 so, that, couldn't   24 ②
25 (1) when (2) if

01 첫 번째 문장에는 '~ 때문에'라는 뜻의 이유를 나타내는 접속사 since, 두 번째 문장에는 '~한 이래로'라는 뜻의 시간을 나타내는 접속사 since가 알맞다.

02 '~할 때'라는 의미의 When이 알맞다.

03 〈보기〉와 ④는 '~하면서'라는 뜻의 시간의 부사절을 이끄는 접속사이다. ① ~대로(접속사) ② ~만큼(원급 비교 / 부사) ③ ~ 때문에(접속사) ⑤ ~로서(전치사)

04 as soon as: ~하자마자

05 「원인 + so + 결과」의 문장은 이유의 접속사 because를 써서 「결과 + because + 원인」으로 나타낼 수 있다.

06 문맥상 첫 번째 빈칸에는 '~할 때'라는 뜻의 시간의 접속사가 알맞고, 두 번째 빈칸에는 '~ 때문에'라는 뜻의 이유를 나타내는 접속사가 알맞다.

07 until은 '~할 때까지'라는 뜻을 나타내는 접속사이고, 접속사 다음에는 「주어 + 동사」가 이어진다.

08 시간의 부사절에서는 현재 시제가 미래 시제를 대신한다.

09 ②는 간접의문문(명사절)을 이끄는 의문사이다. 나머지는 모두 시간의 부사절을 이끄는 접속사이다.

10 '만약 ~하지 않으면'이라는 뜻의 if ~ not은 unless로 바꿔 쓸 수 있다.

11 '~에도 불구하고, 비록 ~이지만'이라는 뜻의 접속사 Though가 알맞다.

12 ③의 if는 '~인지 아닌지'의 뜻으로 명사절을 이끈다. 나머지는 모두 '만약 ~라면'이라는 뜻으로 조건을 나타내는 부사절을 이끈다.

13 시간의 부사절에서는 현재 시제가 미래 시제를 대신한다.

14 의미상 내가 여동생에게 내 옷을 입지 말라고 말했음에도 불구하고 여동생이 옷을 입고 나갔으므로 양보를 나타내는 부사로 바꿔 쓸 수 있다.

15 상반되는 두 문장을 한 문장으로 연결하므로 '~에도 불구하고, 비록 ~이지만'이라는 뜻의 접속사 even though가 알맞다.

16 '조심하지 않으면 칼에 베일 수 있다.'라는 뜻이 자연스러우므로 if ~ not이나 unless를 써서 조건의 부사절을 나타낸다. 조건의 부사절에서는 현재 시제가 미래 시제를 대신한다.

17 문맥상 '너무 ~해서 …할 수 없다'라는 뜻의 「so ~ that + 주어 + can't ….」를 쓴다.

18 「so ~ that ….」: 매우 ~해서 …하다 / 「so as + to부정사」: ~하기 위해

19 '너무 ~해서 …할 수 없다'라는 뜻의 「so ~ that + 주어 + can't ….」로 나타낸다.

20 '매우 ~해서 …하다'라는 뜻의 「so ~ that ….」 구문을 사용한다.

21 「so that + 주어 + can ~」은 '~하기 위해'라는 뜻으로 목적을 나타낸다.

22 「so that + 주어 + can ~」은 '~하기 위해'라는 뜻으로 목적을 나타낸다.

23 「too ~ to부정사」는 「so ~ that + 주어 + can't ….」로 바꿔 쓸 수 있다.

24 접속사 because, though, while 뒤에는 「주어 + 동사」가 오고, 전치사 because of, despite, during 뒤에는 명사(구)가 온다.

25 (1) 나는 연설을 할 때 긴장한다. (2) 네가 거짓말을 하지 않으면 그녀는 속상하지 않을 것이다.

01 ①   02 ④   03 ③   04 ①, ②   05 ①, ④
06 ⑤   07 ③   08 don't apologize → apologize 또는
unless → if   09 Though[Although / Even though] it rained
10 (1) while (2) so that (3) As soon as   11 because of
12 so that I could exchange   13 boring that   14 (1) 우
리가 극장에 들어갔을 때 그 영화는 이미 시작했다. (2) 그녀는 나이
가 들면서 더 현명해졌다. (3) 어두워지고 있어서 우리는 서둘러 버스
정류장으로 갔다.   15 Tony was so healthy that he could
leave the hospital.

01 ①은 '~인 반면'이라는 의미로 대조를 나타내고, 나머지는 모두 '~하
는 동안'이라는 의미로 시간을 나타낸다.

02 ④ 접속사 뒤에는 「주어+동사」를 쓰고, 전치사 뒤에는 명사(구)를 쓰
므로 while 대신 during을 쓴다.

03 ③ 문맥상 '휴식을 취하기 위해서'라는 목적의 의미가 되어야 하는데
뒤에 절이 쓰이지 않았으므로 「so that」을 쓸 수 없다. 「so as + to
부정사」 구문이 되도록 빈칸에는 as to가 들어가야 한다.

04 '너무 ~해서 …할 수 없다'라는 뜻의 「so ~ that + 주어 + can't ...」
또는 「too ~ to부정사」 구문을 사용한다.

05 「(in order) + to부정사」와 「so that + 주어 + can + 동사원형」은 '~하
기 위해, ~하도록'이라는 목적의 의미를 나타낸다.

06 첫 번째 빈칸에는 '~하는 동안'이라는 뜻의 시간의 접속사 while이,
두 번째 빈칸에는 '만약 ~하지 않으면'이라는 뜻의 접속사 unless가
알맞다.

07 ③ '~에도 불구하고'라는 의미를 나타내는 양보의 접속사 Though
[Although / Even though]가 와야 알맞다.

08 unless는 '~하지 않으면'의 뜻으로 if ~ not의 의미이다. 조건절을
긍정문으로 바꾸거나, 접속사 unless를 '만약 ~하면'의 뜻인 if로 고
쳐 쓴다.

09 양보의 의미를 나타내는 접속사 though[although / even though]
를 이용한다.

10 (1) 앞뒤 문장이 서로 대조되는 내용이므로 while이 알맞다. (2) 뒤에
이어지는 내용이 목적을 나타내고 있으므로 so that이 알맞다. (3) '~
하자마자'라는 의미의 as soon as가 알맞다.

11 because는 뒤에 「주어+동사」를 쓰고 because of 뒤에는 명사(구)
를 쓴다.

12 「in order+to 부정사」는 목적을 나타내며 「so that + 주어 + can + 동
사원형」으로 바꿔 쓸 수 있다.

13 「so ~ that ....」은 '매우 ~해서 …하다'라는 의미로 결과를 나타낸다.

14 (1) '~할 때'라는 뜻의 시간의 접속사로 쓰였다. (2) '~함에 따라서, ~
할수록'이라는 뜻의 시간의 추이를 나타내는 접속사로 쓰였다. (3) '~
때문에'라는 뜻의 이유를 나타내는 접속사로 쓰였다.

15 「형용사 + enough + to부정사」는 「so + 형용사 + that + 주어 + can
...」으로 바꿔 쓸 수 있다.

01 ③   02 ③   03 ②, ④   04 ③   05 ②, ③
06 ②   07 ①, ⑤   08 When I meet Suji this Sunday, I'll
remind her to call you.   09 burned myself while I was
preparing dinner   10 I haven't seen her since I had
lunch with her   11 (1) ⓑ: will stop → stops (2) ⓒ:
because → because of   12 If she does not agree with
our proposal, we cannot make a contract. / Unless she
agrees with our proposal, we cannot make a contract.
13 She turned on the lantern so that we could see much
better.   14 The fog was so thick that the plane couldn't
land. / The fog was too thick for the plane to land.
15 The trunk is so big that it can hold lots of things.

01 ③은 '~한 이래로'라는 의미의 시간을 나타내는 접속사이고, 나머지
는 모두 '~ 때문에'라는 의미의 이유를 나타내는 접속사이다.

02 '~하는 동안에(첫 번째 빈칸)'와 '~인 반면(두 번째 빈칸)'이라는 의미
의 접속사 while이 알맞다.

03 ② even though → despite 또는 in spite of ④ If it will be → If
it is

04 ① 빈칸 다음에 명사구가 쓰였으므로 because of가 알맞다.

05 ②, ③ so (that)은 목적을 나타내는 접속사이다. ①, ④ 「so ~ that
...」은 '매우 ~ 해서 …하다'라는 의미로 결과를 나타낸다. ⑤ 「가주어
It ~ to부정사」 구문이다.

06 '~하기 위해, ~하도록'이라는 목적의 의미를 나타내는 「so that + 주
어 + can + 동사원형」 구문은 「so as + to부정사」, 「(in order) + to부
정사」로 바꿔 쓸 수 있다.

07 「so ~ that + 주어 + can ...」은 '매우 ~해서 …할 수 있다'라는 뜻으
로 결과를 나타내며 「enough + to부정사」로 바꿔 쓸 수 있다.

08 시간의 부사절에서는 현재 시제가 미래 시제를 대신한다.

09 '~하는 동안'이라는 뜻의 시간을 나타내는 접속사 while이 이끄는 부
사절을 쓴다. 전치사 during 뒤에는 명사(구)를 쓰는 것에 유의한다.

10 접속사 since가 '~ 한 이래로, ~ 이후로'라는 뜻으로 쓰일 때 주절에
는 현재완료 시제를 쓰고, 부사절에는 과거 시제를 쓴다.

11 ⓑ 조건의 부사절에서는 현재 시제가 미래 시제를 대신한다.
ⓒ 명사구 its beauty가 있으므로 because of가 알맞다.

12 '만약 ~하지 않으면'이라는 뜻의 조건의 부사절은 if ~ not이나
unless를 써서 나타낸다.

13 목적을 나타내는 「so that + 주어 + can + 동사원형」으로 바꿔 쓸 수
있다.

14 「so ~ that + 주어 + can't ...」는 '너무 ~해서 …할 수 없다'라는 뜻으
로 「too ~ to부정사」로 바꿔 쓸 수 있다. 의미상 주어는 to부정사 앞
에 쓴다.

15 「so ~ that + 주어 + can...」: 매우 ~해서 …하다, 목적을 나타내는
「so that + 주어 + can + 동사원형」 구문과 혼동하지 않도록 유의한다.

01 ③　　02 Though [Although / Even though] I was a stranger, he treated me in a friendly way.　　03 ⑤
04 ①　　05 My room was so messy that I decided to clean it up.　　06 (1) so that I can keep myself warm (2) though the alarm clock rang many times (3) when I heard the thunder

01 ⓐ as ⓑ Though ⓒ since ⓓ Unless
02 문맥상 양보의 접속사인 though, although, even though 등을 쓴다.
03 ⑤ although는 '~에도 불구하고'라는 양보의 의미이고, in case는 '~할 경우에는'이라는 조건을 나타낸다.
04 ⓑ because → because of ⓓ Although → Despite[In spite of] ⓕ I'll know → I know
05 「so ~ that ...」: 매우 ~해서 …하다
06 제시된 주절과 종속절의 의미를 파악한 다음 문맥이 가장 자연스러운 것끼리 연결한다.

최종 선택 QUIZ

01 b　02 b　03 a　04 a　05 b　06 a　07 b　08 a

UNIT 18 접속부사

✅ 바로 체크

01 For example　　02 As a result　　03 However
04 In addition　05 Otherwise　06 Above all　07 On the other hand

STEP 1 · 만만한 기초

01 ③　02 ④　03 ②, ③　04 ④　　05 As a result
06 ⑤　07 ④　08 Otherwise → For example[instance]
09 ①　10 ③　11 ⑤　12 In addition　13 ①, ②
14 ①　15 ②, ④　16 ⑤　17 Moreover　18 ④
19 ②　20 ④, ⑤　21 In contrast　22 ①　23 ④
24 ①　25 Furthermore → Nevertheless

01 빈칸 뒤에 동물들의 놀라운 능력에 대한 예가 나왔으므로 빈칸에는 예시를 나타내는 접속부사 For example(예를 들면)이 알맞다.
02 thus는 '따라서, 그러므로'라는 뜻으로 결과를 나타내는 접속부사이므로 therefore와 바꿔 쓸 수 있다.
03 빈칸 뒤에 다른 언어에서 온 단어의 예로 cafe를 제시하고 있으므로,

빈칸에는 예시를 나타내는 접속부사인 For instance나 For example이 알맞다.
04 빈칸 앞에는 원인, 빈칸 뒤에는 결과가 나오므로 빈칸에는 결과를 나타내는 접속부사 Therefore(그러므로)가 알맞다.
05 therefore는 '그러므로, 그 결과'라는 뜻의 결과를 나타내는 접속부사 as a result로 바꿔 쓸 수 있다.
06 ⑤ 앞뒤 문장이 인과관계를 나타내므로 However를 Thus 또는 Therefore 등으로 고쳐 써야 한다.
07 첫 번째 빈칸: 앞뒤 문장이 인과관계를 이루므로 결과를 나타내는 접속부사 Therefore나 Thus가 알맞다. 두 번째 빈칸: 뒤에 사람들을 돕는 것에 대한 예가 나왔으므로 예시를 나타내는 접속부사 For example이나 For instance가 알맞다.
08 일상생활에서 환경을 보호할 수 있는 예로 자전거 타기가 제시되어 있으므로, Otherwise를 예시를 나타내는 접속부사인 For example이나 For instance로 고쳐 써야 한다.
09 앞 문장과 뒤 문장의 내용이 서로 대조를 이루므로 빈칸에는 역접을 나타내는 접속부사 However가 알맞다.
10 In addition은 '게다가'라는 의미로 첨가를 나타내는 접속부사이므로 Besides와 바꿔 쓸 수 있다.
11 빈칸 앞뒤 내용이 서로 대조를 이루므로 '한편으로는, 반면에'라는 뜻의 역접을 나타내는 접속부사 On the other hand가 알맞다.
12 '게다가'라는 의미로 첨가를 나타내는 접속부사는 in addition이다.
13 빈칸 뒤에 앞 문장과 상반되는 내용이 연결되므로 역접의 접속부사 yet 또는 however가 알맞다.
14 첫 번째 빈칸: '우리 팀이 졌지만 멋진 경기였다'는 의미가 되어야 하므로 though(하지만)가 알맞다. 두 번째 빈칸: '대답을 하지 않는 대신에 돌아서 방을 나갔다'는 의미가 되어야 하므로, Instead(그 대신에)가 알맞다.
15 문맥상 빈칸에는 '게다가, 더욱이'라는 의미로 첨가를 나타내는 접속부사가 알맞다.
16 〈보기〉, ⑤ 역접을 나타내는 접속부사(하지만) ①, ②, ④ (의문문, 부정문에서) 아직 ③ (의문문에서) 벌써
17 '노래도 잘하고 춤도 잘 추고 게다가 바이올린도 잘 연주할 수 있다'는 의미가 되어야 하므로, However를 첨가를 나타내는 접속부사 Moreover로 고쳐 써야 한다.
18 '더 열심히 하지 않으면 시험에 떨어질 것이다'라는 의미가 자연스러우므로 빈칸에는 '그렇지 않으면'이라는 의미의 Otherwise가 적절하다.
19 '무엇보다도'라는 의미를 나타내는 접속부사는 above all이다.
20 앞뒤 문장이 대조되는 내용이므로 양보의 접속부사가 알맞다.
21 앞뒤의 내용이 서로 대조를 이루므로 '대조적으로'라는 의미를 나타내는 접속부사 In contrast가 알맞다.
22 일주일 전에 Barbara에게 이메일을 보내고 답장을 기다려왔는데 마침내 오늘 답장을 받았다는 내용이 되도록 빈칸에는 '마침내'라는 뜻의 At last가 알맞다.
23 빈칸 앞에 언급한 내용을 다른 말로 부연 설명하고 있으므로 빈칸에는 '다시 말해서'라는 뜻의 접속부사 In other words가 알맞다.
24 '코트를 입어라, 그렇지 않으면 감기에 걸릴 것이다'라는 의미이므로, or는 otherwise와 바꿔 쓸 수 있다.
25 furthermore는 '더욱이'라는 의미로 첨가를 나타내는 접속부사이다.

‘그럼에도 불구하고’라는 의미로 양보를 나타내는 접속부사는 nevertheless이다.

STEP 2 · 오답률 40~60% 문제
pp. 182 – 183

01 ②, ④   02 ⑤   03 ④   04 ③   05 ⑤   06 ③
07 ①   08 However → For example[instance]   09 in addition   10 As a result   11 though   12 Moreover → Otherwise   13 Finally, At last, In the end   14 (B)–(C)–(A)   15 Therefore[Thus]

01 해외여행 전에 할 일을 언급한 뒤 또 다른 할 일을 덧붙여 언급하고 있으므로 ‘게다가’라는 의미의 접속부사가 알맞다.

02 세상을 지배하려던 지도자들에 대한 예를 들고 있으므로 For example(예를 들면)이 알맞다.

03 첫 번째 빈칸: 앞뒤 문장이 원인과 결과에 해당하므로 접속부사 Therefore가 알맞다. 두 번째 빈칸: 앞 문장과 뒤 문장의 내용이 서로 대조를 이루므로 역접의 접속부사 However가 알맞다.

04 ③ 뒤 문장이 앞 문장의 결과에 해당하므로 역접을 나타내는 접속부사가 아니라 결과를 나타내는 접속부사(As a result, Therefore 등)가 알맞다.

05 at last는 ‘마침내’라는 뜻으로 in the end와 바꿔 쓸 수 있다.
① 적어도 ② 대조적으로 ③ 요컨대 ④ 우선

06 ③ nevertheless는 ‘그럼에도 불구하고’라는 뜻으로 양보를 나타내는 접속부사이다.

07 ‘서두르지 않으면 지하철을 놓쳐서 회의에 늦을 것이다’라는 의미가 되어야 내용이 자연스러우므로, 빈칸에는 ‘그렇지 않으면’이라는 의미의 접속부사 Otherwise가 알맞다.

08 두 번째 문장에 에너지를 절약하는 예가 제시되었으므로 However를 예시를 나타내는 접속부사 For example 또는 For instance로 고쳐 써야 한다.

09 besides는 ‘게다가’라는 의미로 첨가를 나타내는 접속부사이므로 in addition과 바꿔 쓸 수 있다.

10 ‘그 결과’라는 의미를 가진 접속부사는 as a result이다.

11 though가 접속부사로 문장 끝에 사용되면 ‘하지만, 그러나’의 의미를 나타낸다.

12 ‘그렇지 않으면’이라는 의미의 접속부사 otherwise를 써야 한다.

13 finally, at last, in the end는 모두 ‘마침내, 결국’이라는 의미를 나타내는 접속부사이다.

14 친구들과 시험에 관해 이야기했는데(B), 친구들은 시험이 쉬웠다고 하지만(C) 나는 그렇게 생각하지 않는다는 내용이다(A).

15 노래를 잘 못해서 올해 최악의 가수로 선정되었다는 내용으로 빈칸에는 결과를 나타내는 Therefore 또는 Thus가 알맞다.

STEP 3 · 오답률 60~80% 문제
pp. 184 – 185

01 ⑤   02 ⑤   03 ②   04 ①   05 ⑤   06 ④
07 ⑤   08 In other words   09 For instance   10 In contrast   11 yet → therefore[thus]   12 Otherwise   13 On the other hand   14 Moreover   15 The school was old and badly heated. Besides, it was too far from their house.

01 ‘긍정적인 사고는 우리를 성공으로 이끄는 반면, 부정적인 사고는 우리를 실패로 이끌 것이다’라는 의미가 되어야 하므로, 빈칸에는 ‘반면에’라는 의미로 역접을 나타내는 On the other hand가 알맞다.

02 ‘(C) 폭풍우로 인해 (A) 모든 항공이 취소되고, (D) 게다가 호텔도 방이 다 차서 (B) 하룻밤 동안 공항에서 자야 했다’라는 내용이 되어야 자연스럽다.

03 ② 빈칸 뒤에 온 문장은 앞 문장의 결과에 해당하므로, 결과를 나타내는 접속부사(Therefore, As a result 등)가 알맞다.

04 ‘온종일 아무것도 먹지 못해서 그들은 배가 매우 고팠다’는 것이 가장 자연스럽다.

05 ‘Edward는 똑똑하지만 대부분의 동아리 회원들이 그를 지지하지 않는다’는 의미로, Yet은 ‘그럼에도 불구하고’라는 양보의 의미로 쓰였다.

06 첫 번째 빈칸: 앞 문장과 뒤 문장의 내용이 서로 대조를 이루므로 빈칸에는 역접의 접속부사 though가 알맞다. 두 번째 빈칸: ‘비가 그치지 않아 걱정했는데, 마침내 5일째 비가 멈추었다’라는 의미가 자연스러우므로 At last가 알맞다.

07 〈보기〉, ⑤ 그럼에도 불구하고(접속부사) ① 고요한 ② 여전히 ③ 훨씬 ④ 움직이지 않는

08 in other words는 ‘다시 말해서’라는 의미로 앞에서 언급한 내용을 다른 말로 표현할 때 쓴다.

09 몸짓이 문화마다 다른 의미를 나타낸다는 예로 OK 손짓을 들고 있으므로, 빈칸에는 ‘예를 들어’라는 의미로 예시를 나타내는 For instance가 알맞다.

10 빈칸 앞뒤의 내용이 대조를 이루므로 빈칸에는 ‘대조적으로’라는 뜻의 In contrast가 알맞다.

11 yet은 ‘하지만’이라는 의미의 역접을 나타낸다. ‘따라서, 그러므로’라는 의미로 결과를 나타내는 접속부사는 therefore[thus]이다.

12 조건을 나타내는 if가 not과 함께 쓰이면, ‘그렇지 않으면’이라는 의미로 otherwise와 바꿔 쓸 수 있다.

13 ‘아르바이트가 별로 만족스럽지 않았지만 보수는 좋았다’라는 의미이므로, ‘반면에’라는 의미로 역접을 나타내는 On the other hand가 알맞다.

14 ‘더욱이’라는 의미로 첨가를 나타내는 접속부사는 moreover이다.

15 ‘게다가’라는 의미로 첨가를 나타내는 접속부사 besides를 쓰는 것이 의미상 자연스럽다.

STEP 4 · 실력 완성 테스트
p. 186

01 ③   02 ⑤   03 ①   04 (1) She got lost. Moreover, her car broke down. (2) They thought that the plan sounded risky. Nevertheless, they were willing to try. (3) There are some foods that dogs cannot have. For instance,

chocolate is harmful to dogs. 05 However, As a result, For example, Also

01 (A) nevertheless: 그럼에도 불구하고(양보) (B) besides: 게다가 (첨가) (C) in fact: 사실은

02 빈칸에는 '비록 ~이긴 하지만'이라는 의미의 접속사와 '그렇지만, 하지만'이라는 의미의 접속부사로 모두 쓰일 수 있는 though가 알맞다.

03 ⓐ 앞 문장이 원인, 뒤 문장이 결과를 나타내고 있으므로 Therefore, Thus 등이 알맞다. ⓑ 앞뒤의 내용이 서로 대조를 이루고 있으므로 However, In contrast 등이 알맞다.

04 (1) 첨가의 의미를 나타내는 Moreover(더욱이)가 알맞다. (2) 양보의 의미를 나타내는 Nevertheless(그럼에도 불구하고)가 알맞다. (3) 예시를 나타내는 For instance(예를 들면)가 알맞다.

05 대부분의 사람은 공기, 물, 그리고 토양 오염에 익숙하다. 하지만, 빛 공해도 다른 형태의 오염만큼 심각하다는 것을 아는 사람은 적다. 한 조사에 따르면, 세계 인구의 약 80퍼센트가 밤에 충분히 어둡지 않은 하늘 아래에서 살고 있다. 그 결과 종종 사람들은 수면 방해로 고통 받고, 그것은 사람들을 온종일 피곤하게 만든다. 야생 생물들 또한 빛 공해에 의해 위협 받는다. 예를 들면, 밤에 이동하는 수백만 마리의 새들은 높은 건물의 창에서 나오는 빛에 혼란을 느껴 건물에 부딪혀 죽게 된다. 또한 많은 새끼 바다거북들은 인공 빛이 그들을 바다로부 터 멀어지게 하기 때문에 죽는다.

최종 선택 QUIZ   p. 187

01 a   02 b   03 a   04 a   05 b   06 a   07 b   08 a

UNIT 19 원급 비교 / 비교급 비교

✔ 바로 체크   p. 188

01 tall   02 could   03 twice   04 as   05 bigger
06 wise   07 much   08 the better   09 and
10 the more

STEP 1 · 만만한 기초   pp. 189 – 191

01 ②   02 ③   03 ②   04 ④   05 as expensive as
06 cute   07 ④   08 ③   09 ②, ⑤   10 quiet →
quietly   11 ⑤   12 ⑤   13 popularer → more
popular   14 ①   15 (m)ore   16 (1) shorter than (2)
taller than   17 ④   18 The[the]   19 ③   20 higher,
colder   21 ⑤   22 more careful   23 ③   24 bigger
25 four times larger than

01 '~만큼 …한'의 의미를 나타내는 원급 비교의 형태는 「as + 형용사의 원급 + as」이다.

02 「not as + 형용사/부사의 원급 + as」의 형태로 원급 비교의 부정이다.

03 원급 비교는 「as + 형용사/부사의 원급 + as」로 쓴다.

04 ④ 원급 비교 구문은 형용사의 원급을 쓴다. more important → important

05 '~만큼 …한'의 의미를 나타내는 원급 비교이므로 「as + 원급 + as」의 형태로 쓴다.

06 원급 비교인 「as ~ as」에서는 비교급이 아닌 원급을 써야 한다.

07 '~만큼 …하지 않은'이라는 뜻의 원급 비교의 부정은 「not as[so] + 원급 + as」로 표현한다.

08 as soon as possible은 '가능한 한 빨리'라는 의미로 「as soon as + 주어 + can」으로 바꿔 쓸 수 있다. 명령문의 주어는 you이다.

09 「배수사 + as + 원급 + as」이고, '두 배'는 twice 또는 two times로 나타낸다.

10 '가능한 한 조용하게 말하라'는 의미이므로 형용사 quiet 대신 동사 speak를 수식하는 부사 quietly로 써야 한다.

11 「as + 원급 + as + 주어 + can」으로 쓸 수 있고, high는 '높게, 위로'라는 뜻의 부사로 쓰였다.

12 than이 있으므로 「비교급 + than」 구문이다.

13 3음절 이상인 단어의 비교급은 단어 앞에 more를 붙인다.

14 ① very는 원급을 강조할 때 쓰는 부사로 비교급 앞에 쓸 수 없다.

15 두 문장 뒤에 모두 than이 있으므로 비교급 문장이다. creative의 비교급은 more creative이고, many의 비교급은 more이다.

16 그림을 보면 Monica < Judy < Annie의 키 순서이므로 tall과 short을 이용하여 비교급 구문으로 나타낼 수 있다.

17 「the + 비교급 ~, the + 비교급 …」 표현이므로 ④의 원급은 쓸 수 없다.

18 첫 번째 문장: '~할수록 더 …하다'라는 의미의 「the + 비교급 ~, the + 비교급 …」이다. 두 번째 문장: '둘 중에서 더 ~한'이라는 의미의 「the + 비교급 + of the two」 구문이다.

19 '~보다 더 …한'이라는 의미는 「형용사의 비교급 + than」으로 쓴다. hard의 비교급은 harder이다.

20 '더 높이 올라갈수록 더 추워진다.'는 뜻으로 「the + 비교급 ~, the + 비교급 …」으로 바꿔 쓸 수 있다.

21 her는 소유격으로 단독으로 주어 자리에 올 수 없으므로 Daniel이 주어가 되어야 하며, much는 비교급 앞에서 비교급을 강조한다.

22 careful 뒤에 than이 있으므로 more careful로 쓴다.

23 very는 원급을 강조할 때 쓰는 부사이다.

24 '점점 더 ~한'이라는 의미의 「비교급 + and + 비교급」 구문이다.

25 「배수사 + 비교급 + than」의 형태로 비교급 문장을 완성할 수 있다.

STEP 2 · 오답률 40~60% 문제   pp. 192 – 193

01 ②   02 ④   03 ⑤   04 ③   05 ③   06 ②
07 ⑤   08 she could   09 smaller than   10 more
carefully than me[I]   11 more   12 less crowded than
13 The more, earn, the more, spend   14 The weather is
much warmer than last spring.   15 ⓐ more expensive ⓑ
cheaper

01 B의 대답으로 보아 Ron과 Harry의 나이가 같은지 묻는 말이 와야 한다. 따라서 원급 비교 as old as가 알맞다.

02 A의 질문에 B가 Edward라고 답했으므로 Stephen은 Edward만큼 '빠르지 않다'라는 내용이 이어져야 한다. 따라서 원급 비교의 부정인 not as fast as로 써야 한다.

03 「배수사 + as + 원급 + as」 형태로 써야 한다. '세 배'는 three times이고, 내 것(my book)은 소유대명사 mine으로 쓸 수 있다.

04 누구나 가능한 한 오래 건강하길 원한다.

05 밑줄 친 단어 뒤에 than이 있으므로 모두 비교급으로 써야 한다.

06 주어진 문장은 'Bob은 Teddy보다 더 부지런하다.'는 의미로 ②의 'Teddy는 Bob만큼 부지런하지 않다.'인 원급 비교의 부정으로 나타낼 수 있다.

07 '~할수록 더 …하다'라는 의미이므로 「the + 비교급 ~, the + 비교급 …」 형태로 써야 한다.

08 「as + 원급 + as possible」은 「as + 원급 + as + 주어 + can [could]」으로 바꿔 쓸 수 있다.

09 '내 남동생의 방은 내 방보다 작지 않다.'는 '내 방은 내 남동생의 방보다 작다.'와 같은 의미이므로 「비교급 + than」으로 바꿔 쓸 수 있다.

10 「부사의 비교급 + than」 구문이다. carefully의 비교급은 more carefully이고, 비교 대상이 '나'이므로 me 또는 I를 쓴다.

11 '한국을 방문하는 여행객들이 점점 더 많아지고 있다.'는 의미로 many의 비교급 more를 쓴다.

12 '~보다 덜 …한'은 「less + 원급 + than」 구문을 사용한다.

14 '~보다 훨씬 더 …하다'라는 의미이므로 「much + 비교급 + than」의 어순이 되어야 한다.

15 뒤에 than이 있으므로 expensive와 cheap의 비교급 형태로 쓴다.

STEP 3 · 오답률 60~80% 문제　　　pp. 194 – 195

01 ③　　**02** ⑤　　**03** ②　　**04** ④　　**05** ①　　**06** ③
07 ①　　**08** My bag is not as[so] heavy as yours[your bag].
09 Time is as precious as gold.　　**10** three times longer than　　**11** as soon as I can　　**12** Peter is much more intelligent than Matt.　　**13** three years older than　　**14** Is she more cheerful than her brother?　　**15** Does he cook better than his wife?

01 대화의 흐름상 '~만큼 …한'이라는 의미의 「as + 원급 + as」를 쓴다.

02 '가능한 한 일찍'은 as early as possible이고, 「as early as + 주어 + can」으로 바꿔 쓸 수 있다. 명령문이므로 주어는 you를 쓴다.

03 much의 비교급은 more이고, fast의 비교급은 faster이다.

04 ④ 형용사의 원급을 강조할 때는 so나 very 등을 사용한다. ①, ②, ③, ⑤ 비교급을 강조할 때는 much, far, even, still, a lot 등을 쓴다.

05 ⓒ the many mistakes → the more mistakes

06 ③ Chris의 점수가 점점 더 나빠졌으므로 앞에는 공부를 점점 덜 했다는 내용이 오는 것이 자연스럽다.

07 ①은 비교급을 강조하는 much이고, 나머지는 모두 불가산명사를 수식하여 '많은'의 의미를 나타내는 much이다.

08 '~만큼 …하지 않다'의 의미의 「not as[so] + 원급 + as」 구문을 쓴다.

09 '~만큼 …한'은 원급 비교로 쓴다.

10 「배수사 + as + 원급 + as」는 「배수사 + 비교급 + than」으로 바꿔 쓸 수 있다.

11 「as + 원급 + as possible」은 「as + 원급 + as + 주어 + can[could]」으로 바꿔 쓸 수 있다.

12 '~보다 더 …한'이라는 의미는 「비교급 + than」으로 나타내고, 비교급을 강조하는 much는 비교급 앞에 쓴다.

13 '그가 나보다 세 살이 더 어린(younger)' 것이므로 '나는 그보다 세 살이 더 많다(older)'는 의미의 문장이 되어야 한다.

14 more cheerful을 이용하여 be동사 의문문을 쓴다.

15 better than을 이용하여 일반동사 의문문을 쓴다.

STEP 4 · 실력 완성 테스트　　　p. 196

01 ②　　**02** ⑤　　**03** The older you get, the wiser you will become.　　**04** ③, ⑤　　**05** (1) Edward is taller than Aaron. (2) Edward is heavier than Lisa. (3) Lisa got a higher score than Aaron.　　**06** [예시 답] (1) I run faster than my friend. (2) Junsu has as many friends as me. (3) I am more careful than my friend. (4) I feel happier than my friend. (5) I am more interested in English than my friend.

01 ②는 '더 많은 것'이라는 의미의 대명사로 쓰였고, 나머지는 모두 much의 비교급으로 쓰여 '더 많은'의 의미를 나타낸다.

02 ①, ② → more and more excited ③ → twice as large as ④ that은 앞에 있는 population을 지칭하며 비교 대상이 동일해야 하므로 that of는 필요하다. ⑤ 본동사(hurried)가 과거이므로 can을 could로 써야 한다.

03 '~할수록 더 …한'은 「the + 비교급 ~, the + 비교급 …」으로 쓴다.

04 very는 원급을 수식하는 데 사용되며, even과 a lot은 모음으로 시작되므로 빈칸 앞에 an이 있어야 한다.

05 세 사람의 키(height), 몸무게(weight), 점수(score)를 묻는 비교급 질문에 비교급 문장으로 답한다.

최종 선택 QUIZ　　　p. 197

01 a　**02** b　**03** b　**04** a　**05** b　**06** b　**07** b　**08** b

UNIT 20　최상급 비교

✔ 바로 체크　　　p. 198

01 tallest　**02** in　**03** as　**04** smarter　**05** faster
06 parks　**07** the richest　**08** of　**09** No　**10** artists

STEP 1 · 만만한 기초

01 ③　　02 sourest 또는 most sour　　03 ④　　04 (1) the oldest of the three (2) the heaviest of the three　　05 the worst　　06 ⑤　　07 ②　　08 the best, have, read　　09 ③　　10 ④　　11 ②　　12 ③　　13 stronger than　　14 higher than　　15 ⑤　　16 ②　　17 Nobody is as brave as　　18 ⑤　　19 ②　　20 ④　　21 ①　　22 ③　　23 ③　　24 ④　　25 higher than any other boy

01 최상급의 비교 범위를 한정할 때 「of + 복수 명사」로 나타낼 수 있다.

02 '가장 신[시큼한]'이라는 최상급의 의미가 되어야 하므로 sour의 최상급인 sourest로 써야 한다. most sour도 가능하다.

03 최상급의 비교 범위를 한정할 때 최상급 뒤에 「in + 장소 / 집단」, 「of + 복수 명사」를 쓴다.

04 나이는 Sam = Greg < Paul, 체중은 Sam < Paul < Greg 순이다.

05 '최악'이라는 의미는 bad의 최상급 the worst로 써야 한다.

06 ⑤ 「one of the + 최상급 + 복수 명사」이므로 scientists로 쓴다.

07 ② KN-2는 가장 인기 있는 품목이므로 the most popular가 알맞다.

08 「the + 최상급 + 명사(+ that) + 주어 + have ever + 과거분사」의 형태로 써야 한다.

09 ③ 빈칸 앞에 most가 있으므로, good의 최상급인 best는 쓸 수 없다.

10 ④는 비교급으로 more를 쓰고, 나머지는 모두 most를 써야 한다. ① '대부분'이라는 뜻의 대명사 ②, ③, ⑤ 최상급

11 최상급 뒤에 「of + 복수 명사」를 써서 최상급의 비교 범위를 나타낼 수 있다.

12 「부정주어 + as + 원급 + as」는 최상급의 의미를 나타내므로 빈칸에는 light의 최상급인 lightest가 들어가야 한다.

13 「부정주어 + 비교급 + than」 구문으로 최상급의 의미를 나타낸다.

14 「부정주어 + 비교급 + than」 구문으로 최상급의 의미를 나타낸다.

15 「There is nothing + 비교급 + than」 구문은 「Nothing is + 비교급 + than」으로 바꿔 쓸 수 있다.

16 원급과 비교급을 이용한 최상급 표현으로 동사 sing을 수식하는 부사 well(두 번째 빈칸)과 well의 비교급인 better(첫 번째 빈칸)를 쓰는 것이 알맞다.

17 최상급의 의미를 나타내는 「부정주어 + as + 원급 + as」의 어순으로 쓴다.

18 '어떤 —도 …만큼 ~하지 않다'는 「부정주어 + as + 원급 + as」로 쓸 수 있다.

19 「비교급 + than any other + 단수 명사」 또는 「비교급 + than all the other + 복수 명사」로 쓸 수 있다.

20 최상급의 의미를 나타내는 「부정주어 + as + 원급 + as」 형태로 쓴다.

21 ① 부정주어인 nobody와 can't는 이중부정이므로 can't 대신 can을 쓴다.

22 최상급을 의미하는 「No other + 명사 ~ as + 원급 + as」와 「비교급 + than any other + 단수 명사」이다.

23 There ⓐ is ⓑ nothing ⓒ easier ⓓ than ⓔ cooking for her.

24 Nothing is worse than bullying.

25 「비교급 + than any other + 단수 명사」로 최상급의 의미를 나타낼 수 있다.

STEP 2 · 오답률 40~60% 문제

01 ⑤　　02 ⑤　　03 ④　　04 ①, ④　　05 ①　　06 ③　　07 ②　　08 (1) thickest (2) thicker　　09 one of the funniest teachers　　10 the most frightening movie, watched　　11 the hottest month of the year　　12 No student, as witty　　13 No sport, more popular　　14 islands → island　　15 worker → workers

01 ⑤ 「one of the + 최상급」이 주어일 때는 단수 취급한다. are → is

02 「the + 최상급 + 단수 명사」의 형태가 알맞다.

03 문맥상 모두 최상급을 써야 한다. do one's best: 최선을 다하다

04 ① No → Nothing 또는 No other thing, ④ 「비교급 + than any other + 단수 명사」이므로 planet이 알맞다.

05 첫 번째 문장: 「비교급 + all the other + 복수 명사」이다. 두 번째 문장: is가 있으므로 단수 주어가 알맞다. 세 번째 문장: 빈칸 뒤에 있는 all은 복수를 의미하므로 of를 쓴다.

06 No other mountain in the world is higher than Mt. Everest.
　　① ② ③ ④ ⑤ ⑥ ⑦

07 ②는 '가장 ~한 것 중 하나'라는 의미이고, 〈보기〉와 나머지는 모두 '가장 ~한'의 의미이다.

08 대화의 흐름상 (1)은 최상급 표현이, (2)는 than으로 보아 비교급 표현이 되어야 한다.

09 「one of the + 최상급 + 복수 명사」로 쓴다.

10 방금 전에 본 영화가 정말 무서웠다는 내용으로 frightening은 most를 써서 최상급을 만든다.

11 '8월은 일 년 중 가장 더운 달이다.'라는 의미의 최상급 문장을 써야 한다.

12 최상급 의미이고 비교 대상 앞에 as가 있으므로 「No (other) + 명사 ~ + as + 원급 + as」로 쓴다.

13 최상급의 의미이고 비교 대상 앞에 than이 있으므로 「부정주어 + 비교급 + than」 구문으로 쓴다.

14 최상급의 의미를 나타내는 「No (other) + 명사 ~ + as + 원급 + as」에서 명사는 단수 명사로 써야 한다.

15 최상급의 의미를 나타내는 「비교급 + than + all the other + 복수 명사」이다.

STEP 3 · 오답률 60~80% 문제

01 ④, ⑤　　02 ⑤　　03 ③, ⑤　　04 ②　　05 ①　　06 ③　　07 ③　　08 Today is the happiest day in[of] my life.　　09 the most polite person, have ever met　　10 is as amazing as an aurora　　11 (A) the most important (B) more important than any other　　12 Is he the best singer?[Does he sing best?]　　13 Is water the most necessary for them?　　14 Nothing can please her as much as this song.　　15 He is kinder than any other boy at school.

→ most ② diligentest → most diligent ③ friend → ~~f~~riends

02 첫 번째 빈칸에는 '그가 그녀를 가장 많이 필요로 했을 때'의 의미인 when he needed her most가, 두 번째 빈칸에는 '~의 인생에서 가장 좋은 시기'의 의미인 the best time of one's life가 적절하다.

03 「부정주어 + 비교급 + than」을 이용한 최상급 표현은 「부정주어 + as + 원급 + as」, 「There is nothing + 비교급 + than」 등으로 바꿔 쓸 수 있다.

04 ⓑ doctors 또는 any other doctor ⓓ snake를 snakes로 고친다.

05 ① → all the plants 또는 all the other plants

06 ③ 첫 번째 문장은 비교급을 강조한 문장이고, 두 번째 문장은 최상급을 나타내는 문장이다.

07 ③은 'Dean은 우리 반에서 가장 유머러스하지 않은 학생'이라는 의미이고, 나머지는 모두 'Dean이 우리 반에서 가장 유머러스한 학생'이라는 의미이다.

08 '~의 인생에서 가장 행복한 날'은 the happiest day in[of] one's life라고 쓴다.

09 「the + 최상급 + 명사 + that + 주어 + have ever + 과거분사」의 순서로 쓴다.

10 최상급 표현이므로 「부정주어 + as + 원급 + as」로 바꿔 쓸 수 있다.

11 (B) 빈칸 뒤에 단수 명사인 thing이 있으므로 비교급을 이용한 최상급 표현으로 「비교급 + than any other + 단수 명사」를 쓴다.

12 B의 대답으로 보아 '그가 가장 노래를 잘하니?'라는 의미의 질문이 와야 한다.

13 B의 대답으로 보아 '그들에게 물이 가장 필요하니?'라는 의미의 최상급 표현을 써야 한다.

14 「부정주어 + as + 원급 + as」의 어순이 되어야 한다.

15 「비교급 + than any other + 단수 명사」는 최상급의 의미를 나타낸다.

STEP 4 · 실력 완성 테스트 p. 206

01 ⑤ 02 ② 03 Nothing is more convenient than a smartphone. 04 (1) Sumin is the smartest (of the three). (2) Minsu is the tallest (of the three). (3) Dongho is the youngest (of the three). 05 ④ 06 [예시 답] (1) I am the funniest of all my friends. (2) I have the most figures in my class. (3) I am the most popular person in my class. (4) I have the most supporters in my school. (5) I run fastest in the class.

01 나는 의사로부터 최악의 소식을 들었다. 그것은 나에게 일어났었던 것 중 가장 비참한 것이었다. / ⓒ 주절의 시제가 was로 과거이므로 종속절의 시제는 과거 완료로 쓴다.

02 ⓑ 「one of + 최상급 + 복수 명사」이므로 show → shows, ⓒ 「비교급 + than any other + 단수 명사」이므로 the most impressive를 more impressive로 고치거나 또는 than any other를 삭제

03 「부정주어 Nothing + 비교급 + than ~」의 형태로 쓴다. Nothing은 단수 취급하므로 동사는 is, '편리한'은 convenient로 비교급은 more convenient이다.

04 세 사람의 IQ, 키, 나이를 묻는 최상급 질문에 해당하는 정보를 표에서 찾아 최상급으로 답한다.

05 맥락상 '최악의 가뭄'이라는 뜻으로 bad의 최상급 worst를 쓴다.

최종 선택 QUIZ p. 207

01 b 02 a 03 b 04 b 05 a 06 b 07 a 08 b

UNIT 21 가정법 과거

✔ 바로 체크 p. 208

01 could 02 traveled 03 were 04 did not 05 were 06 were 07 would fail 08 were not

STEP 1 · 만만한 기초 pp. 209 – 211

01 ④ 02 were 03 ② 04 ② 05 If I knew his address, I would send him a gift. 06 ④ 07 ③ 08 don't have, can't 09 ③ 10 ⑤ 11 you were 12 ② 13 ⑤ 14 don't have 15 ② 16 ② 17 ③ 18 knows → knew 19 ① 20 ③, ④ 21 ⑤ 22 were not for 23 ① 24 ④ 25 (1) liked (2) owned (3) were not sitting

01 if절의 동사가 과거형이므로 주절의 동사는 「조동사의 과거형 + 동사원형」의 형태가 되어야 한다.

02 주절의 동사가 「조동사의 과거형 + 동사원형」이므로 if절은 과거형이 되어야 한다. 가정법 과거 문장에서 if절에 be동사가 쓰일 경우 주어의 인칭이나 수에 관계없이 주로 were를 사용한다.

03 실현 가능성이 거의 없는 일을 가정하고 있고 주절의 동사가 「조동사의 과거형 + 동사원형」이므로 if절의 동사는 과거형이 와야 한다.

04 현재 사실과 반대되는 상황을 가정할 때는 가정법 과거로 나타낸다.

05 가정법 과거는 「If + 주어 + 동사의 과거형/were ~, 주어 + 조동사의 과거형 + 동사원형 .....」의 형태로 나타낸다.

06 현재 사실에 반대되는 가정을 하는 것이므로 가정법 과거로 나타내야 한다. if절에는 동사의 과거형을 쓰고, 주절에는 「조동사의 과거형 + 동사원형」으로 쓴다.

07 현실에 대한 아쉬움을 나타낼 때 가정법 과거를 사용할 수 있으며 가정법 과거의 형태는 「If + 주어 + 동사의 과거형/were ~, 주어 + 조동사의 과거형 + 동사원형 .....」이다.

08 가정법 과거 문장이므로 반대 의미의 직설법 현재로 바꿔 쓴다.

09 현재 사실과 반대되는 소망을 나타내므로 I wish 다음에는 동사의 과거형이 와야 한다. be동사의 경우 과거형은 주로 were를 쓴다.

10 현재 사실에 대한 아쉬움을 나타내고 있으므로 I wish 가정법 과거를 사용한다. I wish 가정법 과거는 「I wish + 주어 + 동사의 과거형」으로 표현하므로 직설법의 조동사 can은 could로 바꾼다.

11 현재 사실과 반대되는 소망을 나타내므로 I wish 가정법 과거로 표현하며, be동사는 were를 쓰는 것에 주의한다.

12 직설법 문장에 현재 시제가 쓰였으므로 「I wish + 주어 + 동사의 과거형」으로 표현한다.

13 현재와 반대되는 소망을 표현하고 있으므로 I wish 가정법 과거를 사용한다. I wish 가정법 과거는 「I wish + 주어 + 동사의 과거형 / were」로 나타낸다.

14 I wish 가정법 과거는 현재 사실과 반대되는 소망을 나타내므로 직설법에서는 동사를 현재형으로 바꾸고, 가정법이 긍정이므로 직설법에서는 부정으로 쓴다.

15 as if 가정법 과거는 '마치 ~인 것처럼'이라는 의미로 주절과 같은 시점의 사실과 반대되는 상황을 가정할 때 쓴다.

16 as if 가정법 과거는 「as if + 주어 + 동사의 과거형 / were」로 쓴다.

17 주절과 같은 시점의 사실에 반대되는 가정이 되어야 하므로 as if 가정법 과거를 써야 한다. 이때 be동사는 주어의 인칭과 수에 관계없이 주로 were를 쓴다.

18 직설법과 주절의 시점이 같으므로 as if 가정법의 시제는 과거가 되어야 한다. 직설법의 부정 표현은 가정법에서 긍정으로 나타내므로 knew로 고쳐 쓴다.

19 주어진 문장은 'Peter는 마치 그의 새 삶을 즐기는 것처럼 보였다.'라는 의미로 as if 가정법 과거를 사용해 사실과 반대되는 상황을 가정하고 있다. 따라서 'Peter는 사실 새 삶을 즐기지 않았다.'라는 의미이다.

20 '태양이 없다면 지구상에 아무것도 살 수 없을 것이다.'라는 내용이 되어야 하므로 빈칸에는 '~이 없다면'을 뜻하는 Without 또는 But for가 와야 한다.

21 현재 있는 것이 없다고 가정할 때는 without 가정법을 이용하고, without 대신 but for나 if it were not for로 바꿔 쓸 수 있다. 주절은 「조동사 과거형 + 동사원형」을 쓴다.

22 가정법 과거에서 Without 대신 If it were not for나 But for를 쓸 수 있다.

23 ① 현재 사실과 반대되는 일에 대한 소망을 나타내고 있으므로 I wish 가정법 과거를 써야 한다. (→ had)

24 ④는 단순 조건문이므로 know가 알맞고 나머지는 모두 동사의 과거형인 knew가 알맞다.

25 (1) '내가 만약 해산물을 좋아한다면 그의 식당에 자주 갈 텐데.'라는 의미가 되도록 가정법 과거로 나타낸다.
(2) '내가 요트를 가지고 있다면 좋을 텐데.'라는 의미가 되도록 I wish 가정법 과거로 나타낸다.
(3) 'Clara는 마치 내가 그녀의 옆에 앉아 있지 않은 것처럼 나를 무시했다.'라는 의미가 되도록 as if 가정법 과거로 나타낸다.

STEP 2 · 오답률 40~60% 문제   pp. 212 – 213

01 ③   02 ⑤   03 ③   04 ②   05 ②   06 ①
07 ⑤   08 were in Korea, could invite him to my wedding

09 If I had a million dollars, I could build a new house.
10 I lived near the beach   11 were old   12 as if
13 (1) as if he were not interested in money (2) as if he understood what his mom said   14 were not for my bad cold   15 Without, But for, were not for

01 '내가 용돈을 더 받는다면 새 휴대전화를 살 수 있을 텐데.'라는 의미가 되도록 현재 사실과 반대되는 일을 가정하는 가정법 과거를 써야 한다. 따라서 빈칸에는 각각 동사의 과거형과 조동사의 과거형이 알맞다.

02 뒤에 너무 비싸다는 말이 이어지므로 빈칸은 '내가 너라면, 난 그것을 사지 않을 텐데.'라는 의미가 되어야 자연스럽다. 가정법 과거는 「If + 주어 + 동사의 과거형 / were ~, 주어 + 조동사의 과거형 + 동사원형 .....」으로 쓴다.

03 ③ 직설법 현재를 가정법 과거로 바꿀 때「If + 주어 + 동사의 과거형 / were ~, 주어 + 조동사의 과거형 + 동사원형 .....」으로 쓴다. (don't → didn't)

04 ② 가정법 과거로 나타내려면 if절의 동사를 과거형으로 고치고 (have → had) 단순 조건문으로 나타내려면 주절의 조동사를 현재형으로 고친다. (would → will)

05 I wish 가정법 과거 문장과 as if 가정법 과거 문장에서 주어와 수에 관계없이 be동사는 were를 쓴다.

06 I wish 가정법 과거 문장과 as if 가정법 과거 문장에서는 동사의 과거형을 써야 한다.

07 as if는 '마치 ~인 것처럼'이라는 의미로 주절과 같은 시점의 사실과 반대되는 상황을 나타낼 때 쓴다. 따라서 In fact, Kelly was responsible for the accident.와 같은 의미이다.

08 가정법 과거 문장의 if절에서 be동사가 쓰일 때 주어와 수에 관계없이 were를 쓴다.

09 가정법 과거는 「If + 주어 + 동사의 과거형 / were ~, 주어 + 조동사의 과거형 + 동사원형 .....」으로 쓴다.

10 '내가 바닷가에 살면 좋을 텐데.'라는 의미의 현재 사실과 반대되는 소망을 I wish 가정법 과거로 나타낼 수 있으며 「I wish + 주어 + 동사의 과거형 / were」의 형태로 쓴다.

11 나이가 어려서 혼자 여행할 수 없다고 했으므로 이어지는 문장은 '혼자 여행할 수 있을 만큼 나이가 들었으면 좋겠다.'라는 내용이 자연스럽다.

12 'Kevin은 어른이 아닌데, 어른인 것처럼 행동한다.'라는 의미가 되도록 as if 가정법 과거를 이용한다.

13 as if 가정법 과거는 '마치 ~인 것처럼'이라는 의미로 주절과 같은 시점의 사실과 반대되는 상황을 가정할 때 쓴다.

14 without 가정법 과거에서 Without 대신 If it were not for를 쓸 수 있다.

15 '만약 ~이 없다면'은 without 가정법 과거로 쓸 수 있고, Without을 But for 또는 If it were not for와 바꿔 쓸 수 있다.

01 ⑤　02 ②　03 ③　04 ③　05 ①, ④　06 ②
07 ⑤　08 If she were not afraid of heights, she could go to the top of the Eiffel Tower.　09 If doctors found a cure for all diseases, people would live much longer than now.　10 I didn't have so much homework tonight　11 (1) I were popular with girls (2) I had a chance to meet my favorite singer　12 (1) she[Maria] were wearing a raincoat, wouldn't (2) he didn't know me　13 (1) as if he agreed with her (2) If it were not for Emily　14 (1) he were rich (2) it snowed, we could go skiing (3) our school uniforms looked cool　15 as if she is → as if she were, speak → spoke[could speak]

01 ⑤ '만약 차가 더 적다면, 오염이 덜할 텐데.'라는 의미로 동사 are를 과거형 were로 고쳐야 한다.

02 가정법 과거는 「If + 주어 + 동사의 과거형 / were ~, 주어 + 조동사의 과거형 + 동사원형 .....」의 형태로 쓴다.

03 현재 사실에 대한 유감을 나타내므로 I wish 가정법 과거로 쓸 수 있다. 직설법이 부정이면 가정법은 긍정으로 나타낸다.

04 더울 때 바깥에서 일하는 것을 좋아하지 않으므로 바깥에서 일하지 않고 싶다는 소망을 I wish 가정법 과거로 나타내야 한다.

05 ② → He talked as if he were a doctor. ③ → As it is not warm, we won't go camping. ⑤ → As I work full-time, I can't exercise more.

06 ②는 단순 조건문이므로 빈칸에 is가 들어가야 하고 나머지는 모두 were가 알맞다.

07 ⓐ will → would ⓒ disappears → disappeared

08 가정법 과거는 현재 사실과 반대되는 내용을 가정할 때 쓰이므로 직설법의 내용과 반대로 써야 한다.

09 가정법 과거 문장으로 쓰려면 동사 find와 will을 과거형으로 써야 한다.

10 I wish 가정법 과거는 현재의 사실과 반대되는 내용을 소망할 때 쓰고, 이때 동사는 과거형으로 써야 한다.

11 I wish 가정법 과거는 「I wish + 주어 + 동사의 과거형 / were」의 형태로 쓴다.

12 가정법 과거는 현재와 반대되는 사실을 가정할 때 쓴다. as if 가정법 과거는 '마치 ~인 것처럼'이라는 의미이므로 In fact 다음에 이어지는 문장과 반대되는 내용으로 써야 한다.

13 (1) 주절과 같은 시점의 사실과 반대되는 상황을 가정할 때 as if 가정법 과거를 써야 한다. (2) '~이 없다면'은 If it were not for를 이용하여 나타낼 수 있다.

14 각각 as if 가정법 과거, 가정법 과거, I wish 가정법 과거를 이용하여 나타내야 하고, 이때 동사의 형태에 주의한다.

15 가정법 과거가 되도록 as if와 I wish 다음에 동사를 과거형으로 고쳐야 한다.

01 ①　02 ④　03 (1) They treat her as if she were a child. (2) I wish you drove more carefully.　04 were smart[smarter], (I) knew the answer to the question　05 If I were rich and had enough time, I would travel around the world.　06 it were not for, would not be

01 ⓒ can → could ⓓ have → had ⓔ has been → were

02 ④ '비가 많이 오지 않는다면, 사무실로 운전해 갈 텐데.'라는 의미는 '비가 많이 와서 사무실로 운전해 가지 않을 것이다.'라는 의미이다. (→ As it rains a lot, I will not drive to the office.)

03 (1) '마치 ~인 것처럼'을 의미하는 「as if + 주어 + were」를 쓴다. (2) '~라면 좋을 텐데'는 I wish 가정법 과거, 즉 「I wish + 주어 + 동사의 과거형」으로 쓴다.

04 현재 똑똑하지 못해 그 문제에 대한 답을 알지 못하는 것을 유감스러워하고 있으므로, I wish 가정법 과거를 써서 표현한다. 직설법이 부정이면 가정법은 긍정이 되어야 한다.

05 가정법 과거는 「If + 주어 + 동사의 과거형 / were ~, 주어 + 조동사의 과거형 + 동사원형 .....」으로 나타낸다.

06 「If it were not for + 명사(구)」, 「Without[But for] + 명사(구)」: 만약 ~이 없다면

최종 선택 QUIZ
p. 217

01 b　02 a　03 a　04 b　05 a　06 b　07 b　08 b

UNIT 22 가정법 과거완료

✓ 바로 체크
p. 218

01 would have gone　02 had caught　03 had accepted
04 had studied　05 had been　06 had met
07 had not been　08 wouldn't be

01 ④　02 had known　03 (1) didn't tell (2) went
04 ④　05 hadn't helped　06 ②　07 had done, I wouldn't have been punished　08 had paid, would have understood　09 ⑤　10 ②　11 ②　12 had taken, would be　13 had been　14 ④　15 ⑤　16 didn't learn　17 wasn't　18 ②　19 ③　20 ②　21 ①　22 it had not been for　23 Without, couldn't have found　24 ②　25 ③

01 주절에 「조동사의 과거형＋have＋과거분사」가 쓰였으므로 과거 사실과 반대되는 일을 가정하는 가정법 과거완료 문장임을 알 수 있다. 가정법 과거완료 문장의 if절에는 「had＋과거분사」를 쓴다.

02 주절의 동사가 「조동사의 과거형＋have＋과거분사」이므로 if절의 동사는 「had＋과거분사」의 형태가 되어야 한다.

03 'Judy가 Kevin에게 경기가 취소된 것을 알렸더라면 그는 경기장에 가지 않았을 텐데.'라는 의미의 가정법 과거완료 문장은 Judy가 Kevin에게 취소 사실을 알리지 않았고, Kevin이 경기장에 갔다는 사실을 나타낸다.

04 가정법 과거완료는 과거 사실에 반대되는 것이므로, 직설법으로 바꿀 때 동사는 과거형으로 쓰고 가정법과 반대의 의미가 되게 한다.

05 가정법 과거완료이므로 if절의 동사는 「had＋과거분사」가 되어야 한다.

06 과거 사실과 반대되는 일을 가정할 때는 가정법 과거완료로 나타낸다. if절에는 동사를 「had＋과거분사」 형태로 쓰고, 주절의 동사는 「조동사의 과거형＋have＋과거분사」 형태로 쓴다.

07 가정법 과거완료는 「If＋주어＋had＋과거분사 ~, 주어＋조동사의 과거형＋have＋과거분사 .....」의 형태로 쓴다.

08 직설법을 가정법 과거완료로 바꿀 때 형태는 「If＋주어＋had＋과거분사 ~, 주어＋조동사의 과거형＋have＋과거분사 .....」로 하고, 의미는 반대가 되게 한다.

09 ⑤ '그녀가 아프지 않았더라면 모임에 참석했을 텐데.'라는 의미가 되어야 자연스러우므로 hadn't been으로 고쳐야 한다.

10 '어젯밤 눈이 오지 않았더라면 오늘 길이 미끄럽지 않을 텐데.'라는 의미를 나타내는 혼합 가정법이 되도록 if절에는 가정법 과거완료를, 주절에는 가정법 과거를 쓴다.

11 'Mia가 발목을 삐지 않았더라면 지금 친구들과 스케이트를 타고 있을 텐데.'라는 의미를 나타내는 혼합 가정법이다. 혼합 가정법의 주절에는 가정법 과거를 쓴다.

12 과거에 실현되지 못한 일이 현재까지 영향을 줄 때 혼합 가정법을 사용하며, if절에는 가정법 과거완료를, 주절에는 가정법 과거를 쓴다.

13 과거에 이루지 못한 일에 대한 유감은 I wish 가정법 과거완료로 나타내므로 빈칸에는 「had＋과거분사」로 쓴다.

14 ①, ②, ③, ⑤는 모두 '과거에 너무 많이 먹은 것'에 대한 유감을 나타내고, ④는 '과거에 너무 많이 먹었음이 틀림없다'는 확실한 추측을 나타낸다.

15 'Fred는 런던을 간 적이 없는데 방문했던 것처럼 말한다.'라는 의미가 되도록 as if 가정법 과거완료로 나타내야 한다. 따라서 「had＋과거분사」 형태가 알맞다.

16 I wish 가정법 과거완료는 과거에 이루지 못한 일에 대한 유감을 나타내므로 직설법에서는 동사를 과거형으로 쓰고, 가정법이 긍정이므로 직설법에서는 부정으로 쓴다.

17 as if 가정법 과거완료는 '마치 ~이었던 것처럼'이라는 의미로 주절보다 앞선 시점의 사실과 반대되는 상황을 가정한다.

18 as if 가정법 과거완료가 쓰였으므로 '사실은 그는 과거에 그녀의 소설을 읽지 않았다'라는 것을 알 수 있다.

19 과거에 이루지 못한 일에 대한 유감을 나타내는 I wish 가정법 과거완료 형태가 알맞으므로 「I wish＋주어＋had＋과거분사」가 알맞다.

20 주절보다 앞선 시점의 사실과 반대되는 내용을 가정할 때 as if 가정법 과거완료로 나타낸다.

21 「Without＋명사(구)」가 가정법 과거완료 구문에 쓰이면 '만약 ~이 없었다면', '만약 ~이 아니었다면'의 뜻을 나타내고, 「But for＋명사(구)」나 「If it had not been for＋명사(구)」와 바꿔 쓸 수 있다.

22 '~이 없었다면'을 뜻하는 가정법 과거완료의 「But for＋명사(구)」는 「If it had not been for＋명사(구)」와 바꿔 쓸 수 있다.

23 「Without＋명사(구)」가 가정법 과거완료와 함께 쓰여 '만약 ~이 없었다면'이라는 의미를 나타낸다.

24 ① → could help ③ → had gone ④ → had driven ⑤ → could see

25 ③ 주절에 「조동사의 과거형＋have＋과거분사」가 쓰였으므로 가정법 과거완료 문장임을 알 수 있고, 따라서 빈칸에는 had had가 와야 한다. 나머지는 모두 had가 알맞다.

STEP 2 · 오답률 40~60% 문제   pp. 222 – 223

01 ①　　**02** ⑤　　**03** ④　　**04** ②　　**05** ③　　**06** ②
07 ①, ⑤　　**08** had missed, would have been late
09 If the dress[it] had been on sale, Ruth would have bought it[the dress].　　**10** stayed → had stayed, would finish → would have finished　　**11** I wish I hadn't drunk so much coffee last night.　　**12** I wish I had prepared
13 as if she had seen　　**14** Without, couldn't have graduated　　**15** If it had not been for your advice, I wouldn't have applied for the job.

01 가정법 과거완료는 과거 사실에 반대되는 것이므로 직설법으로 바꿀 때 동사는 과거형으로 쓴다.

02 과거 사실에 반대되는 가정이므로 가정법 과거완료를 사용한다. 가정법 과거완료는 if절에는 동사를 「had＋과거분사」 형태로 쓰고, 주절에는 「조동사의 과거형＋have＋과거분사」 형태로 쓴다.

03 가정법 과거완료는 「If＋주어＋had＋과거분사, 주어＋조동사의 과거형＋have＋과거분사」로 쓴다.

04 ⓐ는 혼합 가정법이고, ⓑ는 가정법 과거완료로 옳은 문장이다. ⓒ apologized → had apologized 또는 would have forgiven → would forgive ⓓ hasn't → hadn't

05 ③ '내가 미리 예약을 했더라면 좋을 텐데.'라는 의미로 I wish 가정법 과거완료를 이용하는 것이 알맞다.

06 as if 가정법 과거완료는 '마치 ~이었던 것처럼'이라는 의미로 주절보다 앞선 시점의 사실과 반대되는 상황을 가정할 때 쓴다.

07 ① didn't change → hadn't changed ⑤ wouldn't had quarreled → wouldn't have quarreled

08 가정법 과거완료는 「If＋주어＋had＋과거분사 ~, 주어＋조동사의 과거형＋have＋과거분사 .....」의 형태로 쓴다.

09 '드레스가 세일 중이었다면 Ruth는 그것을 샀을 텐데.'라는 의미가 되도록 가정법 과거완료를 이용해야 한다.

10 어제 있었던 일을 반대로 가정하고 있으므로 가정법 과거완료로 나타내야 한다.

11 I wish 가정법 과거완료는 '~했더라면 좋을 텐데'라는 의미로 「I wish＋주어＋had＋과거분사」로 나타낸다.

12 과거에 이루지 못한 일에 대한 아쉬움을 나타내고 있으므로 I wish 가정법 과거완료를 이용한다.

13 'Jasmine은 사고를 목격하지 않았는데 마치 목격했던 것처럼 말했다.'라는 의미가 되도록 as if 가정법 과거완료로 나타낸다.

14 without 가정법 과거완료는 「Without+명사(구), 주어+조동사의 과거형+have+과거분사」 형태로 쓴다.

15 if it had not been for ~: 만약 ~이 없었다면

STEP 3 · 오답률 60~80% 문제   pp. 224 – 225

01 ①   02 ⑤   03 ①   04 ①   05 ④   06 ①
07 ③, ④   08 If I had known Alex was such a terrible driver, I wouldn't have lent him my car.   09 If she had had more money, she would have opened a restaurant.
10 If I had brought my swimsuit, I could have swum.
11 I wish I hadn't spent so much money on the car.
12 (1) [모범 답] I'm sorry[I regret] I threw away the receipt. (2) [모범 답] In fact, Laura hadn't come up with the idea first.
13 (1) I wish you had seen[watched] this movie. (2) She talked as if she hadn't heard the news.   14 (1) I wish my dad had let me go to the concert. (2) If the shop owner had caught him stealing the jewelry, he would have been arrested.   15 (1) had rained (2) 없음 (3) hadn't sent (4) had not been

01 '내 자전거가 고장 나지 않았더라면 나는 버스를 타지 않았을 텐데.'라는 의미가 되는 것이 알맞다.

02 가정법 과거완료는 「If+주어+had+과거분사 ~, 주어+조동사의 과거형+have+과거분사 .....」의 형태이므로 have 다음에 과거분사 been이 알맞다.

03 과거에 실현되지 못한 일이 현재까지 영향을 줄 때 혼합 가정법을 사용하며, if절에는 가정법 과거완료를, 주절에는 가정법 과거를 쓴다.

04 ① now가 있으므로 과거에 있었던 일이 현재까지 영향을 미칠 때 쓰는 혼합 가정법이 알맞다. (would have felt → would feel)

05 ⓐ는 I wish 가정법 과거완료, ⓑ는 as if 가정법 과거, ⓒ는 가정법 과거완료, ⓓ는 혼합 가정법이고 제시된 문장은 모두 옳다.

06 ①은 가정법 과거 문장으로 'Lucy가 나를 도와주지 않는다면, 나는 꿈을 포기할 텐데.'라는 의미이고, 나머지는 모두 'Lucy가 도와주지 않았더라면, 나는 꿈을 포기했을 것이다.(Lucy가 도와주었기 때문에 나는 꿈을 포기하지 않았다.)'라는 의미이다.

07 ① → I wish I hadn't forgotten Mom's birthday. ② → Jonathan acts as if he had met Suji before. ⑤ → If she hadn't had a car accident, she wouldn't be in the hospital now.

08 과거 사실과 반대되는 가정을 할 때 가정법 과거완료로 나타낸다.

09 가정법 과거완료는 「If+주어+had+과거분사 ~, 주어+조동사의 과거형+have+과거분사 .....」의 형태로 쓴다.

10 '내가 수영복을 가져갔더라면, 수영할 수 있었을 텐데.'라는 의미가 되도록 가정법 과거완료로 나타낸다.

11 「should have+과거분사」는 '~했어야 했는데'라는 의미로 과거 사실에 대한 후회를 나타내는 표현이므로, I wish 가정법 과거완료인 「I wish+주어+had+과거분사」로 바꿔 쓸 수 있다.

12 I wish 가정법 과거완료와 as if 가정법 과거완료는 모두 과거 사실에 대한 반대를 가정한다.

13 I wish 가정법 과거완료: 「I wish+주어+had+과거분사」/ as if 가정법 과거완료: 「as if+주어+had+과거분사」

14 (1) '아빠가 나를 콘서트에 가도록 허락하셨더라면 좋을 텐데.'라는 의미로 I wish 가정법 과거완료를 이용해야 한다. (2) '상점 주인이 그가 보석을 훔치는 것을 알았더라면 그는 체포되었을 텐데.'라는 의미로 가정법 과거완료를 이용해야 한다.

15 (1) 주절이 「조동사의 과거형+have+과거분사」이므로 가정법 과거완료임을 알 수 있다. (2) if절은 「had+과거분사」이고 주절에는 now가 있으므로 혼합 가정법이다. (3) 앞 문장이 과거 시제이므로 I wish 가정법 과거완료로 나타내야 한다. (4) 주절이 「조동사의 과거형+have+과거분사」이므로 가정법 과거완료임을 알 수 있다.

STEP 4 · 실력 완성 테스트   p. 226

01 ③   02 as if he had written the paper   03 ①
04 (1) If I hadn't overslept this morning, I could have seen the sunrise. (2) If I had put the eggs back in the fridge, they wouldn't have gone bad.   05 (1) Lisa talked as if she had been to China. (2) Without the seat belt, the driver would have been hurt. (3) I wish I hadn't forgotten to call you.   06 went → had gone, didn't ignore → hadn't ignored

01 ③ 의미상 '구조선이 없었다면, 나는 익사했을 것이다.'라는 의미가 되도록 If it had not been for a lifeboat가 되는 것이 알맞다.

02 Tom이 보고서를 쓴 것처럼 행동한 것이므로 as if 가정법 과거완료인 「as if+주어+had+과거분사」의 형태로 표현한다.

03 ⓑ '그가 모자를 벗지 않았더라면 나는 그를 몰라봤을 텐데.'라는 의미이므로 모자를 벗어서 그를 알아보았다는 뜻이다. (→ As he had his hat off, I recognized him.)

04 과거에 있었던 일을 반대로 가정하는 가정법 과거완료로 나타낸다.

05 각각 as if 가정법 과거완료, without 가정법 과거완료, I wish 가정법 과거완료를 이용한다.

06 과거의 사실과 반대되는 일을 가정할 때는 가정법 과거완료를 사용해야 한다.

최종 선택 QUIZ   p. 227
01 b 02 b 03 a 04 b 05 b 06 a 07 b 08 b

UNIT 23 일치

✓ 바로 체크
p. 228

01 has 02 is 03 need 04 are 05 is 06 are
07 had studied 08 is

STEP 1 · 만만한 기초
pp. 229 – 231

01 ③ 02 is 03 ⑤ 04 were → was 05 are →
is 06 ① 07 ② 08 ① 09 helps you (to)
improve your English 10 ② 11 ③ 12 is, is
13 ⑤ 14 ③, ④ 15 will[is going to] go 16 travels
17 ② 18 ① 19 ④ 20 ② 21 ④ 22 lied
23 ① 24 ③ 25 ②

01 「a number of+복수 명사」는 '많은 ~'라는 의미로 복수 취급을, 「the number of+복수 명사」는 '~의 수'라는 의미로 단수 취급을 한다.

02 「A and B」가 하나의 개념을 나타내면 단수 취급한다.

03 ① 「every+명사」는 단수 취급한다.(→ has) ② -one으로 끝나는 대명사는 단수 취급한다.(→ knows) ③ 학문 이름은 단수 취급한다.(→ is) ④ 「one of+복수 명사」는 단수 취급한다.(→ sings)

04 -body로 끝나는 대명사는 단수 취급한다.

05 나라 이름은 복수형이어도 단수 취급한다.

06 거리나 금액을 나타내는 명사구가 하나의 개념을 나타내고 있으므로 단수 취급한다.

07 「분수 / the rest+of+복수 명사」는 복수로 취급한다.

08 ② the rich는 rich people을 의미하므로 복수 취급한다.(is → are) ③ glasses(안경)는 쌍으로 된 물건으로 복수 취급한다.(looks → look) ④ 「every+단수 명사」는 단수 취급한다.(like → likes) ⑤ 「the number of+복수 명사」는 '~의 수'라는 의미로 단수 취급한다.(are → is)

09 동명사구는 단수 취급하므로 helps로 쓰고, 준사역동사 help는 목적격 보어로 동사원형과 to부정사를 모두 쓸 수 있다.

10 has는 3인칭 단수 동사이므로 Each를 쓴다. 동사가 are이므로 '많은 ~'을 의미하는 A number of를 쓴다. Bread and butter는 '버터를 바른 빵'이라는 하나의 개념이므로 단수 취급한다.

11 「every+단수 명사」는 단수 취급하므로 wants가 와야 하고, want는 목적어로 to부정사만을 취하므로 ③이 알맞다.

12 동명사구와 관계대명사 what이 이끄는 명사절은 단수 취급한다.

13 ⑤ 「half of+복수 명사」는 복수 취급하므로 is를 쓸 수 없다.

14 주절의 시제가 과거이므로 종속절에는 과거(③) 또는 과거완료(④) 시제를 쓸 수 있다.

15 주절이 현재 시제인 경우 종속절에 모든 시제를 쓸 수 있는데, 종속절에 next Friday가 있으므로 미래 시제가 알맞다.

16 '빛은 소리보다 더 빨리 이동한다'는 것은 불변의 진리이므로 주절의 시제와 상관없이 현재 시제로 쓴다.

17 과거의 한 시점에 동시에 일어난 행동이므로 종속절에는 주절과 마찬가지로 과거 시제를 쓴다.

18 '물은 수소와 산소로 이루어져 있다'는 내용은 과학적 사실이므로 주절의 시제와 상관없이 현재 시제로 쓴다.

19 ①, ⑤ 가정법으로 were를 쓴다. ② 종속절에 yesterday가 있으므로 were를 쓴다. ③ 주절의 시제에 맞춰 과거 시제인 were가 알맞다. ④ that절의 내용이 격언이므로 현재 시제인 is를 쓴다.

20 주절의 시제가 과거이면 종속절에는 과거 또는 과거 완료를 쓸 수 있다. 원래 문장에서 주절과 종속절의 시제가 현재로 같으므로 주절이 과거로 바뀌면 종속절에도 과거 시제를 쓴다.

21 주절의 시제가 과거인 경우 종속절에는 과거, 과거 진행형, 조동사의 과거형, 과거 완료를 쓸 수 있다.

22 주절의 시제가 현재이면 종속절에 모든 시제를 쓸 수 있다. 종속절에 yesterday가 있으므로 과거 시제로 쓴다.

23 습관(첫 번째의 경우), 보편적 사실(두 번째의 경우), 불변의 진리(세 번째의 경우)를 나타내는 문장에서 동사는, 시제 일치의 예외에 해당되어 주절의 시제와 상관없이 항상 현재 시제를 쓴다.

24 주절의 시제가 과거이므로 종속절의 시제를 일치시켜 can의 과거형을 쓴다.

25 주절의 시제가 과거이면 종속절에는 과거와 과거완료가 올 수 있다. ①, ⑤ 주절의 시제가 현재이면 종속절에는 모든 시제를 쓸 수 있다. ③ '불변의 진리'이므로 주절의 시제에 상관없이 현재 시제로 쓴다.

STEP 2 · 오답률 40~60% 문제
pp. 232 – 233

01 ④ 02 ① 03 ③ 04 ⑤ 05 ② 06 ③
07 ④ 08 Half of the participants seem to enjoy the program. 09 (1) The number of bees has been declining for years. (2) Six to eight hours of sleep is good for your body. 10 Two-fifths of Julia's income is spent on clothes. 11 solved, was solving, had solved 12 had done 13 had gone 14 had broken out → broke out
15 made, was making, had made

01 ④ 「all + of + 단수 명사」는 단수 취급한다. of 뒤가 복수 명사일 때는 복수 취급한다.

02 ⓓ 「퍼센트 + of + 복수 명사」는 복수 취급하므로 is를 쓸 수 없다.

03 '~의 수'라는 의미는 「the number of + 복수 명사」로 쓰고 단수 취급하므로 is가 알맞다.

04 ① 학문 이름은 단수 취급한다.(affect → affects) ② scissors는 짝을 이루는 명사로 복수 취급한다.(looks → look) ③ 「A and B」의 형식이 별개의 사물이면 복수 취급한다.(differs → differ) ④ 「a number of + 복수 명사」는 '많은 ~'라는 의미로 복수 취급한다.(is → are)

05 ② '기름이 물보다 가볍다'는 내용은 과학적 사실이므로 주절의 시제와 상관없이 현재 시제로 쓴다. (was → is)

06 금액을 나타내는 명사구가 하나의 단위처럼 쓰일 때는 단수 취급한다. 주절의 시제가 과거이므로 종속절에도 과거 시제를 쓴다.

07 ④ 역사적 사실인 경우에 주절의 시제와 상관없이 항상 과거 시제로 쓴다. (had ended → ended)

08 「half of + 복수 명사」는 of 뒤의 명사에 동사의 수를 일치시킨다.

09 (1) '~의 수'는 「the number of + 복수 명사」로 나타내고 주어가 the number이므로 동사는 단수 취급한다. (2) 시간을 나타내는 명사구가 하나의 단위로 사용되는 경우 동사는 단수 취급한다.

10 「분수 + of + 단수 명사」에서 of 뒤에 있는 명사 income이 셀 수 없는 명사이므로 단수 취급한다.

11 주절이 과거 시제인 경우 종속절에는 과거, 과거 진행형 또는 과거 완료를 모두 쓸 수 있다.

12 주절의 동사를 현재 시제에서 과거 시제로 바꿀 때, 종속절의 시제가 과거이면 과거 완료로 바뀐다.

13 주절의 동사를 현재 시제에서 과거 시제로 바꿀 때, 종속절의 시제가 현재 완료이면 과거 완료로 바뀐다.

14 역사적 사실은 주절과 상관없이 항상 과거 시제로 쓴다.

15 주절의 시제가 과거이므로 종속절에 과거, 과거 진행형, 과거 완료 시제를 쓸 수 있다.

STEP 3 · 오답률 60~80% 문제   pp. 234 – 235

01 ④   02 ③   03 ①, ②   04 ⑤   05 ②   06 ①
07 ④   08 Mathematics is my favorite subject.   09 (1) The rest of the money (2) Two-thirds of the students
10 (1) A number of tourists visit (2) The number of elephants is   11 ⓐ → will have ⓑ → freezes ⓒ → would go ⓓ → missed[had missed]   12 the police had not found the missing boy   13 whether she arrived
14 the sun sets in the west   15 ⓐ have fed → fed 또는 had fed ⓑ went → goes

01 「the rest of + 단수 명사」는 단수 취급한다. / 「all + 복수 명사」는 복수 취급한다. / '실을 꿸 바늘'이라는 뜻으로 단수 취급한다.

02 ① are → is로 고친다. ② 「not only A but also B」는 B에 동사의 수를 일치시키므로 is를 쓴다. ④ '배우이자 가수인 한 사람'의 의미로 단수 취급한다. ⑤ 「분수 + of + 단수 명사」는 단수 취급한다. three quarters: 4분의 3

03 ① 「most of + 복수 명사」는 of 뒤에 오는 명사에 수를 일치시킨다. (is → are) ② to부정사구는 단수 취급한다. (are → is) ⑤ 시간을 나타내는 Five years는 하나하나 세는 의미이므로 복수 취급하여 올바른 문장이다.

04 ⓑ 동명사구는 단수 취급한다. (are → is) ⓒ the elderly는 '노인들'이라는 의미로 복수 취급한다. (is → are)

05 ② 주절의 시제가 과거이면 종속절에는 과거, 과거 완료를 쓴다.

06 주절은 현재 시제이고, 역사적 사실은 주절의 시제에 상관없이 과거 시제로 쓴다.

07 ④ 속담은 주절의 시제와 상관없이 현재 시제로 쓴다. (were → are)
백지장도 맞들면 낫다.

08 복수형 학문 이름은 단수 취급한다.

09 '양'을 나타내는 표현에서는 of 뒤에 있는 명사에 동사의 수를 일치시킨다.

10 (1) '많은 ~'는 a number of로 나타내고 복수 취급한다. (2) '~의 수'는 the number of로 나타내고 단수 취급한다.

11 ⓐ 주절의 시제가 현재이면 종속절은 모든 시제가 가능한데, soon이 있으므로 미래 시제가 알맞다. ⓑ 불변의 진리는 항상 현재 시제로 쓴다. ⓒ·ⓓ 주절의 시제가 과거이면 종속절의 시제는 과거 또는 과거완료가 올 수 있다. will의 과거형은 would이다.

12 주절을 현재 시제에서 과거 시제로 바꿀 때 종속절의 시제가 과거이면 과거완료로 바꾼다.

13 주절의 시제를 과거에서 현재로 바꾸면 종속절의 과거완료를 과거로 바꾼다.

14 불변의 진리는 주절의 시제에 상관없이 현재 시제를 쓴다.

15 ⓐ 주절의 시제가 과거이므로 종속절에는 과거 또는 과거완료를 쓴다. ⓑ 습관은 주절의 시제와 상관없이 현재 시제로 쓴다.

STEP 4 · 실력 완성 테스트   p. 236

01 ③   02 ④   03 ②   04 (1) The number of, is (2) One-fifth of the students are (3) Half of the students are
05 Here is → Here are, are → is, took → will take   06 I think every person has to follow

01 ⓐ 쌍을 이루는 명사는 복수 취급한다. (is → are) ⓓ 복수형 학문 이름은 단수 취급한다. (are → is)

02 ① of 뒤에 단수 명사가 오면 단수 취급한다. (are → is) ② 주절의 시제가 과거일 때 종속절의 시제는 과거 또는 과거완료가 올 수 있다.(likes → liked 또는 had liked) ③ 보편적 사실은 항상 현재 시제로 쓴다.(made → makes) ⑤ 역사적 사실은 항상 과거 시제로 쓴다. (discovers → discovered)

03 ① 격언이므로 현재 시제로 쓴다.(makes) ③, ④, ⑤도 불변의 진리·보편적 사실이므로 현재 시제로 쓴다.(③ has ④ is ⑤ fly) ② 주절의 시제가 과거일 때 종속절의 시제는 과거 또는 과거완료를 쓸 수 있으므로 needed 또는 had needed가 들어간다.

04 (1) 「the number of + 복수 명사」는 '~의 수'라는 의미로 단수 취급한다. (2), (3) 분수와 부분 표현이 복수 명사와 쓰였으므로 복수 취급한다.

05 Here is[are]는 뒤에 있는 주어에 동사를 일치시킨다. 주어(menus)가 복수이므로 Here are로 쓴다. / either는 '(둘 중) 어느 것이나'의 의미로 단수 취급하므로 Either is가 되어야 한다. / 마지막 B의 말은 '좋아요, 그것으로 할게요.'라는 의미로 미래 시제가 되어야 하므로 will take로 고친다.

06 '모든 사람들'은 every person이고 단수 주어이므로 has to로 쓴다.

최종 선택 QUIZ   p. 237

01 a   02 a   03 a   04 b   05 a   06 b   07 b   08 a

UNIT 24 화법 / 특수 구문

✓ 바로 체크
p. 238

01 told　　02 she was　　03 if　　04 not to　　05 want
06 that　　07 did I dream　　08 Neither

STEP 1 · 만만한 기초
pp. 239 – 241

01 ⑤　　02 ①, ⑤　　03 ⑤　　04 ④　　05 told, that she would　　06 not to eat　　07 was the report → the report was　　08 ③　　09 does worry　　10 ③　　11 ②, ④　　12 did decide　　13 It was, that[which]　　14 It was the accident that[which] changed my plan.　　15 ⑤　　16 ④　　17 ④　　18 ②　　19 ③　　20 so she did → so did she　　21 were two little boys　　22 ③　　23 Not, did we stay　　24 ①　　25 ③, ⑤

01 평서문의 화법을 전환할 때에는 전달할 말을 that절로 바꿔 쓴다. 이때 인칭대명사, 시제, 부사(구) 등을 알맞게 바꿔야 한다.

02 의문사가 없는 의문문은 간접 화법에서 if나 whether로 연결한다.

03 인용부호 안의 문장이 의문사가 있는 의문문인 경우 said to를 asked로 바꾸고, 「의문사 + 주어 + 동사」의 어순으로 쓴다.

04 인용부호 안의 문장이 긍정명령문일 때 to부정사로 바꾼다.

05 평서문을 간접 화법으로 바꿀 때 접속사 that으로 연결하고 인칭대명사와 시제 등을 알맞게 바꾼다.

06 인용부호 안의 문장이 부정명령문일 때「not + to부정사」로 바꾼다.

07 의문사가 없는 의문문은 간접 화법에서「if[whether] + 주어 + 동사」의 어순으로 쓴다.

08 ③ 의문사가 없는 의문문은 간접 화법에서「if[whether] + 주어 + 동사」의 어순으로 쓴다. 따라서 that을 if나 whether로 고쳐야 한다.

09 주어가 3인칭 단수이고, 현재 시제이므로 동사 앞에 does를 쓴 다음 동사원형을 쓴다.

10 〈보기〉와 ③의 do는 동사를 강조하는 do이다. ①, ④ 일반동사 ② 부정문을 만들 때 쓰는 조동사 ⑤ 의문문을 만들 때 쓰는 조동사

11 ② 동사를 강조하기 위해 동사 앞에 do[does / did]를 쓸 경우 바로 뒤에는 동사원형을 써야 한다. hates → hate ④ 주어가 복수이므로 do를 써서 동사를 강조한다. does → do

12 동사를 강조할 때는 동사 앞에 do[does / did]를 쓰는데, 과거 시제이므로「did + 동사원형」을 쓴다.

13 주어나 목적어, 부사(구)를 강조할 때는「It is[was] ~ that ....」을 쓴다.

14 과거 시제이므로「It was ~ that ....」으로 써야 한다.

15 ⑤ 동사를 강조할 때는 주어의 인칭과 수, 시제에 맞추어「do[does/ did] + 동사원형」을 쓴다. → Mary did watch the soccer game in the living room.

16 ④는「It(가주어) ~ that(진주어) ...」구문이고, 나머지는 모두 강조 구문이다.

17 부사 here가 문장 앞에 왔으므로「동사 + 주어」의 어순이 되어야 한다.

18 주어가 3인칭 단수이고, 앞의 동사가 일반동사의 현재 시제인 lives이므로 does를 써야 한다.

19 앞 내용에 동의할 때 앞 내용이 긍정문이면「So + 동사 + 주어」, 부정문이면「Neither + 동사 + 주어」를 쓴다.

20 앞 내용에 동의할 때 앞 내용이 긍정문이면「so + 동사 + 주어」의 어순으로 쓴다.

21 「부사구 + 동사 + 주어」의 어순이다.

22 부정어 never가 문장의 맨 앞으로 도치되어 강조되면, 주어와 be동사의 위치가 바뀐다.

23 부정어 not과 함께 a single day를 강조해 문장 앞에 쓸 때는「부정어구 + do동사 + 주어 + 동사」로 쓴다.

24 ① 앞 문장의 동사가 be동사이므로 응답에서도 be동사를 주어에 일치시켜 써야 한다. So do I. → So am I.

25 ③ 앞 내용이 부정문이면「neither[nor] + 동사 + 주어」를 쓴다. so → neither[nor] ⑤ 부정어가 문장 앞에 올 때「부정어 + do동사 + 주어 + 동사」로 어순이 도치된다. we talked → did we talk

STEP 2 · 오답률 40~60% 문제
pp. 242 – 243

01 ②　　02 ③　　03 ①　　04 ③　　05 ⑤　　06 ④　　07 ①　　08 Lisa said that she would go hiking the next[following] day.　　09 (1) how she spent her holiday (2) us not to feed the animals in the zoo　　10 if[whether] she had ever visited, she hadn't　　11 (1) I did tell him the truth. (2) It is a new laptop that[which] Jack wants to buy.　　12 It was last night that Steve called me.　　13 did I dream of winning the first prize　　14 (1) felt guilty, too (2) can't drive a car, either　　15 neither[nor] did Amy

01 인용부호 안의 문장이 명령문이면 전달동사 said to는 의미에 따라 told, advised 등으로 쓰고, 부정명령문인 경우에는「not + to부정사」로 바꿔 쓴다.

02 ③ that → if[whether]

03 주어가 3인칭 단수이고 현재 시제이므로「does + 동사원형」을 이용하여 동사를 강조한다.

04 ③의 do the dishes는 '설거지하다'라는 의미의 일반동사이고 나머지는 모두 동사를 강조하는 do이다.

05 ① does makes → does make ② do believe → did believe ③ It is → It was ④ who → that[which]

06 ④ 앞에서 쓴인 동사가 be동사이므로 does를 is로 고쳐야 한다.

07 ① 의문사가 없는 의문문이므로 if나 whether로 연결한다. 나머지는 모두 that이 알맞다.

08 주절의 시제가 과거이므로 종속절의 will은 would로 바꾸고 문맥에 맞게 인칭대명사와 부사를 바꾼다.

09 (1) 의문문을 간접 화법으로 바꿀 때 의문사가 있으면「의문사 + 주어 + 동사」의 어순으로 쓴다.
(2) 인용부호 안의 문장이 부정명령문인 경우에는「not + to부정사」로 바꿔 쓴다.

10 의문사가 없으므로 「if[whether]+주어+동사」의 어순으로 쓰고, 시제는 과거완료로 바꾼다.

11 (1) 동사를 강조할 때는 do동사를 이용해야 하고 과거 시제이므로 「did+동사원형」을 쓴다.
   (2) It is와 that 사이에 강조하는 말을 쓴다.

12 시제가 과거이며, 강조하고자 하는 말이 last night이므로 is와 who를 제외하고 「It was ~ that ....」의 형태로 쓴다.

13 「부정어(Never)+do동사+주어+동사원형」의 어순으로 쓴다.

14 「so+동사+주어」는 '~도 역시 그렇다'라는 의미이고, 「neither+동사+주어」는 '~도 역시 아니다'라는 의미로 각각 too와 either를 이용하여 바꿔 쓸 수 있다.

15 앞 내용이 부정이므로 「neither[nor]+동사+주어」의 어순으로 쓴다.

12 부정어를 강조할 때는 「부정어(Never)+조동사+주어+동사」의 어순으로 쓴다.

13 앞 문장이 긍정일 때는 so를, 부정일 때는 neither를 이용하며 주어와 동사를 도치시켜야 한다.

14 ⓐ 「부정어+do동사+주어+동사」의 어순으로 쓴다. ⓒ neither는 부정어로 '~도 역시 아니다'라는 의미를 나타내므로 neither 다음에 긍정의 동사가 와야 한다.

15 (1), (2) 화법을 전환할 때 동사 전환, 주절과 피전달문 연결, 시제, 대명사와 부사(구) 전환 등에 주의한다.
   (3) 동사를 강조할 때는 do동사를 이용한다.
   (4) 「부정어+조동사+주어+동사」의 어순으로 쓴다.

STEP 3 · 오답률 60~80% 문제
pp. 244 – 245

01 ①　02 ④　03 ④　04 ①, ②　05 ①, ⑤
06 ③, ⑤　07 ①　08 He ordered her not to park her car there.　09 if[whether] she could take care of his dog while he was away, when he was coming back　10 The doctor did try to save her.　11 It was the zookeeper that was attacked by the lion.　12 Never have I heard such a strange story.　13 (1) so did my sister (2) neither has Max　14 (1) ⓐ: they eat → do they eat (2) ⓒ: doesn't Steve → does Steve　15 (1) He asked Mary if[whether] she wanted to get a refund. (2) She said to me, "I moved here a year ago." (3) He did take the medicine after dinner. (4) Seldom have his films received positive reviews.

01 Sam은 파티에 왔고 파티에 오지 않은 것은 바로 Kevin이었다는 것을 강조한다. 첫 번째 빈칸에는 시제가 과거이므로 「did+동사원형」을 쓰고, 두 번째 빈칸은 강조 구문으로 that 또는 who가 알맞다.

02 ④는 「It(가주어) ... that(진주어) ~」 구문이고 나머지는 모두 강조 구문이다.

03 「부정어(Hardly)+조동사+주어+동사원형」의 어순이 알맞다.

04 1형식 구문에서 주어가 대명사인 경우 부사(구)를 문장 앞에 쓰더라도 주어와 동사가 도치되지 않는다.

05 ① to not swim → not to swim ⑤ he had → had he

06 ① did wanted → did want ② not being → not to be ④ so Kate has → so does Kate

07 ⓓ did → have

08 간접 화법에서 부정명령문은 「not+to부정사」로 쓰고, 부사 here는 there로 바꿔 쓴다.

09 의문문을 간접 화법으로 바꿀 때 의문사가 없으면 「if[whether]+주어+동사」의 어순으로 쓰고, 의문사가 있으면 「의문사+주어+동사」의 어순으로 쓴다.

10 동사를 강조할 때는 do동사를 이용하며, 과거 시제이므로 「did+동사원형」을 써야 한다.

11 「It ~ that」 구문에서 강조할 말은 It is[was]와 that 사이에 쓴다.

STEP 4 · 실력 완성 테스트
p. 246

01 ②　02 ②　03 (1) She warned me to keep the door locked. (2) They asked him how long he had been waiting there. (3) Sally asked Jack if[whether] he could give her a ride home the next[following] day.　04 ①, ④　05 (1) so does Paul (2) neither does Lydia　06 (1) It was Diana that[who] found a cat under the car yesterday. (2) Diana did find a cat under the car yesterday. (3) It was a cat that[which] Diana found under the car yesterday. (4) It was under the car that[where] Diana found a cat yesterday. (5) It was yesterday that[when] Diana found a cat under the car.

01 앞 사람의 말에 동의할 때, 앞 내용이 긍정이면 So를, 부정이면 Neither[Nor]를 쓴다. ②는 앞의 말이 긍정이므로 So를, 나머지는 모두 Neither[Nor]를 써야 한다.

02 ⓐ did made → did make ⓓ imagined John → did John imagine

03 화법을 전환할 때 동사 전환, 주절과 피전달문 연결, 시제, 대명사와 부사(구) 전환 등에 주의한다.

04 ① neither Sam will → neither will Sam ④ Hardly I can → Hardly can I

05 「so+동사+주어」는 '~도 역시 그렇다'라는 의미이고, 「neither+동사+주어」는 '~도 역시 아니다'라는 의미이다.

06 (2)는 동사를 강조해야 하므로 do동사를 이용하고, 나머지는 모두 「It was ~ that ....」 강조 구문을 이용한다.

최종 선택 QUIZ
p. 247

01 a　02 b　03 a　04 a　05 a　06 a　07 b　08 b

48 · UNIT 24

중·고등

바로 영어 시리즈

우리가 찾던 책이 바로 이거야!

문법

바로 문장 쓰는 문법 기본
쓰기가 쉬워지는 중학 문법서(개념+교과서 문장 쓰기)

바로 문제 푸는 문법 N제 실전
실전 N제형 문법 기출서(난이도별 기출 유형 훈련)

독해

바로 읽는 배경지식 독해 기본
수능의 배경지식을 쌓는 중학 독해서

바로 읽는 구문 독해 실력
문장의 구조와 정확한 해석을 훈련하는 구문 독해서

듣기

바로 Listening 중학영어듣기 모의고사
최신 듣기 유형과 시험 형식을 완벽 분석한 듣기 평가 대비서

어휘

바로 VOCA
중학 필수 어휘 및 고등 모의평가 & 수능 필수 어휘 학습

정답은
이안에
있어!

배움으로 행복한 내일을 꿈꾸는
천재교육 커뮤니티 안내

교재 안내부터 구매까지 한 번에!
천재교육 홈페이지

자사가 발행하는 참고서, 교과서에 대한 소개는 물론
도서 구매도 할 수 있습니다. 회원에게 지급되는 별을 모아
다양한 상품 응모에도 도전해 보세요!

다양한 교육 꿀팁에 깜짝 이벤트는 덤!
천재교육 인스타그램

천재교육의 새롭고 중요한 소식을 가장 먼저 접하고 싶다면?
천재교육 인스타그램 팔로우가 필수!
깜짝 이벤트도 수시로 진행되니 놓치지 마세요!

수업이 편리해지는
천재교육 ACA 사이트

오직 선생님만을 위한, 천재교육 모든 교재에 대한 정보가 담긴
아카 사이트에서는 다양한 수업자료 및 부가 자료는 물론
시험 출제에 필요한 문제도 다운로드하실 수 있습니다.

https://aca.chunjae.co.kr

천재교육을 사랑하는 샘들의 모임
천사샘

학원 강사, 공부방 선생님이시라면 누구나 가입할 수 있는 천사샘!
교재 개발 및 평가를 통해 교재 검토진으로 참여할 수 있는 기회는 물론
다양한 교사용 교재 증정 이벤트가 선생님을 기다립니다.

아이와 함께 성장하는 학부모들의 모임공간
튠맘 학습연구소

튠맘 학습연구소는 초·중등 학부모를 대상으로 다양한 이벤트와 함께
교재 리뷰 및 학습 정보를 제공하는 네이버 카페입니다.
초등학생, 중학생 자녀를 둔 학부모님이라면 튠맘 학습연구소로 오세요!